Lecture Notes in Computer Science 6267

Commenced Publication in 1973
Founding and Former Series Editors:
Gerhard Goos, Juris Hartmanis, and Jan van Leeuwen

Kim Normann Andersen Enrico Francesconi
Åke Grönlund Tom M. van Engers (Eds.)

Electronic Government and the Information Systems Perspective

First International Conference, EGOVIS 2010
Bilbao, Spain, August 31 – September 2, 2010
Proceedings

Springer

Volume Editors

Kim Normann Andersen
Center for Applied ICT (CAICT) and Copenhagen Business School (CBS)
Frederiksberg, Denmark
E-mail: andersen@cbs.dk

Enrico Francesconi
Institute of Legal Information, Theory and Techniques, ITTIG-CNR, Florence, Italy
E-mail: francesconi@ittig.cnr.it

Åke Grönlund
ESI/Informatics, Örebro University, Örebro, Sweden
E-mail: ake.gronlund@oru.se

Tom M. van Engers
University of Amsterdam, Faculty of Law, Leibniz Center for Law
Amsterdam, The Netherlands
E-mail: vanEngers@uva.nl

Library of Congress Control Number: 2010932204

CR Subject Classification (1998): K.5.2, H.4, H.5, J.1, K.4, K.4.2

LNCS Sublibrary: SL 3 – Information Systems and Application, incl. Internet/Web and HCI

ISSN 0302-9743
ISBN-10 3-642-15171-X Springer Berlin Heidelberg New York
ISBN-13 978-3-642-15171-2 Springer Berlin Heidelberg New York

springer.com

Printed in Germany

Typesetting: Camera-ready by author, data conversion by Scientific Publishing Services, Chennai, India
Printed on acid-free paper 06/3180

Preface

In front of you are the proceedings of the First International Conference on Electronic Government and Information Systems Perspective, EGOVIS. This conference builts on the tradition of its predecessors, the Electronic Government Conferences (EGOV) under the DEXA umbrella, which have been ongoing for nine years, but it also included some innovations. In view of the large number of electronic government conferences, we found it important to focus the scope of the conference a little and to increase the quality requirements. Hence this year's conference featured a tougher review process and a smaller set of accepted papers. As a result, these proceedings contain the very best papers of 2010 covering various important aspects of electronic government and information systems used in the public sector. With an acceptance rate of less than 20% EGOVIS belongs to the top ten conferences in the world. The Program Committee accepted 13 full papers and 11 short papers, covering the most recent research trends in electronic government implementations, such as ICT for eGovernment services and monitoring, knowledge and content management systems for temporal and geo-spatial applications, interoperability for electronic government integrated architectures, decision and support tools for eDemocracy and direct participation of citizens in the policy-making strategies, and Web 2.0 and 3.0 approaches for collaborative and transparent public sector services.

The Chairs of the Program Committee wish to thank all the reviewers for their valuable work. We know that reviewing is time consuming, but it is also rewarding to be involved in discussions with fellows about issues raised, and this makes the review process as much a learning process as the conference itself. We also want to thank Gabriela Wagner for supporting us with all the administrative work involved and stimulating us to get things done in time.

We regret that we were informed that one of the keynote speakers we hoped to welcome at EGOVIS had to decline because of a serious health problem. We wish Trevor Bench-Capon a quick recovery and hope to welcome him back in our network of colleagues soon.

To the readers of these proceedings we wish a pleasant learning experience. We hope that the presentations and exchange of ideas may stimulate you to keep submitting your papers.

Tom van Engers
Enrico Francesconi
Åke Gronlund
Kim Normann Andersen

Organization

Honorary Chairs

Wichian Chutimaskul	King Mongkut's University of Technology, Thailand
Fernando Galindo	University of Zaragoza, Spain
Roland Traunmüller	University of Linz, Austria

General Chair

Roland Wagner	University of Linz, Austria

Conference Program Chairs

Kim Normann Andersen	Copenhagen Business School, Denmark
Enrico Francesconi	Italian National Research Council, Italy
Åke Grönlund	Örebro University, Sweden
Tom van Engers	University of Amsterdam, The Netherlands

Program Committee

Ignacio Aedo	Universidad Carlos III de Madrid, Spain
Jan Aidemark	Växjö University, Sweden
Kim Normann Andersen	Copenhagen Business School, Denmark
Majed Ayyad	NextLevel Technology Systems, Palestine
Carlo Batini	University of Milano Bicocca, Italy
Victor Bekkers	Erasmus University Rotterdam, The Netherlands
Trevor Bench-Capon	Liverpool University, UK
Alejandra Cechich	Universidad Nacional del Comahue, Argentina
Wojciech Cellary	Poznan University of Economics, Poland
Wichian Chutimaskul	King Mongkut's University of Technology, Thailand
Flavio Corradini	University of Camerino, Italy
Vytautas Cyras	Vilnius University, Lithuania
Annelie Ekelin	Blekinge Institute of Technology, Sweden
Fernand Feltz	Centre de Recherche Public - Gabriel Lippmann, Luxembourg
Enrico Francesconi	Italian National Research Council, Italy

Fernando Galindo	University of Zaragoza, Spain
Johann Gamper	Free University of Bozen, Italy
Stefanos Gritzalis	University of the Aegean, Greece
Åke Grönlund	Örebro University, Sweden
Henning Sten Hansen	Aalborg University, Denmark
Helle Zinner Henriksen	Copenhagen Business School, Denmark
Patrik Hitzelberger	Centre de Recherche Public - Gabriel Lippmann, Luxembourg
Hannakaisa Isomaki	University of Jyväskylä, Finland
Christos Kalloniatis	University of the Aegean, Greece
Nikos Karacapilidis	University of Patras, Greece
Dimitris Karagiannis	University of Vienna, Austria
Vagelio Kavakli	University of the Aegean, Greece
Jaroslav Kral	Charles University of Prague, Czech Republic
Irene Krebs	Brandenburg University of Technology in Cottbus, Germany
Josef Küng	University of Linz, Austria
Hun-yeong Kwon	Kwangwoon University, Korea
Fabio Luiz Leite Júnior	University Federal de Campina Grande, Brazil
Marian Mach	Technical University of Košice, Slovakia
Francisco Javier García Marco	University of Zaragoza, Spain
Pedro Rafael Muro-Medrano	University of Zaragoza, Spain
Sinisa Neskovic	University of Belgrade, Serbia
Mara Nikolaidou	Harokopio University of Athens, Greece
Javier Nogueras	University of Zaragoza, Spain
Monica Palmirani	University of Bologna, Italy
Christos Papatheodorou	Ionian University & "Athena" Research Centre , Greece
Peter Parycek	Danube University Krems, Austria
Aljosa Pasic	Atos Research, Spain
Günther Pernul	University of Regensburg, Germany
Andrea Polini	University of Camerino, Italy
Reinhard Posch	Technical University Graz, Austria
Gerald Quirchmayr	University of Vienna, Austria
Peter Regner	FAW, Austria
Siegfried Reich	Salzburg Research, Austria
Aires J Rover	Federal University of Santa Catarina, Brazil
Luis Álvarez Sabucedo	University of Vigo, Spain
Erich Schweighofer	University of Vienna, Austria
Jan Stanek	University of South Australia, Australia
Daniela Tiscornia	ITTIG Institute for Theory and Techniques for Legal Information, Italy
A Min Tjoa	Vienna University of Technology, Austria
Roland Traunmüller	University of Linz, Austria
Gonzalo Valdes	University of Santa Maria (UTFSM), Chile

External Reviewers

Table of Contents

E-Government Services Analysis

Decision Support Tools

Invited Talk

ICT in E-Government (I)

Information Modelling and Integration

E-Government Services and Web 2.0 (I)

E-Government Services Design, Implementation and Monitoring

ICT in E-Government (II)

E-Government Services and Web 2.0 (II)

Knowledge Management

Stakeholders' Views on Government Enterprise Architecture: Strategic Goals and New Public Services

Katja Penttinen and Hannakaisa Isomäki

Faculty of Information Technology, University of Jyväskylä,
PO Box 35 (Agora), 40014 Jyvaskyla, Finland
katja.penttinen@jyu.fi, hannakaisa.isomaki@jyu.fi

Abstract. This paper introduces different stakeholders' views on enterprise architecture development within the Finnish government. The data is gathered from 21 interviews accomplished during spring 2007 among participants of the Interoperability Programme. The interviewees represent different sectors and levels of the Finnish government and IT companies. On the basis of a qualitative data analysis we discuss the notions that different actors connect to EA work. The key conclusions are that the ongoing EA work is seen as technically oriented and more emphasis should be put to activities and contents. On the basis of the data, it seems easier to develop government EA and interoperability on the level of state administration and ministries than in the agency level.

Keywords: State Administration, Enterprise Architecture, Interview Research.

1 Introduction

At present, public administrations all over the world promote costly e-government programmes to provide electronic access to government services. However, e-government approaches have often not been able to solve organisations' concern how to utilise ICT to its fullest strategic extent. Difficulties have been encountered and many e-government initiatives are described as chaotic and unmanageable [1]. One solution has been to initiate an enterprise architecture (EA) programme. EA is seen as a comprehensive approach, for example: "*enterprise architecture is a coherent whole of principles, methods and models that are used in the design and realisation of an enterprise's organisational structure, business processes, information systems, and infrastructure*." [2] Further, Enterprise architecture is used to descripe how different elements in an organisation – systems, processes, organisations, and people – work together as a whole [3]. By identifying, structuring and categorizing these elements, EA can increase the potential for cross-public sector reuse and reduce duplication and hence reduce costs.

In taking EA into use as a holistic development tool for e-government, it is of utmost importance to take into account the views of the stakeholders involved. In particular, it is necessary to notice their views in order to guarantee acceptance of the

K.N. Andersen et al. (Eds.): EGOVIS 2010, LNCS 6267, pp. 1–8, 2010.

new information systems. From an information-legal basic rights viewpoint, the most pivotal issues of catering for the stakeholders' concern the right to receive information, the right to communicate, the right to free information, to exchange information freely, and the right to information sovereignty. Thus, when using EA as a tool for e-government, attention should be paid on the informativeness of the approach, and especially, how the stakeholders understand EA in the context of developing e-government. However, there is little research that discloses how the stakeholders actually understand EA as a tool for the development work of e-government.

In this paper, we introduce results from an empirical study concerning different stakeholders' views on government EA development initiated within the Interoperability Programme of the Finnish state administration. In the following, we first depict the research setting and method. Second, we present the results as stakeholders' views on government enterprise architecture. Third, the strategic goals of enterprise architecture work are described. Forth, we present interviewees ideas for new public services. Finally, we state the conclusions and topics for the future research.

2 Research Method

According to its aim to understand different stakeholders' views in particular organizational context, the study merges with the principles of interpretive research that is seen to produce deep insights into human thought and action [4]. An interpretive analysis was carried out with data from semi-structured, in-depth interviews. The interviewees were asked a written informed consent, and the questions were asked in a manner that excludes interviewer bias [5]. The method has been applied also in our prior study [6].

The interview themes and related questions were derived from an underlying theoretical EA framework developed for the Finnish state administration. The framework consists of four generally known EA viewpoints:

- Business (e.g., clients, organisation, stakeholders, services, processes)
- Information (e.g., strategic knowledge capital, vocabulary)
- Information systems (e.g., information system portfolio, systems' life-cycles)
- Technology (e.g., technology and standard policies, model architectures)

These issues are placed within three levels in the framework. The highest is the level of state administration, which is the top level of decision making. The second level is the level of administrative sector, which includes independent decision-making bodies under state administration level. The lowest level refers to civil service department level. This structure was implemented in this study by selecting interviewees from each level. The interview questions concerned the respondents' views of current and future condition of state EA. These levels form the basis for interconnections between the different sectors in that the level of state administration operates in a cross-sectional manner, and thus is able to delegate cross-sectional tasks to the lower levels.

In this way also the participants from the state administration level possess essential decision making power.

The data is collected from 21 interviews accomplished during the spring 2007 among participants of an Interoperability Programme of the Finnish state administration. At the time of the interviews, the Programme was just started, and was in its planning phase. The interviewees represent stakeholders from different levels and also sectors of Finnish government and IT companies. Their concern related to the development of EA varied according to their occupational position (Table 1). The selection of interviewees was based on purposeful sampling [7] in order to capture variation in the data in terms of both assumed information intensiveness and stakeholder population. The interviewees consisted of 11 state employees and 10 IT company employees. Six of them were female and 15 were male. Purposeful sampling together with the number of interviews is regarded to provide for saturated analysis of the information available [e.g. 8].

The transcribed interviews were analysed. During analysis an interpretation of the interviewees' utterances was carried out by iterating between the interdependent meaning of parts and the whole that they form [4]. In this way the whole data was the source of the results, which indicate the various meanings that the respondents assign to EA. In the following, the citations from data are selected on the basis of representativeness within data.

Table 1. Interviewees by organisational level, occupation, experience in EA, and number

Organisational level	Occupation	Experience in EA (yrs)	No
State administration	Administrative Counselor	25	1
	Chief Secretary	10	1
	Operations Manager	7	1
	Vice Director	30	1
Administrative sector	Senior Lawyer	1	1
	Information Specialist	7	1
	Senior Adviser	4	1
Civil service department	Data Administration Manager (city)	2	1
	Data Administration Manager	15-30	3
Management level of IT companies	Director	6	1
	Sales Director	10	1
	Consulting Manager	10-25	2
Consultants	Senior Consultant	8	1
	Management Consultant	0-9	2
	Consultant	10-16	3

Next we present results of the study. We have selected the business architecture as our viewpoint in this paper. The results depict interviewees' opinions on current and target business architecture of Finnish state government.

3 Views on Government Enterprise Architecture

The Finnish government enterprise architecture work is carried out by various different stakeholder groups. This was also reflected in the interviews. We categorized the representatives of the public administration in three organisational levels that are also present in the Finnish EA framework. These are state administration, administrative sector and civil service department. The interviewees where from different sectors of the government, such as the Ministry of Finance, Ministry of Defence, Ministry of Social Affairs and Health and, Ministry of Employment and the Economy. The representatives of the IT companies were categorized in two levels: management and consultants.

At the general level stakeholder group's views varied in relation to the organisational viewpoint. At the level of civil service department the interviewees discussed the EA work through the lens of the department or municipality they represented. Interviewees from administrative sector viewed EA through their own organisation or sector of administration. The interviewees from the state administration had the viewpoint of administrative sector or the state as a whole. One interviewee had the viewpoint of a municipality.

The interviewees from IT companies discussed the EA work solely from the viewpoint the whole government. They did not consider administrative sectors or civil service departments as separate wholes. One representative of an IT company discussed the viewpoint of municipalities.

We believe that these differences in EA views elicit an important notion for the government EA work. The government EA work is holistic and the results are aimed for the whole government. The somewhat narrow views of people participating in the EA work may lead to unexpected or unwanted outcomes. Representative of administrative sector delineates how he views EA:

"...from the viewpoint of my own organisation and then also from the holistic...at least should be viewed."

The view of a consultant:

"...we look the government as a whole and how the...organisation, the whole system, would work in the best possible way."

These different views on government enterprise architecture are visible throughout the data. They are reflected in the answers to other questions as well. Next we discuss the strategic goals of the government EA work.

4 Strategic Goals of Enterprise Architecture Work

The main goal of the Finnish Interoperability Programme is to create EA to be used as a tool for steering the development of operations and information systems (IS) at all levels of state administration. In addition, the goal is to create and introduce a governance model for EA maintenance and utilisation of EA descriptions in steering of development and IS projects. With the EA it is easier to take into account strategic goals in the development of public services. These goals are: customer orientation, sustainable development, enhancement of service production. Hence, EA is defined as a tool for strategic management through which the operational development and use of IS are harmonised in the level of state administration. These strategic goals of EA work are very holistic and require substantial changes in the work practices within the government and in the customer interface.

From the interviewees presenting Finnish government, we asked what kind of strategic goals should their organisation or the government generally set for the EA work. At the civil service department level increasing interoperability was seen as the key strategic goal. Interoperability is defined as *an ability of information systems and of the business processes they support to share and exchange information* [9]. Interoperability was mentioned from the viewpoints of building shared services and facilitating information transfer. However, technical interoperability was often in the center of the discussions.

Interviewee from the administrative sector brought up that attention should be paid in interoperability of the operational processes at the organisational level. Interviewees representing state administration emphasized viewpoints of productivity and efficiency:

"It should be based on nationally centered systems, because we must remember that we have only 5,2 million citizens...In Finland the volume is extremely small...that is why...we must avoid building overlapping systems..."

Another interviewee emphasized the productivity viewpoint. In his opinion it accelerates the functioning of the administration, improves its quality and enhances the ability to service citizens.

From the interviewees representing IT companies, we asked what kind of strategic goals should be set to the government EA work. They brought up, for example, that guidelines and recommendations are needed in state administration but from the other hand there should also be freedom to do the core functions. IT professionals conceived the role of communications significant in order to achieving success in Ea work. They felt that there is a need for a corporal strategy for the government as a whole. Currently such is lacking.

IT professionals highlighted improving interoperability as an important goal for rationalizing the administrative work but as well in a wider societal framework. This means the qualitative change brought up by aging of the population and as a need for new type of service production.

Representatives of IT companies underlined the importance of customer viewpoint which did not come up in the interviewees of administrative people. In sales directors words:

"Well in the end everything concludes in this customer viewpoint thus why the state exists and why the services are produced...therefore first the strategic goal needs to be...producing better services here for these customers."

The stakeholders of the state administration emphasized interoperability as the main strategic goal for the enterprise architecture work. This was seen important from the viewpoint of using the common information resources and establishing coherent business processes in the state level. All stakeholders repeatedly elicit the need for rationalizing the operations as a strategic goal.

Next we present interviewees proposals for new public services.

5 New Public Services

New public services emerged as a significant goal for the government EA work. For many interviewees perceiving new type of services was troublesome. We asked: "What kind of new services public administration could produce" and the answers were general, when new public services were conceived solely as electronic services.

Representatives of civil service departments perceived electronic services as a substantial challenge and at the same time they saw a great development potential in them. As concrete development matter they brought up, for example, user identification. Currently in Finland, there is a lack of a reliable and widely used identification method. This was seen as an obstacle for the development of electronic public services.

At the administrative sector level the interviewees highlighted coherent service production and jointly development.

The transition into centralized solutions, particularly in financial and personnel administration, was seen important in the level of state administration. Centralized solutions would have substantial efficiency benefits. This does not mean merely cost savings; furthermore it would result in producing better services with available monetary resources. In addition, they perceived producing electronic services in a way that takes into account the important democratic principles:

"...legal protection and then requirements of democracy, transparency and all these are secured. The way we now work at paper is transformed into electronic...This is where the focus is. Certainly we can produce new services, but to keep public sector's costs together...then this adaptation and productivity require...making these as efficient as possible."

The requirement for democracy and efficiency in new services comes up in other interviews also. Interviewee saw it problematic that during elections politicians promised new services and lower taxes and citizens do expect to get new welfare services. He stated:

"It might be that the public administration is condemned to cut down services instead of extending them."

Representatives of IT companies had varying opinions. Consulting manager wished better services instead of new services:

"Well, I do not know, there are little that citizens would need. Most of these current, so called, services are such that no one ever asked for...I think it would be most important to get the existing services to function even better."

Consultant disclosed the need for proactive service concept and one-stop shop services.

New services were essential for the interviewees. Representatives of administration defined services generally as electronic services without concrete examples or customer perspective. Developing electronic services is a major challenge which requires a lot of work from actors in public administration. Representatives of IT companies had concrete ideas for new services and ways of servicing.

6 Conclusions

Data analysis elicit different stakeholders' views in all the four EA viewpoints. In this article, we concentrated on the business architecture, because it is the fundamental function in transforming governmental traditional administrative processes into public services. Stakeholders' views varied in regard to the interviewees' background organisation.

The uttermost important strategic goal for the government EA work was interoperability. Interoperability was defined both technically and functionally. Representatives of IT companies brought up more strongly than administrative people the need for improving customer orientation and developing service production. All stakeholders emphasized the need for rationalisation.

Representatives of public administration perceived new electronic services as the most important type of services, but developing them was seen challenging and laborious. They also saw the possibility of reducing services. The improvement of existing services was found more important by the IT professionals than creating new services.

Differences in the interviewees background organisations were visible, for example, as follows. At the level of civil service departments the viewpoint was more narrow than the viewpoint in the level of state administration and IT companies. The views of people in state administration and IT companies were closer than of other groups. Based on the data promotion and development of government EA and interoperability is presumable easier in the state administration and administrative sector than in the civil service department level. In the civil service departments the focus is more in developing their own EA than participating in creating a government wide EA.

The interviewees saw the ongoing government EA work as technically oriented and more emphasis should be put to activities and contents. The need for productivity goals, concrete policies and common guidelines was recognised. Some interviewees were skeptical on the possibility of success in the EA work itself. According to the interviewees there are challenges in regards of marketing and communicating EA work, hence these are the requirements for advancement of the EA thinking.

This article focused on the business architecture viewpoint. In future research, the other three architectural viewpoints: information, information systems and, technology are covered. This is a requirement for constituting a more holistic picture on stakeholders' view on government enterprise architecture. In addition, follow up interviews would give important knowledge on development of stakeholders views.

Acknowledgments. The authors would like to thank the interviewees for participating the study and Katariina Valtonen for her assistance in data collection. This study is an adjunct project of FEAR (Finnish Enterprise Architecture Research) project. The project was funded by the Finnish Ministry of Finance and IT companies.

References

1. Layne, K., Lee, J.W.: Developing Fully Functional E-Government: A Four Stage Model. Government Information Quarterly 18(2), 122–136 (2001)
2. Lankhorst, M., et al.: Enterprise Architecture at Work –Modeling, Communication, and Analysis. Springer, Heidelberg (2005)

3. Morganwalp, J.M., Sage, A.P.: Enterprise Architecture Measures of Effectiveness. International Journal of Technology, Policy and Management 4(1), 81–94 (2004)
4. Klein, H.K., Myers, M.D.: A Set of Principles for Conducting and Evaluating Interpretive Field Studies in Information Systems. MIS Quarterly 23(1), 67–94 (1999)
5. Kvale, S.: To Validate is to question. In: Kvale, S. (ed.) Issues of Validity in Qualitative Research, Studentlitteratur, Lund, pp. 73–92 (1989)
6. Isomäki, H., Liimatainen, K.: Challenges of Government Enterprise Architecture Work – Stakeholders' Views. In: Wimmer, M.A., Scholl, H.J., Ferro, E. (eds.) EGOV 2008. LNCS, vol. 5184, pp. 364–374. Springer, Heidelberg (2008)
7. Patton, M.Q.: Qualitative evaluation and research methods. SAGE, Newbury Park (1990)
8. Sandberg, J.: Understanding human competence at work: An interpretive approach. Academy of Management Journal 43(1), 9–25 (2000)
9. IDABC: European Interoperability Framework for pan-European eGovernment Services, version 1.0 (2004)

An Investigation into Critical Determinants of e-Government Implementation in the Context of a Developing Nation

Nahid Rashid[1] and Shams Rahman[2]

[1] Department of Management, Monash University, Melbourne, Victoria, Australia
[2] School of Business IT and Logistics, RMIT University, Melbourne, Victoria, Australia

Abstract. Over the last decade governments of many developing nations have undertaken initiatives to adopt e-Government. There is evidence that these nations faced many challenges during the phase of implementation. The aim of this research is to investigate the critical determinants associated with the implementation of e-Government in Bangladesh. The results indicate that currently there exist a high degree of political commitment and administrative leadership. What is required is to improve skills of the human resources within the implementing agencies, and to develop awareness of both public agencies and general citizens. The results also highlight that the implementing agencies must develop right organisational structures and formulate appropriate regulatory framework. Previous studies on e-Government predominantly used case studies and qualitative approaches. This is one of the rare studies which applied a quantitative method using data from four categories of stakeholders. The findings of the research can be applied in many developing nations.

Keywords: e-Government, Public sector, Critical determinants, ICM analysis

1 Introduction

There is evidence that a successful electronic-Government (e-Government) can facilitate speedy, transparent, efficient and effective interaction with citizens, businesses and other stakeholders [1, 2, 3]. As in developed countries, people and businesses in developing nations also require more efficient services from public sectors. Recently, many developing nations have undertaken initiatives to adopt e-Government. Studies suggest that a coordinated effort by political leaders, bureaucrats, and private entrepreneurs is important to facilitate the growth of e-Government [4].

The aim of this study is to investigate the critical determinants associated with the implementation of e-Government in Bangladesh. The paper is organised as follows. A review of literature on determinants preventing the implementation of e-Government is presented in section 2. Based on the literature review, a conceptual framework for e-Government implementation in Bangladesh is proposed in section 3. An outline of the research methodology is given in section 4. The results of the analysis are given in

K.N. Andersen et al. (Eds.): EGOVIS 2010, LNCS 6267, pp. 9–21, 2010.

section 5 which is followed by a discussion in section 6. The paper ends with a conclusion and recommendation in section 7.

2 Literature Review

The implementation of e-Government in developing nations faces many challenges. For example, Ndou [5] suggests political commitment as the most important factor for the implementation of e-Government in developing nations. Dalal [6] views laws regarding openness as the backbone of the success for e-Government. Chen and Knepper [7] propose a set of elements for successful adoption of e-Government. Many other authors have contributed to this issue. Literature suggests that a vast majority of the studies used case studies and qualitative approaches. Based on the existing body of knowledge, our research classifies determinants into four categories, e.g. institutional, resource-related, access-related and legal aspects. Each of these categories is briefly discussed in the following sub-sections.

2.1 Institutional Factors

Institutional factors such as political commitment, administrative leadership and organisational structure are considered critical for e-Government implementation. For example, Coursey and Norris [8] and Koh et al. [9] view political commitment and appropriate organisational structure as the two key factors for e-Government adoption. A similar view is expressed by Kettle [10]. According to OECD [11], the most important element for successful reform is the strength and consistency of support from the highest political level. For any reform to materialise, political commitment is considered to be the most important success criterion especially in the context of developing nations [5, 12]. CEG [13, p.7] suggests that 'public sector leaders must embrace e-Government as a tool to transform and improve government and connect it to the people it serves'. Singh [14] asserts that the top officials within a department are the main driving forces for making any sustainable changes. Therefore, it is critical that they have a clear understanding of the definition and scope of e-Government. While political commitment is the milestone of any change, administrative leadership with effective management process is crucial [15]. A summary of the studies related to institutional factors is given in Table 1.

2.2 Resource-Related Factors

Resource-related factors such as technical, financial and human resources are critical for e-Government implementation. The shortage of IT skills is identified as a major constraint for introducing e-Government in developing nations [17, 18, 19]. Moreover, there is a lack of institutional support to develop expertise and skills related to e-Government application. Hence, many e-Government projects in developing nations suffer from acute shortages of skilled human resources [20, 21, 22].

Table 1. Literature related to institutional determinants

Higher level determinant	Determinants	Source
Institutional	Political commitment	Bonham et al. [4]; CEG [13]; Coursey and Norris [8]; OECD [11]; Kettle [10]; Koh et al. [9]; Mahmood [12]; Ndou [5]
	Administrative leadership and commitment	Coursey and Norris [8]; Kettle [10]; CEG [13]; Mahmood[12]; Koh et al. [9]; Singh [14]; Bonham et al. [4]
	Organisational structure	Hasan [16]; Koh et.al [9]; Coursey and Norris [8]; O'Dell and Garyson [15]

Generally, e-Government projects are inter-sectoral or inter-organisational in nature. Dawes and Pardo [23] suggest that inter-organisational projects often lack adequate financing. Caffery [24] highlights that resource-shared projects are often implemented on an ad-hoc basis where financial and man power supports are generally inadequate to sustain these projects. A similar view has also been expressed by Edmiston [25] and Norris et al. [26].

Technical capability is related to the computer hardware, software, and expertise required for implementing projects. E-initiatives demand investments for securing hardware, software, and expertise. Bonham et al. [4] and Bourn [27] indicate the lack of technical infrastructure as a significant barrier to deliver e-services. The ICT (information and communication technology) infrastructure in developing nations is generally weak and at the same time the use of ICT is low [28, 29]. Hence, the e-Government adoption becomes more challenging when sub-optimal use of available infrastructure is added to inadequate technical infrastructure [21, 30]. A summary of the relevant literature regarding resource-related determinants is given in Table 2.

Table 2. Literature related to resources issues

Higher-level determinant	Determinant	Source
Resource	Technical	Bonham et al. [4]; Bhatnagar and Bijorn-Andersen [28]; Bourn [27]; Dawes and Pardo [23]; MOSICT [30]; Taifur [21]; Yong [29]
	Human resources	BEI [22]; Chen and Gant [18]; Dawes and Pardo [23]; Heeks [17]; Moon [19]; Morshed [20]; Taifur [21]
	Financial	Caffery [24]; Dawes and Pardo [23]; Edmiston [25]; Norris et al. [26]

2.3 Access-Related Factors

Access related determinants in the context of e-Government implementation include education and basic technical knowledge, awareness, and purchasing capacity. According to UNDP [31] e-Government implementation efforts in Bangladesh have been facing challenges in three A's areas: Access, Awareness, and Applications. This report highlights that ICT (e-mail and the Internet) is still considered to be something meant for the elites in the society and the majority of the people are ignorant about the usefulness of ICT in their lives. The effective use of ICT requires not only literacy but also technical skills, computer literacy and language skills [32]. The importance of education and purchasing capacity has been highlighted in many studies [16, 20, 33, 34]. Heeks [35] suggests that e-Government has little relevance for a developing nation like Bangladesh where it is hard to satisfy the basic economic needs. While implementing e-Government in developing nations, the ability of the users to make use of the benefit of e-Government needs to be considered. For example, according to Thomas and Streib [36], digital divide may hinder users' willingness to use the websites. Further, Rice [37, p.74] cautions that the 'Digital divide among the LDCs appears to be widening despite globalisation, which are failing to keep pace with the growing ICT race of OECD countries'. Table 3 provides a summary of the studies related to accessibility issues.

Table 3. Literature related to accessibility issues

Higher-level determinant	Determinant	Source
Access	Education and technical knowledge	Fors and Moreno [32]; Rice [37]; Thomas and Streib [36]
	Awareness	Heeks [35]; Rice [37]; Thomas and Streib [36]; UNDP [31]
	Purchasing capacity	Cecchini and Raina [34]; Morshed [20]; Hasan [16]; Hossain [33]; Thomas and Streib [36]

2.4 Legal Factors

Legal barriers include regulatory framework, privacy and security. A sound legal or policy guidance with clear indications regarding accessibility of information and issues related to risk and trust is essential [38, 39]. The absence of legislation hampers a congenial environment for knowledge sharing. The regulatory framework for e-Government in Bangladesh is not adequate. An e-mail has no official value in the existing government and legal system. Cyber crime, electronic authentication are not protected by laws. Dalal [6] views laws regarding openness as the backbone of success of e-Government. Transparency and accountability mechanisms should be strengthened in the form of legislation, regulation and policy.

Breach of privacy and security may harm public trust in e-Government. Generally, trust determines whether or not users will choose to receive services through the Internet. Hence, organisations need to be aware that they have to be trustworthy in handing all information during the delivery of services. Kubicek [40] cautions that in order to achieve the goal of transparency and openness, the risk of breaking citizens' privacy may arise from ethical and legal perspectives. Another important aspect is the maintenance of official secrecy for the sake of so called national security and integrity. Regulatory provisions are often in place to control information flow and maintain confidentiality. Table 4 gives a summary of the literature related to legal issues concerning e-Government.

Table 4. Literature related to legal issues

Higher-level determinant	Determinant	Source
Legal	Regulatory framework	Dalal [6]; Lane and Buchanan [38] ; Marquette [41]; Rousseau et al. [39]
	Privacy	Dawes [42]; Dalal [6]; Edmiston [25]; Marquette [41]; Kubicek [40]; Rousseau et al. [39]
	Security	Belanger et al.[44]; Coursey [43] ; NECCC [45]

3 Conceptual Framework

Based on the discussion in section 2, a conceptual framework is proposed to assess critical determinants of e-Government implementation in Bangladesh. The framework is shown in Figure 1 which is described by twelve determinants and four higher-level determinants.

Four higher-level determinants are institutional, resource, access, and legal aspect related. Determinants included in the institutional, resource, and legal category represent the supply-side while determinants within access category represent the demand-side of e-Government implementation. Institutional weakness can be seen as lack of political commitment, administrative leadership, and unaligned organisational structure to introduce e-Government. Resource implies shortage of human resources in terms of skilled and trained professional, inadequate ICT infrastructure, and lack of financial support. Legal aspect includes inadequate regulatory framework and privacy-security concerns, and access denotes lack of education and technical skills, and awareness among the general people about ICT and lack of economic capacity.

4 Research Methodology

4.1 Respondents

The aim of this research is to identify critical determinants of e-Government implementation in Bangladesh. To address this objective from the real-world perspective, respondents were chosen on the basis of their capacity to generate information ensuring that research objectives are met. Using a survey questionnaire a total of 65 senior officials was interviewed. These respondents hold key positions and work closely with broad range of e-Government efforts of the government of Bangladesh, including formulation of e-Government strategy, management of e-Government projects and development of change management programs. They were selected using convenience sampling plan and they belong to four categories of organization such as public officials and policy makers, implementing agency, ICT task force and development partners. The distribution of respondents is shown in Table 5. The survey was conducted in late 2008.

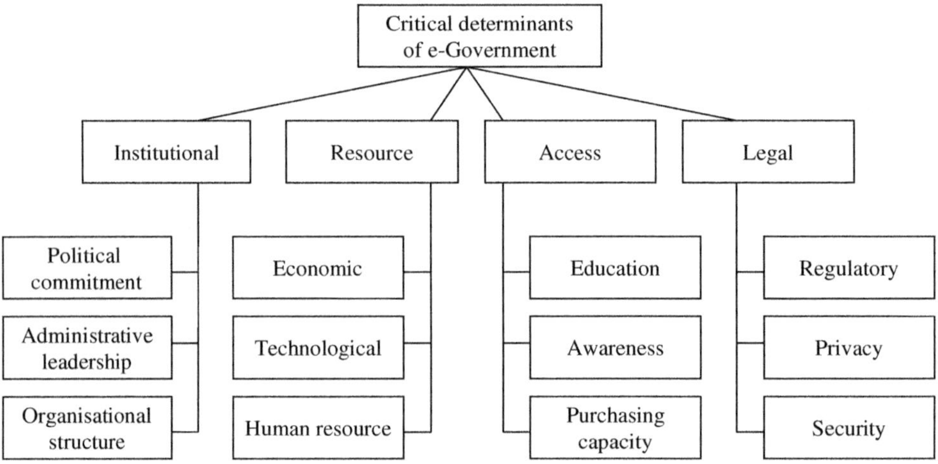

Fig. 1. The proposed conceptual framework

4.2 Data Analysis Method

Importance-Commitment Matrix Analysis. An Importance-Commitment Matrix (ICM) analysis uses a 2 X 2 format. An example is shown in Figure 2. The vertical axis represents the perceived importance of the determinants from low to high, and the horizontal axis represents the perceived commitment of the determinants from low to high. Thus, it generates four quadrants such as 'low priority', 'possible overkill', 'concentrate here', and 'keep up the good work' (Figure 2). This is one of the more widely known importance-performance gap-based methods proposed by Martilla and James [46]. The utility of the ICM analysis lies in its capacity to represent both importance and commitment perspectives with regards to the relative improvement priorities required in a competitive environment. In recent times the method has been applied widely in service operations. For example, Clarke [47] and Skok et al. [48] applied ICM type gap analysis to develop marketing strategies for organisations within the health care industry. Babakus et al. [49] applied the method to assess the perceptions of customers in order to improve the service quality of a catering firm and Lai and Cheng [50] applied ICM type analysis to assess supply chain performance in transport logistics.

Table 5. Distribution of respondents

Respondent category	Member	Description	Number of Respondents
Category-1	Public officials and Policy makers	Senior public officials who work closely with broad range of e-Government efforts of the government, including formulation of e-Government strategy, management of e-Government projects, and development of change management programs	44
Category-2	Implementing agencies		10
Category-3	Member, ICT Task Force and others	Representatives from the National ICT Task Force (highest ICT policy making body of the country). They are responsible to identify and priorities ICT-related needs. Within others are the representatives from selective professional groups such as Transparency International (Bangladesh), Anti-corruption Commission	7
Category-4	Representatives, Development partners	They are the representatives from different development partners who are actively involved in e-Government implementation in Bangladesh. They belong to organisations such as UNDP, World Bank, Asian Development Bank, and Asia Foundation.	4

The respondents were asked to provide their perception on the level of importance and commitment for each of the twelve determinants. A likert scale of 1 – 5 was used to measure the levels of importance and commitment.

5 Results of Analysis

The ICM analysis was applied to twelve determinants of e-Government implementation in Bangladesh. The analysis was conducted in the following manner. The mean

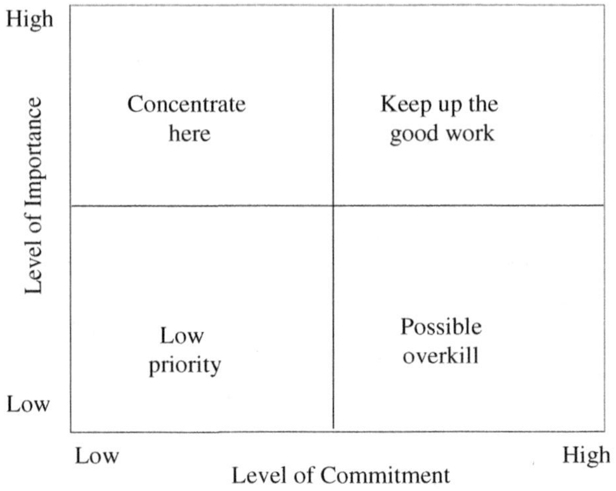

Fig. 2. Importance-Commitment matrix [46]

values for twelve assessment determinants on importance and commitment were calculated. A *t*-test was conducted to ascertain the significance of difference between what is important and what has so far been committed for e-Government implementation as perceived by the respondents.

As is apparent from the analysis that the top three determinants as perceived by the respondents are 'political commitment' (mean = 4.88), 'human resource' (mean = 4.80), and administrative leadership (mean = 4.37). From the commitment perspective, the top three determinants are political commitment (mean = 3.46), economic resource (mean = 3.24), and administrative leadership (mean = 3.05). Overall, the mean importance values of all determinants are higher than the mean values of commitment except for the 'economic resource' and 'technical resource' determinants. These differences are found to be statistically significant for all determinants except for the 'technical resource' determinant (see Table 6).

Table 6. Mean and standard deviation of determinants' importance and commitment ratings

	Determinant	Importance		Commitment		Performance - Commitment	
No.		Mean	SD	Mean	SD	Mean	t-value
1	Political commitment	4.88	0.33	3.46	0.71	1.42	14.59*
2	Administrative leadership	4.37	0.49	3.05	0.81	1.32	11.22*
3	Organisational structure	4.14	0.58	2.11	0.36	2.03	23.91*
4	Economic resource	2.98	0.60	3.24	0.49	-0.26	-2.64 **
5	Technical resource	3.03	0.47	3.04	0.44	-0.01	-0.10 +
6	Human resource	4.80	0.50	2.50	0.50	2.30	26.23*
7	Purchasing power	3.10	0.30	2.80	0.60	0.30	2.96**
8	Education	4.00	0.30	2.40	0.60	1.60	19.66*
9	Awareness	4.70	0.60	2.70	0.60	2.00	18.10*
10	Regulatory framework	3.98	0.33	1.90	0.61	2.08	24.31*
11	Security	3.91	0.34	1.68	0.77	2.23	21.32*
12	Legal	3.74	0.44	1.64	0.65	2.10	21.60*

* significant at 0.001; ** significant at 0.01; $^{+}$ not significant.

Similar analysis was conducted for the higher-level determinants. The results show that the most important higher-level determinant is 'institutional' issues (mean = 4.46), followed by 'access' (mean = 3.93) and 'legal' aspect of e-Government implementation (mean = 3.88). The least important higher-level determinant is 'resource' (mean = 3.60) (Table 7), whereas, the current commitment- level is highest for the 'resource' determinant (mean = 2.93), closely followed by the 'institutional' determinants (mean = 2.87). The respondents perceived that currently the least commitment is being given to the 'legal' aspects of e-Government (mean = 1.74). The difference between means of importance and means of commitment are statistically significant expect for 'resource' (Table 7).

Table 7. Mean and standard deviation of higher-level determinants' importance and commitment ratings

	Higher-Level determinant	Importance		Commitment		Importance - Commitment	
No.		Mean	SD	Mean	SD	Mean	t-value
1	Institutional	4.46	0.38	2.87	0.4	1.59	3.49*
2	Resource	3.60	1.04	2.93	0.38	0.67	1.06+
3	Acecess	3.93	0.80	2.63	0.21	1.30	2.71*
4	Legal	3.88	0.12	1.74	0.14	2.14	19.83**

* significant at 0.001; ** significant at 0.01; + not significant

The overall mean values of importance and commitment were calculated. The low and high values used to draw the vertical and horizontal axis were decided based on the relative rather than the absolute levels of importance and commitment. The position of the cross-hairs that divide the matrix into four quadrants is critical as it since influences the interpretation of the results (Figure 3). Since mean and median values are close, mean values were used as the dividing points in this study, to avoid discarding useful information [46]. Twelve determinants of e-Government implementation that were located in the four quadrants of importance-commitment map are shown in Figures 3. The analysis shows that two determinants fall into quadrant 'low priority', three into 'possible overkill', two into 'keep up the good work', and five into 'concentrate here' category. Figure 3 also shows an iso-rating line, where commitment equals importance. The distance from the iso-rating line is the gap identified in Table 6.

6 Discussion

This study provides an assessment on the determinants of e-Government implementation in Bangladesh. The results indicate that the current commitment level perceived by the respondents is lower than the importance level. Ten out of twelve determinants' commitment ratings are lower than their corresponding importance ratings. The gap between importance and commitment of a specific determinant indicates its strength or weakness. The largest two gaps identified are for determinants such as 'human resource' and 'security'.

The distribution of twelve determinants is shown in Figure 3. Determinants in the quadrant 'high importance and high commitment' indicates that existing system have strengths in these determinants and it is government's responsibility to make sure that

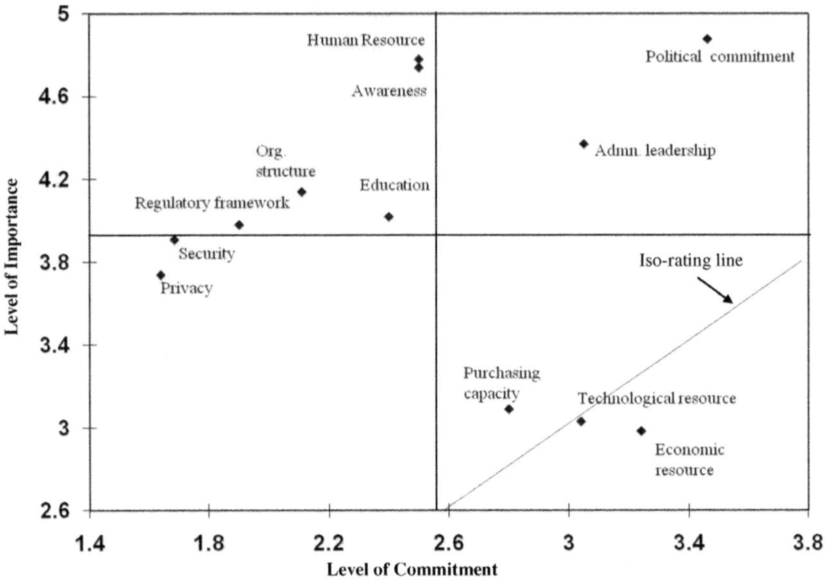

Fig. 3. An importance-commitment matrix for e-Government in Bangladesh

these important determinants remain in this quadrant. This quadrant is termed as 'Keep up the good work'. Determinants such as 'political commitment' and 'administrative leadership' fell in this quadrant.

On the contrary, two determinants such as 'security' and 'privacy' fell in the 'low priority' (low importance and low commitment) quadrant which indicates that at the current situation the policy-makers are not required to assign a great deal of importance to these two determinants while implementing e-Government in Bangladesh.

The 'concentrate here' quadrant of the ICM map represents the determinants which needs more attention. Determinants such as 'human resource', 'awareness, 'organisational structure', 'education' and 'regulatory framework' fell into this quadrant. These determinants are highly rated in importance but were rated low in commitment scale, and hence should be given top priority. What it means is that for successful implementation of e-Government in Bangladesh a further improvement of skills of human resources within the implementing agencies, and development of awareness of both public agencies and general citizens through education and training is critical. The results also indicate that the implementing agencies must develop appropriate organisational structure for e-Government implementation and formulate appropriate regulatory framework for monitoring the system. In general, implementation of e-Government urgently requires the determinants belong to 'concentrate here' along with the factors under the 'keep up the good work' quadrant.

Finally, the quadrant 'possible overkill' denotes low importance and high commitment. Out of twelve determinants employed in this study for e-Government implementation, three determinants fell in this quadrant. These are 'purchasing capacity', 'technological resource', and 'economic resource'. This shows that relatively more resources than necessary are committed towards these determinants. It would be more useful to divert some of the resources from these determinants to elsewhere.

7 Conclusion and Recommendation

Based on extensive literature, a framework for e-Government implementation has been proposed with twelve determinants and four higher-level determinants. Data were collected against these determinants using 65 respondents who belong to four categories of organisations such as government policy makers and public officials, development partners, implementing agencies, and ICT task force members. Twelve determinants of the proposed e-Government framework were subjected to the ICM analysis. This research is one of the rare studies which apply a quantitative approach using data from four categories of stakeholders.

The results indicate that from the supply perspective the critical determinants of e-Government are political commitment, administrative leadership, human resource, organisational structure and regulatory framework. The critical determinants from the demand perspective include education in general and education in IT in particular, and awareness. It appears from the results that currently there is a high degree of political commitment, and administration leadership to introduce e-Government in Bangladesh. From these results the following recommendations can be suggested:

- build awareness of e-Government among government officials through training.
- develop awareness and improve access to citizens: e-Government to be accessible to all users, the government should invest resources and introduce necessary policies to extend ICTs.
- recruit ICT skilled human resource in government agencies to ensure the sustainability of the projects.
- Develop appropriate organisational structures for e-Government implementation and formulate appropriate regulatory framework for monitoring systems.
- results of this research can easily be transferred to other developing nations.

References

1. Schware, R., Deane, A.: Deploying e-Government Programs: The Strategic Importance of 'I' before 'E'. Info. – J. Policy, Regulation and Strategy for Telecommunications 5, 10–19 (2003)
2. Bhatnagar, S.: E-government: From Vision to Implementation: A Practical Guide with Case Studies. Sage Publication, Thousand Oaks (2004)
3. Lam, W.: Barriers to e-government. J. Enterprise Information Management 18, 511–530 (2005)
4. Bonham, G., Seifert, J., Thorson, S.: The transformational potential of e-government: at the role of political leadership. In: 4th Pan European International Relations Conference, University of Kent (2001)
5. Ndou, V.: E-Government for Developing Countries: Opportunities and Challenges. Electronic J. Information Systems in Developing Countries 18, 1–24 (2004)
6. Dalal, P.: Cyber Law Forum: Electronic Governance and Transparency, `http://perry4law.blogspot.com/2005/06/electronic-governance-andtransparency.html`
7. Chen, Y.C., Knepper, R.: Digital Government Development Strategies. Lessons for Policy Makers from a Comparative Perspective. In: Electronic Government Strategies and Implementation. Idea Group publishing, USA (2005)

8. Coursey, D., Norris, D.: Models of e-Government: Are They Correct? An Empirical Assessment. PAR 68, 523–536 (2008)
9. Koh, C.E., Ryan, S., Prybutok, V.R.: Creating Value through Managing Knowledge in an E-Government to Constituency (G2C) environment. J. Computer Information Systems 45, 32–41 (2005)
10. Kettle, D.F.: The Transformation of Governance, Public Administration for Twenty-First Century America. John Hopkins University Press, U.S.A. (2002)
11. OECD: The E-Government Imperative (2003), `http://www1.worldbank.org/publicsector/egov/E-GovernmentImperative.pdf`
12. Mahmood, R.: Can Information and Communication Technology Help Reduce Corruption? How So and Why Not: Two Case Studies from South Asia. Perspectives on Global Development and Technology 3, 347–373 (2004)
13. Council For Excellence in Governance: e-Government, the Next American Revolution. Council for Excellence in governance, Washington, DC (2001)
14. Singh, S.H.: Government in the Digital Era and Human Factors in e-Governance. In: Regional Workshop on e-Government (2003)
15. O'Dell, C., Grayson, C.J.: If Only We Knew What We Know: Identification and Transfer of Internal Best Practices. California Management Review 40, 154–174 (1998)
16. Hasan, S.: Introducing E-government in Bangladesh: Problems and Prospects. International Social Science Review 78, 111–125 (2003)
17. Heeks, R.: e-Government as a Career of Context. J. Public Policy 25, 51–74 (2005)
18. Chen, Y., Gant, J.: Transforming Local e-Government Services: the Issue of Application Service Providers. Government Information Quarterly 18, 343–355 (2001)
19. Moon, M.J.: The Evolution of E-government Among Municipalities Rhetoric or Reality. PAR 62, 424–433 (2002)
20. Morshed, K.: E-Governance: Bangladesh Perspective, Bangladesh ICT Policy Monitor Network, `http://bangladeshictpolicybytesforall.net`
21. Taifur, SASM: SICT's Steps Towards Good Governance through ICTs: e-Governance Strategies. Ministry of Planning, Bangladesh (2006)
22. BEI: Study of e-Government in Bangladesh. Bangladesh Enterprise Institute and Asia Foundation, Dhaka (2004)
23. Dawes, S.S., Pardo, T.: Building Collaborative Digital Government Systems. In: Mclver, W.J., Elmagarmid, A.K. (eds.) Advances in Digital Government Technology, Human Factors, and Policy. Kluwer Academic Publishers, Norwell (2002)
24. Caffrey, L.: Information Sharing Between and within Governments. The International Council for Technology in Government Admin, London, A study group report of the Commonwealth Secretariat (1998)
25. Edmiston, K.D.: State and Local e-Government: Prospects and Challenges. American Review of Public Administration 33, 20–45 (2003)
26. Norris, F., Fletcher, P.D., Holden, S.H.: Is Your Local Government Plugged in? Highlights of the 2000 Electronic Government Survey, University of Maryland, Baltimore, MD (2001)
27. Bourn, J.: Better Public Services Through E-Government.The National Audit Office, London (2002)
28. Bhatnagar, S.C., Bjorn-Andersen, N.: Information Technology in Developing Countries. Elsevier Science, Amsterdam (1990)
29. Yong, J.S.L.: E-government in Asia: Enabling Public Service Innovation in the 21st Century. Times Media, Singapore (2003)

30. MOSICT (Ministry of Science and ICT). E-governance activities, http://www.mosict.gov.bd/what_new.htm
31. UNDP: e-Governance Horizon Scan Report. An Assessment Study of e-Governance in Bangladesh, Access to Information (A2I) Programme, Chief Advisor's Office, Government of the People's Republic of Bangladesh (2001)
32. Fors, M., Moreno, A.: The Benefits and Obstacles of Implementing ICTs Strategies for Development from a Bottom-up Approach. In: ASLIB Proceedings, vol. 54, pp. 198–206 (2002)
33. Hossain, F.: E-Governance Initiatives in Developing Countries: Helping the Rich? Or, Creating Opportunities for the Poor. Asian Affairs 27, 5–23 (2005)
34. Cecchini, S., Raina, M.: Electronic Government and the Rural Poor: The Case of Gyandoot. Information Technologies and International Development 2, 65–75 (2004)
35. Heeks, R.: Understanding E-governance for Development, Institute for Development Policy and Management, Manchester, UK (2001)
36. Thomas, J.C., Streib, G.: The New Face of Government: Citizen-initiated Contacts in the Era of E-government. J. Public Administration Research and Theory 13, 83–102 (2003)
37. Rice, M.: Information and Communication Technologies and the Global Digital Divide. Comparative Technology Transfer and Society 1, 72–88 (2003)
38. Lane, C., Buchanan, R. (eds.): Trust Within and Between Organisation: Conceptual Issues and Empirical Applications. Oxford University Press, Oxford (1998)
39. Rousseau, D.M., Sitkin, S.B., Burt, R.S., Camerer, C.: Not so Different After All: a Cross Discipline View of Trust. Academy of Management Review 23, 393–404 (1998)
40. Kubicek, H.: Third-generation Freedom of Information in the Context of E-Government: The Case of Bremen, Germany. In: Aichholzer, G., Burkert, H. (eds.) Public Sector Information in the Digital Age: Between Markets, Public Management and Citizens' Rights, pp. 275–286. Edward Elgar, Cheltenham (2004)
41. Marquette, H.: Corruption, Democracy and the World Bank. Crime, Law and Social Change 36, 395–407 (2001)
42. Dawes, S.S.: Interagency Information Sharing: Expected Benefits, Manageable Risks. J. Policy Analysis and Management 15, 377–394 (1996)
43. Coursey, D.: E-Government: Trends, Benefits, and Challenges. In: The Municipal Yearbook, pp. 14–21. International City/County Management Association, Washing (2005)
44. Belanger, F., Hiller, J.S.: A Framework for E-government: Privacy Implication. Business Process Management Journal 12, 48 (2006)
45. NECCC: E-Government Strategic Planning, National Electronic Commerce Coordinating Council, Las Vegas, NV (2000)
46. Martilla, J.A., James, J.C.: Importance-Performance Analysis. Journal of Marketing 41, 77–79 (1977)
47. Clarke, R.N.: Health Plan Marketing and Reproductive Health Services. Western Journal of Medicine 163, 64–70 (1995)
48. Skok, W., Kophamel, A., Richardson, I.: Diagnosing Information Systems Success: Importance-performance Maps in the Health Club Industry. Information and Management 38, 409–419 (2001)
49. Babakus, E., Pedrick, D., Richardson, A.: Assessing Perceived Quality in Industrial Service Setting: Measure Development and Application. J. Business to Business Marketing 2, 47–68 (1995)
50. Lai, K.-H., Cheng, T.C.E.: Supply Chain Performance in Transport Logistics: an Assessment by Service Providers. International Journal of Logistics: Research and Applications 6, 151–164 (2003)

"What We Cannot Speak about We Must Pass over in Silence" – (In)correctly Arguing and Comparing the Costs of IT Investments in Public Sector

Samuli Pekkola and Kimmo Wideroos

Department of Business Information Management and Logistics
Tampere University of Technology, PO Box 541, 33101 Tampere, Finland
{samuli.pekkola,kimmo.wideroos}@tut.fi

Abstract. In our era of increasing capitalism a cost-based reasoning is often used, also in public sector, for arguing and comparing the costs within and between different institutions. One of the approaches is the total cost of ownership (TCO) where the costs are approached holistically so that, for example, IT costs per workstation, per person, or per IT staff can be presented. TCO is then used in arguing that a certain IT investment is needed because their TCO is better, worse, or different than of the others' TCO. In this paper we argue that this approach is incorrect and does not provide reliable basis for arguments or comparisons. We demonstrate this through analyzing three ministries' IT expenditures and a purchaser-provider split model and its pricing structure. We propose that as we cannot provide a reliable basis for cost-based reasoning, we should not speak about it but pass it over in silence. The need for new metrics and methods is thus evident.

Keywords: E-government, TCO, costs, purchaser-provider split, IS management.

1 Introduction

Currently public sector is facing a crisis. Taxes shrink while unemployment is increasing. Desperate need to cut the costs puts public services at risk, while citizens urge for both the supply of old services and the development of new ones. Information technology (IT) is seen as a means to rationalize or improve the services and appropriate processes but also as a cutting target. Every new investment ought to be carefully analyzed before an investment decision is made. For instance in Norway, every new IT project in public sector should result better services (for citizens), more effective operations, or cost savings [1]. Counter-intuitively, it seems that IT expenditures in Finnish public sector are increasing despite that more services are outsourced [2-4].

Different costs range from acquisition costs (hardware and software) and control costs (centralization and standardization) to operations costs (support, evaluation, installation or upgrade, training, downtime, personal use, auditing, security, and power consumption) [5]. Often a total cost of ownership (TCO; [6]) approach is used

K.N. Andersen et al. (Eds.): EGOVIS 2010, LNCS 6267, pp. 22–31, 2010.

in arguing the costs. For example, TCO can be calculated per workstation, per server, per employee, or per IT staff. This provides means for comparing the organizations or departments, and of their IT expenditures. Then the organizations reason that certain investment need to made because their TCO is less, more, or different than the others. In other words, they make some assumptions, calculate and acquire TCO's from different organizations, and compare the results. The cost estimation may prove difficult due to the hidden costs related to the investments [7].

In this paper, we present several issues why utilization of TCO in reasoning IT investments, particularly in public sector, is misleading. We will demonstrate this by an analysis of IT budgets of different Finnish ministries, and by examining the impact of the purchaser-provider split of organizing public services. By so doing, we argue that reasoning the costs and prices for functional purchaser-provider split model is practically impossible, and leads to a sub-optimized and inefficient situation from the public sector point of view.

The paper is organized as follows. First TCO and related research are presented. Then, an analysis of Finnish government IT costs and organization is performed in order to illustrate the differences between the TCOs. Third, purchaser-provider model is elucidated. The paper ends with discussion and concluding chapters.

2 TCO and Related Research

Usually, and as the latter analysis of Finnish government ICT reviews reveal, the reasoning behind the IT investments is first to ensure certain level of quality for each potential solution, after which their prices and costs can be compared. Also the benefits can be considered [8]. Yet the public servants have lost interest in detailed analysis of the benefits [1]. This lack of interest of measuring and evaluation the benefits of IT investments has been widely demonstrated (e.g. [8-12]). Frisk and Plantén [8] stated that the benefits are usually evaluated at the feasibility stage, not later. This is supported by Ashurst et al. [12] statement that benefits should be monitored throughout the lifecycle of an IT investment – although in practice they are not. These studies show that the focus of IT investments and IT projects is on costs leaving the benefits with lesser interest.

The focus on costs, particularly on public sector, is understandable as there is a constant pressure to save money and provide better or at least same quality services. Particularly purchaser-provide split [13] has been seen as a mean to reduce costs. To make the cost calculations and comparisons possible, TCO has been adapted to measure the effectiveness of organizations expenditures. It has been utilized in several domains (e.g. [14-16]) although in IS domain it has been seldom studied. This is surprising as TCO provides "*a holistic view of costs related to IT acquisition and usage at an enterprise level*" [6]. Yet the attempts to measure the effectiveness of IT on such level of details has proven to be difficult – many of the effects and implications are not quantifiable or comparable, or benefits, values and indirect implications have been ignored (c.f. [17, 18]), or it is focusing solely on technology costs [19]. However, for the purpose of this study, the utilization of TCO as a basic metric is feasible as our focus is only on the costs and their conceptualization.

TCO makes a holistic approach to a context. For example, it has been used to measure the costs of communities of practice [19], to analyze different software platform options [20] or application service providers [21], to identify the measures of business intelligence [22], and to analyze network and systems management in general [23] and at schools [24]. David et al. [5] performed a comprehensive literature review on different cost factors implying on IT TCO. They divided the costs on three categories: acquisition costs, control costs and operations costs. Acquisition costs include all costs spent on hardware and software while operations costs consists of support, evaluation, installation or upgrade, training, downtime, futz (personal use; [25]), auditing, virus, and power consumption costs. Control costs consider the costs of centralization and standardization.

Yet, although these studies, among many others, attempt to partially conceptualize the costs and value of IT (investments), the complexity of the issue makes it very difficult to evaluate (c.f. [26-28]). For instance David et al. [5] stated that different costs are related to one another in a complex way. This argues for simpler measures. Reichman and Staten [28] proposed the use of relative cost of operations/ownership (RCO), which, instead of trying to encapsulate the whole TCO of IT investment, focuses on factors that distinguish different alternatives.

The costs in general have been tackled very seldom in e-government research. One rare example is the procurement of IT, where the costs have been seen as a rationale behind the investment (e.g. [29-31]) but they are not on focus *per se*. Usually, in e-government literature, the costs are seen only as an impact of information systems implementation aiming to improve the processes' cost-effectiveness (c.f. [32, 33]).

3 An Analysis of IT Budgets of Finnish Ministries

In order to illustrate the difficulties of evaluating and comparing IT investment costs, we analyzed IT budgets of Finnish ministries by utilizing public data from Ministry of Finance (see e.g. [4]). We collected the data from annual reports in 2000-2009. For instance, in 2008, the IT budgets were 802,5M€, that being in average 9,8% of the ministries' total budgets. In IT departments there were 4281 employees (3,9% of all employees), with labor input 5071 person years. These people were administrating more than 166 000 workstations and 9000 servers.

According to the ICT reviews, total IT budgets increased rapidly from 2000 to 2008 (from 458,3M€ in 2000 to 802,5M€ in 2008)[1]. The ministries have also started to acquire more IT solutions as services thus outsourcing and consultancy costs have boomed for every ministry. However, at the same time personnel costs became stable. However, this is just an example. The only "fact" is that outsourcing and consultancy is getting more popular and expensive. The figure or data does not provide any means to evaluate whether outsourcing and consultancy costs are absolutely greater or relatively more expensive between ministries, or whether the ministries have changed their IT service structure or model. Figure 1 illustrates the development of TCO per workstation in three ministries. It provides a theoretical basis for comparative analysis whether a ministry is organizing their IT "better" than the other ministries.

[1] Inflation rate no considered. Inflation rate corrected budget for 2008 should be 528,4M€. This means that the costs have increased 59,8%.

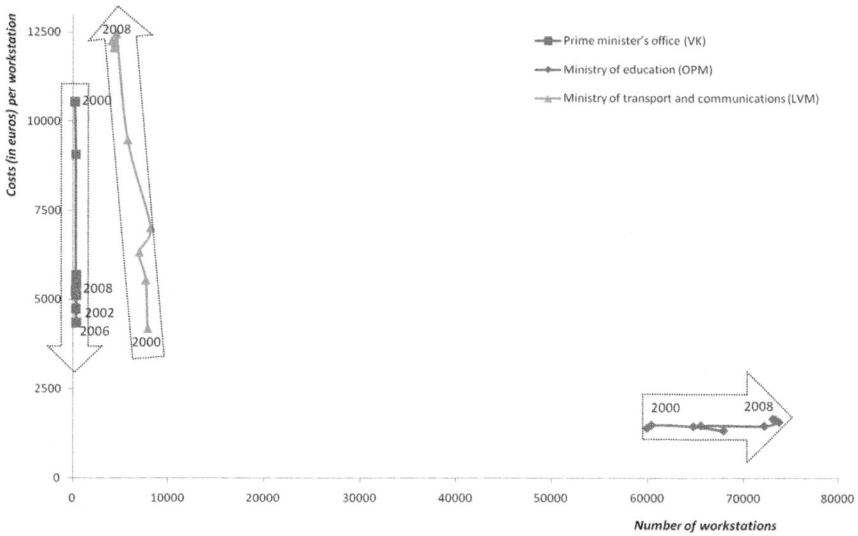

Fig. 1. Time series of total number of workstations (x-axis) and TCO / workstation (y-axis) in three different ministries (big arrows illustrating general trend from 2000 to 2008)

Figure 1 presents the development of TCO per workstation over time for each ministry. For instance, Ministry of Education has managed to keep their IT costs per workstation quite stable over nine years – although their number of workstations has increased from 60000 to 75000. On the other hand, Prime minister's office has managed to cut down their IT costs during the first three years after which they have increased moderately. The number of workstations has remained about the same. Third, Ministry of Transportation and Communication had 8000 workstations and TCO of 4100€ in 2000. In 2008 they had about the same number of workstations while TCO per workstation had trebled.

What do these numbers tell us? Is Ministry of Education organizing their IT better than others as their TCO per workstation has remained stable even the number of workstations has increased? Is Ministry of Transportation and Communication wasting the taxpayers' money for poor IT? Has Ministry of Finance been successful in reorganizing their IT management? We argue that these numbers tell us nothing. We know Ministry of Education has had constant TCO. Yet their activities have not changed much – or they might have but we do not know it as it is not reported in the annual ICT reviews. Meanwhile Ministry of Transportation and Communication might have got new tasks, new systems, or new responsibilities that have presumed new IT investments. Ministry of Finance, for ones part, first might have re-organized their IT, and then better utilized it for their tasks. Basically, for each and every ministry, we do not know whether new systems have been acquired, or whether new systems are operating as intended.

Consequently the graphs and TCO's do not provide us an adequate basis for reasoning that one ministry is doing their IT management and investments better or worse than the others. Every ministry provides different services for citizens, companies, its employees, other ministries, or other actors. They have different organizations, objectives, volumes, cultures, and resources thus arguments and comparisons between the ministries and their TCOs are misleading and provide incorrect results for sure. Yet they are presented and compared in official ICT reviews that are used as a basis for decision making in different institutions.

4 Purchaser-Provider Split

The purchaser-provider split model (illustrated in Figure 2) has been approved in public sector in Sweden [13] and in Finland. The model aims at rationalizing public service production by allowing external companies to compete with the departments of a municipality or a ministry in service production. For example, a municipality opens up their IT management services to external competition, potentially including an external company owned by the municipality itself. After bidding, an agreement is created with a company winning the bid. The municipality then stipulates the company to obey a service level agreement, where, e.g. the prices are explicitly defined. Then each department, such as hospitals or schools, may purchase their services according to their needs, following predefined agreement and prices. The municipality (purchaser) monitors the provider for adequate services, service level, and that they follow the agreement. The purchaser also instructs the customers to purchase their services from that particular service provider. The fundamental idea is to lower public administration costs as each department (customer) purchases only the services they need, with the prices that are transparent to the customers.

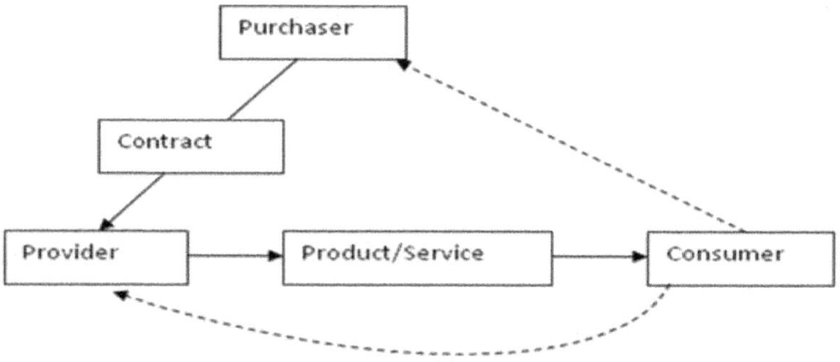

Fig. 2. Purchaser-producer split model

The transparency of the prices creates problems for sophisticated services, such as IT management or maintenance services. The price should cover all the costs – just like in every business. This means that TCO of each service should be calculated. However, as demonstrated earlier with the ministries, the context, spread and spectrum of IT services make it very difficult to compare them even within one provider. Similarly to ministries, also municipalities have different services for their employees, citizens and companies. Hence, IT costs should be evaluated according to the role of IT in specific service production.

The challenge of providing reasonable metrics for IT investments is illustrated in Figure 3, which is a fictive case of three services A, B and C. Service A could be, for instance, an access to ERP services, production costing 1000€[2], while service B includes an administration of database servers, production costing 100€ + 10€ for each server. Service C is workstation maintenance, production costing 1000€ + 1€ for each workstation. Three consumers want to utilize these services for their operations. Consumer I wants an ERP (service A), 10 servers (service B), and 10 workstations (service C). Consumer II wants an ERP, 2 servers and 100 workstations, and Consumer III just the maintenance of 1000 workstations. This means that an ERP with two accesses points, 12 servers, and the maintenance of 1110 workstations need to be provided. This necessitates resources worth for 3330€ (A=1000€ + 0€*2, B=100€+10€*12, C=1000€+1€*1110). Let us assume that the pricing structure is based on the number of workstations as such figure provides an easy way to monitor and charge for the service usage. Consequently the provider needs to charge for each service unit at least 3330€ / 1110 workstations = 3€/workstation. This means that Consumer I pays 30€, Consumer II pays 300€ and Consumer III pays 3000€.

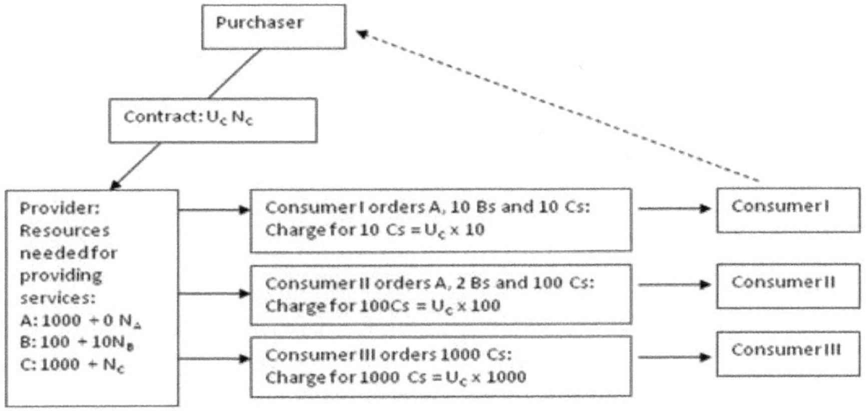

Fig. 3. Example of 3 services, A, B and C and Consumer I, II and III

It can be easily deduced that the provider is unable to optimize its service levels and costs for every service and customer. The inappropriateness of TCO measure for service pricing becomes apparent when we scrutinize the case from Customer III's point of view. Customer III only consumes service C (workstation maintenance), paying 3000€ for it. For the provider the same service costs 1000€ + (N_C=1000€) = 2000€. Thus, Customer III supplements the costs of other services which it does not utilize. Customer III could possibly find another less expensive provider for service C. As the principle of purchaser-producer model is to make the pricing transparent, Customer III should, in fact, try to change the provider.

---

[2] Services, sums and cost models are fictious, not based on any study or data. They are chosen just to illustrate our argument. Also, for simplicity, we have excluded all other costs that are common for A, B, and C (e.g. common management, offices, etc).

If this change-over takes place, the basis for the provider changes (Figure 4). Now the provider needs resources for 2*A + 12*B + 110*C making it to cost 2330€, with a cost of 2330€ / 110 = 21,18€ per workstation. Thus, Consumer I pays 218€, II pays 2118€ and III pays, to a new service provider, let say 2500€, totaling 4836€. This makes sense to Consumer III who saves 500€. However, from the systemic point of view, costs increase 4836€ – 3330€ = 1506€ for the purchaser, the owner of Consumers I, II and III.

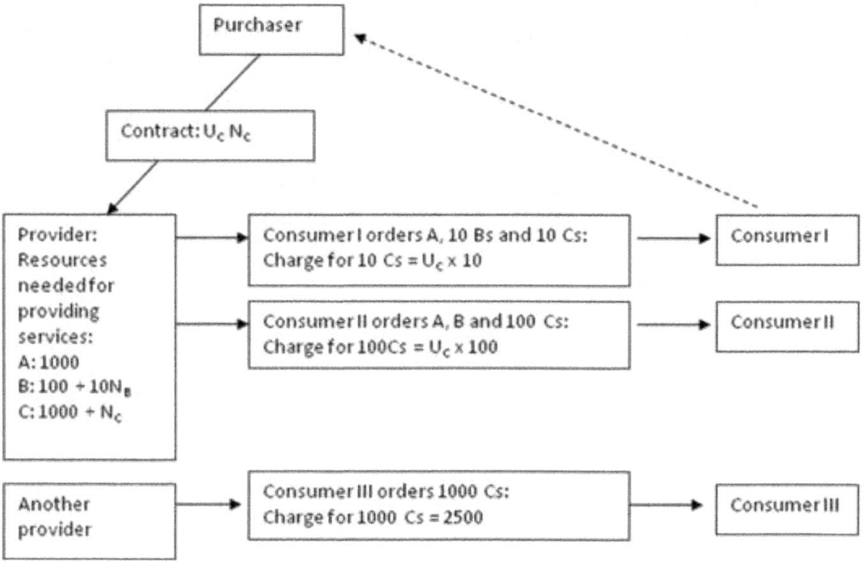

Fig. 4. Situation after Consumer III has changed the provider

What does this mean from the TCO perspective? Easily one may price oneself out from the market by incorrectly pricing their services – all services, including the costs of service A and service B. How to do it correctly? How can the costs be disentangled from one or another? Following the arguments of Lucas [26], Brynjolfsson [27] and Reichman and Staten [28] it cannot be done. This means that the provider has to include "extra" services and the development of new services and their costs to the pricing structure. Under the circumstances, the costs of a service are not based on its actual costs, but include the costs of other services.

5 Discussion, Implications, and Conclusions

The analysis of the ministries' IT budgets shows that an accurate comparison of the costs to others in different context is impossible even if we precisely know how the costs are composed. The analysis of the purchaser-producer split shows that TCO-based pricing will not provide an optimal situation for all consumers. As a matter of fact, purchaser-provider split and coarse TCO calculations make it possible to shift costs from one service to another, consequently sweeping possibly conflicting interests under the carpet. Yet, as the pricing (of IT services) should be transparent, the price should reflect the real expenses, not hidden or estimated ones. This implies that either the service providers need to specialize to some narrow area, which would correspondingly increase the number of service providers, or the basis for pricing needs to be changed. Yet changing the pricing structure is difficult as purchaser-provider split is based on an assumption of charging actual, transparent costs. To be able to do it, calculating the total costs of a service is needed.

The analysis also questions the utilizations of private sector models for public sector (also in [34]). As Caudle et al. [35] show, public sector differs fundamentally from private companies by environmental factors (e.g. less market information, more legal and formal constrains), by organization/environment transactions (e.g. sanctions and powers of government, "public interest"), and by internal structures and processes (e.g. less delegation, no ultimate authority, more politics). Although currently internal structures and processes have been tried to be changed – as the popularity of purchaser-provider split shows – many characteristics of environmental factors, organization/environment transactions, and internal structures have been left intact. In order to properly apply the models, fundamental changes needs to be done throughout the system. To apply the purchaser-producer split model properly, there needs to be enough competition and freedom for consumers to select their preferable services. This necessitates experienced and professional procurement in public sector.

We have analyzed two different examples of utilizing TCO as a basis for comparing "the quality of IT management" or for arguing the basis for service prices. As we have shown, in both cases the use of TCO has resulted invaluable, incorrect, or expensive results. This implies that cost-based reasoning should not be used in public sector – or elsewhere. However, unfortunately cost-based reasoning is often used as a decision criterion as quality-factors (efficacy and efficiency) are much more difficult to quantify and compare. This sets a need for developing new, reliable, quantifiable, comparable, and real metrics for arguing both for IT investments and of their costs, and reasoning for the prices of different services.

Thus, our contribution to practice is to warn the practitioners of not using TCO for comparative purposes. The results will be incorrect for sure. Only if the basis of TCO calculation and the context are known in-depth, it can be used, for instance, to compare the shifts of costs between different years within one institution, municipality, or ministry. Our contribution to research is to urge for the development of more reliable metrics for comparing different institutions and their cost structures, and for arguing for the correctness of certain pricing principles. Currently we do not have such tools. If we cannot develop them, we should stop talking about TCO and costs as they do not form reliable data. Wittgenstein's famous words "What we cannot speak about we must pass over in silence" should be remembered.

References

1. Päivärinta, T., Dertz, W.: Pre-determinants of Implementing IT Benefits Management in Norwegian Municipalities: Cultivate the Context. In: Wimmer, M.A., Scholl, H.J., Ferro, E. (eds.) EGOV 2008. LNCS, vol. 5184, pp. 111–123. Springer, Heidelberg (2008)

2. VM 2007, Tietoja valtion tietohallinnosta ja tietotekniikasta (Finnish government ICT review 2006), Valtionvarainministeriön julkaisuja 5a/2007 (2007), http://www.vm.fi/vm/fi/04_julkaisut_ja_asiakirjat/01_julkaisut/04_hallinnon_kehittaminen/20071004Tietoj/name.jsp
3. VM 2008, Tietoja valtion tietohallinnosta ja tietotekniikasta (Finnish government ICT review 2007), Valtionvarainministeriön julkaisuja 26/2008 (2008), http://www.vm.fi/vm/fi/04_julkaisut_ja_asiakirjat/01_julkaisut/04_hallinnon_kehittaminen/20080618Tietoj/name.jsp
4. VM 2009, Tietoja valtion tietohallinnosta ja tietotekniikasta (Finnish government ICT review 2008), Valtionvarainministeriön julkaisuja 25a/2009 (2009), http://www.vm.fi/vm/fi/04_julkaisut_ja_asiakirjat/01_julkaisut/04_hallinnon_kehittaminen/20090612Tietoj/name.jsp
5. David, J.S., Schuff, D., St. Louis, R.: Managing your IT total cost of ownership. Communications of the ACM 45(1), 101–106 (2002)
6. Cappucio, D., Keyworth, B., Kirwin, W.: Total Cost of Ownership: The Impact of System Management Tools. Gartner Group, Stanford (1996)
7. Willcocks, L., Lester, S.: How do organizations evaluate and control information systems investments? Recent UK survey evidence. In: Avison, D.E., Kendall, J.E., DeGross, J.I. (eds.) Proceedings of the IFIP WG8.2 Working Group Information Systems Development: Human, Social, and Organizational Aspects, Noordwijkerhout, The Netherlands, pp. 15–39 (1993)
8. Frisk, E., Plantén, A.: IT investment evaluation – a survey on perceptions among managers in Sweden. In: Proceedings of 11th European Conference on Information Systems Evaluation (2004)
9. Lin, C., Pervan, G.: The Practice of IS/IT Benefits Management in Large Australian Organizations. Information Management 41(1), 13–24 (2003)
10. Ward, J., Daniel, E.: Benefits Management: Delivering Value from IS and IT Investments. Wiley, Chichester (2006)
11. Bennington, P., Baccarini, D.: Project Benefits Management in IT Projects – an Australian Perspective. Project Management Journal 35(1), 20–30 (2004)
12. Ashurst, C., Doherty, N., Peppard, J.: Improving the impact of IT development projects: the benefits realization capability model. EJIS 17(4), 352–370 (2008)
13. Siverbo, S.: The Purchaser-Provider Split in Principle and Practice: Experiences from Sweden. Financial Accountability & Management 20(4), 401–420 (2004)
14. Ellram, L.M.: Total cost of ownership: an analysis approach for purchasing. International Journal of Physical Distribution & Logistics Management 25(8) (1995)
15. Degraeve, Z., Labro, E., Roodhooft, F.: Total Cost of Ownership Purchasing of a Service: The Case of Airline Selection at Alcatel Bell. European Journal of Operational Research 156(1), 23–40 (2004)
16. Wilmering, T.J., Ramesh, A.V.: Assessing the Impact of Health Management Approaches on System Total Cost of Ownership. In: Proceedings of the IEEE Aerospace Conference, Big Sky, MT (2005)
17. Irani, Z., Ghoneim, A., Love, P.E.D.: Evaluating Cost Taxonomies for Information Systems Management. European Journal of Operational Research 173(3), 1103–1122 (2006)
18. Rosemann, M., Wiese, J.: Measuring the Performance of ERP Software: A Balanced Scorecard Approach. In: 10th Australasian Conference on Information Systems, Wellington, New Zealand (1999)
19. Millen, D.R., Fontaine, M.A., Muller, M.J.: Understanding the Benefit and Costs of Communities of Practice. Communications of the ACM 45(4), 69–73 (2002)

20. Taudes, A., Feurstein, M., Mild, A.: Options Analysis of Software Platform Decisions: A Case Study. MIS Quarterly 24(2), 227–243 (2000)
21. Bennett, C., Timbrell, G.: Application Service Providers: Will they Succeed? Information Systems Frontiers 2(2), 195–211 (2000)
22. Lönnqvist, A., Pirttimäki, V.: The Measurement of Business Intelligence. Information Systems Management 23(1), 32–40 (2006)
23. Blum, R.: Network and Systems Management Total Cost of Ownership. Lucent Technologies, Murray Hill, NJ (2001)
24. Lei, K., Rawles, P.: Strategic Decisions On Technology Selections for Facilitating A Network/Systems Laboratory Using Real Options & Total Cost of Ownership Theories. In: Conference on Information Technology Education archive: Proceedings of the 4th conference on information technology curriculum on Information technology education, ACM Press, New York (2003)
25. Dryden, P.: 'Futz factor' measurement tough to pin down in TCO. Computerworld (April 13, 2003), `http://www.computerworld.com/cwi/story/0,1199,NAV47_STO30535,00.html`
26. Lucas, H.: The Management of Information Technology: Strategic Decision Making for Managers. Wiley & Sons, Chichester (2004)
27. Brynjolfsson, E.: The Productivity Paradox of Information Technology. CACM 36(12), 66–77 (1993)
28. Reichman, A., Staten, J.: TCO is overrated. Forrester Research (2008), `http://www.forrester.com/Research/Document/Excerpt/0,7211,44545,00.html`
29. Moe, C.E.: E-procurement, determinants towards adoption. In: DEXA EGov Conference, Zaragoza, September 2004, pp. 3–6 (2004)
30. Moe, C.E., Risvand, A.C., Sein, M.K.: Limits of Public Procurement: Information Systems Acquisitions. In: DEXA EGOV Conference, Krakow, Poland (2006)
31. Moe, C.E., Päivärinta, T.: Procurement Of IS in the Public Sector – A Preliminary Study. Paper Presented in Scandinavian Workshop on E-Government SWEG 2010. Örebro, Sweden (2010)
32. Yildiz, M.: E-government research: Reviewing the literature, limitations, and ways forward. Government Information Quarterly 24(3), 646–665 (2007)
33. Gupta, M.P., Jana, D.: E-government evaluation: a framework and case study. Government Information Quarterly 20(4), 365–387 (2003)
34. Henriksen, H.Z.: The beauty and the beast: IT in government. Paper Presented in Scandinavian Workshop on E-Government SWEG 2010. Örebro, Sweden (2010)
35. Caudle, S.L., Gorr, W.L., Newcomer, K.E.: Key information systems for the public sector. MIS Quarterly 15(2), 171–188 (1991)

Small-Area Population Projections - A Key Element in Knowledge Based e-Governance

Henning Sten Hansen

Aalborg University
Department of Development and Planning
Lautrupvang 2B
DK-2750 Ballerup
Phone: +45 99 40 24 06
Fax: +45 98 15 57 75
HSH@LAND.AAU.DK

Abstract. Population is an important part of regional and local economy due to the population's role as labour force (tax payers), consumers, and users of public services. Consequently, the size, the age structure and the spatial distribution of population are essential factors in knowledge based e-Governance especially regarding the mid and long term planning of land-use and service facilities. Therefore, population projections are important inputs to decision-making at local and regional level. However, in order to be useful in a spatial decision-making context, the projections must be available for a subdivision of the territory to be managed. This requires a detailed and robust population projection model, plus reliable and up-to-date data. The current paper describes a Danish approach to small-area population projections based on the well-known cohort-component principle supplied with some structural elements, and demonstrate how the results can be used to serve the decision making concerning school planning.

Keywords: Population projections, decision support systems, knowledge-based e-governance.

1 Introduction

Detailed information about future population development in the form of projections and scenarios are needed at regional and local level. Especially for various planning purposes like locating new kinder gardens, schools, hospitals, roads and even expanding the capacity of sewage system and electrical power plants, you need knowledge about the future population at detailed spatial and temporal levels. Besides, a growing population will enhance the environmental impact due to increasing noise, and air pollution. Every year the national statistical offices make population projections for nations, regions, and municipalities, but for most detailed planning purposes, projections at lower spatial level are absolutely needed. Therefore, many municipalities make population projections at district level.

K.N. Andersen et al. (Eds.): EGOVIS 2010, LNCS 6267, pp. 32–46, 2010.

All over the world, many approaches to population projections have been developed, but lack of appropriate data may cause the user to choose a method, which is different from the method chosen under optimum circumstances. Especially, when making projections at sub-municipal levels, access to data may be a serious obstacle. According to Smith et al. [1] we can classify the various approaches to population modelling into three different overall categories: 1) trend extrapolation, 2) cohort-component methods, and 3) structural models. The extrapolation methods applied can be based on simple linear or exponential curve fitting or more advanced methods based on polynomial methods or the so-called ARIMA developed by Box and Jenkins [2]. Usually, no analysis is made of factors that cause population changes, e.g., births, deaths, and migration. The cohort-component model has been utilised successfully at national and regional levels [3], but very often the model is difficult to implement due to lack of detailed data at smaller spatial levels – like for example school districts or even lower spatial units. However, especially the Nordic countries keep registers recording all demographic events at personal level, and such information is of high value in making detailed population projections. The structural models assume that people will migrate to areas in which their economic opportunities are expected to be highest, but economic factors are not the only ones that influence the migration decision.

Population projections have too often been carried out by small specialist groups with only minor interaction with other parts of the organisation. What is needed today with increasing efficiency demands in the public sector is knowledge about the future population development and the derived consequences for kindergartens, schools, elderly care etc, and to make this knowledge available for as well the other departments in the organisation as the public.

The aim of the current research has been to develop a framework for knowledge based e-Governance in local authorities using small area population projections. This requires a detailed model for population projections at sub-municipal level with a sufficient spatial and temporal resolution to support medium-range to long-range planning. The paper is divided into four parts. After the introduction follow a description of the knowledge based framework and the developed population projection model. The third section presents the data employed and some examples from a Danish case area. The paper ends with some conclusions and an outline for subsequent work.

2 Methods

Information about the future population development plays an important role in the management process in local authorities, where the main objectives are to serve the citizens as expected in the Western-European welfare societies. The most important services from a citizen point of view and the most costly services from the authority point of view are related to small children (kindergartens), school children, and elderly people. Especially for the first two groups the services have an important geographic dimension, where the kindergartens and schools serve the families living in the neighbourhood of these facilities. The Danish Government has declared that the municipalities are obliged to fulfil the demand for child care through kindergartens or similar, and rearrangements of the school structure is one of the politically most thorny issues. Therefore it is of vital importance with detailed information about the population structure today and particularly in the near future. Investments in kindergartens, schools and senior housing are costly and require knowledge about population for the next 10 – 20 years at one-year intervals and for small geographic units. Accordingly, the local authorities must set up an IT infrastructure serving this purpose, and this requires as well economic resources as a well educated staff. These requirements are facilitated by the structural reform of local and regional authorities from January 2007, where 273 municipalities were merged into just 98 municipalities [4].

The flow of communication between different departments using population projections is illustrated in figure 1. In most municipalities the population projections are made by the Finance department, but in some municipalities the projections are made by the Environment & Planning department. The planning department provides residential development plans, which is important base information for the population projections. The projection data are then made available for the Town Council as well as the main user departments – the Childcare & Education department, and the Social Services department, which use the population data to analyse the future needs for kindergartens, schools, elderly care and health care. Based on the analysis work these departments send their request for resources to the Town Council, which finally nominate an official population forecast, which is made available to the public through the web site of the municipality. In addition to the authorities mentioned above, population forecasts have received strong attention among the citizens – not so much as individuals as members of different local community associations – related to for example kindergartens and schools. Below, we describe rather detailed the various elements in making small area population forecasts.

2.1 The Population Projection Model

The future population development is generally referred to as either population projections or population forecasts. A projection is a rather strict calculation of the future population based on a certain set of assumptions. Thus, the results of a projection show the future population development, if the set of assumptions is correct. Population forecasts are closely related to population projections by adding a probability dimension. In this context, a population forecast can be defined as the most likely of several population projections (scenarios). Very often a population forecast is a combined result of numerical results and political decisions, where for example the city council decides which of several projections shall be nominated to be the official population forecast for that particular local authority.

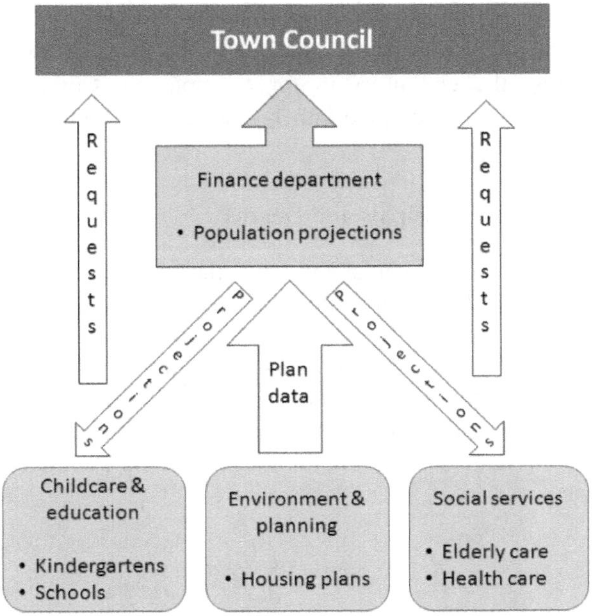

Fig. 1. The information flow between various units

The cohort-component projection models are the most advanced tool for population projection by providing a theoretically complete model treating the various demographic components individually. The method is suitable at all geographic scales – from global over national to local – and even sub-local scales. The current model aims at making population projections for small-scale areas representing subdivisions of municipalities.

The current implementation employs the gross-migration method – i.e. handling in-migration and out-migration separately - instead of the often used net-migration method. There are two reasons for choosing the gross-migration method. First, a separate modelling of in- and out-migration facilitates a more detailed analysis of the modelling results in order to identify potential errors behind strange looking results. Second, the net-migration method is criticised for making growing areas grow faster, and declining areas decline faster [5].

The population projection model applied is based on the cohort-component principle and can be described by the following general population equation, where the superscript *d* refers to the district:

$$P^d_{t+1,i,s} = P^d_{t,i,s} + B^d_s - D^d_{i,s} + I^d_{i,s} - O^d_{i,s} + \Delta H^d_{i,s}$$

The variables $P_{t,i,s}$ and $P_{t+1,i,s}$ refer to the population of sex *s*, age *i* at the time *t* and t+1 respectively. B_s is the number of new-born boys (s=1) and girls (s=2), whereas $D_{i,s}$ denotes the number of deaths for each age group and sex. The last two variables $I_{i,s}$

and $O_{i,s}$ refer to In-migration and Out-migration. The last term ΔH refers to changes in the population within a district due to changes in the stock of dwellings. Due to the requirements among the end users in for example the Childcare and Education department, the population is divided into 1-year cohorts. Below, the various components are described in detail.

2.2 Estimating Number of Births and Deaths

The number of births can be calculated from the number of women in the child-bearing age (15-49) and the age-specific birth rates. However, fertility rates and age-specific birth rates seldom remain constant, but rise or decline from year to year depending on various factors and conditions. Calculating the fertility rates by age of mother requires data on the number of women in each age group and the number of births by age of mother. Currently we have used regionalised fertility rates from Statistics Denmark. The number of births for each district is calculated according to the following formula:

$$B_{t+1,s}^{d} = F^{d} \cdot \sum_{i=15}^{49} P_{i,2}^{d} \cdot f_i \cdot c_s$$

where f_i is the age-specific birth rate and c_s is the proportion of boys and girls of born children. For each district the real number of births differs considerably from the expected number of births. Some districts – mainly in the city centres – have births numbers less than expected, whereas other districts – mainly in the countryside – have births numbers above the expected. Therefore we have added a district dependant correction factor F_d, which is estimated from the observed ratio between the realised and expected births for the previous 3 – 5 years.

The long-term trend in age-specific mortality rates is downward because of the continual improvement in living conditions, and increasing control of disease and prolongation of life by the advancement of medical science [6]. Future mortality rates will probably show some improvement, but it will be very slight and, in fact, many age-specific rates may remain constant. The number of deaths for each district is calculated according to the following formula:

$$D_{t+1,i,s}^{d} = D^{d} \cdot P_{t,i,s}^{d} \cdot m_{i,s}$$

where m is an age and sex specific mortality rate. Nevertheless, it is a fact that even within a rather little and homogeneous country like Denmark we can observe different life durations for different parts of the country. What is more surprising is that we can even observe the same differences – but in smaller scale – between different districts within a (larger) municipality. Therefore, we have added a district dependant correction factor D, which is estimated from the observed ratio between the realised and expected deaths for the previous 3 – 5 years.

2.3 Migration

Migration has huge impact on the population development – not at least the age composition at local levels. Causes of migration are many and varied. Migration is considered as a process with close connection to economic development, labour markets and housing markets. When young people want to start their education they are often forced to move to the bigger cities with sufficient education possibilities. Thus we can observe an outmigration of young people from smaller towns and rural districts to the bigger cities, and this migration is reversed when they have finalised their education and being married and want to settle down.

The current model divides migration into three different elements. The first migration element – the intra-district migration - concerns change of addresses within a district, and they are ignored in the further calculation process. They of course do not make any changes to the population structure for the districts. The second element – the inter-district migration – deals with change of addresses within the municipality, but between districts. Those two internal types migration account for about two thirds of all migration events in Danish municipalities. The third element – the external migration – refers to the migration to the outside world and migration from the outside world and to the municipality.

Out-migration is generally less complicated to calculate compared to in-migration. We assume that an out-migration event solely is dependent on a decision taken by an individual or family to move from one location to another. The frequency of taken that decision is dependent on age, sex and district. Based on this assumption, the internal out-migration *OI* – i.e. the out-migration from one district to another within the municipality - is calculated by

$$OI_{t+1,i,s}^{d} = P_{t,i,s}^{d} \cdot oi_{i,s}^{d}$$

oi is an age, sex and district specific *internal* out-migration coefficient, which is estimated from observed historical out-migration data. The coefficient is calculated as the ratio between observed internal out-migration and the population for each age, sex and district. Similarly, the external out-migration OE – i.e. the out-migration from one district to a location outside the municipality - can be determined by the following formula

$$OE_{t+1,i,s}^{d} = P_{t,i,s}^{d} \cdot oe_{i,s}^{d}$$

where *oe* is an empirical derived age and sex specific *external* out-migration coefficient. The calculation of this coefficient is carried out similarly to the internal coefficient, but where the internal out-migration is replaced by the external out-migration.

In-migration is a much more complicated process to model. Thus a free dwelling unit is a pre-assumption for an in-migration event to take place, and this can for example be obtained through an out-migration event or a death event – or a combination of both. Accordingly, the in-migration into a district is considered to be a function of the number of adult people leaving the district and the number of adult dead. The reason why we only consider adult people is that taking away children or young people will not free dwellings for in-migration.

The first step is to create a pool *R* with in-migrants. The internal out-migrants constitute one part of this pool, due to the requirement of balance between internal out-migration and internal in-migration. The other part of the in-migration pool is made of external in-migration – i.e. in-migration from the outside world and into the municipality– and this figure can be calculated as follows

$$R_{i,s} = ie_{i,s}\left[\sum_{d}\left(\sum_{i=20}^{99} OE_{t,i,s}^{d}\right)+\sum_{d}\left(\sum_{i=20}^{99} D_{t,i,s}^{d}\right)\right]$$

The external in-migration coefficient *ie* is estimated based on historical data from the previous 5 years, where observed in-migration is related to observed external adult out-migrants and dead adults. The last step in estimating the in-migration is to allocate the in-migration pool to the various districts. This is done by weighting the individual districts by their 'demand' as expressed through the number of adult out-migrants (internal and external) and the number of dead adults within each district.

2.4 Changes in the Dwelling Structure

The migration figures dealt with above were concerned with a fixed number of dwellings. However, this is seldom the situation in the real world, where new settlements are established frequently, and some dwellings are even abolished. Therefore, we have enhanced the migration component by adding the possibility to incorporate expected changes in the dwelling stocks within each district. However, in this respect new challenges will arise. Firstly, and most importantly, they are policy based rather than trend based. Thus, the precise location of new dwelling areas and the type of dwellings are a result of political decisions. Second, you must know the characteristics of the people moving into the new dwellings. Currently, we have derived those characteristics from observed events through the previous 3 – 5 years for 5 different dwelling types (detached houses, terrace houses, flats, houses for elderly people, and youth residences). The derived characteristics for the three first more general dwelling types are shown in figure 2.

The municipality lays out development policies for the forthcoming 10 – 20 years, and the plans give guidelines about preferred locations of dwellings but do not detail specific housing sites or the timing of development. The exact location and timing of new housing is determined through what is called the Local Plan process. However, it is still one of the big challenges in making population projections to define the location and not at least the year where people real move to these new dwellings. This is often based on a best guess among the planners and economists doing the projection effort in practice.

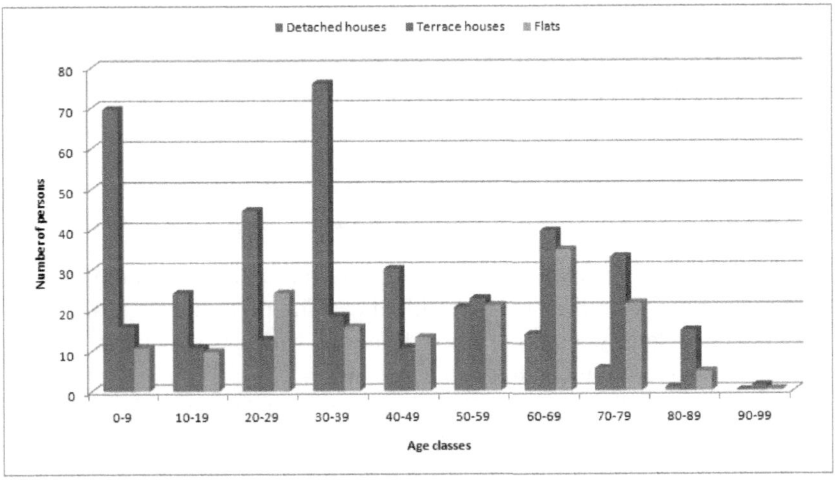

Fig. 2. Number of persons to new dwellings. The numbers refer to 100 building units.

The last challenge is related to the fact that in practice the total population in a municipality will *not* increase as much as expected from the number of new dwellings. The reason behind this is what's normally called the thinning-out' effect, where each person statistically requires more and more floor space. For example, when young people leave home they often move into a normal flat and not into the dedicated single-room flat targeted to the young people. The same can be said about the elderly people, who often spend their whole life in a normal flat or house, in contrast to earlier, where they moved to special old people's home when they became old. In the model this effect is handled by a so-called split factor, which expresses the share of people coming from outside the municipality and into the new dwellings.

2.5 A Scenario Based Approach

Making forecasts of the future population development is a challenging effort. Although the model has been tested and found valid, we must address the fact that the forces driving behind population development are extremely difficult to predict [7]. One way of solving this problem is to use a scenario based approach. Scenarios can provide a multi-dimensional decision-space for the user community of population projections. Fertility, mortality and external migration are the demographic components entering the scenario building. Regarding the fertility component, Statistics Denmark provides three different levels for the general fertility rate until 2030: a) the rate increases with 4.4%, b) the rate increases with 14.2%, c) the rate decreases with 5.3%. There is a general trend that life expectancy is increasing steadily , and we use two different data sets for the age specific mortality rate: a) one data set with a very moderate decrease in the rate, and another b) with a more optimistic decrease in the age specific mortality rate – particularly for the elderly people. Finally, three scenarios are developed for the external migration: a) reduced net migration due to slow regional economic development where the business sector loses competitiveness; b) net migration as in the previous years as a result of a stable regional economic development; c) increased net migration due to enhanced economic competitiveness where the business sector can expand and create provisions for new jobs.

3 Results

The developed model is generic by nature, but its precise implementation will depend on the spatial scales as well as the available data. The performance of the developed model is demonstrated by a case study in Randers, which is a medium sized Danish municipality. Randers municipality is located north of Aarhus - Denmark's second largest city - and accordingly some of the growth around Aarhus will also hit Randers. Thus the population increased from 91666 in 2001 to 93644 in 2007. Randers municipality is divided into 133 basic projection districts, where the population size ranges from 23 persons in the 'smallest' district to 2913 persons in the 'largest' district. Figure 3 illustrates settlement structure and population density in Randers municipality in 2007. The settlement structure is characterised by Randers town, which has about half of the total population, and several smaller villages.

3.1 Data Layers

The Danish Central Person Register (CPR) is the main data source to be used in the population projections. CPR was originally developed in 1968 but its roots go back to 1924, where the first Danish Population Register was established [8].

The register is updated daily through the municipal registration of people. All registered persons have a unique person identification number made up of 10 digits, where the first 6 digits refers to the birthday, and the last 4 digits represent a serial number, of which the last digit indicates the sex of the person. An odd number refers to a male person, and an even number refers to a female. The most important information contained in CPR is Name, Address, Marital status, and Place of birth. The raw ASCII file contains utilised in the current population projection research includes the following columns: code for demographic event type, personal identification number, address1, and address2. The two addresses are necessary to register migration events.

The Danish national Address Register (AR) is needed to assign a spatial reference to the events in the CPR. The Danish address system has traditionally been managed by the municipalities, but recently since the beginning of the century an address reform aiming at standardisation and quality improvements was launched, and a central address register was established [9]. Each address is composed of the following elements: a municipality code, a road code, a house number plus eventually a letter. Also floor number and side are included. Thus a unique identification of each residential unit is available. Besides the proper address the Address Register contains an x-coordinate and a y-coordinate. Recently, cell identification to the Danish national square grid is added to the Address Register.

As mentioned above the population projection model deals with people within districts and not individuals. Therefore a district map is needed. Generally most municipalities have subdivided their territory into smaller units – e.g. statistical districts, school districts etc. Alternatively, a neutral subdivision using grid squares can be used. First of all, the municipality should subdivide their territory into a system of districts, which are flexible enough to adapt to needed changes in for example the school structure. Therefore the municipalities are encouraged to define a spatial subdivision, so the basic population projection districts can easily be aggregated into larger districts regarding school planning, elderly care planning etc. This means quite many – often several hundred - small districts.

Assigning district identifications to each person can thus be performed through a two-step procedure. First, spatial references are assigned to the persons in CPR through an attribute join between Central Personal Register and the Address Register with the address as join key. Second the new point based CPR can be assigned district identifications through a point-in-polygon operation. Finally, we can summarise the state of population and the various demographic events into a set of tables with age representing the columns and districts representing the rows. However, in order to maintain the statistical quality of the coefficients described above, we have defined much larger so-called parameter districts for the purpose of estimating the different migration coefficients as well as the fertility and mortality level coefficients. Generally, the number of parameter districts are rather low (less than ten), and the basic districts entering a parameter district are characterised by similar demographic properties. However, defining the parameter districts is a tough and time consuming exercise, but not at least a very important one, because the quality of the derived coefficients are much dependant on this task.

3.2 Examples

We ran the model from 2008 and until 2020, which are the typical decision-making range in a Danish municipality. Beyond that range, there is too much uncertainty about the pre-assumptions behind the projections. The scenario parameters used are moderate increase in the general fertility rate, slow improvement in the mortality rate, and external net migration as described in the previous years. The main output from a population forecast is two tables for each sex – one for male population and one form female population. The rows and columns represent districts and ages respectively. In addition several other tables regarding in-migration, out-migration, number of born and death, and number of persons to new dwellings etc. are produced. This supports the transparency of the modelling results and facilitates further analysis and visualisation. Below, we will present and discuss some results from the population projection.

Figure 4 illustrates the spatial distribution of population change between 2007 and 2020. The main growth districts are located near the main town Randers. Additionally we can observe that the growing districts are located in the south-western part of the municipality – near the motorway towards Aarhus. The declining districts are located towards the north-eastern part dominated by farmland and smaller villages. Some areas show growth rates on several hundred percent, and this is due to strong urban development in these districts (shown in black).

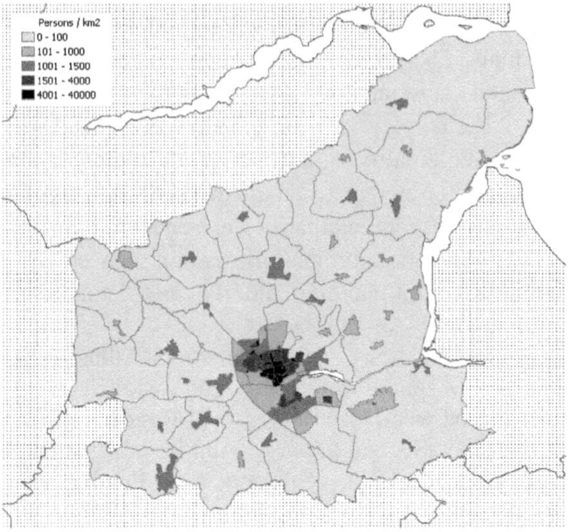

Fig. 3. Settlement structure and population density

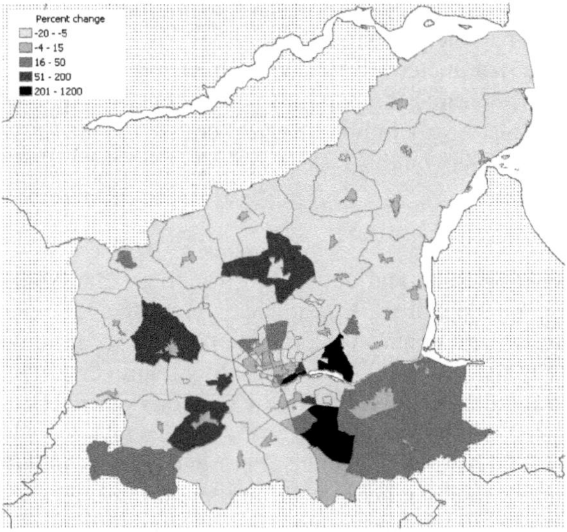

Fig. 4. Estimated population change (in %) between 2007 and 2020

Next we go into more detail and analyse the future spatial distribution of two groups, which have special political attention. The two groups are school children and elderly people. Figure 5 shows each district's projected change (in %) for school children between 2007 and 2020. The projected number of school children in 2020 compared with the observed number of school children in 2007 varies considerably over the municipality. However, there are many similarities between the projected changes for school children and the population in general, and again the extremely high growth rates for some districts are closely related to heavy urban development in those parts of the municipality. From a decision point of view the projected spatial redistribution of school children will have dramatic consequences for the future school structure, where schools will be closed in the declining north-east, whereas there will be a need for new schools in the expanding south-western part of Randers municipality.

The spatial distribution of elderly people in 2020 compared with the base year 2007 is illustrated in figure 6. With longer duration of life it is obvious that we will have an overall growth of elderly people in all parts of the municipality, and with the lower migration rates in this age group compared with younger people we can expect a rather spatially homogeneous distribution of elderly people. This expectation is partly in accordance with the map in figure 6, but especially south-east from the main town Randers (the bigger black coloured districts in figure 5) we can expect in 2020 a significant growth in the number of elderly people compared with the observed number in 2007. The reason for this is that the municipality in these districts has planned many new terrace houses (about 400), and especially this type of dwelling is very popular among people between 60 and 75 (see fig. 2). When the young people leave their home, their parents do not need so much floor space any longer, and with terrace houses they can (partly at least) avoid staircases. Also in this case the map can be used in health care planning – especially in long term investment planning.

3.3 Discussions

The examples shown above are just a very limited number of maps, tables, graphs etc, which can be produced using the result of a population projection using the described model, and it is up to the user to decide among the many possibilities. Clearly, maps illustrating the need for future changes in the school structure have high political interest, but the huge amount of output from the model support the possibility of producing other maps giving further insight into the deeper reason behind this development. Next, these explaining maps can perhaps even be used as outset for political discussions on how decisions can be taken to counteract against a possible unwanted development.

Population projections by their very nature are uncertain. We cannot know precisely what the population will be one year from now, much less 10, 20, or 30 years from now. This is especially true, when we are dealing with small-area population projections as in the current research project. Thus local political decisions concerning for example new urban development can make significant changes to the spatial distribution of people within a municipality. One way of handling this uncertainty is to use spatial scenarios as mentioned above. Population projections are conditional ("if, then") statements about the future [10].

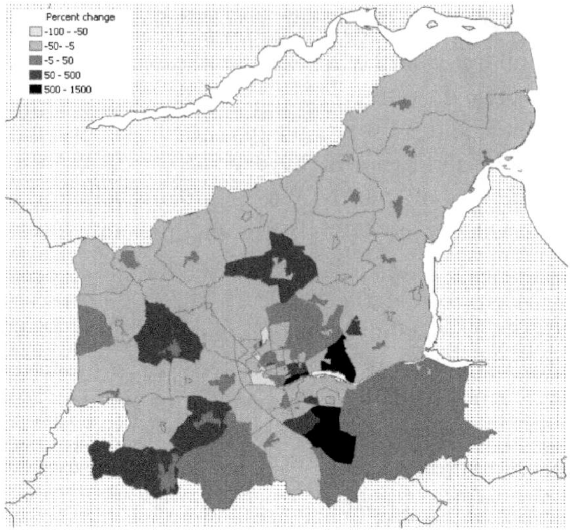

Fig. 5. Projected changes (in %) for school children between 2007 and 2020

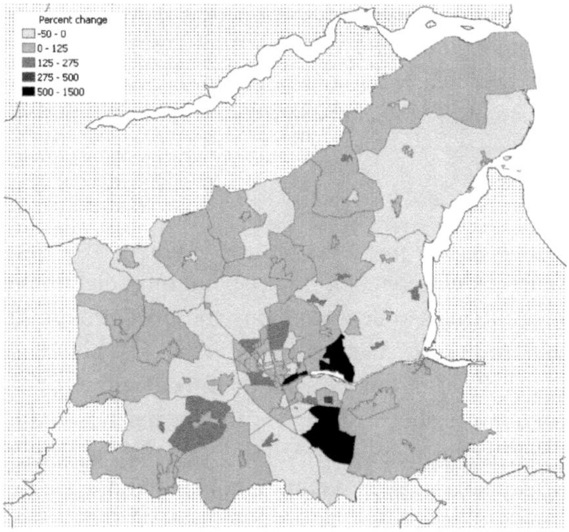

Fig. 6. Projected changes (in %) elderly people between 2007 and 2020

They are combinations of numerical calculations and underlying assumptions, and each scenario has its own assumptions. Then politicians and other decision-makers can discuss the various scenarios and nominate one of these as the official population forecast for the municipality. However, there are also other risks in making population projections. Political pressure may influence the projections, especially if population growth is a strong political objective – and this is often the case – there may be a risk to overestimate the future growth [11].

Generally the model performs very well were the projected values on the short term – less than 5 years – differ less than 1% from the observed values, and currently 37 out of 98 Danish municipalities are using the described approach to make population projections. One remarkable exception is 2009 where the migration figures and particularly the building of new houses nearly stopped due to the economic crisis. The model described has been used in Randers municipality since 2003, and currently 37 out of 98 Danish municipalities are using the described approach to make population projections.

4 Concluding Remarks

Public budget are general under pressure, and at the same time the citizens are expressing their 'rights' much more than just a few years ago. Therefore, it is important for the decision-makers to be well prepared with sufficient knowledge – not at least about the future - to take the right decisions. We have introduced the term knowledge-based e-governance to underline the importance of knowledge and not just information. Knowledge here been considered as an appropriate collection of information, such that it's intent is to be useful for understanding the development and challenges and to support decision-making.

Local and regional population projections are an important tool for today's politicians and other decision-makers. This is contrary to the rather little research performed in this field, and the main publication in this field is the book entitled 'State and local population projections' by Smith et al. [1]. Furthermore, very few have seen the connection between GIS and local population projections, although population projection is a clear spatio-temporal modelling effort. One reason can be the lack of detailed and reliable data to carry out small-are population projections using a comprehensive 1-year cohort-component model.

The aim of the current research project has been to develop a detailed spatio-temporal population projection model based on the cohort-component method with an additional structural element. The main requirement for the decision-makers is that the model produces reliable results, and that the model is transparent – not a black box – so the analysts can understand the result and explain it to the politicians and today even the public. Next, the model must be able to work on a very detailed subdivision, supporting the spatial planning of new public facilities, shops and other services. Both requirements are fulfilled by the described model and several (currently 37 out of 98) mainly larger Danish municipalities have used the model during the last ten years.

Although the described model is used frequently as an important tool in many Danish local authorities, there is still need for further research and development. One of the main challenges using the model today is the identification of parameter districts, which is a critical part of the preparation efforts, because those districts are used to estimate the various migration coefficients as well as the fertility and mortality levels. Currently, the identification process is carried out by comparing tables and graphs to identify districts with similar demographic characteristics. We are currently, working on a (semi-)automatic procedure to identify the parameter districts by applying cluster analysis techniques. This will reduce the huge effort for the manual identification, and will also make the results more reliable.

Population development is probably the most important key element in knowledge-based e-Governance but besides the obvious derived knowledge concerning children and elderly care, the estimated population projections can provide knowledge about future needs for water, sewage, public transport etc. thus contributing to enhanced efficiency and quality in the decision making process.

References

1. Smith, S., Tayman, J., Swanson, D.: State and Local Population Projections – Methodology and Analysis. Springer, Heidelberg (2001)
2. Box, G., Jenkins, G.: Time Series Analysis – Forecasting and Control, San Fransisco, Holden Day (1970)
3. Cannan, E.: A Review of Economic Theory (1963) (reprint)
4. Ministry of Interior and Health. The Local Government Reform – in Brief. The Ministry of Interior and Health, Department of Economics, Copenhagen (2006)
5. Isserman, A.M.: The Right People, the Right Rates – Making Population Estimates and Forecasts with an Interregional Cohort-Component Model. Journal of the American Planning Association 59, 45–64 (1993)
6. Lundström, H., Quist, J.: Mortality Forecasting and Trend Shifts: An Application of the Lee-Carter Model to Swedish Mortality Data. International Statistical Review 72, 37–50 (2004)
7. Wilson, T., Rees, P.: Recent Developments in Population Projection Methodology: A Review. Population, Space and Place 11, 337–360 (2005)
8. Nielsen, H.: CPR – The Danish National Population Register. Ministry of Interior (1991) (in Danish)
9. Lind, M.: Developing a System of Public Addresses - as a "language" for location dependent information. In: URISA Proceedings 2001 (2001)
10. Isserman, A.M.: Projection, Forecast, and Plan – On the Future of Population Forecasting. Journal of the American Planning Association 50, 208–221 (1984)
11. Laakso, S.: The Use of Regional and Local Population Projections in Public Policy Planning. Report Urban Research no. 1/2005 (2005)

From Policy-Making Statements to First-Order Logic

Adam Wyner[1,*], Tom van Engers[2], and Kiavash Bahreini[2]

[1] Institute of Communication Studies, University of Leeds, LS2 9JT, UK
adam@wyner.info
http://wyner.info/LanguageLogicLawSoftware/
[2] Leibniz Center for Law
Oudemanhuispoort 4-6 1012 CN Amsterdam, The Netherlands
{vanengers,k.bahreini}@uva.nl
http://www.leibnizcenter.org

Abstract. Within a framework for enriched on-line discussion forums for e-government policy-making, pro and con statements for positions are input, structurally related, then logically represented and evaluated. The framework builds on current technologies for multi-threaded discussion, natural language processing, ontologies, and formal argumentation frameworks. This paper focuses on the natural language processing of statements in the framework. A small sample policy discussion is presented. We adopt and apply a controlled natural language (Attempto Controlled English) to constrain the domain of discourse, eliminate ambiguity and unclarity, allow a logical representation of statements which supports inference and consistency checking, and facilitate information extraction. Each of the policy statements is automatically translated into first-order logic. The result is a logical representation of the policy discussion which we can query, draw inferences (given ground statements), test for consistency, and extract detailed information.

Keywords: Policy-making, eGovernment, first-order logic.

1 Introduction

In the European Union, it is widely recognised that it is important to promote and reinforce democratic institutions and build support for regulations by, in part, broadening participation and making policy efficiently. Consultation and dialogue about policy encourages natural compliance as the policy which consequently arises more accurately relates to and bears on the people which the policy affects. The policy would be more effective and less expensive to enforce. In many cases, governments already consult stakeholder representatives and experts in policy-making processes, for example, when deciding on creating new regulations or adapting existing regulations. The tools typically used are face-to-face meetings, rounds of consultation/commenting, and written position reports.

* Corresponding author.

K.N. Andersen et al. (Eds.): EGOVIS 2010, LNCS 6267, pp. 47–61, 2010.

However, these tools limit the number of participants, constrain the base of support, miss the opportunity to leverage "the wisdom of crowds", and are difficult to apply further analytic processes to.

Online forums have been used to broaden participation and make policy more efficiently ([1] and [2]), but they have not been designed or used to support public policy-making. Our use case starts with a policy problem or question that requires the modification or introduction of a regulation. In order to get a clearer picture of the issues, stakeholders are consulted using an online forum wherein they contribute statements pro and con with respect to previous statements given by other stakeholders. While such forums generate a wealth of information, the data needs to be structured, represented, extracted, reasoned with, and analysed in order to be useful. Moreover, as participants use natural language to express and understand policy, the tools must process natural language to some extent and at some level. Yet, by and large, natural language processing (NLP) techniques are not applied to such forums, which might explain in part why they are not used to co-create policies and regulations to the extent they could be.

Though online forums help to gather and store information, they must be analysed further, whether manually or automatically, in order to summarise, extract information, draw inferences, or create argument maps ([3] and [4]). One comment may or may not refer to an immediately preceding comment or use some index to a preceding comment. A range of different topics may be introduced within a comment. The relationship between one comment and the next is not overt. Consequently, it is difficult to reconstruct the overall argument, the relationships among statements, and the conclusions that might follow from the give set of statements. Indeed, the longer the list of comments, the more problematic the task. In addition, it is difficult to prevent or filter out redundancy, to require grammatically well-formed statements, or to encourage the discussion to be bound within a given domain of discourse.

In addition to online forums, tools have been developed to support debates such as Debategraph[1], Debateopedia[2] and for argument representation such as Araucaria [5], Carneades [6], and ArguMed [7]. In all these systems the participant is responsible for indicating the semantic relationship between one statement and the next, e.g. whether a statement is a premise, an exception, a conclusion, or a contradiction with respect to some other statement. As a consequence of this, these systems require that the participants have a clear understanding of the semantic relationships between statements. None of these systems provide for an internal analysis of the statements put forward by its users.

Useful as these tools are, they do not supplant knowledge engineering. In practice, knowledge engineers translate the users' natural language expressions into a formal representation that is then processed further using automated reasoning and information extraction [8]. However, this "knowledge acquisition bottleneck" has limited the adoption and use of powerful AI-technologies [9].

---

[1] `http://debategraph.org/`

[2] `http://debatepedia.idebate.org/en/index.php/Welcome_to_Debatepedia!`

To help overcome the bottleneck, we develop tools which use NLP techniques, allowing those who are being consulted to enter their issues and concerns more directly. NLP techniques for information extraction have been applied to legal texts *after* the texts have been constructed [10], but this does not address the construction of the input information, nor its formalisation, nor broaden the base of participants. While some commercial applications support translation of policy from natural language into a proprietary, restricted, formal, executable language[3], we focus on applying an open, flexible NLP system which allows users to input statements dynamically into a policy-making debate and translates the statements into formal knowledge base. Such an approach broadens the base of parties responsible for constructing the knowledge base.

To make online forums and debate tools useful for policy-making, [11] propose and outline a framework which extends multi-threaded discussion forums, integrating NLP, ontologies, and argumentation. In contrast to existing debate and argumentation support systems, our support tool for policy-making makes the semantic *content* of comments formal and explicit as well as to makes formal and explicit the range of fine-grained *relationships between the statements*, where the semantic relationships might be agreement, disagreement, introduction of a premise or exception, refinement, pronominal anaphora, and others.

In this paper, we develop one of the key modules of the tool – the syntactic and semantic processing of the input statements so as to support information extraction, inference, consistency testing, and argumentation. There are other aspects of policy-making that are relevant in the broad scope, but which we do not consider here such as drafting rules, explanatory portions for motives and goals, measures of intended and unintended effects to determine the effectiveness of the policy, bridging strategies during implementation of the new policy.

Processing natural language gives rise to a range of expectations, which it is important address. As we describe in Section 4, we work with a *controlled natural language* which has an extensive vocabulary and an expressive, yet normalised, syntax; the sentences written in this language appear as natural English sentences. They can be automatically parsed and (with some limits) translated into first order logic, giving rise to a knowledge base. The language can be used to express an ontology and rules. To some extent, as we discuss later, the user must accommodate to the restrictions of the language; however, this is no unduly difficult. Yet, it does imply that users cannot use just any way of communication with which they are familiar, and in this regard, our approach is significantly different from prior debate support tools. For our purposes, we work with a (large) fragment of natural language, incrementally adding further linguistic capabilities as they become needed or developed. Finally, it is our assumption that the system is used in "high value" contexts by participants who are willing and able to adapt to some of the constraints (topic, expressivity, explicit marking of statement relations) in order to gain the advantages of collaboratively building a

[3] See, for example, RuleBurst `www.ruleburst.com`, now part of Oracle Policy Modelling `www.oracle.com`

clear, explicit knowledge base which represents a range of diverse, and possibly conflicting statements (See [12] for a related exercise).

In Section 2, we provide a sample policy-making discussion. In Section 3, we outline the modules of our policy-making support tool. The NLP component is reviewed in Section 4. The novel sections are Section 5, the discussion of how we apply ACE to the sentences from our sample, and Section 6, the discussion of logical issues. Future work is outlined in Section 7.

2 Example

[11] present a sample policy discussion concerning recycling and taxation, based on a BBC *Have Your Say* discussion of *Should people be paid to recycle?* From this discourse, we select some key statements in more simplified forms. We assume that each statement is made separately by a participant on the discussion list. In the source discussion, participants informally relate one statement to another. In our version, participants select the argumentative role that relates one statement to another such as whether one statement is the premise of another statement (which then also has the role of a conclusion), whether one statement contradicts another, among other roles. The participant ascribes the role to the statement using a pull-down menu.

This discussion is not a complete representation either of the answers to the question *Should people be paid to recycle?* much less all the domain knowledge and logical statements that might be relevant to the discussion. Rather it represents a fragment. Moreover, the relationships among the statements are not strictly logical in some cases; rather, there is some informal sense in which one statement supports, implies, or attacks another statement. But as in natural discussion, much is left implicit – argumentative discussion proceeds by such partial steps with implicit information that might be filled in later.

The statements were:

(1) Every householder should pay tax for the garbage which the householder throws away.
(2) No householder should pay tax for the garbage which the householder throws away.
(3) Paying tax for garbage increases recycling.
(4) Recycling more is good.
(5) Paying tax for garbage is unfair.
(6) Every householder should be charged equally.
(7) Every householder who takes benefits does not recycle.
(8) Every householder who does not take benefits pays for every householder who does take benefits.
(9) Professor Resnick says that recycling reduces the need for new garbage dumps.
(10) A reduction of the need for new garbage dumps is good.
(11) Professor Resnick is not objective.
(12) Professor Resnick owns a recycling company.

(13) A person who owns a recycling company earns money from recycling.
(14) Supermarkets create garbage.
(15) Supermarkets should pay tax.
(16) Supermarkets pass the taxes for the garbage to the consumer.

When the participants input the statements, they select the argumentative relation which they claim holds between the statements. We leave for future work exactly what linguistic properties of the statements are used to determine the relation. The argumentative relationships among the statements are: some participant makes statement (1), then some other participant gives (4) as a premise for (1); another participant states (3) as an additional premise for (1). Statements given as premises of a statement (e.g. (4) is a premise of (1)) can themselves the conclusion which follows from other premises, as (9) is a premise of (4). On the other hand, (9) is criticised by statement (11), so one might infer that (9) does not hold. In (2), we have a counter-proposal to (1) along with its premises reasons. (16) criticises (15), where (15) is a premise of (2).

In the next section, we outline the framework, focusing the discussion on the syntactic and semantic analysis of the input sentences.

3 Framework Outline

In this section, we outline the framework in [11], setting the analytic context. There are four components: multi-modal multi-threaded discussion forums, a controlled language, an ontology (related to the controlled language), and an argumentation framework. These are outlined and related in Figure 1.

We have a *participant* and a *discussion forum*. The participant reads the statements on the forum, selects a statement to respond to, and clicks on a response trigger. The response has two aspects. First, the user selects a *mode* which indicates the relation between the input statement and some previous statement, where the sorts of roles are *premise*, *conclusion*, *exception*, and *rule* (among others). Second, an editing text box opens for the user to input the statement. The editor supports a controlled language system, which guides the user to input only a well-formed statement that respects a restricted vocabulary and grammar (discussed in Section 4). The system automatically parses and semantically represents the statement, allowing the participant to check whether the resulting interpretation accurately represents the users intended interpretation. The two aspects gather statements about a policy, which is effectively a knowledge base with inconsistencies. Given statements and their argumentative relations, the discussion is input to an *argumentation framework*, which we do not discuss in this paper [13]. Further processes can be applied to the knowledge base (after processing by an argumentation framework) - inference, query, redundancy and consistency checks, and information extraction.

The policy statements have three related semantical representations: the semantics *of* each sentence (given by the controlled language), the semantic relationships (e.g. premises, conclusions, contradictions) *between* each sentence

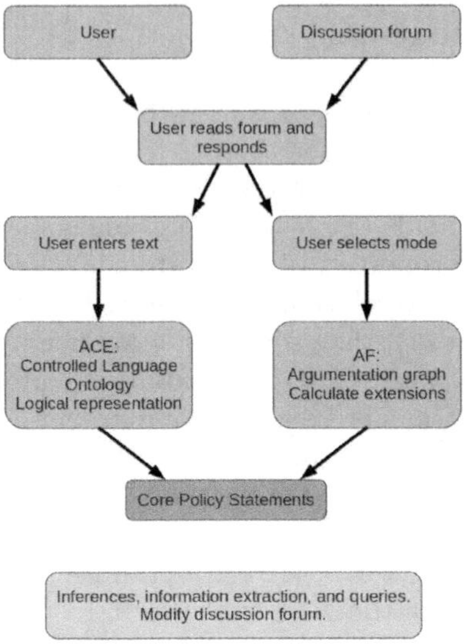

Fig. 1. Flow of Input

(given by the selection of the mode), and the semantics of the arguments and their evaluation in an argumentation framework (given *after* sentences in their relationships have been constructed into arguments and attack relations). In this paper, we focus on issues about the input of the sentences and their semantics.

4 Overview of Attempto Controlled English

To facilitate the processing of sentences, we use a well-developed controlled natural language system – Attempto Controlled English (ACE)[4]. Our objective is to give enough of an overview of ACE to understand its capabilities and to make sense of the semantic representations in Section 5. A controlled language has a specified vocabulary and a restricted range of grammatical constructions so as to provide a consistent linguistic expression, which can then be used to formally represent knowledge. The vocabulary and grammatical constructions are a subset of a natural language (e.g. English) so that sentences written and read in the controlled language appear as normal sentences, allowing the user to read and write English sentences, but to translate them into a formal representation. ACE provides a range of support tools to input statements, represent them in different forms, and process them further such as for reasoning, information extraction, or information interchange using XML. To use ACE, the user has to have some familiarity with the vocabulary, grammar, and interpretation rules.

Consider a simple sentence such as "Bill is happy." A user enters in the sentence to an ACE interface such as the online web server; different representations

[4] http://attempto.ifi.uzh.ch/site/description/

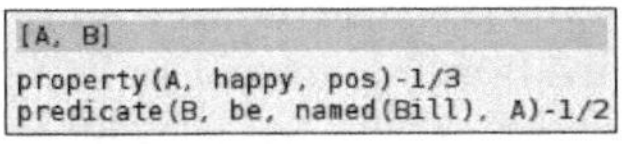

Fig. 2. Semantic Representation of *Bill is happy*

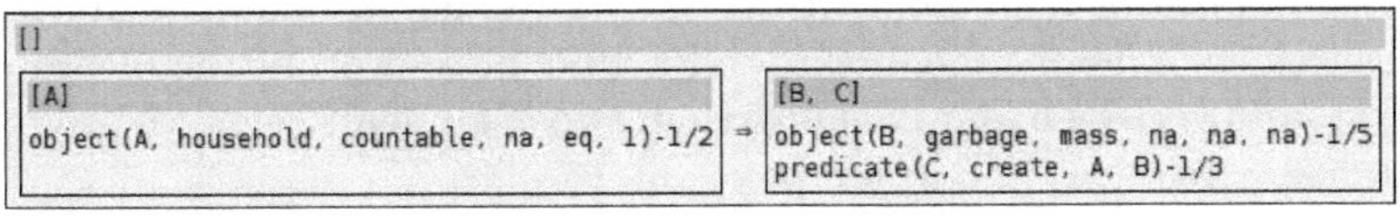

Fig. 3. Semantic Structure of *Every household creates some garbage*

can be requested such as a syntactic phrase structure tree or semantic representation graphically shown in Figure 2. In the semantic representation, we use a *Discourse Representation Structure* (DRS see [14] and [15]), which is a variant of first order logic and supports the semantic representation of aspects of discourse such as pronominal anaphora. In Figure 2, discourse referents (objects) A and B are introduced (some of the details of the representation are discussed further below). With respect to these objects, A is indicated to be the property *happy*, and B is the predicate *be* which predicates the property *happy* of an entity named *Bill*. Within a box, the statements are interpreted as conjuncts. We overlook other details that are not relevant.

ACE supports a large lexicon, a range of grammatical constructions, and correlated semantic interpretations: negation on nouns or verbs, conjunction, disjunction, conditionals, quantifiers, adjectives, relative clauses, discourse anaphora, modals ("necessity", "possibility", "permission", and "recommendation"), possessives, prepositional phrases, verbs with three arguments, and verbs with subordinate clauses.[5] Consider a sentence such as "Every household creates some garbage.", which is interpreted as a conditional rule. As we are primarily interested in the semantic representation, we omit the syntactic parse. The DRS in Figure 3 is equivalent to the first order expression $\forall x[[household'(x)] \rightarrow \exists y[garbage'(y) \wedge create'(x,y)]]$, where the box to the left of the conditional symbol => is understood to have a universal quantifier with scope over the antecedent and consequent, while the box to the right of => is understood to have an existential quantifier. Objects in the box on the right are the same as those introduced in the box on the left.

ACE checks that the sentences input to the system satisfy the constraints of the syntax and semantics of the language, thus the user is only able to input grammatically acceptable and semantically interpretable sentences in building the knowledge base. For instance, every common noun (e.g. household, dog, etc) must appear in a noun phrase with a quantifier (e.g. a, some, every, at least two, etc); a transitive verb must appear with a direct object; adjectives

[5] We discuss several of these later. However, while most of ACE is first order, the modals ("must", "can", "should", and "may") and verbs which take a sentential complement (e.g. "say") are not semantically interpretable.

which modify nouns must precede the noun. While there are a range of such constraints, most of them are familiar from English grammar or from guidelines to good English expository style. Other constraints may be less familiar such as anaphoric reference is to the most recent noun phrase (in *A dog chased another dog. It was black and white.*, the pronoun "it" is linked to the second dog.), definite noun phrases must be introduced by an indefinite noun as in a discourse *A dog walked in. The dog lay down.*, differences of interpretation of prepositions *of* and *for*, and verbs which take more than two arguments (e.g. *give*). We discuss these issues as relevant in Section 5.

5 Analysis of Example Sentences with ACE

In Section 2, sixteen sentences were presented as representative of a policy discussion. In working with ACE, it was found that these sentences either cannot be parsed by ACE or do not yield the intended interpretation. We therefore modified the sentences, resulting in the following set of sentences. Below, we discuss considerations that went into the revisions of the sentences as well as present and briefly discuss the semantic representations.

(1) Every household should pay some tax for the household's garbage.
(2) No household should pay some tax for the household's garbage.
(3) Every household which pays some tax for the household's garbage increases an amount of the household's garbage which the household recycles.
(4) If a household increases an amount of the household's garbage which the household recycles then the household benefits the household's society.
(5) If a household pays a tax for the household's garbage then the tax is unfair to the household.
(6) Every household should pay an equal portion of the sum of the tax for the household's garbage.
(7) No household which receives a benefit which is paid by a council recycles the household's garbage.
(8) Every household which does not receive a benefit which is paid by a council supports a household which receives a benefit which is paid by a council.
(9) Tom says that every household which recycles the household's garbage reduces a need of a new dump which is for the garbage.[6]
(10) Every household which reduces a need of a new dump benefits the household's society.
(11) Tom is not objective.
(12) Tom owns a company that recycles some garbage.
(13) Every person who owns a company that recycles some garbage earns some money from the garbage which is recycled.
(14) Every supermarket creates some garbage.

[6] We have substituted "Tom" for "Professor Resnick", which would have to be introduced to the ACE lexicon.

(15) Every supermarket should pay a tax for the garbage that the supermarket creates.
(16) Every tax which is for some garbage which the supermarket creates is passed by the supermarket onto a household.

5.1 Guidelines

In revising the sentences, we observed a range of issues. Broadly speaking, while all of the initial sentences are grammatical and have the intended interpretation to a native English speaker, not all of them are also grammatical and have the intended interpretation in ACE. There may be constructions and interpretive rules that English speakers have which ACE does not yet have. Thus, our objective was to find a way to present the intended interpretation in a syntactic expression that accommodates ACE. Given practice, this is not difficult. Indeed, one may claim that the exercise demonstrates not only the functionality of ACE, but the value in formulation of the sentences which made explicit information that otherwise might have been implicit in the sentences. We outline the issues, then further discuss them with respect to the examples.

- Simplify the lexicon and syntax where possible.
- Use simple morphological forms rather than:
  - Gerunds – verbs as nouns, e.g. *Recycling is good.*
  - Participles – verbs as adjectives, e.g. *Recycled garbage is good*
  - Complex noun morphology – tax versus taxation.
- Noun-noun combinations are not available in ACE such as *garbage dump* unless they are hyphenated as *garbage-dump* and appear in the lexicon; rewrite such combinations as a relative clause *a dump which is for some garbage.*
- Use determiners on nouns - *some, a, every* - and follow the constraint on the definite determiner *the* in a countable noun phrase. For mass noun phrases, this constraint does not apply.
- Use common nouns that have a mass interpretation such as *garbage* with a determiner as in *the garbage* or possessive *the household's garbage.*
- Use possessive nouns rather than pronouns. Pronouns refer to the most recent noun and can give an unintended interpretation.
- Observe the interpretations that arise with different propositions *of, for, on*, etc, particularly with respect to verbs that take two or more arguments such as *give, pay*, and others. Where the arguments of verbs may appear in different syntactic orders – *diathesis alternations* as in the passive or in *Bill gave a present to Jill* versus *Bill gave Jill a present* – follow the canonical word order (active and using the prepositional phrase).
- Make implicit knowledge explicit and state all relevant participants.
- Where ACE finds some word or phrase unacceptable, seek an alternative synonymous word or phrase. While ACE can accept new lexical items, we have chosen to keep to the lexicon ACE provides.
- Consider scope of quantifiers, modals, and negation.

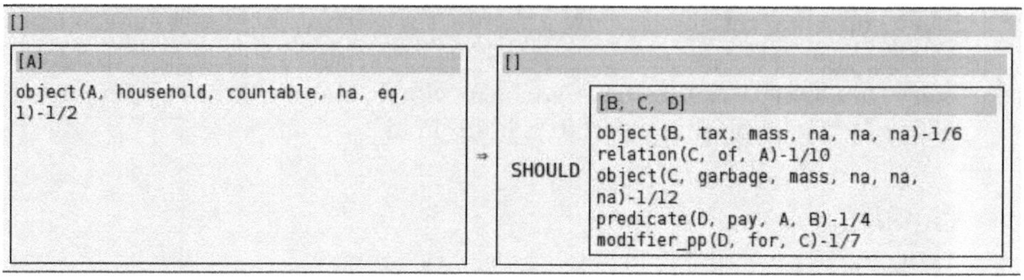

Fig. 4. Every household should pay some tax for the household's garbage

In developing the sentence forms, we discussed alternative representations and their interpretations. This highlighted the importance of working with participants who have some *expert* knowledge in the analysis of sentences or of developing and working with a *monitoring and support* system for less expert participants. A monitoring and support system would generate questions which the participant can use to check whether the interpretation given by ACE corresponds to the intended interpretation. Such a system is a *meta* level tool but is not a functionality yet provided by ACE.

We discuss alternative representations. We illustrate sentences (1) and (2) and highlight points about others, abbreviating the discussion to avoid redundancy. Each of the sentences can be input to ACE, resulting in an interpretation which we find acceptable. We do not discuss the details of the semantic representations, leaving this as an exercise for the reader.

5.2 Discussion of Sentences

In Figure 4, we revise *Every householder should pay some tax for the garbage which the householder throws away*, changing *householder* to *household* to give a more general statement, eliminating *throws away* (a complex verb), and making the relative clause a possessive. Alternatives such as *Every householder should pay tax for garbage which the householder throws away* or *Every householder should pay some tax for all of the garbage which the householder throws away* are unacceptable in ACE. An alternative sentence *Every household should pay some tax for its garbage* is grammatically well-formed, but it yields the unintended interpretation in ACE of *Every household should pay some tax for the tax's garbage*; while speakers use pragmatics to determine the antecedent of pronouns, ACE uses the most recent pronoun. Replacing the possessive pronoun with a possessive noun clarifies the meaning. Finally, the subject noun phrase *every household* is outside the scope of the modal *should*, indicating what should hold for each household (distributively) rather than what should hold for all the households together (collectively).

With Figure 5, we considered alternatives with negation such as *Every household should pay no tax for some garbage* or *Every household should pay no tax for any garbage.* In our view, the sentence meaning is more clearly expressed with negation on the subject rather than the object. ACE does not provide for

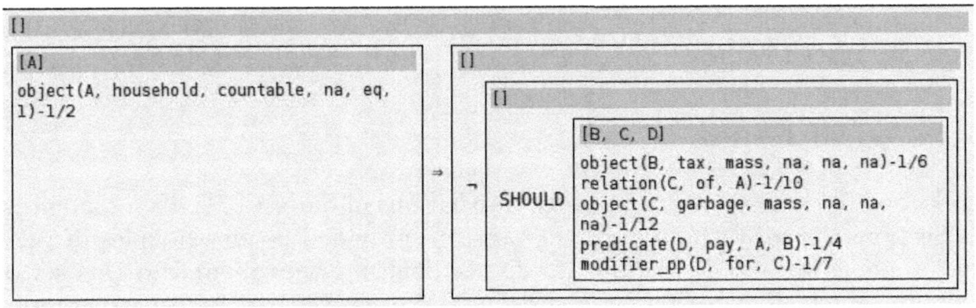

Fig. 5. No household should pay some tax for the household's garbage

quantifiers such as *any* under the scope of negation (referred to as *negative polarity items*). Note that negation takes scope over the modal operator *should.*

For sentence (3), we revise a sentence *Paying tax for garbage increases recycling* which contains a participle and a gerund, misses a determiner, and leaves implicit which participants played what role (who pays the tax and who recycles) as well as a notion of *amount* that is relevant to *increase.* While the revised sentence is longer, contains two relative clauses, introduces explicit participants, and introduces an explicit phrase for *amount,* it is syntactically clear and yields the intended interpretation. For sentence (4), a revision of *Recycling more is good,* we have removed the gerund, the unacceptable quantifier *more* (which leave implicit what is quantified over), and added a specific verb and benefactor *benefactor* tied to the participant *the household.* Similar issues apply to (5). (6), based on *Every household should be charged equally,* removes the adverb *equally* and introduces a noun for equal portions of the sum of a tax; moreover, the tax is on all the garbage which is produced by the society. In this example, it is important to be specific about who pays what. For (7), we made explicit (with a passive relative clause) who are the beneficiaries and sources of of the benefit. A *council* is that government organisation in the United Kingdom which pays out state benefits. (8) distinguishes the houses which do not receive benefits from those which do, then specifies that the first pays for the second. (9) introduces a subordinate clause, what the speaker "says". Titles and some proper names are not intrinsic to ACE, so we have simplified to a recognisable proper name. We have used a relative clause rather than a noun-noun combination. An object that is reduced is introduced *a need....* While the preposition "for" might intuitively be acceptable in *a need for a new dump....,* ACE does not relate the *need* and the *dump*; this is corrected by using the preposition "of" instead. In (10), we have used not only a *need,* but a verb that expresses benefit (rather than the term *good* in the source text) and an explicit beneficiary *the household's society.* In (12), we have an alternative formulation of the source sentence that used a participle *Professor Resnick owns a recycling company.* Finally, in (16), we have a statement about supermarkets and taxes. In this example, taxes are the topic of the sentence, and a passive verb form *is passed* makes a rule about taxes rather than supermarkets. Note as well that we have used the prepositional phrase *onto* rather than *to* since ACE provides a more accurate semantic relationship using the first rather than the second.

6 Logical Issues

In Section 5, there are the first-order translations of our set of sixteen sentences. In Sections 2 and 3, the set of sentences are provided as an examples of rules and arguments. In this section, we discuss logical issues related to this set of sentences such as consistency, query, inference as well as the construction of rules and arguments.

One of the tools allied with ACE is the first-order RACE inference engine. ACE sentences can be input to RACE, which can be tested for consistency and queried; inferences can be drawn from the sentences, that is, theorems can be proven. However, as a first-order reasoner, RACE cannot reason with modal operators such as *should* or verbs which take sentential complements such as *say*; to reason with these expressions requires a modal logic, which has not been implemented with ACE.[7] To side step these issues, statements with *should* ((1), (2), (6), and (15)) are revised as generic statements with the simple, present tense; the verb *say* is removed from (9), making the subordinate clause a main clause and leaving the speaker implicit. Neither of these moves substantively impact on our analysis since it is common for statements of law to be expressed in terms of generics rather than with modal operators [16], generics have modal interpretations [17], and one might claim that every statement has an implicit speech act and speaker [18]. However, these issues remain to be explored further.

Given the revised sentences, we can input our set of ACE sentences into RACE. For example, we can input the set of (modified) sentences {(1), (3), (4), (9), (10)}. To this set of sentences, we add a sentence which makes an assertion about a house so that we have a non-null model:

> Every household pays some tax for the household's garbage. Every household which pays some tax for the household's garbage increases an amount of the household's garbage which the household recycles. If a household increases an amount of the household's garbage which the household recycles then the household benefits the household's society. Every household which recycles the household's garbage reduces a need of a new dump which is for the garbage. Every household which reduces a need of a new dump benefits the household's society. A household pays some tax for the household's garbage.

These are consistent. We can use natural language for querying or as output of proven theorems:

(1) Is a household which recycles the household's garbage a household which benefits the household's society?

---

[7] Automated reasoning with modal logic is under active development. See `http://www.cs.man.ac.uk/~schmidt/tools/` on various tools and related literature.

(2) There is a household which benefits the household's society.
(3) Every household benefits the household's society.

The query (1) returns the answer *true*, (2) is proven with respect to the statements, and (3) cannot be proven. Other sets of sentences can similarly be consistent, be queried, and be used to prove theorems.

In Section 3, the objective of our framework is to not only provide logical translations of policy statements, but to support formal argumentation. This requires: (a) relating the statements into structures comprised of premises, exceptions, conclusions, and rules; (b) identifying arguments; and (c) identifying *attack* relations among the arguments. Point (a) is addressed by the user selecting a *mode* of relationship using the forum tool. The intention is that the modes correspond to relations required to instantiate basic components of complex arguments, which can then be structured related and evaluated in an *argumentation framework* (See [13], [19], [20], and [21]). [11] provide an example of a structure of the example sentences and arguments, following [20]. While further discussion of these issue are beyond the scope of this paper, some remarks are relevant.

Broadly, the tool we propose supports the *acquisition* from *users* of statements and their relationships. Other than controlling the form and meaning of the input statements and constraining the available modes of relationships among them, it is the user who determines the relationships among statements. From a database of statements and relationships, we can study what may underlie the selection of the relationships. For instance, while logic may define different notions of semantical incompatibility such as classical negation, negation as failure, or contrariness, these notions are not regularly, explicitly represented in natural language; indeed, the identification of semantical incompatibility in natural language is an ongoing research area [22] and may require the formalisation of pragmatic information. Nonetheless, contributors to the policy-making forum likely will find strong agreement about why one natural language sentence is semantically incompatible with another, though this may have as yet no formal realisation. While contributors will agree and disagree, discussion at all presumes some intuitive common understanding. For example, intuitively, *Tom is not objective* is in some sense semantically incompatible with *Tom says that every household which recycles the household's garbage reduces a need of a new dump which is for the garbage.* Yet, the logical form of these statements does not give rise to any incompatibility, and the representations must be augmented. Moreover, it is essential to identify semantical incompatibility to determine attack relationships in an argumentation framework. Similar remarks may be made concerning the premise or exception relationships, for example, *Tom says that every household which recycles the household's garbage reduces a need of a new dump which is for the garbage* may be a statement given in support of *If a household increases an amount of the household's garbage which the household recycles then the household benefits the household's society.*, but logical form does not make this explicit. While our approach does not solve the issues of the semantic relationships among statements, it does contribute to understanding the issues by providing a way to build a knowledge base of statements and arguments that can be further studied. In addition, our approach makes it feasible to instantiate arguments and reason with them formally so as to support policy-making.

7 Future Work

In this paper, we have focused on the analysis of the sentences input to a policy-making discussion forum. In future work, we will explore other aspects of the overall proposal as outlined in Section 3. The components of the framework will be developed and integrated. While ACE is a well developed tool, ACE will be utilised as the back-end for the editor tool of the forum. We will examine theoretical issues about the representation of arguments derived from the statements and their mode of relation as well as inputting the arguments to automated argumentation frameworks, allowing us to generate attacks among arguments and sets of consistent statements. Together, the output of the system will be the core policy statement. Beyond the theoretical analysis and implementation, the tool will be tested on a topic with a pool of contributors, examining a range of usability issues. Finally, we will consider ways to extend ACE and argumentation to cover additional aspects that may be relevant to a policy-making forum such as voting on statements, ranking the strength of attack, additional linguistic expressions, and others.

Acknowledgements. During the writing of this paper, the first and third authors were supported by the IMPACT Project (Integrated Method for Policy making using Argument modelling and Computer assisted Text analysis) FP7 Grant Agreement No. 247228.

References

1. Macintosh, A.: Moving toward "intelligent" policy development. IEEE Intelligent Systems 24(5), 79–82 (2009)
2. Cartwright, D., Atkinson, K.: Using computational argumentation to support e-participation. IEEE Intelligent Systems 24(5), 42–52 (2009)
3. Thelwall, M., Hasler, L.: Blog search engines. Online Information Review 31(4), 467–479 (2007)
4. Prabowo, R., Thelwall, M., Hellsten, I., Scharnhorst, A.: Evolving debate in online communication: A graph analytical approach. Internet Research 18(5), 520–540 (2008)
5. Reed, C., Rowe, G.: Araucaria: Software for argument analysis, diagramming and representation. International Journal on Artificial Intelligence Tools 13(4), 961–980 (2004)
6. Gordon, T., Prakken, H., Walton, D.: The carneades model of argument and burden of proof. Artificial Intelligence 171, 875–896 (2007)
7. Verheij, B.: Argumed - a template-based argument mediation system for lawyers. legal knowledge based systems. In: Hage, J.C., Bench-Capon, T., Koers, A., de Vey Mestdagh, C., Grtters, C. (eds.) JURIX: The Eleventh Conference, Nijmegen, pp. 113–130. Gerard Noodt Instituut (1998)

8. van Engers, T.: Legal engineering: A structural approach to improving legal quality. In: Macintosh, A., Ellis, R., Allen, T. (eds.) Applications and Innovations in Intelligent Systems XIII, Proceedings of AI-2005, pp. 3–10. Springer, Heidelberg (2005)
9. Forsythe, D.E., Buchanan, B.G.: Knowledge acquisition for expert systems: some pitfalls and suggestions. In: Readings in knowledge acquisition and learning: automating the construction and improvement of expert systems, pp. 117–124. Morgan Kaufmann Publishers Inc., San Francisco (1993)
10. Engers, T., van Gog, R., Sayah, K.: A case study on automated norm extraction. In: Gordon, T. (ed.) Legal Knowledge and Information Systems. Jurix 2004: The Seventeenth Annual Conference, Frontiers in Artificial Intelligence and Applications, pp. 49–58. IOS Press, Amsterdam (2004)
11. Wyner, A., van Engers, T.: A framework for enriched, controlled on-line discussion forums for e-government policy-making. In: Proceedings of eGov 2010, Lausanne, Switzerland (August 2010) (to appear)
12. Shiffman, R.N., Michel, G., Krauthammer, M., Fuchs, N.E., Kaljurand, K., Kuhn, T.: Writing clinical practice guidelines in controlled natural language. In: Fuchs, N.E. (ed.) Proceedings of the Workshop on Controlled Natural Language (CNL 2009). LNCS. Springer, Heidelberg (2010)
13. Baroni, P., Giacomin, M.: Argumentation in Artificial Intelligence. In: Semantics of Abstract Argumentation Systems, pp. 25–44. Springer, Heidelberg (2009)
14. Kamp, H., Reyle, U.: From Discourse to Logic: Introduction to Model-theoretic Semantics of Natural Language: Formal Logic and Discourse Representation Theory. Springer, Heidelberg (1993)
15. Asher, N.: Reference to Abstract Objects in Discourse. Kluwer Academic Publishers, Dordrecht (1993)
16. de Maat, E., Winkels, R.: Automatic classification of sentences in dutch laws. In: Legal Knowledge and Information Systems. Jurix 2008: The 21st Annual Conference, Frontiers in Artificial Intelligence and Applications, pp. 207–216. IOS Press, Amsterdam (2008)
17. Pelletier, F., Carlson, G.: The Generic Book. The University of Chicago Press, Chicago (1995)
18. Horn, L., Ward, G. (eds.): Handbook of Pragmatics. Blackwell, Malden (2004)
19. Besnard, P., Hunter, A.: Argumentation based on classical logic. In: Rahwan, I., Simari, G. (eds.) Argumentation in Artificial Intelligence, pp. 133–152. Springer, Heidelberg (2009)
20. Prakken, H.: Formalising ordinary legal disputes: a case study. Artificial Intelligence and Law 16, 333–359 (2008)
21. Prakken, H.: An abstract framework for argumentation with structure arguments. Argument and Computation (to appear, 2010)
22. Voorhees, E.M.: Contradictions and justifications: Extensions to the textual entailment task. In: Proceedings of ACL-08: HLT, Columbus, Ohio, June 2008, pp. 63–71. Association for Computational Linguistics (2008)

A Fuzzy Recommender System for eElections

Luis Terán and Andreas Meier

Information Systems Research Group, University of Fribourg,
Boulevard de Pérolles 90, 1700 Fribourg, Switzerland
{luis.teran,andreas.meier}@unifr.ch
http://diuf.unifr.ch/is/

Abstract. eDemocracy aims to increase participation of citizens in democratic processes through the use of information and communication technologies. In this paper, an architecture of recommender systems for eElections using fuzzy clustering methods is proposed. The objective is to assist voters in making decisions by providing information about candidates close to the voters preferences and tendencies. The use of recommender systems for eGovernment is a research topic used to reduce information overload, which could help to improve democratic processes.

Keywords: Recommender Systems, eDemocracy, eElections, Fuzzy Logic, Fuzzy Clustering.

1 Introduction

Recommender systems are computer-based techniques used to reduce information overload and to provide recommendations of products likely to interest a user. This technique is mainly used in eCommerce to suggest items that a customer is assumably going to buy.

In [4], Yager makes a distinction between "recommender systems" and "targeted marketing". Yager considers that recommender systems are "participatory" systems, where users intentionally provide information about their preferences. In contrast, targeted marketing methods are based on extensional information, which refers actions or past experiences on specific objects.

The definition of recommender systems as introduced by Yager is used in this paper. In addition, it is assumed that users are willing to provide information about their preferences. It is important to mention that recommender systems for eElections make no use of past actions where each event is consider as unique.

The paper introduces a fuzzy-based architecture of a recommender system for eElections. First, a description of recommender systems for eCommerce and eGovernment is presented in Sect. 2 and 3. Sect. 4 gives a brief introduction to fuzzy logic, fuzzy sets, and fuzzy clustering methods used in the recommendation approach. The fuzzy recommender system architecture is described in Sect. 5. Finally, the conclusions are drawn in Sect. 6.

K.N. Andersen et al. (Eds.): EGOVIS 2010, LNCS 6267, pp. 62–76, 2010.

2 Recommender Systems for eCommerce

According to Yager [4], recommender systems used in eCommerce are targeted marketing methods, which rely on past experiences to increase the sales of products. The main problems, and the more widely used techniques of recommender systems in eCommerce are described in this section for better understanding of their use and scope.

In [1], Vozalis and Margaritis describe the challenges and problems of recommender systems used in eCommerce. The most relevant are the *sparsity* and *first rater* problems. *The sparsity problem* refers to the number of recommendations made by customers. This problem occurs when the number of items rated is small compared to the total number of items. *First rater problem* refers to a product which can be the subject of a recommendation only if another user has previously rated it.

According to [1], the more widely used techniques in recommender systems are based on Collaborative Filtering (CF) methods. The goal of CF is to recommend or to predict the benefit of a specific product based on previously ranked items by the user and the opinions of other users with similar likings.

In a CF scenario there is a list of users $U = \{u_1, u_2, \dots, u_m\}$ and a list of items $I = \{i_1, i_2, \dots, i_n\}$. Each user has a list of items I_{ui} for which other users have provided their opinions (rating score). There exists a user $u_a \in U$ called the *active user* from whom the recommendation or prediction is computed. A matrix $\boldsymbol{R}$ ($m \times n$ user-item matrix), where each entry r_{ij} represents the ratings of user u_i about a specific item i_j. The rating is a numerical value from 0 to a maximum value (0 value means no ranking).

According to [2] and [3], the more widely used techniques in recommender systems based on CF methods are: *Memory-based* (*user-based*), and *Model-based* (*item-based*). These techniques use a calculation of similarities between individuals (Memory-based) or items (Model-based).

2.1 Memory-Based Collaborative Filtering Algorithms

Memory-based algorithms compute neighborhood formations using the user-item matrix $\boldsymbol{R}$, which contains the ratings of items by user. Nevertheless, users have no obligation to provide their opinion on all items.

In order to compute the similarity between users u_i and u_k from $\boldsymbol{R}$, two methods are more widely used: *Pearson Correlation Similarity* and *Cosine/Vector Similarity*.

Using the *Pearson Correlation Similarity* or *Cosine/Vector Similarity*, a $m \times m$ *similarity matrix* $\boldsymbol{S}$ is generated including the similarity values between users. Using $\boldsymbol{S}$, neighborhood formation is computed based on several schemas. The most common according to [1] are: *Centered-based Schema* and *Aggregate Neighborhood Schema*.

The final step in the recommendation process is to generate either *prediction* or a *Top-N recommendation*. Prediction P_{aj} is a numerical value that expresses the possible opinion of active user u_a about an item i_j for which the active user has yielded no opinion. Top-N recommendation is a list of N items that the active user u_a would like the most.

2.2 Model-Based Collaborative Filtering Algorithms

In the model-based CF algorithm, a set of items ranked by the active user u_a is used to compute similarities between these items and a target item i_j to select the n most similar items. The first step in the computation of similarities between items i_i and i_j is to isolate users that rated both items.

The second step is the computation of similarities between items i_i and i_j. The main techniques used to compute the similarity sim_{ij} according to [3] are Cosine/Vector Similarity, Pearson Correlation, and Adjusted Cosine Similarity. After the computation of the similarities of items, the computation of the n most similar items to a target item i_j from its neighborhood N of items is performed.

According to [1], the more widely used technique to compute predictions is the *Weighted Sum* method. It generates a prediction of item i_j for an active user u_a.

Recommender systems used in eCommerce can be classified as "Targeted Marketing", according to [4], since they use the past experiences of users. In this approach, the accuracy of the recommendation depends directly on the participation of users. These type of recommender systems are only suitable for the repeat-appeared items mentioned in [2], where a user can purchase an item even though some have been sold.

3 Recommender Systems for eGovernment

In [13], the term eGovernment refers to the use of information technologies to improve the interaction between public administrations, citizens, and the private sector. Three types of relationships are defined for eGovernment: Administration to citizens (A2C), Administration to Business (A2B), and Administration to Administration (A2A). In [9], Meier introduces an eGovernment framework consisting of three levels: Information and Communications, Production, and Participation. It is shown in Fig. 1.

The lowest level provides information and communication for eGovernment; it focuses on the design of communal web portals. The second level consists of the actual public services (electronic procurement, taxation, and electronic payments, among others). The third level refers to citizen participation. This paper focuses on the participation level, specifically on eDemocracy.

In [9], Meier mentions the importance of citizen participation in eDemocracy (eElection and eVoting). Meier defines *eDiscussion* as a stage where citizens could know more about the candidates or the subject in a voting process. It uses information and communication technologies such as forums, decision aids, and subscription services, among others, to aid voters in making decisions. In the same way, once an eVoting or eElection process has been completed, another stage defined as *ePosting* is required [9]. This stage facilitates the publication of

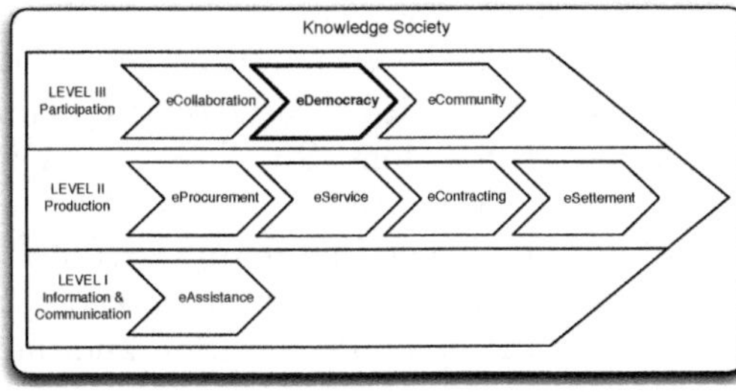

Fig. 1. eGovernment Process Oriented Maturity Model

results, and it gives voters the possibility to open discussion channels about the process. Fig. 2 shows the stages of eVoting and eElection as part of a process chain.

This paper proposes a fuzzy recommender system for eElections used by voters to establish the most similar candidates according to their preferences and tendencies. In addition, it is used after a voting/election process to establish the preferences and tendency of the new elected authorities.

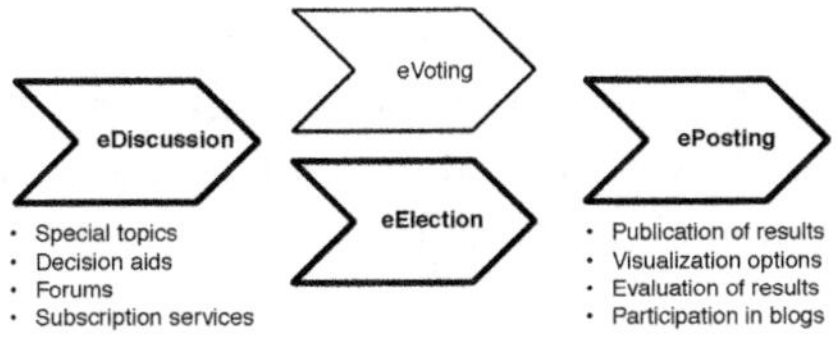

Fig. 2. Stages of eVoting and eElection as part of a Process Chain

According to Yager in [4], and assuming that users are willing to collaborate in providing information about their preferences, recommender systems used in eGovernment are classified as "Participatory" systems. These types of recommender systems are suitable for the one-and-only item [2], where the *recommendation target* is a unique item/event. Examples of one-and-only items are selling a house, trade exhibitions, elections, and voting, among others, where the recommendation makes no use of their past actions since these events occur only once.

3.1 Smartvote

Smartvote [11] is an online recommendation system for communal, cantonal and national elections in Switzerland. Smartvote system is based on profile comparison between candidates and voters. Smartvote recommendation is based on similarities between voters and candidates.

In order to compute their similarities, voters and candidates must create their profiles using a questionnaire of 30 to 70 questions about values, attitudes and political issues. Smartvote questionnaire is based on two main types of questions: standard questions and budget questions. Standard questions are related to the acceptance or rejection of specific political issues, and budget questions intend to establish whether voters would spend more or less in certain areas.

Smartvote questionnaire is composed of eleven categories: 1) welfare, familly and health, 2) education and research, 3) migration and integration, 4) society, culture and ethics, 5) finances and taxes, 6) economy and work, 7) environment, transport and energy, 8) state institutions and political rights, 9) justice, police and army, 10) foreign policy and foreign trade, and 11) fields of activity. Each category contains different questions related to that topic. Those questions could be either standard questions or budget questions (For more information about Smartvote questionnaire refer to [11]).

In order to generate the recommendations, Smartvote computes the "Match Points" using (1).

$$MP_i(v, c) = 100 - |a_{iv} - a_{ic}| + b \tag{1}$$

where a_{iv} and a_{ic} are the answers of voter v and candidate c to questions i respectively, $MP_i(v, c)$ represents the number of points of agreement ("Match Points") of voter v and candidate c to questions i, and b represents a bonus which applies if and only if there is a perfect match ("Yes-Yes" and "No-No" combinations). Table 1 shows the values given in standard questions (similar procedure is used for budget questions).

Table 1. Points of agreement on Standard Questions

V(⇓) C(⇒)	Yes	Prob. Yes	Prob. No	No	Total
Yes	100+50	75	25	0	250
Prob. Yes	75	100	50	25	250
Prob. No	25	50	100	75	250
No	0	25	75	100+50	250
Total	250	250	250	250	

The next step in the calculation of matching is to take into account the relevance of each question to voters. For each question there is selection by weighting "+", "=", and "-", the corresponding match points are multiplied by the factors 0.5, 1 and 2, as shown in (2)

$$MP_i(v, c, W) = MP_i(v, c) * W_i \tag{2}$$

where $MP_i(v, c, W)$ is the weight scored match of voter v and candidate c to question i.

Finally, (3) is used to compute the match between a voter v and candidate c to the n questions:

$$MP(v, c, W) = \sum_{i=1}^{n} MP_i(v, c, W) \quad (3)$$

Additionally, a matching value as percentage between voter v and candidate c is calculated using (4) and (5).

$$MP(v)_{Max} = \sum_{i=1}^{n} a_{vi} * W_i \quad (4)$$

$$MP(v, c, W) = \frac{MP(v, c, W)}{MP(v)_{Max}} * 100 \quad (5)$$

where $MP(v)_{Max}$ is the theoretical maximum possible match score depending only on the answer and weights of voter v, and $MP(v, c, W)$ represents the matching value as percentage between voter v and candidate c.

The computation of Matching Point depends on the maximum possible match score which, in turn, depends on the answer given by voters. Smartvote can be used to generate recommendations by full lists, in this case the matching values are computed using the mean average of all candidates in the list.

4 Fuzzy Logic, Fuzzy Sets and Fuzzy Clustering

Fuzzy Logic is a multi-value logic which allows a better understanding of the result of a statement more approximate than precise in real life. In contrast with "sharp logic", where results of a statement are binary ("true or false", "one or zero"), fuzzy logic admits a set of truth values in the interval $[0, 1]$. Fuzzy logic is derived from fuzzy set theory introduced by Zadeh in [6], where a fuzzy set is determined by a membership function with a range of values between 0 and 1. In [6], Zadeh gives a **definition** of fuzzy sets, shown below:

Definition 1. *A fuzzy set is built from a reference set called universe of discourse. The reference set is never fuzzy. Assuming $U = \{x_1, x_2, ..., x_n\}$ as the universe of discourse, then a fuzzy set A ($A \subset U$) is defined as a set of ordered pairs:*

$$\{(x_i, \mu_A(x_i))\}$$

where $x_i \in U, \mu_A : U \rightarrow [0, 1]$ is the membership function of A and $\mu_A(x) \in [0, 1]$ is the degree of membership of x in A.

Fig. 3 shows an example of three fuzzy sets with the expressions "young", "middle-age", and "old" as function of the age of a citizen. $\mu_{young}(t)$, $\mu_{middle}(t)$, and $\mu_{old}(t)$ are the membership functions for age t and the fuzzy sets. It is clear that age t_1 belongs to three sets with different degrees of membership.

Fuzzy clustering is an unsupervised learning task which aims to decompose a set of objects into "clusters" based on similarities, where the objects belonging

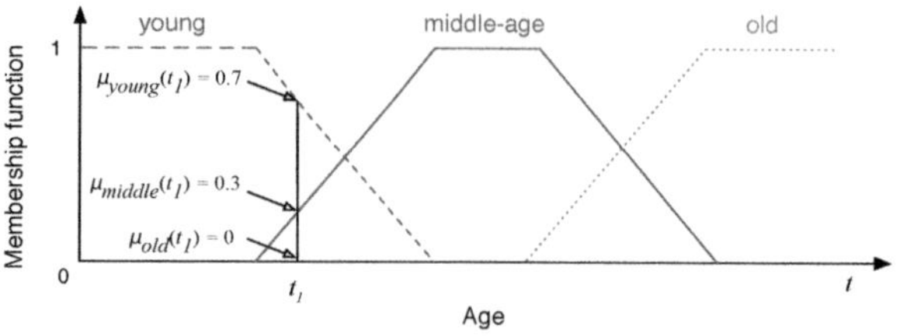

Fig. 3. Example of Fuzzy Set *Age*

to the same cluster are as similar as possible. In sharp clustering, each element is associated to just one cluster.

The main algorithms used to generate clusters are c-means (sharp clustering) and fuzzy c-means (fuzzy clustering). The fuzzy recommender system proposed in this paper uses the fuzzy c-means algorithm explained below.

4.1 Fuzzy C-Means Algorithm (FCM)

The c-means algorithm originally proposed by Jim Bezdek [7] is a method of cluster analysis which aims to partition n observations into c clusters. Each observation belongs to one and only one cluster. Fuzzy c-means is an extension of the c-means algorithm which allows gradual membership of data points to clusters with different degrees of membership according to fuzzy set theory introduced by Zadeh [6]. Thus, fuzzy c-means defines a given set of samples $X = \{x_1, ..., x_n\}$, a set of clusters Γ_i ($i = 1, ..., c$ and $2 \leq c < n$), and a $c \times n$ fuzzy partition matrix $\boldsymbol{U} = [u_{ij}]$. The membership degree u_{ij} of an observation x_i in a cluster Γ_i is such that $u_{ij} = \mu_{\Gamma_i(x_j)} \in [0, 1]$.

A probabilistic cluster partition defined by the constraints in (6) and (7) guarantee that clusters are not empty, and that the sum of the membership for each x is equal to 1

$$\sum_{j=1}^{n} u_{ij} > 0, \forall i \in \{1, ..., c\} \tag{6}$$

$$\sum_{i=1}^{c} u_{ij} = 1, \forall j \in \{1, ..., n\} \tag{7}$$

Thus, the FCM algorithm is based on minimization of an objective function shown in (8)

$$J_m = \sum_{i=1}^{c} \sum_{j=1}^{n} u_{ij}^m \parallel x_j - y_i \parallel^2 \tag{8}$$

where x_j is the jth of d-dimensional measured data, y_i is the d-dimensional center of cluster i, m is any real number greater than 1 (m determines the level of "fuzziness", $m = 2$ is a typical value used), and $\parallel * \parallel$ is any norm expressing the similarity between any measured data and the center. In (8), $\boldsymbol{Y} = [y_i]$ is the matrix of cluster centers ($i = \{1, ..., c\}$).

The membership function u_{ij} and the center of clusters y_i are computed taking the derivative of the objective function J_m with respect to the parameters to optimize equal to zero, taking in to account constraint (7), equations (9) and (10) are obtained.

$$u_{ij} = \frac{1}{\sum_{l=1}^{c} \frac{\|x_j - y_i\|}{\|x_j - y_l\|}^{\frac{2}{m-1}}} \tag{9}$$

$$y_i = \frac{\sum_{j=1}^{n} u_{ij}^m x_j}{\sum_{j=1}^{n} u_{ij}^m} \tag{10}$$

The FCM algorithm is a two-step iterative process defined as follows. First, set the input variables c, m and ϵ (ϵ is a termination criteria, normally $\epsilon \in [0, 1]$). Second, set an iteration number $k = 0$. Third, generate randomly a matrix of cluster centers $\boldsymbol{Y}^{(k)}$. Then, given the initial matrix $\boldsymbol{Y}^{(k)}$, compute the fuzzy partition matrix $\boldsymbol{U}^{(k)}$.

Finally, using a repeat-until loop, update $\boldsymbol{Y}^{(k+1)}$ using $\boldsymbol{U}^{(k)}$ then, update $\boldsymbol{U}^{(k+1)}$ using $\boldsymbol{Y}^{(k+1)}$. Repeat this process until the termination criteria is reached ($|\boldsymbol{U}^{(k+1)} - \boldsymbol{U}^{(k)}| \leq \epsilon$). The termination criteria could be also a predefined number of iterations. FCM algorithm it is presented in Algorithm 1.

Algorithm 1. FCM

Input: c, m, ϵ
Output: $\boldsymbol{U}^{(k+1)}$

1: Set iteration number: $k \leftarrow 0$
2: Generate matrix of cluster centers: $\boldsymbol{Y}^{(k)} \leftarrow$ random
3: Compute $\boldsymbol{U}^{(k)} \leftarrow \boldsymbol{Y}^{(k)}$
4: **repeat**
5:     Update $\boldsymbol{Y}^{(k+1)} \leftarrow \boldsymbol{U}^{(k)}$
6:     Update $\boldsymbol{U}^{(k+1)} \leftarrow \boldsymbol{Y}^{(k+1)}$
7: **until** $|\boldsymbol{U}^{(k+1)} - \boldsymbol{U}^{(k)}| \leq \epsilon$
8: **return** $\boldsymbol{U}^{(k+1)}$

5 Recommendation Approach

5.1 Problem Statement

Although Collaborative Filtering based approaches are the more widely used, they are only suitable in the repeat-appeared scenario, which is described in [1]. As mentioned in Sect. 3, recommender systems for eGovernment have to be suitable also in the one-and-only items scenario, where the *recommendation target* is a unique item/event (a voter v wants to receive a recommendation of n candidates close to his preferences in an election E).

In the voting/election scenario, the recommendation makes no use of past events given that candidates could be different for each election or even they can change their political orientation.

This paper yields no discussion about political issues. However, it assumes candidates behavior and that their postulation in election is different for each election process.

Furthermore, in recommendation generation, it is necessary to define the elements needed and the output of the system developed. As mentioned previously, a recommender system used on eElections must be able to recommend a list of n candidates close to the preferences of an specific voter.

This paper introduces a Fuzzy Recommender System (FRS) for eElections which provides information about closest candidates to a voter, and it provides the distribution of political parties organized in fuzzy clusters.

5.2 Fuzzy Recommender System Architecture

The recommendation process is given in three steps. In the first step, voters and candidates must create their profiles using a fuzzy interface, described in more detail in the following section, to be stored in a database.

In the second step, once all necessary profiles have been created, the user selects the recommendation target and the type of output (Top-N Recommendation or Fuzzy Cluster Analysis). In the final step, once all information has been computed by the recommendation engine, the user receives the recommendation in the pre-established format. The architecture of the FRS is presented in Fig. 4, each element is discussed in depth in following sections.

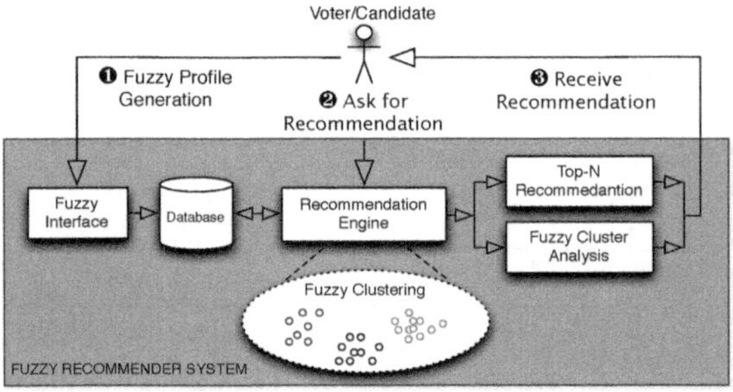

Fig. 4. Fuzzy Recommender System Architecture

Fuzzy Interface. The fuzzy interface is comparable to the Smartvote interface used by candidates and voters to complete a questionnaire regarding political issues (each question has different possible responses). In spite of the flexibility provided by the Smartvote interface, it can be considered as a sharp interface. For this reason, and to guaranty flexibility, a convenient tool is used to determine the level of agreement/disagreement and relevance for a specific question. Fig. 5 shows an example of Fuzzy Interface.

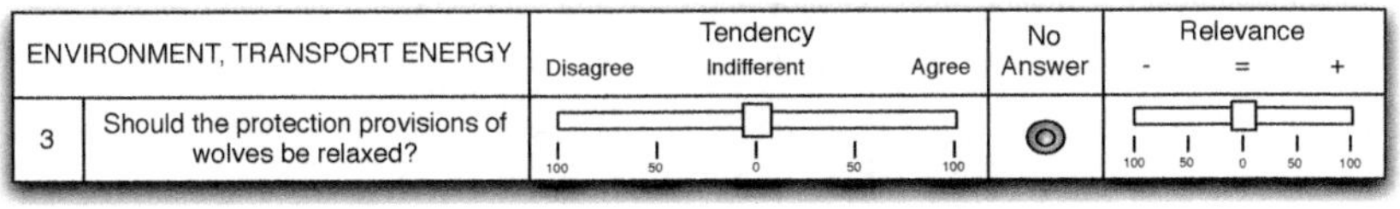

Fig. 5. Fuzzy Interface

Fuzzy Profile. In order to generate a recommendation, voters and candidates have to generate a profile which describes their preferences. This paper makes no reference about profile generation. However, it assumes that profile can be generated and evaluated. This paper proposes a profile representation called "Fuzzy Profile"(FP), a multi-dimensional Euclidean space defined by:

$$FP_i = (fpc_{i1}, ..., fpc_{in})$$

where FP_i is the FP vector of user i, and fpc_{ij} is the *j-th* "fuzzy profile component" (fpc). Each fpc is the norm of a multi-dimensional Euclidean space defined by:

$$fpc_{ij} = ||(q_{ij1}, ..., q_{ijl})|| = \sqrt{\sum_{k=1}^{l} q_{ijl}^2}$$

where fpc_{ij} is the *j-th* fuzzy profile component of FP_i, and q_{ijk} is the *k-th* component of fpc_{ij}.

In order to illustrate the use of a FP, a Smartvote profile instance of user i (FP_i) composed by n questions ($FP_i = (fpc_{i1}, ..., fpc_{in})$) is used. Each question has two components: "tendency" and "relevance" (q_{ij1} and q_{ij2}), where $fpc_{ij} = ||(q_{ij1}, q_{ij2})|| = \sqrt{q_{ij1}^2 + q_{ij2}^2}$. Fig. 6 shows the computation of "fuzzy profile component" for a general question in the Smartvote system.

Recommendation Engine. The FRS is based on fuzzy cluster generation as shown in Fig. 4. Once the FP is generated, the next step is to ask for a recommendation. At this point the user selects a particular event and the type of recommendation (Top-N Recommendation or Fuzzy Clustering Analysis). The request is sent to the recommendation engine which processes the query.

To provide a graphical representation of results that users can easily analyze, the recommendation engine transforms the high-dimensional space of FP to a bi-dimensional space which reduces the complexity of data analysis. The recommender engine uses a mapping method originally proposed by Sammon in [8] which is described in more detail in below.

Sammon Mapping. This technique tries to preserve the inter-pattern distances. It is a well-know technique for transforming a high-dimensional space (n-dimensions) to a space with lower dimensionality (q-dimensions), finding N points in the q-dimensional space.

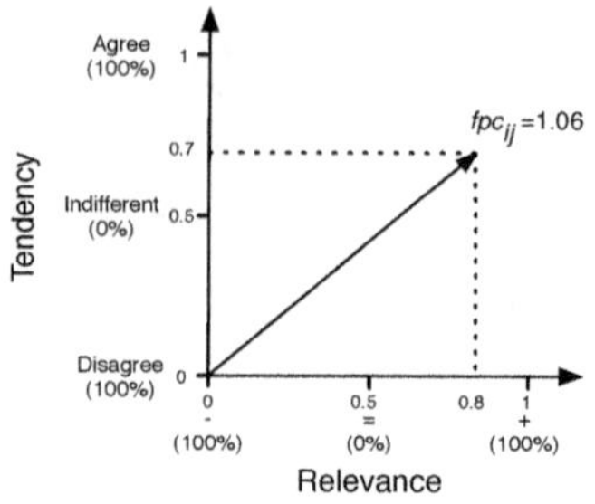

Fig. 6. Fuzzy Profile Component Computation

Denoting the distances between two different points x_i and x_j $(i \neq j)$ in the original space as d_{ij}, and the distance between points y_i and y_j in the mapped space as d'_{ij}, then the mapping becomes a minimization problem of the called Sammon's stress E defined in (11)

$$E = \frac{1}{\lambda} \sum_{i=1}^{N-1} \sum_{j=i+1}^{N} \frac{(d_{ij} - d'_{ij})^2}{d_{ij}}, \lambda = \sum_{i=1}^{N-1} \sum_{j=i+1}^{N} d_{ij} \tag{11}$$

In order to minimize E, Shammon applied a steepest descent technique, where the new y_{i_l} at iteration $t+1$ is given in (12)

$$y_{i_l}(t+1) = y_{i_l}(t) - \alpha \left[\frac{\frac{\partial E(t)}{\partial y_{i_l}(t)}}{\frac{\partial^2 E(t)}{\partial^2 y_{i_l}(t)}} \right] \tag{12}$$

where $y_{i_l}(t)$ is the *l-th* coordinate of point y_i in the mapped space, α is a constant computed empirically to be $\alpha \approx 0.3$ or 0.4. The partial derivatives in (12) are given by:

$$\frac{\partial E(t)}{\partial y_{i_l}(t)} = -\frac{2}{\lambda} \sum_{k=1,k\neq i}^{N} \left[\frac{d_{ki} - d'_{ki}}{d_{ki} d'_{ki}} \right] (y_{i_l} - y_{k_l})$$

$$\frac{\partial^2 E(t)}{\partial^2 y_{i_l}(t)} = -\frac{2}{\lambda} \sum_{k=1,k\neq i}^{N} \frac{1}{d_{ki} d'_{ki}} \cdot \left[(d_{ki} - d'_{ki}) - \left(\frac{(y_{i_l} - y_{k_l})^2}{d'_{ki}} \right) \left(1 + \frac{d_{ki} - d'_{ki}}{d_{ki}} \right) \right]$$

Fig. 7 shows an illustration of Sammon mapping from a three-dimensional space to a bi-dimensional space.

Fuzzy Cluster Analysis. Once the FP is mapped to a low-dimensional space, FRS generates fuzzy clusters using fuzzy c-means algorithm (refer to Sect. 4.1) which requires two main inputs: the number of clusters and a random matrix of cluster centers. For this reason, prior knowledge about the dataset is required. In the eElection scenario, FRS considers the number of clusters equal to the number of political parties.

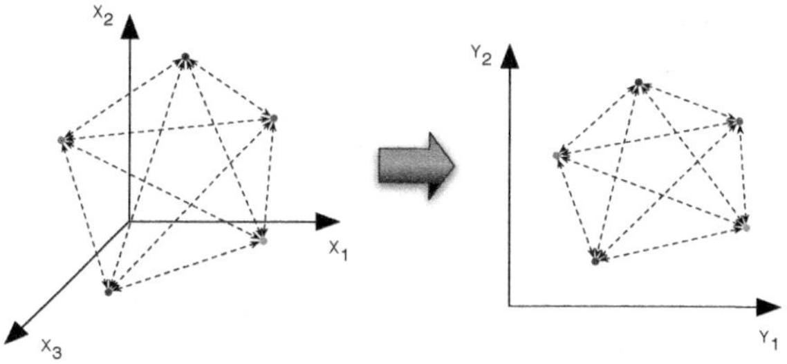

Fig. 7. Illustration of Sammon Maping

The second input required by the fuzzy c-means algorithm is the matrix of initial centers which is generated randomly. Consequently, the algorithm may converge to a local minima given the random nature of the algorithm.

In order to avoid this problem, a modified version of FCM algorithm is introduced in this paper which initializes the matrix of centers with a random member of each political party. The initialization process is based on two assumptions: First, cluster formation relies on the existence of political parties. Second, members of political parties have the same ideology [12]. Algorithm 2 shows the modified FCM.

Algorithm 2. FCM Modified

Input: c, m, ϵ
Output: $\boldsymbol{U}^{(k+1)}$

Set iteration number: $k \leftarrow 0$
for $i = 1$ to c **do**
  $y_i \leftarrow$ random member from P_i
end for
Compute $\boldsymbol{U}^{(k)} \leftarrow \boldsymbol{Y}^{(k)}$
repeat
  Update $\boldsymbol{Y}^{(k+1)} \leftarrow \boldsymbol{U}^{(k)}$
  Update $\boldsymbol{U}^{(k+1)} \leftarrow \boldsymbol{Y}^{(k+1)}$
until $|\boldsymbol{U}^{(k+1)} - \boldsymbol{U}^{(k)}| \leq \epsilon$
return $\boldsymbol{U}^{(k+1)}$

The output of Algorithm 2 is a fuzzy partition matrix $\boldsymbol{U}^{(k+1)}$ which contains the membership degree of voter and candidates with respect to each cluster.

Top-N Recommendation. The top N candidates similar to voter v are generated using the bi-dimensional FP. The distances of all candidates with respect to voter v are computed and the N closest candidates are displayed. The similarity percentage ($S_{vc_i}(\%)$) of a voter v and the *i-th* candidate (c_i) is computed using the most distant candidate (d_{max}) as reference. The computation of similarity percentage is shown in (13)

$$S_{vc_i}(\%) = 100 - (\frac{100 * d_{vc_i}}{d_{max}}) \tag{13}$$

where d_{vc_i} is the distance between voter v and the i-th candidate.

The output of this algorithm are the n closest candidates and their similarity percentage with respect to voter v.

5.3 Recommendation Output

In our research, a Fuzzy Recommender System Prototype (FRSP) has been developed to display the results of a recommendation. FRSP has the following input variables: number of clusters (political parties), Top-N candidates, total number of candidates, number of questions, number of components of each question, and voter responses. FRSP uses typical parameters of fuzzy c-means algorithm ($m = 2$, and $\epsilon = 1 * 10^{-4}$) and Sammon mapping algorithm (total iterations = 500, and relative tolerance = $1 * 10^{-9}$).

The first step is to generate a Fuzzy Profile (FP) of candidates randomly. Then, the FP (multi-dimensional space) is mapped to a bi-dimensional space using the Sammon algorithm. The bi-dimensional FP is normalized in $[0, 1]$ to facilitate the visualization of results. After the normalization, and using the fuzzy c-means algorithm, the FRSP computes the fuzzy partition matrix $\boldsymbol{U}$ which contains the membership degree of voter and candidates.

In order to generate the Top-N candidates and similarity percentage (refer to Top-N Recommendation in Sect. 5.2.), the FRSP computes a vector of distances between voter and all candidates using the normalized FP.

Finally, FRSP provides two graphical interfaces: Fuzzy Cluster Analysis Graphical Interface (FCAGI) and Top-N Recommendation Graphical Interface (TNRGI). FCAGI displays the location of voter, location of candidates (labeled by political parties), and a level diagram of clusters. TNRGI displays the location of voter, the N closest candidates, similarity percentage, and a level diagram of clusters.

Fig. 8 shows the recommendation output of the FRSP.

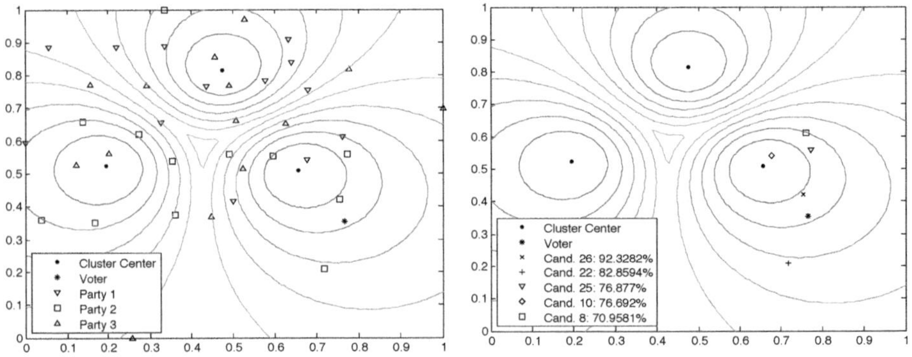

(a) Fuzzy Cluster Analysis **(b)** Top-N Recommendation

Fig. 8. Recommendation Output

6 Conclusions

This research paper introduces an architecture of a fuzzy recommender system for eElections used in eGovernment to increase participation of citizens, could possibly improve democratic processes.

The recommender system approach differs from collaborative filtering methods in that they are based on past experiences. It is also suitable in the one-and-only scenario where events such as voting and election processes occur only once.

Another important feature introduced in the proposed recommendation system is the fuzzy clustering analysis. It provides a graphical representation of political parties distributed in clusters, helping citizens to analyze politicians behavior based on similarities among them.

Fuzzy clustering analysis differ from classic clustering (sharp clustering) in that the observations belong to one and only one cluster. Moreover, classic clustering makes no use of gradual membership. A prototype of the fuzzy recommender system has been developed to visualize the results of a recommendation using profiles of candidates generated randomly.

The main differences between the recommender system proposed and the Smartvote system are the computation of similarities and the way recommendations are displayed to users.

The Smartvote system computes similarities based on "Match Points" (Sect. 3.1), and the recommendations are displayed as a list of the closest candidates with a percentage of similarity.

The FRS computes similarities based on distances in a high-dimensional space. In addition, it computes fuzzy clusters based on the number of political parties which are part of the eElection process (Sect. 5.1), where candidates and voters described in a finest granularity can belong to several clusters.

The recommendations in the FRS are displayed in a bi-dimensional space, which includes the percentage of similarity of the n closest candidates (Fig. 8). Therefore, relationships to closest "neighbors" can be derived and analyzed.

It should be noted that although the prototype is used for eElections, it can be applied for other domains such as community building, and public memory, among others. In the case of "Public Memory", described in [9], past behaviors could be taken in to account with the use of voting records to assess what the elected authorities claimed before the elections, or in the case of candidates that were elected previously. Thus, past behaviors can be used as more reliable profile information.

In future research, the prototype will be extended and tested with real data to address issues such as impacts, acceptance, and quality of the approach. In addition, to further validate the FRS, a more in-depth analysis and comparisons with classical clustering methods, including the Smartvote system, will be performed.

Acknowledgments

We wish to thank the members of the Fuzzy Marketing Methods Research Center (`htt://www.FMsquare.org`) and the Information System Research Group (`http://diuf.unifr.ch/is/`) at the University of Fribourg for contributing with valuable thoughts and comments.

We specially thank Andreas Ladner, Barry Burns, Jonathan Velasquez, Juan Carlos Altamirano, and Stefani Gerber for their support and collaboration.

References

1. Vozalis, E., Margaritis, K.: Analysis of Recommender Systems' Algorithms. In: The Sixth Hellenic European Conference on Computer Mathematics and its Applications (HERCMA 2003), Athens, Greece (2003)
2. Guo, X., Lu, J.: Intelligent E-Government Services with Personalized Recommendation Techniques. International Journal of Intelligent Systems 22, 401–417 (2007)
3. Sarwar, B., Karypis, G., Konstan, J.: Item-based Collaborative Filtering Recommendation Algorithms. In: 10th International World Wide Web Conference, Hong Kong, pp. 285–295 (2001)
4. Yager, R.: Fuzzy Logic Methods in Recommender Systems. Fuzzy Sets and Systems 136, 133–149 (2003)
5. Mobashe, R., Burke, R., Sandvig, J.: Model-Based Collaborative Filtering as a Defense Against Profile Injection Attacks. In: Proceedings of the 21st National Conference on Artificial Intelligence (AAAI'06), Boston, Massachusetts (2006)
6. Zadeh, L.: Fuzzy Sets. Department of Electrical Engineering and Electronics Research Laboratory, Berkeley, California (1965)
7. Bezdec, J.C.: Pattern Recognition with Fuzzy Objective Function Algorithms. Plenum Press, New York (1981)
8. Sammon, J.W.: A Nonlinear mapping for Data Structure Analysis. IEEE Transactions on Computers C-18(5) (1969)
9. Meier, A.: eDemocracy & eGovernment. Springer, Berlin (2009)
10. Valente de Oliveira, J., Witold, P.: Advances in Fuzzy Clustering and its Aplications. Wiley, West Sussex (2007)
11. Smartvote, `http://www.smartvote.ch/`
12. ACE Project, `http://aceproject.org/ace-en/topics/pc/pca/pca01/pca01a`
13. European Commission, `http://ec.europa.eu/information_society/activities/egovernment/index_en.htm`

Web 2.0 Creates a New Government

Roland Traunmüller

Johannes Kepler Universität Linz
Altenbergerstrasse 69
4040 Linz, Austria
traunm@iwv.jku.at

Abstract. Innovating Government is high on the agenda and has been proven as successful by using Web 2.0. This label includes a new wave of web-based applications that rely on the concept of the user as a producer. Web 2.0 provides means to create a better Government. As first point, improvements are regarded that are based on providing feedback to agencies. Examples include service ratings, law enforcement and budget allocations. A next type of improvements concerns citizen participation in order to reconnect citizens with politics and policy making as to improve responsiveness. For this aim social media are great in sustaining all kind of civic society activities. Prominent examples include campaigning, petitioning, monitoring and urban planning. Another way is agency staff persons using the Web 2.0 for cross-agency collaboration. Collaboration at large leads to good practice exchange and knowledge management.

Keywords: E-Government, Digital Government, Web 2.0, Social Media, Social Networks, Innovation, Public Governance, Participation.

1 Innovation Calls for Involving the Citizens

Competition is growing among countries, companies and institutions. Feeling the pressure from competition innovation is regarded as panacea. Also for Government innovation has become essential. It gives the State the ability for coping with societal needs posed in economics, welfare, health, education, environment etc. Thus, Government has to be open for innovating Government. In innovation processes users play a growing role. Thus, involving the citizens as well as agency staff is a key advantage for innovating Government.

To make involvement happen having adequate tools and methods is a necessary condition. Now, with Web 2.0 such means have become available. Social media can be used in several government-related activities. First we discuss the Web 2.0 and its enabling power. Then the influence of Web 2.0 on Public Governance is treated in several aspects: feedback to administration; democratic deliberation and participation of citizen in policy making; staff collaboration; exchange of expertise and managing knowledge. As the literature is vast, citations are given in a paradigmatic way. Citations on e-Government in general comprise the e-Europe Awards overviews ([1], [2]) and the recent EGOV-conference proceedings [3, 4]. Further citations are on Government and Web 2.0 [5, 6, 7], about Government and Knowledge Management [8] and concerning e-Participation [9, 10, 11, 12].

K.N. Andersen et al. (Eds.): EGOVIS 2010, LNCS 6267, pp. 77–83, 2010.

2 The Web 2.0 – A Way to Bring in the User

Under the name of Web 2.0 a new wave of web-based applications has emerged. These applications rely on the concept of the user as a producer of information; so social webs are emerging. The creation of collaborative content is done in several ways: as blogs that are online notes open to comment for other users; as wikis which are knowledge collections built by collaborative edition; as tagging that makes co-sharing of information possible. Web 2.0 is a broad and emerging concept involving technologies, applications, and values. The user roles occurring are diverse ranging from producing content to mere rating or usage. With increasing level of engagement the percentage of users decreases. With a social web new ideas are diffusing much more rapidly. Time (25 Dec 2006) made the User the Person of the Year. Therefore the front-page of that edition had a reflecting foil mirroring the spectator.

3 Social Networks Grow in Power

There are big drivers accelerating the trend. Biggest reason is that both, new ICT possibilities and a new net-friendly generation have come together. So, the labour market has got young people with a proper understanding. Then, more and more employees have become knowledge workers - and have realised that situation. There are further drivers just as to think abut Non-Governmental Organizations (NGOs). In their intention to contribute to the realization and development of democratic societies they entail a broad usage of technology.

There are a lot of hindrances as well. An inherent problem of social websites is privacy and after recent incidents the awareness of vulnerability has grown. In several concrete projects privacy has been neglected and this deficit is somehow inherent in social media - as their main purpose is facilitating communication. Then, there are institutions in power that try to hinder dissemination of information. They fear that with dissemination of information a power-shift may occur. Destructive behaviour is not uncommon, so individuals may write insulting remarks. Also groups may act in systematically influencing ratings or mobbing of users.

4 Networking Will Improve Public Governance

In recent years ways in improving Public Governance have attracted a lot of interest. Public Governance covers three zones, an inner zone with Public Administration as the machinery of Government, a middle zone with the "policy cycle" and an outer one covering the shifting balance of the public and private realm. Here comes in the role of new actors such as intermediaries and NGOs as well as new instruments such as Public Private Partnerships. The discussion on Public Governance has got momentum on diverse grounds, so an ongoing discussion on the co-evolution of Public Governance and e-Transformation. Surely this has been stimulated by the recent corporate governance discussion too.

The scope of Public Governance is rather broad: democratic and cooperative policy formulation; citizen and civil society involvement; a transparent and efficient implementation of policies; a continuous evaluation of their results; an accountability of public decision makers. Ways to improve policy making in the future entail a lot of discussion – so increased interest is cast on particular issues. The matters range from e-Participation, e-Voting, ICT assistance of collaborative work to all kind of evaluation (so with focus on e-Maturity or on good practice projects). Also collecting and disseminating knowledge, knowledge transfer and assisting legal drafting are in discussion. An excellent way to enhance Public Governance is provided by networking applications.

In the following we will treat some clusters of government-related networking activities that are improved by the Web 2.0:

1. Some improvements aim at providing feedback to agencies. Examples include suggestions, service ratings, law enforcement and budget allocations.
2. Further improvements concern citizen participation in all kind of civic society activities. Prominent examples include campaigning, petitioning, monitoring and urban planning.
3. Agency staff persons will use social media for improving formal cooperation with informal cross-agency collaboration.
4. Collaboration at large results in good practice exchange and knowledge collection.

5 Providing Feedback to Public Agencies

There is a common critic that e-Government is not enough demand oriented. In many projects the Web 2.0 is used as a means to improve Public Administration. Now, with social media the citizens may contribute by giving proposals for amendments. This is a valuable feedback to agencies and makes administration more accessible. So the Dutch ministry of the Interior set up a portal posing the question: How would you improve government? From many answers the best three were voted. The winning ideas included: (a) Help me with this e-form; (b) Government makes it possible - a proactive system; (c) a portal that making government services more accessible. Another project with citizens suggesting enhancements has been run at the city of Cologne where citizens made budget allocations for recreational facilities. A project Burgerlink has been organized in The Netherlands suggesting an e-Citizen Charta. The demands that were stated include: Choice of channel, overview of rights and duties, comprehensive procedures and convenient services etc.

There are other forms of contributions by citizens as well. So citizens may provide advice and ratings of public service so helping other citizens. Lay-persons are very skilled in re-writing public information in a form that is better understandable as the official jargon used for. Further, experienced citizens may give hints how to better deal with special administrative problems such as making applications to a certain public agency.

There are many cases where law is enforced and citizens help with monitoring. Such cases may involve negative behaviour such as insults on race. Other cases citizen may be involved in documenting trespasses of the travel code. As an example citizens have posted photos of cars parking in a bike lane.

6 Enhancing Participation in the Civic Society

E-Democracy is the support and enhancement of democracy, democratic processes and institutions. So empowerment is the red thread accompanying most activities. The idea of empowering means: giving someone the power that he was deficient before. Democracy is the goal and participation is the way. Thus e-Participation develops and implements new forms of participation. For the side of participants it brings numerous advantages: promoting more transparency and accountability; giving an increased sense of fulfilment; leading to higher user satisfaction; reaching a burden reduction in administrative terms. Also for the project side advantages are plentiful: giving better information for decision makers; increasing contact with the public; heightening security for the agency.

Today a big challenge is the perceived democratic deficit requiring new relationships between state and citizens. So it is intended to reconnect citizens with politics and policy making in a better way. In this point, e-Participation can improve the nature of representative democracy – as it facilitates more direct and more numerous links between representatives and individual voters. There is a second important argument for e-Participation: Knowledge and capability of citizens should be tapped in as the complexity of decision making demands more expertise. Further, many persons who are concerned by a decision should be directly or indirectly part of the decision making process. So the communication procedures involve citizens, public authorities, and elected representatives.

In the course of recent years, the foci of e-Participation have changed. Initially, e-Participation started with a high interest in e-Voting. Several projects were conducted using the web for voting. But most projects ran without digital signature and were often directed to rather special groups. Later on, other issues have been added. They include fostering local initiatives, improving consultation, enhancing deliberative spaces, supporting community development and developing democratic knowledge. The broad spectrum is illustrated by the list of finalists in the category "Participation and transparency" at the eEurope Awards in Lisbon: Internet voting in Estonia; Mypage self-service citizen's portal (Norway); Citizens' e-consultation in Madrid; VirtuoCity – virtual cities over one thousand words (Apeldoorn); ePetition (UK); e@sy Connects - transformational petitioning (South Yorkshire), Vicky – a virtual assistant for social security (Italy), etc. All in all, one sees success cases and deficiencies. Many projects have been performed isolated and some lack commitment from elected representatives. Lack of connection with other activities on same public-policy issue is common. Therefore for future projects the list of demands is long: active participation; innovative solutions; responding to greater diversity; better outcomes at less cost.

7 A New Impetus for Participation

A Web 2.0 application that has attracted a lot of interest is campaigning. Earlier, campaigning was performed by print media, party meetings, rallies, public speeches etc. Later electronic media such as radio and TV arrived; since the mid-Nineties the Web 1.0 got used. Now with social media there is a change; a new medium has arrived that brings additional messages. Citizens may become quite active in supporting their representatives at elections. E-Campaigning is about raising awareness about issues as well as engaging with people and encouraging people to engage with each other. It channels the power of public opinion to advance a progressive drive. One has to resume that e-Campaigning is quite different from traditional channels; it is citizen-based, decentralised, and individualistic using social micro-networks.

Another application is taking petitions. Several institutions, so the European Parliament or the Prime Ministers Office in the UK have an e-Petitioning system in order to handle complaints or requests on certain issues. There are Petition committees that accept electronic petitions and takes action considered appropriate to resolve the issue in question. Then the initiator of a petition is informed on the process and outcome.

Citizens are not only supporting their representatives, they are also watching and observing them in a critical disposition. Diverse forms of monitoring have become a leading issue in citizen participation. The targets of monitoring are divers. They include: events such as elections, groups such as political unions, persons such as politicians, modes such as proper fund spending and spaces such as parks.

8 Supporting Cooperation in Public Administration

Web 2.0 is an important instrument for improving cooperation. In Public Administration cooperation within and between agencies is a substantial part of work and therefore some institutions have used collaborative tools quite effectively. For this aim the advantages of social media are high with benefits as innovation and idea exchange, employee engagement and sharing of knowledge. A further gain is that the persons involved get a better understanding what other persons of the community do. One has to be aware that there are barriers as well; communication may be hindered from fearing the loss of control and reputational damage. Especially in the public sector cooperation skipping hierarchies earns suspicion. Further sometimes moderation may be needed, when it comes to sharing of rather sensitive data.

A particular field of use is lawmaking. Legal drafting needs instruments, so tools for information retrieval and handling the information flow between diverse stakeholders from the beginning to the authentic publication. Such stakeholders are ministries, parliaments, parties, consulting bodies etc. Connecting stakeholders will make law-making more effectively. Empowered through ICT law making has become more transparent, accessible and accountable. Further, citizens are more engaged in public life when they get better access to Parliament work. In addition electronic handling results in relevant cutbacks with electronic lawmaking in Austria now annually saving 60 tons of paper.

9 Knowledge Exchange and Collection

Besides cooperation in and between particular agencies there is a collaboration at large that accomplishes benefits for a broader public. One example is professional information exchange; another is collecting domain and service knowledge.

Professional knowledge transfer is done in diverse ways, such as in conferences, seeking good practice model cases or virtual communities. The professional community is usually broad and may include quite different stakeholders, such as citizens, politicians, administrators, companies, and researchers. For them a portal may give help of diverse kind: advice, solution to a problem, referral to a source of information, recommendation of experts, etc. For such communities a reasonable level of trust is very important as appreciated connections have to be created. Trust works through ascribing good intentions to other members and having confidence in their words.

For the community of persons interested in e-Government a portal was created under the name www.epractice.eu and promoted by the European Commission. The possibilities of this portal are broad: sharing documents, cases, events and news; posting blogs and commenting; viewing a list of community members with their profile; find persons interested in a topic and viewing tags to content. The portal epractice.eu provides its members with a blogging facility in which all registered users can post opinions, questions and links to news. Further the portal combines online with offline activities. So workshops are held regularly to discuss the latest issues and cases face-to-face. Any member can request the organisation of a workshop. The epractice.eu portal hosts an array of exciting communities which gather members with common interests and give them networking opportunities. The topics of the communities are quite diverse, so public procurement, citizen participation, social computing, identity management, policy modelling, inclusion and benchmarking. The members submit also real life good practice cases and the collection contains already 1400 examples including those cases gathered at awards competitions.

Collecting and managing knowledge is an important point for larger communities of knowledge workers. Social media allow collecting also parts of knowledge which are implicit. This means that part of knowledge that is present only in the heads and becomes visible only in the behaviour of individuals as well as in social practices. In running cooperation a lot of implicit knowledge has to be made explicit. So organizations get access to their internal (often tacit) knowledge. This is a key asset for organisations and managing knowledge is a central task.

Generally, Knowledge management means handling many aspects of information and knowledge: sources, carriers, needs, offers and flows. Knowledge management is an ongoing and adaptive interaction with the instrument of a knowledge base. It entails organized transfer of know-how, skills and expertise in a proactive way. KM-systems are the means; the learning organization is the goal. Knowledge management is a sophisticated issue due to the fact that quite diverse types have to be handled. Just to give some examples: so knowledge about people and society, on documents and relationships, on procedures and structures, about experiences and on lessons learnt. Often also knowledge about knowledge, so in assessments, evaluating experiences and retrieval procedures is involved.

Turning to knowledge management in Government the sophistication even increases as there is a kosmos of varied knowledge types. As basic classes there are repositories on registers, management information and legal norms; then there is a lot of service knowledge that has to be made explicit. That includes knowledge about the policy field to be influenced, about the own means and modalities of action, about the stakeholders, about the internals of the administrative system etc.

References

1. Leitner, C. (ed.): eGovernment in Europe: The State of Affairs. Presented at the eGovernment Conference in Como, EIPA, Maastricht (2003)
2. Millard, J. (ed.): European eGovernment 2005-2007: Taking stock of good practice and progress towards implementation of the i2010 eGovernment Action Plan. Presented at the eGovernment Conference in Lisbon, EC Brussels (2007)
3. Scholl, J., Janssen, M., Traunmüller, R., Wimmer, M. (eds.): Electronic Government, Proceedings EGOV 2009 (within DEXA 2009 in Linz). LNCS, vol.~5693. Springer, Berlin (2009)
4. Wimmer, M., Scholl, J., Janssen, M., Traunmüller, R. (eds.): Electronic Government, Proceedings of Ongoing Research, General Development Issues and Projects of EGOV 2009 (within DEXA 2009 in Linz). Trauner Verlag, Linz (2009)
5. Osimo, D.: Web 2.0 in Government: Why and How?, `http://www.jrc.es/publications/pub.cfm?id=1565`
6. Fages, R., Sanguesa, R. (eds.): State of the art in Good Practice Exchange and Web 2.0 (September 2007), `http://www.epractice.eu`
7. Habbel, F., Huber, A. (eds.): Web 2.0 für Kommunen und Kommunalpolitik. Verlag Werner Hülsbusch, Boizenburg (2008)
8. Traunmüller, R., Wimmer, M.: KM for Public Administration: Focusing on KMS Feature Requirements. In: Karagiannis, D., Reimer, U. (eds.) PAKM 2002. LNCS (LNAI), vol. 2569, pp. 314–325. Springer, Heidelberg (2002)
9. COE, Council of Europe, Good Governance in the Information Society, `http://www.coe.int/T/E/Integrated_Projects/Democracy/`
10. COE, Council of Europe, Reflections on the Future of Democracy in Europe (September 2008) ISBN 92-871-5835-5
11. Smith, S., Macintosh, A., Millard, J. (eds.): Study and supply of services in the development of eParticipation in the EU (May 2008), `http://www.european-eparticipation.eu`
12. Tholeifsdottir, A., Wimmer, M. (eds.): Report on current ICT's to enable Participation (2006), `http://www.demo-net.org`

Elements of Comprehensive Assessments of IT Infrastructure Projects in the Austrian Ministry of Finance

Edward W.N. Bernroider[1], Stefan Koch[2], and Volker Stix[3]

[1] Royal Holloway, University of London, TW20 0EX Egham, United Kingdom
edward.bernroider@rhul.ac.uk
[2] Bogazici University, 34342 Bebek, Istanbul, Turkey
stefan.koch@boun.edu.tr
[3] Vienna University of Economics and Business, Augasse 2-6, A-1090 Vienna, Austria
volker.stix@wu.ac.at

Abstract. This article strives to support research and practice in the application of decision and valuation models to IT infrastructure projects in public administration. The aim is to present the elements needed to flexibly embrace evaluation structure, management and quantification methods. We sketch how different models can work together in a complementary way laying a robust and comprehensive foundation for an integrated analysis of IT impacts. We present design and assessment results from two major IT projects in the Austrian Ministry of Finance.

Keywords: IT evaluation, Public Administration, Decision making, Evaluation frameworks, IT value.

1 Introduction

Enterprises have been facing substantially increasing investments into Information Systems (IS) with costs associated with Enterprise Resource Planning (ERP) systems of millions of USD or EUR [1,2], while the generated value remains widely disputed. The selection and usage of IS evaluation frameworks and methods poses a major challenge to large organizations in particular those in the public sector, where decisions tend to be complex with a myriad of needs to account for [3]. Public administration is concerned about (added) value and consequently about how to effectively assess IT, especially given the large public interest. Frameworks are needed in decision making [4], and popular models such as the DeLone and McLean IS success model [5] are available to structure the problem. However, viewed in isolation they do not provide guidance on how to manage the evaluation process. Existing frameworks often seem either to generic or not sufficiently detailed to provide effective help to the evaluator [6]. Specific methods provide help with quantification in some dimensions such as financial but lack overall context. Research has acknowledged the need for IT evaluation framework building [7] and recommends to use and develop more

K.N. Andersen et al. (Eds.): EGOVIS 2010, LNCS 6267, pp. 84–91, 2010.

advanced, or combined instruments that take into account multi-criteria, multi-stakeholder and systemic streams of OR [8]. In terms of method application in practice, [9] state that the existing literature has identified noticeable gaps. Until today, there seems to be a lack of simple and pragmatic yet generic and plausible frameworks to support IT investment evaluation.

This article aims at reducing the gap between theory and practice by exploring and applying elements of a generic framework including multiple methods and models to two specific IS evaluations. The framework was designed generically in nature to be instantiated with specific investment objects. The model should also enable to explore the causes of certain outcomes. Key was to support flexibility in both structure and methods, so all elements should be substitutable. The context of the evaluation should drive its manifestation, e.g., IT artefact and stakeholder requirements drive structure and methods. This article thereby explores how well a generic approach works for public administration IT evaluation practice. Two large scale IT evaluations, one based on an ERP project, the other on Business Intelligence, are used as cases, each supported by more than twelve months of field research and more than three hundred gathered data sets across all assessed constructs.

2 Empirical Research Method

The Austrian Ministry of Finance served as research environment. We performed an empirical validation of the framework within two different projects: The first one was an ERP project, while the second one was concerned with a BI system. In comparison, the second project was much smaller in scope, both in investment and user base. We used exploratory and explanatory techniques to support our validation. Initial interviews were held with the executive IT management to pinpoint the problem and explore requirements. We initially engaged in an exploratory approach where we asked about what requirements are needed for the various IT evaluation problems faced [10]. In an explanatory setting we asked about how and why the evaluation task was addressed with the support of the developed modular framework. We expected to see if the same framework and process model can be applied to two different types of IT project to support our objective of evaluation generality. The ERP case relates to an IT project implemented from 1998 to 2004 with investment costs of EUR 78 million. The system is being used by approximately 4,000 users. Due to its major and far reaching impact, this case was well suited to test the modular validation framework. The BI case study relates to comparatively smaller project with an investment value of EUR 680,000 and a user base of 200. Next to the size difference, both IT projects also have a significantly different profile and purpose, which in turn helped us to validate our generality claim. A series of open and semi-structured interviews were carried out with the experienced IT management, who expressed a strong willingness to monitor and control IT benefit realisation. For each investment case, background internal documentation and information was provided as well as lists of users, which were contacted with questionnaires to assess the user related constructs. Questionnaires were forwarded to 1,006 users with a return quota of 37% and 17 users with a return quota of 71% for the ERP and BI cases, respectively. The resulting extensive field work was operationally conducted by partners.

3 Framework Design Considerations

3.1 Management Model

According to our objectives we sought to design a holistic measurement system that can be effectively used to assess any IT investment in the public sector. For this purpose we looked for an overarching management approach, and exploited the content, context and process (CCP) idea proposed by [11], for work on organisational change, expanded in the context of IS evaluation [12, 13], and more recently applied by [6]. There is widespread support in academic literature for this approach [9]. The use of CCP provided us with a source for questions to guide the design of the model in relating to what is being measured, by whom and for what purpose.

3.2 Unit of Analysis

The type of IT determines basic orientation of the investment evaluation and consequently also further construction of the framework in terms of model instantiation. This includes all elements, e.g., structure in terms of an underlying multidimensional base model and configuration of its dynamic relationships. Most IT taxonomies differentiate between the breadth of support (from personal production tools to ERP, and inter-organizational systems) and organizational level at which systems are used, cf. [14]. The cases used here are ERP (company-wide breadth and lower level) and Business Intelligence (possibly again company wide, and higher organizational level).

3.3 Structure Model

In decision making and evaluation it is essential to find a structure to understand and outline the problem. It should allow for identification and classification of attributes and reflect influences among them [4]. Literature suggests different choices to structure IS evaluation. We needed models that provide semantically clear dimensions and guidance on cause and effect relationships between them. Examples for established structural models are the IS Success Model [5, 15], Task-Technology Fit [16, 17], or Balanced Scorecard [18]. The output of each base model is a vector of dimensions aggregating underlying measurements. The aggregation task is not trivial but can be supported by approaches available in literature. It should be noted that the taxonomical approach is also criticised, e.g. by [19], who argue that there can be no valid general structure. The validity of the listed measurement models, however, was validated for specific IS, e.g., for ERP systems by [20]. We acknowledge the concerns and suggest keeping the choice of structure open, but request its definition at run time. Here we chose to apply the D&M IS success model in both case studies due to its wide acknowledgement in particular for IS, and also the public sector [21, 22].

3.4 Quantification Model

The area of multiple attributive decision making promises the flexibility to account for the different investment considerations and for the multiple stakeholders involved. We therefore sought to assign quantification to attributes placed within dimensions of the evaluation structure. Based on the evaluation type, e.g., an ERP project, a list of appropriate measures should be presented, connected with appropriate techniques to quantify them. An essential aspect in this design step is to reflect on completeness of dimensions while minimizing overlaps between dimensions. A further requirement is also independence between measures (in a statistical interpretation).

Elementary methods provide the means to quantify each measure, e.g., through simple questionnaires or complex optimisation models. There are a vast number of methods available in literature, some based on simple cost-benefit multiple criteria analysis [23] while most rely on rather complex models and methods at least from the viewpoint of practitioners, like for example the profile distance method [24]. Many methods are summarised in review papers [26-29].

3.5 Aggregation Model

Within the dimensions given by the chosen structure suitable methods are needed to support the aggregation of single measurements into aggregated measures per dimension. Subsequently, these dimensions can be further consolidated in another step where the decision maker or user can include preferences. Commonly considered methods for aggregation of measures are based on simple additive weighting [25] or the Analytic Hierarchy Process [30], which we applied. In order to support practicability we suggest to hardcode the first aggregation mechanism, where attributes are aggregated into single dimensions during design time. Of course, the mechanism needs to able to treat different scale types. We suggest to treat metric and non metric scales separately thereby avoiding many problems and mistakes made with scale transformations.

4 Case Study Results

4.1 Enterprise Resource Planning Case

CCP dictates to determine what is being measured, by whom and for what purpose. Here we refer to an ERP system as unit of analysis and its purpose includes three domains: Integration, process optimisation and functionality. The integration domain embraces technical and behavioural integration, with the latter considered the biggest challenge, as many ERP projects are technically driven [31], which tends to undervalue important behavioural aspects needed in delivering and implementing organisational change [32]. Functional requirements were largely financial accounting area and to support automated workflows across systems for procurement, billing and other areas. Paperless processes are central to the overarching eGovernance strategy, as well as process optimisation for efficiency and effectiveness of operations.

The next step included the definition of a base model and measures that can be used to assess the system. As argued, for both cases we chose the mentioned IS Success Model from DeLone and McLean [5, 15]. Based on the D&M model, the dimensions are grouped into three causal stages where each has an effect on the next. In the first stage the consequences are seen in the quality dimensions (System, Information and Service Quality), which in turn impact Intention to Use and User Satisfaction, and finally Net Benefits. While literature suggests a breadth of different measures, the majority focuses either on technical performance or financial value, so we also considered studies that concentrated on benefits [33, 21]. In terms of quantification of measures, again the decision maker needs to select and identify from a vast list. The final set comprised 37 items. Measures were assigned to different assessors, which conforms to a recommendation of CCP. Four different groups of assessors were identified, comprising active and semi-active system users, decision makers, and domain experts. Each received a set of measures through questionnaires and interviews in the first three groups. Domain experts were included to help with quantification aspects of certain methods such as discounted cash flow analysis.

It has to be defined how and to what extent aggregation should take place within one dimension of the base model and potentially also across dimensions. We suggest a systematic procedure to support aggregation based on AHP, done by experts. The common problem of heterogeneous scale types across measures had impact on aggregation. Solutions are to transform scales, which tends to lose semantics, or to restrict the level of aggregation to uniform groups. Net benefits included a financial measure (Discounted Cash Flow), which was excluded in the aggregation process. All remaining measures are qualitative and can be more easily aggregated into one figure. Hence, after aggregation each dimension of the model is represented by one value apart from Net Benefits with a 2 dimensional figure. Table 1 shows the final ERP assessment results on the highest aggregation level. The decision maker now sees a complete picture on the success of the ERP project, which can be used to explore causal relationships according to the used D&M base model.

Table 1. ERP aggregation assessment results

Model dimension	Aggregation 1	Aggregation 2
Information Quality	2.1	1.98
System Quality	2.13	
Service Quality	1.88	
Intention to Use / Use	2.28	2.34
User Satisfaction	2.53	
Net Benefits: Set 1	2.03	2.03
and eDCF	€ 18-151 mio	€ 18-151 mio

4.2 Business Intelligence Case

The goals of BI focused on reporting from the view of different users with navigation and selection features, as well as data integration and access. Therefore it differed considerably from the ERP case and also the list of measures naturally was different and reduced by 10. This related to system-inherent factors (not many technical measures available), but also context-related factors, e.g., cost of data collection. In the BI project, aggregation also differed, as the initiator decided on different weights for the dimensions: The Net Benefit dimension, the most important one in the ERP case, was of less importance, while quality and user view became more important. The result (Table 2) should not be seen in isolation. It is an aggregated view and an aspect is its ability to decompose the construct again to explore shortcomings or strengths within each dimension. This feature allows use in problem analysis, tracking and controlling.

The decision maker is free to explore aspects of each aggregated dimension back into elemental metrics. Due to insufficient responses service quality dimension was not included in aggregation. As can be seen, the BI project is less successful than the ERP project, in particular system usage is problematic.

Table 2. BI aggregation assessment results

Model dimension	Aggregation results	Aggregation 2
Information Quality	2.45	2.47
System Quality	2.49	
Service Quality	n.a.	
Intention to Use / Use	3.45	3.02
User Satisfaction	2.5	
Net Benefits	2.48	2.48

5 Conclusions and Implications

In this article we answered the need for support for complex evaluation tasks in Governmental bodies. We aimed at providing an overall generic framework with links to models and methods to help more effectively assess major IT projects in the Austrian Ministry of Finance. Both case studies were well supported by the approach. Formal evaluation is needed to account for tangible and intangible aspects of the investment decision not only to support it but also for ongoing evaluation. Controlling and defense of investment decisions are concerns of public administration IT management who welcome a general, modular approach supported by an evaluation process that can be instantiated with specific IT evaluation tasks or projects. With this critic in mind considering that every IS is unique and thus needs specific measures [19], we applied the same structure but a different set of metrics to both case studies. While they had distinctive requirements, the assessment worked well with a similar set of measures within the same structural model. In both cases, a robust and comprehensive foundation for an integrated analysis of IT impacts was achieved and IT management showed every intention to apply continuous assessments.

Besides selecting and applying structural and measurement models, important further elements need to be considered in a management view, where we followed the recommendation of CCP to integrate organisational aspects. Here we see challenges in links of methods to organisational stakeholders as well as the provision of sufficient resources. A further finding is the importance of accurately understanding the type of evaluation project before initiating the framework instance. The AHP approach also used in other hybrid multi-criteria decision aids for IT assessments [34] proved to be a useful and accepted technique for consolidation and weight estimation.

References

1. Jutras, C.: The total cost of ERP ownership in large companies. Aberdeen, Boston (2007)
2. Bernroider, E.: The impact of costs and time on ERP project success. In: European Academy of Management (EURAM) 9th Conference, pp. 1–19. Liverpool (2009)

3. Saaty, T.L.: Multi-decisions decision-making: In addition to wheeling and dealing, our national political bodies need a formal approach for prioritization. Mathematical and Computer Model 46, 1001–1016 (2007)
4. Saaty, T.L., Shih, H.-S.: Structures in decision making: On the subjective geometry of hierarchies and networks. EJOR 199, 867–872 (2009)
5. DeLone, W.D., McLean, E.R.: The DeLone and McLean Model of Information Systems Success: A Ten-Year Update. Journal of Management Information Systems 19, 9–30 (2003)
6. Stockdale, R., Standing, C.: An interpretive approach to evaluating information systems: A content, context, process framework. EJOR 173, 1090–1102 (2006)
7. Björnsson, H., Lundegård, R.: Corporate competitiveness and information technology. European Management Journal 10, 341–347 (1992)
8. Kunsch, P.L., Kavathatzopoulos, I., Rauschmayer, F.: Modelling complex ethical decision problems with operations research. Omega 37, 1100–1108 (2009)
9. Smithson, S., Serafeimidis, V.: Information systems evaluation as an organizational institution - experience from a case study. Information Systems Journal 13, 251–274 (2003)
10. Yin, R.K.: Case Study Research - Design and Methods. SAGE, London (2003)
11. Pettigrew, A.: The Awakening Giant: Continuity and Change at ICI. Blackwell, Oxford (1985)
12. Symons, V.J.: A review of information system evaluation: Content, context and process. European Journal of Information Systems 1, 205–212 (1991)
13. Walsham, G.: Interpretive evaluation design for information systems. In: Lester, L.W.a.S. (ed.) Beyond the IT Productivity Paradox. John Wiley, Chichester (1999)
14. Rainer, R.K., Turban, E.: Introduction to Information Systems – Enabling and transforming Business. Wiley, Hoboken (2009)
15. DeLone, W.H., McLean, E.R.: Information Systems Success: The Quest for the Dependent Variable. Information Systems Research 3, 60–95 (1992)
16. Goodhue, D.L.: Understanding user evaluations of information systems. Management Science 41, 1827–1844 (1995)
17. Zigurs, I., Buckland, B., Connolly, J., Wilson, E.V.: A test of task-technology fit theory for group support systems. Data Base for Advances in Information Systems 3, 34–50 (1999)
18. Kaplan, R.S., Norton, D.P.: The Balanced Scorecard – measures that drive performance. Harvard Business Review, 71–79 (1992)
19. Seddon, P.B., Staples, D.S., Patnayakuni, R., Bowtell, M.J.: The IS effectiveness matrix: the importance of stakeholder and system in measuring IS success. In: International Conference on Information Systems, Helsinki, Finland, pp. 165–177 (1998)
20. Bernroider, E.W.N.: IT Governance for Enterprise Resource Planning supported by the DeLone-McLean Model of Information Systems Success. Information & Management 45, 257–269 (2008)
21. Gable, G., Sedera, D., Palmer, A.: Enterprise Resource Planning Systems Impacts: A Delphi Study of Australian Public Sector Organisations. In: 6th Australasian Conference on Information Systems, pp. 584–600 (2002)
22. Thomas, P.: Information Systems Success and Technology Acceptance within Government Organization. In: 12th Americas Conference on Information Systems (AMCIS '06), Acapulco, Mexico (2006)
23. Olson, D.L.: Evaluation of ERP outsourcing. Computers & Operations Research 34, 3715–3724 (2007)
24. Bernroider, E.W.N., Stix, V.: Profile distance method - a multi-attribute decision making approach for information system investments. Dec. Support Systems 42, 988–998 (2006)

25. Zangemeister, Z.: Nutzwertanalyse in der Systemtechnik. Wittemann, München (1976)
26. Behzadian, M., Kazemzadeh, R.B., Albadvi, A., Aghdasi, M.: PROMETHEE: A comprehensive literature review on methodologies and applications. EJOR 200, 198–215 (2010)
27. Farbey, B., Land, F., Targett, D.: How to Assess your IT Investment. A study of Methods and Practice. Butterworth Heinemann, Oxford (1993)
28. Gunasekaran, A., Ngai, E.W.T., McGaughey, R.E.: Information technology and systems justification: A review for research and applications. EJOR 173, 957–983 (2006)
29. Love, P.E.D., Irani, Z., Edwards, D.J.: Researching the investment of information technology in construction: An examination of evaluation practices. Automation in Construction 14, 569–582 (2005)
30. Saaty, T.L.: The Analytic Hierarchy Process. McGraw Hill, New York (1980)
31. Bernroider, E.W.N.: An empirical reflection on the needs for and consequences of operational and technical integration with ERP projects. In: International DSI / Asia and Pacific DSI, Bangkok, Thailand, pp. 1–9 (2007)
32. Kumar, V., Maheshwari, B., Kumar, U.: ERP systems implementation: best practices in Canadian government organizations. Government Information Quarterly 19, 147–172 (2002)
33. Chang, J.C., King, W.R.: Measuring the performance of Information Systems: A Functional Scorecard. Journal of Management Information Systems 22, 85–115 (2005)
34. Wang, J.-J., Yang, D.-L.: Using a hybrid multi-criteria decision aid method for information systems outsourcing. Computers & Operations Research 34, 3691–3700 (2007)

Updating Official Publications to the Web 3.0: A Quantum Leap in e-Gov Transparency and Citizen Participation Is on Sight

Francisco-Javier García-Marco

Facultad de Filosofía y Letras, Universidad de Zaragoza, 50009 Zaragoza, Spain
jgarcia@unizar.es

Abstract. This paper explores the possibilities that semantic and social web technologies offer for enhancing official publications—and particularly official gazettes—, so that transparency and citizen participation are empowered. It is concluded that a quantum leap is possible by promoting, first of all, the automatic collection, presentation and comparison of data; secondly, the linking and reference of all the relevant evidence and documentation from different sources and, therefore, enhancing its use; and, finally, by allowing the public annotation and discussion around laws, norms and governmental acts. Ensuring the permanence of all this information is a key aspect of this effort. To sum up, promoting law and research programs that support a change in the way that official information and documents are published should get into the political and research agenda of all the parties and agents interested in promoting government for the citizens and from the citizens.

Keywords: Official publications. Official gazettes. Semantic Web. Social Web. Web 3.0. Government transparency. Citizen participation. E-Democracy.

1 What Are Official Publications?

The IFLA Official Publications Section spent three years discussing the definition and scope of official publications. According to Eve Johansson [1], this body established that

> An official publication is any document, printed or produced by any other reprographic method in multiple copies, issued by an organization that may be considered to be an official body, and available to a public wider than that body.

A key aspect of this definition that remains in the twilight is the concept of official body. It was thereafter necessary to define it, and they decided that it was any legislature, executive agency, or other organization created by the previous two ones that maintains a relation with them; and, in addition, any association of the aforementioned bodies.

This kind of publications may have different aims: inform the audience, compel the audience, make available results or data, etc.

K.N. Andersen et al. (Eds.): EGOVIS 2010, LNCS 6267, pp. 92–99, 2010.

Some of these publications are compelled by law, because they have a legal effect, and form a specific kind of official publications in themselves. The most important ones are probably the official gazettes—or official diaries or public journals, as they are known in various countries. They are used to publish the laws enacted by the legislative bodies, the norms established by the governmental agencies, and some administrative acts that must be published to come into effect, like dispositions. In fact, in many countries, the publication in those journals is a prerequisite for an act of government to come into effect.

It is possible, of course, to widen the scope of this definition to include all the publications by which any kind of association or organization that has a public status delivers its agreements to the public. In this sense, NGO, unions, scientific societies, etc., deliver public information by journals and special publications.

In this paper, the stress will be put on governmental official publications, and, especially, on official diaries or gazettes, as they are a keystone of public transparency and accountability.

2 Official Publications, for What?

From the point of view of governments, publishing official acts is a way of ensuring that everybody is aware of a law or act of government, and that nobody might claim ignorance, being, therefore, totally responsible.

From the point of view of citizens, the publication of government agreements is a protection against arbitrary decisions and a warranty of transparency, that is, a prerequisite for governmental accountability and responsibility.

These two approaches are certainly divergent, though they converge to make official gazettes useful and a common ground tool. Several scholars have studied this tension. In the United States, John Spencer Walters's research [2] is one of the main references, having studied them from the foundation of the country until 1970.

3 From Stele to the Web 3.0

Official publications have a very old history. One of the oldest is the stele containing the Code of Hammurabi—a Babylonian king—that was found in 1901 in ancient Susa, and that dates from circa 1790 BC. It is a big stone to stand up in a public square for everybody to know which was the law in the city. This is a very good example to show that publication is a key aspect of law and governance, as everybody knows intuitively.

For many years, the usual way to publicize laws, norms and acts of government was by reading them in public places, and issuing copies, some of which were fixed in those public spaces and even in formats designed specifically for this purpose (stele, posters, etc.).

The invention of printing made issuing copies much easier, and, finally, they were grouped in journals, as it was happening with news diaries, and other proceedings, like those of the scientific societies. This was a perfect way not only of distribution, but also of preservation.

From the invention of the World Wide Web in 1989, all the countries and their official bodies took quick measures to deliver those journals on the Internet. The advantages were the same as these of any other electronic publication: world-wide, immediate, permanent and machine-assisted access.

As Internet use has grown, becoming pervasive, governments have been able to use the web even for cutting in expenses. Many governments and public agencies are now delivering their official publications only throughout the Internet, relying on public libraries and other public offices to avoid the undesired effects provoked by the electronic gap.

The challenge now is to go a step forward and bring official gazettes and, in general, official publications up to the promises that the web is offering.

This future can, at the present moment, be imagined throughout the concept of the "Web 3.0", which Tim Berners-Lee [3] abstracted in this way:

> People keep asking what Web 3.0 is. I think maybe when you've got an overlay of scalable vector graphics—everything rippling and folding and looking misty—on Web 2.0 and access to a semantic Web integrated across a huge space of data, you'll have access to an unbelievable data resource.

To sum up, we can have a glimpse of the future of the web by connecting the impact of its two more important technologies: the semantic web and the social web or web 2.0. Let us discuss in the following pages what this might imply for official publications and the problem of citizen protection, a new horizon—in any case—for a tool as old as civilization (Fig. 1).

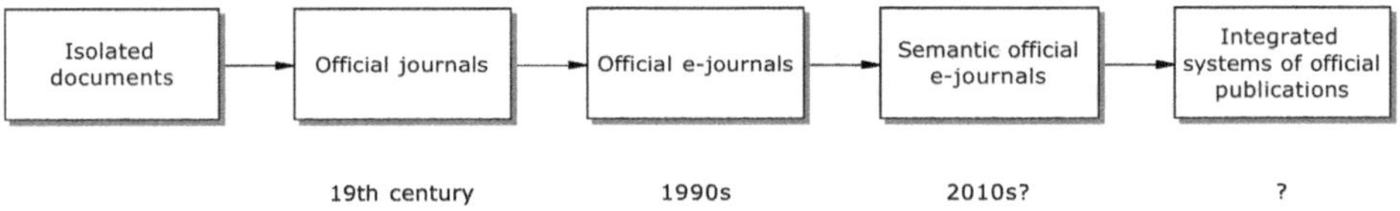

Fig. 1. A prospective history of official publications

4 Official Publications and the Semantic Web

4.1 Semantic Web in e-Government: Towards Demand-Driven Reusability of Public Data

One of the great things about the Semantic Web is that it allows the mark-up and the subsequent automatic processing of data included into otherwise unstructured documents.

Semantic web is being widely researched and used in e-government. Almost every developed country is doing a great work in advancing semantic web applications for enhancing governance and administrative tasks. But the emphasis is put mainly on interoperability among public administrations, which is, of course, a key aspect to ensure the efficacy and efficiency of their activities on behalf of the citizens.

On the contrary, in this article, we will focus on another aspect of the potential offered by these technologies: using semantic web to promote transparency and *empower* citizens to control governmental action in an age of increasing information overload, allowing for the automatic gathering and analysis of data by the citizens and their organizations.

In a recent report for the European Commission, "empowerment" has been situated at the centre of the future political stage of modern societies [4] [5]

> Today, in the 21st century, 'empowerment' seems to be the next great societal value, in response to the massive increase in information and communication permeating society. There is a coming together of new ICT tools with growing competence, ability and incentive to participate in governance by all sections of society. [4]

In the current web-driven information explosion, empowering citizens is no more only about publishing relevant information, but also about preparing this information so that it can be easily processed. Huge quantities of ever-increasing relevant governmental information require, doubtlessly, automatic tools to deal with it.

At this point of the discussion, some sensible criticism should be prospectively addressed. We are going to deal only with two arguments that are more directly used against the public utilization of semantic web in e-government, leaving aside more general arguments about how much transparency is optimal and about the conflicts of transparency with other values as national security or personal privacy.

First, it could be cleverly argued that citizens do not need row data, but that governments must synthesize this information for them; moreover, that this is one of their obligations. But, as in scientific research, the possibility to select, manipulate, summarize and contrast data is essential for government control and proposing sound public policies and projects. It is not the same to provide citizens with a closed discourse and interpretation, that with data they can check and process independently.

Another possible objection is that such an approach is not viable for the general public. It is clear that, just now, we do not see standard citizens using semantic web data to control government action —though some are certainly able and eager to do it—: For many years, this will be the task of non governmental organizations: political parties, labor unions, transparency associations, etc. In the interim, and for sure, new web services will be created by different agents that will enable more people to retrieve and filter semantic data and projecting it into maps and graphics, so that this massive information may be made intelligible to educated people.

4.2 Semantic Web and Official Gazettes: Some Perspectives

Currently, official gazettes are a key tool for ensuring reading-oriented publication, but they are almost impossible to use for automatic gathering and processing.

There are many projects on track regarding the application of semantic web approaches to some types of documents that are published in official gazettes, but systematic ones are still rare.

Laws and legal documents have been probably the kind of documents that have received closer attention, which has resulted in proposals like MetaLex XML and the

Legal Knowledge Interchange Format and several related European projects that have been recently reviewed by Boer, Winkels and Vitali [6] and Martínez and Vicente [7].

But governmental administrative acts are equally of great importance and, in many cases, much easier to be codified, at least step by step. This last approach is, for example, being followed by the *London Gazette* [8], which is actually tagging names and addresses in its insolvency notes (Fig. 2).

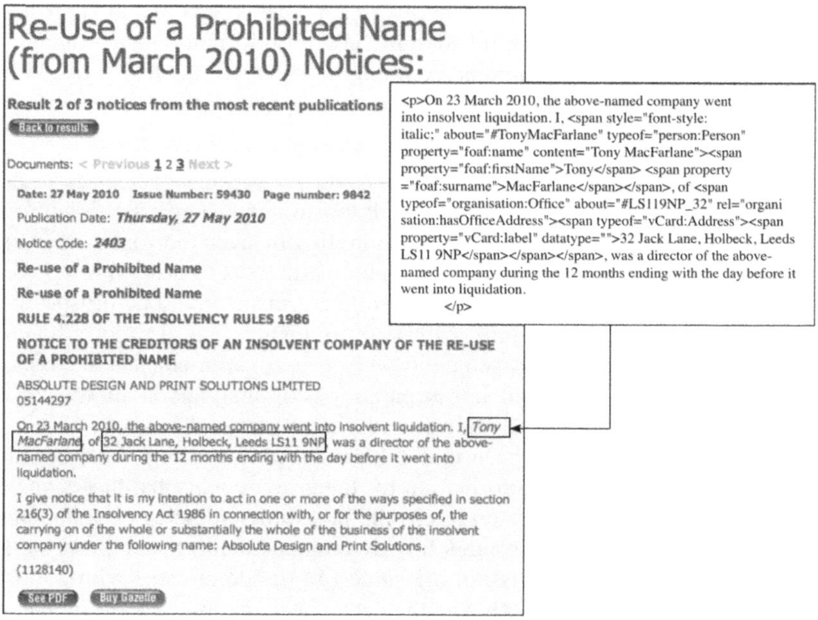

Fig. 2. Semantic tagging at the *London Gazette*

From a very general perspective, it can be stated that laws are about what it is pretended, and dispositions about what the governments are really doing; thereafter, both kinds of information are equally important for controlling them, the heads and tiles of the action of the State.

A transparency-driven use of semantic web in official publications could have four main impacts:

- interconnection with related documents and data;
- widening the scope of information published;
- integration and
- automatic processing.

These possible impacts could be also transformed into lines of action to improve transparency throughout the application of semantic technologies to official publications.

The first of them would be the possibility of interconnecting them with related laws, norms and administrative acts, and, on the other hand, with external evidence and knowledge, like the related work of public bodies, relevant literature, news and public records. This would do the work of non-governmental organizations related to transparency—as Transparency International [9]—and citizens much easier.

The second one would be the possibility of widening the scope of the information published, by ensuring the proper handling of personal—and in general sensitive—data with special protection tags. Besides removing these problems, and once official journals are being published exclusively on the Internet, the problem of cost becomes almost marginal or at least very limited. Many things that were not published because of such costs can now be published or at least easily linked.

Integration is the third big advantage. Official publications in a country can and must stop being isolated publications; and begin to be a system. This is especially important in countries with a great degree of regional or functional autonomy inside the State, where collecting all the related legislation and data is especially difficult, even for insiders. In the best of the worlds, such a system of official publications could be navigated and searched from alternative perspectives—for example, jurisdiction, topic, date, etc.—and linked to related systems of other countries, etc.

Finally, semantic tagging and their interconnection with ontologies would allow the automatic collection and processing of information, making it possible to pass it to any kind of application, which could, reversely, send its output to the Internet under compliance to the same semantic standards. It would be possible, for example, to project the data about public employment or administrative concessions on a map, so that they could be easily assessed, and of course to a statistical package for analysis. In this way, controlling governmental action—and that of the non-governmental agents that suffer or enjoy it—could reach a new level, and could be even automated to a great degree, extending the capability of control by the citizens and their organizations.

Of course, all this will require a huge re-engineering of the whole chain of public information. This cannot be only the task of official gazettes, but a coordinated effort with the governmental agencies providing the data, ensuring a swift interoperabililty in the interchange of information in its different stages.

5 Official Publications and the Web 2.0

Probably because of its official nature, it is very difficult to imagine the level of freedom of expression and informality that it is normally associated to the social web being applied to official publications. Of course, this depends on the level of citizen participation and responsibility of each country, of its democratic commitment and tolerance.

In any case, and despite of this reality, there is a feeling that this world of social communications technologies is the inevitable and desirable future for official publications.

So, some kind of bridge must be imagined for many countries and contexts to overcome this extended incompatibility between official publications and public participation around them.

The semantic web provides the technical solution throughout persistent locators. Thanks to them, the social web could grow outside the governmental sites where official publications reside, but very near—at the distance of a click —on the Internet. Transparency organizations could provide the servers and applications for the citizens to comment, vote, denounce, append information, etc., around the items of the official publications.

This ring of social participation would provide also with very valuable information on the topics about which the citizens are worried, motivated and committed. And this would happen in a transparent and immediate way, available to any interested party, and, of course, to the governments and governmental agencies.

6 Permanent Archiving

If these tools are to be of any use in the context of government control, the information they are conveying must be stored permanently and surely.

It is not only a question of ensuring future research, but of ensuring accountability and transparency in the long term.

After all, the whole strategy of widening the scope of published documents and of linking related information rests on the permanence of all this structured information and their locators. And also of the metadata and the taxonomies/ontologies used to locate and organize them, which keep evolving as the technical, social and political environment changes.

Some solutions are technical, like electronic signatures and digital marks to ensure the authenticity and integrity of the documents, the development of permanent pointers like Uniform Resource Identifiers (URI), historical data in classes, etc. However, the most important problems are of a political and social nature, like inventing the bodies and determining the officers in charge of this task.

7 Conclusions

Up to the moment, and with few and fragmented exceptions, official publications on the Internet are only—but certainly and usefully they are—the electronic surrogates of their predecessors.

This is important, but it is also a retarded form, especially when considering all the possibilities that the current evolution of the World Wide Web is offering.

Advancing in the semantic tagging, organization and publication of the official gazettes and other official publications would certainly allow for their improvement, enlargement, integration and automatic processing; and also for application-enrichment in more specific aspects like confidential access to information and privacy protection.

On the other hand, the application of social web tools would enhance public criticism and empower citizens and their organizations to pursue big improvements in the legal, normative and executive activity of governments; and providing, vice versa, government agencies and agents with fresh and valuable feedback.

Both families of technologies offer together an incredible opportunity to advance the cause of transparency and citizen's participation; and their application in the field of official publications is, because of the reasons that have been previously discussed, a cornerstone of e-democracy.

So, promoting law and research programs that support a change in the way that official information and documents are published should get into the political and research agenda of all the parties and agents interested in promoting government for the citizens and from the citizens.

References

1. Johansson, E.: The definition of official publications. IFLA Journal I(4), 393–395 (1982)
2. Walters, J.S.: U.S. government publication: ideological development and institutional politics from the founding to 1970 / John Spencer Walters. Scarecrow Press, Lanham (2005)
3. Shannon, V.: A more "revolutionary" web. The New York Times. Technology (May 23, 2006), http://www.nytimes.com/2006/05/23/technology/23iht-web.html?_r=1
4. Botterman, M., et al.: Value for Citizens: a Vision of Public Governance in 2020: a Report for the European Commission by Rotterdam, December 2008. Office for Official Publications of the European Communities, Luxembourg (2009), http://ec.europa.eu/information_society/activities/egovernment/studies/docs/final_report_web.pdf
5. Millard, J.: Government 1.5: is the bottle half full or half empty? European Journal of ePractice 9 (March 2010), http://www.epractice.eu/files/European%20Journal%20epractice%20Volume%209.3_1.pdf
6. Boer, A., Winkels, R., Vitali, F.: MetaLex XML and the Legal Knowledge Interchange Format. In: Casanovas, P., Sartor, G., Casellas, N., Rubino, R. (eds.) Computable Models of the Law. LNCS (LNAI), vol. 4884, pp. 21–41. Springer, Heidelberg (2008)
7. Martínez González, M., Vicente Blanco, D.J.: XML legislativo: representación y organización de la información jurídica a través de la tecnología XML. Ibersid, Prensas Universitarias de Zaragoza, Zaragoza (2009), http://ibersid.eu/ojs/index.php/scire/issue/view/187
8. London Gazette, http://www.london-gazette.gov.uk
9. Transparency International, http://www.transparency.org/

One Inch Wide and One Inch Deep: The Role of Policies in Shaping the Adoption of Open Standards and Software in Government

Kim Normann Andersen[1], Daniel Veit[2], Rony Medaglia[1], and Helle Zinner Henriksen[1]

[1] Center for Applied ICT (CAICT), Copenhagen Business School, Howitzvej 60, 1818 Frederiksberg, Denmark
{andersen,rm.caict,hzh.caict}@cbs.dk
[2] Chair of Business Administration and Information Systems, University of Mannheim, Schloss, 68131 Mannheim, Germany
veit@bwl.uni-mannheim.de

Abstract. This paper presents a qualitative and quantitative study on the role of policies in Denmark and Germany in shaping the adoption of open standards and software in government. A comprehensive functionality test, surveys and interviews with suppliers and users in local authorities of both countries have been conducted, together with policy document analyses. While in Denmark open document standards have been bindingly introduced by legislation, Germany adopts a blended top-down and bottom-up approach, only providing recommendations. Although, as a result, it seems that Denmark ranks much higher in the adoption of open document standards, the overall picture is blurrier, as for instance only a small minority of public employees use open source software. The authors also suggest that the need for open standards might actually be overstated, as the rapid adoption of e.g. the PDF document format has made it in practice almost irrelevant.

Keywords: Electronic government, Open standards, Public policy, IT governance.

1 Introduction

International standardization bodies, industry forums, such as the Open Forum Europe, and the open source software community have been seen as aiding government by providing better and cheaper software since the market mechanisms are argued to be more transparent and with less entry and exit barriers, less switching costs, positive network effects, and reduction in path dependency [1]. Massive markets, such as the Chinese public sector, are the best examples of this. To facilitate increased supply-side market competition and smoothen the exchange of data within government and between government and citizens, companies, and NGOs, governments in various countries have pushed for open standards in the exchange of documents. However, governments have been challenged by the diffusion of, for instance, the

K.N. Andersen et al. (Eds.): EGOVIS 2010, LNCS 6267, pp. 100–107, 2010.

PDF format, whereby most of the documents that do not require editing can be exchanged. Moreover, besides open document standards, there are various other open standard challenges that also call for policy attention: the exchange of data between public authorities, document and management systems, e-procurement, digital signature, and IT security [2, 3]. Hence, governments are caught in a prioritization challenge: should policy saliency be given to open document standards, or to open procurement software standards? In the two cases explored in this paper, we argue that, perhaps due to this tricky dilemma, policies on open document standards appear to touch upon only a small part of the challenge, and lack to ground the policies in actionable settings. Therefore we argue that the policies are "one inch wide and one inch deep".

The role of environment and institutional intermediaries to shape and impact the diffusion of information systems are well researched in the information systems community – e.g. [4-7].

Relying on an in-depth qualitative and quantitative study of the Danish and German government initiatives by national parliaments, in which the authors of this paper independently have been involved as national experts [8, 9], we investigate the policies and diffusion of open standards and software in Denmark and Germany. In the Danish case, a comprehensive functionality test, a survey with suppliers and users in the 100 Danish municipalities, as well as an expert group analysis have been conducted [8]. In the German case an extensive survey with 214 municipalities and follow-up interviews, as well as document studies [9] form the empirical foundation for the mapping of governance drivers in this paper.

2 Prior Research and Framework

We have adopted a framework we have earlier used in an analysis of government policies on driving e-commerce adoption forward [4]. Although the objectives of the governance efforts are different, the appeal of the framework is that we take into account global and national environment drivers that are only marginally controlled by national government. We have chosen to categorize the environment drivers into four main categories: industry structure, information infrastructure, financial and human resources, and social/cultural factors.

Various authors have pointed to the role of institutions in innovation and diffusion [5, 10, 11]. We support the notion of institutions and argue that there is a need for conceptually refining our analysis of governmental actions. We have identified four sets of governance actions stimulating open source and document standards diffusion: 1) pedagogical and discourse initiatives (knowledge dissemination e.g. through open source and document standards seminars, materials aiming at improving knowledge, etc.); 2) economic initiatives (e.g. the provision of subsidized pricing for network services, as well as direct subsidies of open source and document standards activities); 3) normative initiatives (e.g. directives and legislation on syntax rules, data dictionaries, etc.); and 4) organizational management [12-14].

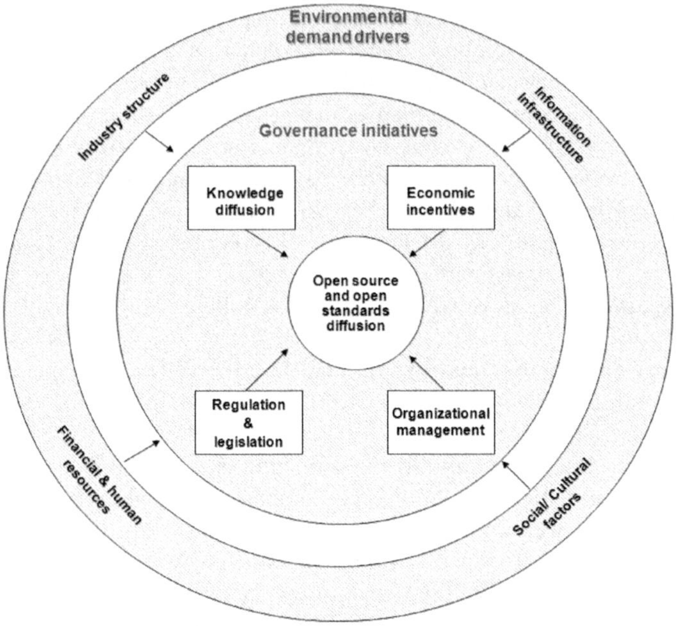

Fig. 1. Framework for identifying demand drivers and policies. Source: Adapted and modified from Andersen et al. [4].

3 The German Case

3.1 Demand Drivers for E-Government Solutions

Germany is a federal republic consisting of 16 federal states. The German e-government initiatives have been fostered in the last years on a federal level. The federal ministry of the interior established an e-government unit, headed by the German federal CIO, which regularly published the Standards and Architectures for E-Government (SAGA) [15] document. This document is made of three main sections: technical standards, data standards and software architectures. The central governance, which is underlying this approach, is the classification of technologies for public usage. The focus of the document is a replacement of proprietary solutions through open source standards. Norms, concepts and architectures are assessed using a pre-defined procedure: 1) suggestion of a norm, standard or architecture through a publicly accessible discussion forum; 2) assessment of the suggestion by the SAGA author team; 3) discussion of the norms, standards and architectures; 4) acceptance of the suggestions by a formal vote of the KBSt; 5) incorporation of the standards into the SAGA document.

Based on the given structure of SAGA and the federal e-government initiatives in Germany, it becomes obvious that the federal structure with the fine granularity of interaction between municipalities, federal states and federal government is creating severe obstacles. Consequently, the acceptance of the SAGA standard in Germany is mediocre [16]. Since the first publication and utilization of SAGA in February 2003, the German government has followed a dual strategy. On the one hand, certain parts of interoperability standards are binding for all federal institutions. On the other hand, in many issues the decision whether to apply the standard or not is left over to the individual IT project leader.

Until 2003 there was no centrally defined standard document available. Hence, a strong "bottom-up" growth of infrastructural decisions has been made.

3.2 Policy Instruments Applied

The state Schleswig-Holstein has, as a first federal state, started to establish an e-government law. This outlook shows, that – next to the federal regulation by the introduction of obligatory standards through SAGA – individual states start to regulate the sector in which the federal rules do not bite.

Knowledge transfer is one of the core issues in e-government development. Therefore, the German ministry of the interior has created several initiatives in which current developments of e-government concepts are fostered through regular exchange of ideas and conferences (e.g. DeutschlandOnline, E-Government 2.0 and BundOnline 2005, and so forth).

3.3 Assessment of Policy Effectiveness

Generally, SAGA e-government standards are well accepted in German municipalities. In the study, conducted by Veit and Parasie in 2007, 214 German municipalities, which are organized in the German Association of Municipalities, were asked about their acceptance of the SAGA standard. The results show that 88.4% of the German municipalities know the SAGA standards. 55.8% actively use them in their IT project implementations (for details cf. Veit and Parasie [9]).

Measured on a 5-point Likert scale (1=strong acceptance; 5=no acceptance) the overall-acceptance of SAGA was 2.66. Technical standards and data standards were accepted slightly better (2.40 and 2.57) where the recommendations of software architectures were taken up worst (2.90). Interestingly, also the "one for all" implementations, which is an initiative to share solutions implemented by one institution for many others is taken up worst (3.74).

The latter issue, together with the question of a stronger utilization of open source in e-government, has been content to another study conducted by Reifsteck, Parasie and Veit [17]. The same German municipalities were asked to what extent they are cooperating while creating e-government solutions.

In the German e-government standard, the use of open source software is suggested. The survey shows that already 74% of German municipalities consider open source software solution when making a decision about infrastructural development, primarily within servers (54%), desktop applications (26%), and internal administrative systems (23%). In the external utilization of open source software at the front-end application at the interface to the citizen and businesses is rather low.

The main obstacles for using open source in e-government applications are seen in the missing interoperability among the open source solutions and between commercial and open source modules (73%), in the lack of support (68%) as well as in a lack of know-how about open source solutions (46%) – see Figure 2.

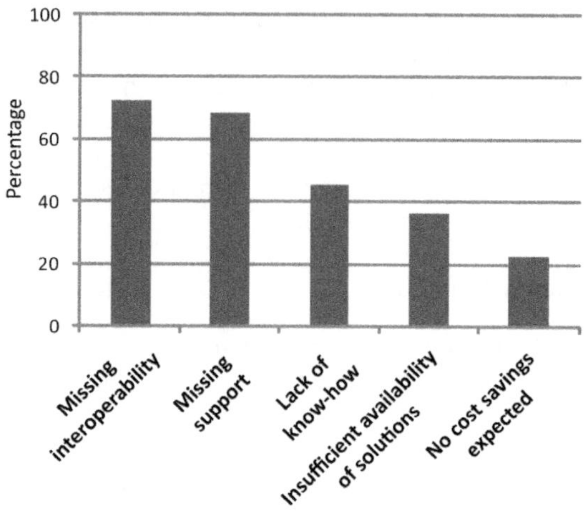

Fig. 2. Obstacles for using open source software in Germany

4 The Danish Case

4.1 Demand Drivers

With 60-70% of the Danish GDP being re-allocated through government and about one third of the workforce employed in the public sector, it is hard to find another case where the public sector plays such an equally critical role in an economy that has, at the same time, managed to stay efficient in the global economy.

In Denmark there has been a long tradition of strong local government, requiring extensive use of IT. Moreover, the 275 municipalities and 14 counties that existed in the 1970s were reduced to 99 municipalities and 5 counties in 2007. These mergers of have been a key driver for an increased awareness of the need to be supported by the use of IT.

In a survey from Statistics Denmark, among the barriers to the use of open source software the failure to adapt to back-office systems has the greatest importance (78%), followed by the barriers of uncertainty about product maturity (75%).

4.2 Policy Instruments Applied

In June 2006 the Danish Parliament adopted on a resolution on mandatory open Standards. Open standards should be part of the basis for government development and procurement of IT software to facilitate competition. The majority of the parties accepted that the resolution should not result in increased costs for the government.

The IT and Telecom Agency has established a software forum (softwarebørsen). As of May 2009, 57 open source software project has been uploaded to this forum. A series of guidelines concerning the use of open standards has been produced.

In the organizational management category, Denmark has established a digital task force directly under the Ministry of Finance and a corresponding board with members from the local authorities, regions, and national government. This tri-part consensus model has the advantage of creating a forum to meet and agree on strategies. However, parallel to this, the Ministry of Science has launched a strategy on open source and open document standards. There are various incidents of disagreement and intense fights between the two units on how and where to push open standards.

4.3 Assessment of Policy Effectiveness

One possible quantitative indicator for whether the Danish open source policy has been effective is the adoption rate of open source software in government. By computing the data collected by Statistics Denmark [18], we have mapped the adoption and use of open source software in the public sector. Also, we have computed data for whether open source software is used on the public sectors' own servers and at the employees' PC. The data covers the period 2004-2008, collected annually.

The adoption rate is impressive in doubling the number of institutions that has bought open source software from about 25% in 2004 to well over 50% in 2008. However, looking at data for employees' use of open software standards at their own PC, only 8% are using open source software.

The data on spread of open document standards are also leaving the effectiveness of the policy in a blurry picture. 86% of the public sector authorities can receive ODF/OOXML document formats but less than 5% of the authorities have any flow of these. Instead the PDF format has been adopted widely as the format to send document back and forth to citizens.

5 Discussion and Conclusion

Policy drivers in Germany and Denmark have very different composition and timing. In Denmark, open document standards have been bindingly introduced by federal legislation. This has a strong positive impact on interoperability. In Germany, on the other hand, open document formats are just a recommendation by the federal IT coordination unit. Hence, a homogeneous interoperability in Germany is far beyond the reach of today's standardization efforts. Although Denmark has had a lot more proactive and early-on regulation, the output is less impressive. Although almost all government authorities have adopted open document standards, the active use in G2C and in G2G is at a lower level than in Germany. The top-down approach followed in Denmark is contrasted by the combination of a bottom-up with a top-down approach taken in Germany. Because if the complexity of IT architectures and infrastructures, this is dangerous and likely prolongs the phase of a highly fragmented, heterogeneous public IT landscape in Germany. However, strong efforts are undertaken in order to empower the central guidelines published by the office of the CIO in the federal ministry of the interior.

Table 1 summarizes the differences between the two countries' policy drivers regarding normative regulation, economic and financial incentives and regulation, knowledge transfer, and government practice.

Table 1. Comparing policy drivers in Germany and Denmark

	Germany	Denmark
Normative regulation	Federal e-government standard document has been published in March. No binding legislation is passed; Intense disputes between software providers, government and consultancies about a resulting market distortion.	Formal regulation passed by Parliament to make open document standards mandatory for all public authorities; Intense disputes between software providers, converter suppliers, and government; International standardization bodies and national regulation at odds.
Economic & financial incentives and regulation	Heterogeneous requirements in different federal states; Heavy disputes between federal institution and federal states; Open source competence center established at the federal IT office; Sharing of "one for all" applications.	Requirement of providing explicit business case calculation for all IT investments larger than 10 million DKK (ca. 1.5 million Euro); Open source software exchange forum established.
Knowledge transfer	Open source has been identified as major contribution to public IT; Knowledge exchange by federal initiatives like E-Government 2.0 and DeutschlandOnline.	Practical guidelines for how to solve converter challenges published at the National Telecom Agency's website; Open source and open document forum established with participants from local, regional, and national/ federal level of government.
Government own practice	Seen as an opportunity to avoid vendor lock-in and create a more diverse software landscape; Strong formalization of data formats and interoperability standards in federal government documents	Seen as vehicle for adoption of open source in other sectors; Relative limited use of open source standards in software developed by government itself; Open document standards are rarely fulfilled in back office or G2G exchanges.

References

1. Zhu, K., Kraemer, K.L., Gurbaxani, V., Xu, S.X.: Migration to Open-standard Interorganizational Systems: Network Effects, Switching Costs, and Path Dependency. MIS Quarterly 30, 515–539 (2006)
2. IDABC. Promotion of Open Document Exchange Format (2007), `http://ec.europa.eu/idabc/en/document/3428/5644`
3. IDABC. TAC Approval on Conclusions and Recommendations on Open Document Formats (2008), `http://ec.europa.eu/idabc/en/document/2592/5588`
4. Andersen, K., Beck, R., Wigand, R., Bjørn-Andersen, N., Brousseau, E.: European E-commerce Policies in the Pioneering Days, the Gold Rush and the Post-hype Era. Information Polity 9, 217–232 (2004)

5. Damsgaard, J., Lyytinen, K.: The Role of Intermediating Institutions in Diffusion of Electronic Data Interchange (EDI): How Industry Associations in the Grocery Sector Intervened in Hong Kong, Finland, and Denmark. The Information Society 17, 195–210 (2001)
6. Henriksen, H.Z., Damsgaard, J.: Dawn of E-government – an Institutional Analysis of Seven Initiatives and their Impact. Journal of Information Technology 22, 13–23 (2007)
7. Rogers, E.M.: Diffusion of Innovations, 5th edn. New Press, New York (2003)
8. Andersen, M.B., Hørlück, J., Kristensen, J., Andersen, K., Pedersen, M.K.: Rapport om implementeringen af ODF og OOXML i offentlige myndigheder fra 1. National IT and Telecom Agency, Ministry of Science, Technology, and Innovation, Copenhagen (January 2008), `http://www.itst.dk/regeringens-it-og-telepolitik/abne-standarder/rapport-fra-ekspertudvalg-vedrorende-abne-standarder-for-dokumentformater/Rapport%20v%201.9%20endelig%20til%20tryk.pdf`
9. Veit, D.J., Parasie, N.P.: Can National E-Government Standards find Acceptance? In: Proceedings of the 42nd Hawaii International Conference on System Sciences (HICSS), E-Government Track (2009)
10. Muir, A., Oppenheim, C.: National Information Policy Developments Worldwide: Electronic government. Journal of Information Science 28, 173–186 (2002)
11. King, J.L., Gurbaxani, V., Kraemer, K.L., McFarlan, F.W., Raman, K.S., Yap, C.S.: Institutional Factors in Information Technology Innovation. Information Systems Research 5, 139–169 (1994)
12. Andersen, K. (ed.): EDI and Data Networking in the Public Sector: Governmental Action, Diffusion, and Impacts. Kluwer, Amsterdam (1997)
13. Andersen, K., Bjørn-Andersen, N., Wareham, J.: Using the Public Sector as a Locomotive for Electronic Commerce: The case of Denmark. In: Bled International Conference on Electronic Commerce, Slovenia (1998)
14. Eckhoff, T.: Statens styringsmuligheter, Tanum-Nori, Oslo (1987)
15. German Federal Ministry of the Interior: Standards and Architectures for eGovernment Applications, Office of the IT-Beauftragten der Bundesregierung, CIO (2008), `http://www.cio.bund.de/cae/servlet/contentblob/77116/publicationFile/3995/saga_4_0_download.pdf`
16. Veit, D.J., Parasie, N.: Umfrage zu E-Government Standards: Empirische Studie in deutschen Kommunen. Fachbericht 20070329 (2007), `http://tinyurl.com/332mux8`
17. Reifsteck, A., Parasie, N., Veit, D.J.: Gemeinschaftliche Entwicklung von E-Government Anwendungen: Empirische Studie in deutschen Kommunen. Fachbericht 20090131 (2007), `http://tinyurl.com/38pa5yg`
18. Statistics Denmark: Den offentlige sectors brug af IT. Annual reports. Statistics Denmark, Copenhagen (2005-2009)

Facilitating E-Government Services through SDIs, an Application for Water Abstractions Authorizations

Miguel Ángel Latre, Francisco J. Lopez-Pellicer, Javier Nogueras-Iso, Rubén Béjar, and Pedro R. Muro-Medrano

Computer Science and Systems Engineering Department,
Aragón Institute for Engineering Research
Universidad de Zaragoza
C/ María de Luna 1, E-50018 Zaragoza, Spain

Abstract. In the last years, there has been a huge increment in the number of e-government services offered to the citizens and companies. However, environment-related permits are among the least developed kind of e-government services in Europe. Environmental management and government requires the use of geographic information and spatial data infrastructures (SDIs) are being providing the framework for optimizing its management, and they are becoming a legal obligation for some countries and institutions.

In order to make profit of geographic information technologies and of the obligation of building SDIs to contribute to the development of e-government services, this paper analyzes an e-government opportunity in the environmental management linked to the use of SDIs and presents how to use them in a real tool: the application for a water abstraction authorization. SDI services are used for the capture, management, and assess of geographical information in a full transactional level e-government service.

Keywords: E-government, Spatial Data Infrastructures, INSPIRE, Water Authorities, Hydrology, Water abstraction requests.

1 Introduction and Motivation

The United Nations Division for Public Economics and Public Administration [24] defines e-government as "utilizing the Internet and the World Wide Web for delivering government information and services to citizens". Evans and Yen [11] add the concepts of "*communication* between the government and its citizens" and stress the advantages "in timeliness, responsiveness, and cost containment". In the last years, there has been a huge increment not only in the number of e-government services provided, but also in their quality and sophistication, due to the fact that many countries are implementing e-government policies, strategies and programs. [1,6,15].

K.N. Andersen et al. (Eds.): EGOVIS 2010, LNCS 6267, pp. 108–119, 2010.

However, environment-related permits are among the least developed e-government services in Europe [15]. As an example, in many countries, both surface and ground waters are public and their use for private purposes requires an authorization given by a governmental authority according to certain conditions. Citizens, companies and other organisms are required to make an application in order to obtain this authorization, providing certain information in order the administration to evaluate it and approve or reject the authorization. In Spain, these water abstraction authorizations are still a paperwork process and it constitutes an excellent example of a governmental service that can be provided electronically to the final users.

In this case, as within any other environmental management process, a lot of data and information involved in the administrative process is geographic information, that is, data that make reference to a location on the Earth surface, being much more complex in aspects related to data creation, maintenance and exploitation than other kinds of data. Not surprisingly, the main creators and users of geographic information are public administrations [3,20], needing it to be of controlled sources and quality, and being required its use for the implementation of e-government services. According to [19], "a *spatial data infrastructure* (SDI) is defined as the infrastructure that provides the framework for the optimization of the creation, maintenance and distribution of geographic information (and environmental data by specialization) at different organization levels (e.g., regional, national, or global level) and involving both public and private institutions [18]". In this line, the European Commission launched INSPIRE (*INfrastructure for SPatial InfoRmation in Europe*) [10], an ambitious legislative directive whose aim is the creation of a European spatial information infrastructure that delivers integrated spatial information services, based on a hierarchy of national, regional and local spatial data infrastructures. The first area where INSPIRE is going to be developed is environmental information.

In Europe, diffusion of information is also an e-government service imposed not only by the INSPIRE directive, but also by pieces of legislation form the environmental domain, such as the Water Framework Directive [9], that identifies information supply as the base to allow consultation and active involvement in the management of river basins to the general public, stakeholders and other authorities.

Geographic information technologies and spatial data infrastructures have to contribute to the success of e-government programmes. Delivering information and government services to the public via internet and other digital means is enabling government agencies to meet the challenges of having to reduce costs, deliver services faster, provide better customer service, and increase productivity. But it is also necessary to take advantage of these infrastructures (taking into account that the obligations derived in Europe from the application of directives such as INSPIRE and the WFD, are pushing towards the creation of SDIs, not only at European or national levels, but also at the regional level) to provide more sophisticated, added-value e-government services.

The rest of the paper is structured as follows. Next section deals with geographic information, spatial data infrastructures and the European directive INSPIRE. Section 3 discuses about e-government opportunities in the environmental management, especially in the case of European Water Authorities. Section 4 shows how e-government services can be developed over a spatial data infrastructure, presenting the process of applying for a water abstraction authorization. This work ends with a conclusions section.

2 Geographic Information and Spatial Data Infrastructures

Geographic information (also known as geospatial data) is information that describes phenomena associated directly or indirectly with a location with respect to the Earth surface. Nowadays, there are available large amounts of geographic data that have been gathered with different purposes by different institutions and companies. For instance, geographic information is vital for decision-making and resource management in diverse areas (natural resources, facilities, cadastre, economy), and at different levels (local, regional, national or even global) [4]. Furthermore, the volume of this information is growing significantly [21,12] due to, for instance, sensors at monitoring sites, automatically collecting and transmitting measurements at small time intervals, technology advances in high-resolution satellite imagery or GPS georeferenced data. Even more, it is possible to also georeference complex collections of a broad range of resource types, including textual and graphic documents, digital geospatial map and imagery data, real-time acquired observations, legacy databases of tabular historical records, and multimedia components such as audio or video.

One feature that makes geographic information different from other information resources is the complexity of the processes involved in data creation, maintenance and exploitation. As a result of this continuous generation of elaborated information, the need for effective data access, sharing, services, and processing becomes increasingly important.

Spatial data infrastructures are the paradigm for the new management and distribution of geographic information. Spatial data sets, metadata, spatial data services form part of spatial data infrastructures, together with network services and technologies, agreements on sharing, access and use; and coordination and monitoring mechanisms [10]. Discovery, access and distribution of up-to-date information is achieved by means of a set of standard web services: among others, catalogue services (that enable the search and retrieval of geographical metadata), web map services (WMS, that provide geographic visualization of the data in the form of maps), web feature services (WFS, that allow for querying for data satisfying certain characteristics or attribute values and provide the requested data in GML format) and gazetteer services (that enable the search and retrieval of geographical names). Ideally, this should be done at any public administration level that has the responsibility of creating and maintaining geographic information.

In the field of spatial data infrastructures, the European Union approved in 2007 the INSPIRE Directive (*INfrastructure for SPatial InfoRmation in Europe*) [10], an ambitious legislative directive whose aim is the creation of a European spatial information infrastructure in order to support Community environmental policies, and policies or activities which may have an impact on the environment. It is being build hierarchically based on the infrastructures for spatial information established and operated by the member states, while these ones, should be organized into a hierarchy that includes infrastructures developed at different political-administrative levels [22], including regional, environmental-related agencies.

3 E-Government Opportunities in the Hydrological Management

It is interesting to take into account that environmental protection is one of the interests of the European Union. Different initiatives and pieces of legislation in the environmental field are taking place in the European Union, with a strong focus and need of environmental data. A considerable amount of these initiatives affect directly to Water Authorities, such as the Water Framework Directive (WFD) [9], which is considered to be the most important piece of legislation in this aspect [25]. The main objective of the WFD is to achieve an accurate management of all water bodies and it expects to reach a *good status* for them by 2015. Diffusion of information to the public is an e-government service imposed to the water authorities by its 14th article [9] and by the *Guidance on Public Participation in Relation to the Water Framework Directive* [7,8], considering that information supply is the base to allow consultation and active involvement in the management of the river basin to the general public, stakeholders and other authorities. In addition to this, the *Guidance Document on Implementing the GIS Elements of the Water Framework Directive* [26] recommends the use of the SDI mechanisms proposed by INSPIRE in order to communicate data among the member states and the European Commission and to disseminate this information to the public.

The most basic e-government application consists clearly in providing citizens with access to information [16]. Governments produce huge volumes of information and an increasing amount of it is now available through the web and other electronic means. In this sense, each spatial data infrastructure provides a first set of standardized, organized core services associated with the public administration level that has the responsibility of creating and maintaining the corresponding infrastructure level. Regarding this subject, each public administration is offering implicitly a minimum set of e-government services [20]. But this is only an e-government service at the basic level of maturity (*web presence* [2,23] or *information dissemination* [5,17]). However, these services provide a good base for developing more sophisticated services oriented to the satisfaction of specific functionality. A higher level of sophistication is desired, such as the level of *interaction*, [2,23] where governments provide help and assistance to citizens (e-mail, official forms downloads and help to fill them), although paperwork is needed to finalize any application; or *transaction* [2,5,17,23] level, where users can perform complete, legally valid, online transactions. In the case of environmental agencies, these levels can be achieved by using spatial data infrastructures to deal with the geographic information needed for these transactions, as it is exemplified in the next section.

This means that a spatial data infrastructure can provide interesting services for e-government. So, if there are many initiatives to built spatial data infrastructures, and they offer services that can be used by developing e-government services, spatial data infrastructures can be considered as the first step for developing e-government in the case of environmental agencies, where they are more developed than e-government services.

4 Water Abstraction Requests at the Ebro River Basin Authority

The Ebro River Basin Authority (*Confederación Hidrográfica del Ebro*, CHE) is the Spanish organization in charge of physically and administratively managing the hydrographical basin of the Ebro River, according to the Water Framework Directive requirements. Part of its administrative work deals with the analysis and approval or refusing of water abstractions that are applied by particulars, companies and other public authorities, in conformance with the river basin management plan objectives.

The initial GIS infrastructure at the CHE evolved into a Spatial Data Infrastructure (IDE-Ebro[1]). The mere existence of this SDI implies that a certain level of e-government services are being provided, enough to cover, for instance, the requirements of the 14th article of the Water Framework Directive about public information supply. IDE-Ebro gives public access to data related to the WFD (surface waters, groundwater bodies and protected areas), their inventory of water points (including wells, springs and monitoring points) and other data of reference of the Ebro River basin district. This access is provided through a set of standard web services, as described previously in section 2: a catalogue service, web map services, web feature services and a gazetteer service.

However, this kind of e-government service belong to the most basic levels of the e-government stage models proposed in the literature, named *web presence* or *interaction* [2], *enhanced presence* or *interactive presence* [24], *information publishing/dissemination* [5], *catalogue* [14] or *simple information dissemination* [13,17].

The SDI infrastructure should be also used to provide to the citizens and companies with more sophisticated services. In the case of application for water abstractions, an e-government service can be provided that can achieve the level of *transaction* [23], built on top of the services provided by the SDI.

The specific administrative process the requests of water abstractions follow depends on characteristics such as water use, amount, source (surface or groundwater) and geographical location. Among the requested information, a

[1] `http://ide-ebro.chebro.es`

map showing the location of abstraction and discharge points, the demand unit (a polygon for an irrigated area, a point for any other demand unit: centre of population, farm ...) and any other infrastructure irrigated area (if any) must be provided. The administrative process also involves a great amount of time because the user has to wait until being informed whether the application is granted or not. Due to a large queue of requests and the fact that some queries have to be redirected to other authorities, this delay can be estimated at about twelve months.

The introduction of a web tool, based on SDI services, to provide this service electronically, improves this administrative process and allows for the elimination of the paper work and related to the user following the process is eliminated, achieving a *full transactional* service [23]. Additionally, by using an electronic tool, stakeholders can make use of the official information the organization is sharing through its own SDI, increasing the reliability of the data and parameters provided with the request. It is also possible to provide users with immediate feedback about the request, informing them about the kind of processing their request will follow, and providing an estimate of the feasibility of the request based on objective criteria included in the process. This feasibility report cannot be legally binding (only the competent authorities can legally inform about a water abstraction request, after their staff have carefully and individually analyzed each request) but by providing it, users can get a straightaway estimate of the result. Finally, by making use of electronic signature services, the request is formally submitted, and its processing at the water authority starts.

4.1 Functionality and Architecture

The architecture of the application is presented in Fig. 1. The core of the tool is a web service (*water abstraction service*), in charge of coordinating the whole process: acquisition and storage of data, generation of the feasibility report, validation of electronic sign, management of users' feedback, ...

The graphical user interface of the tool (*web water abstraction service*) is in charge of acquiring in an on-line manner the parameters of the request, both non-spatial data (such as water use: human supply, irrigation, industrial, aquiculture recreational, navigation, or other; requested amount of water; and water abstraction nature: surface or groundwater) together with the geographical elements of the request (location of the water abstraction points, discharge points, demand units: irrigated areas, centre of population, farms, or others), by pointing onto the map the requested locations or by drawing the perimeter of the irrigation area.

This geographical data capture component (Fig. 2) is based on the services provided by the subjacent spatial data infrastructure, and presented previously, e. g.:

– The location of the area of interest is done by means of the gazetteer service for searching for administrative features by name and/or by zooming in on an interactive map provided by web map services.

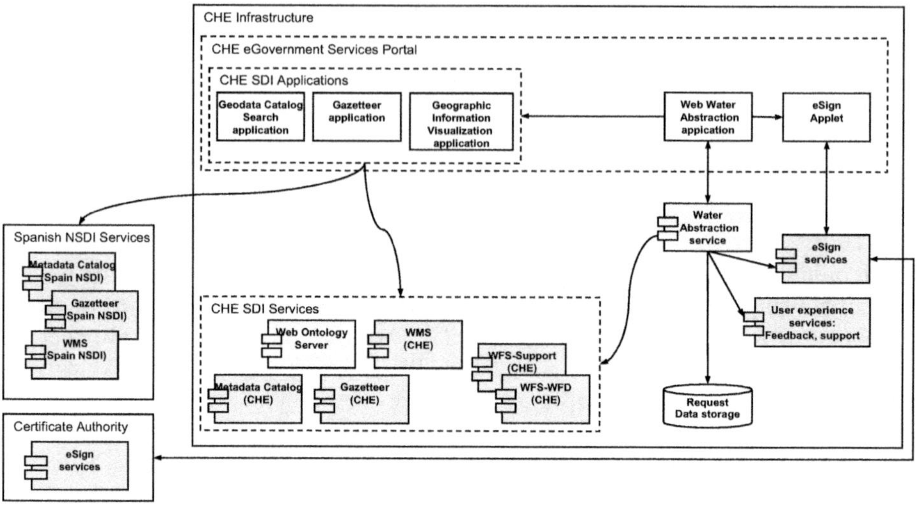

Fig. 1. Architecture of the application for water abstractions requests

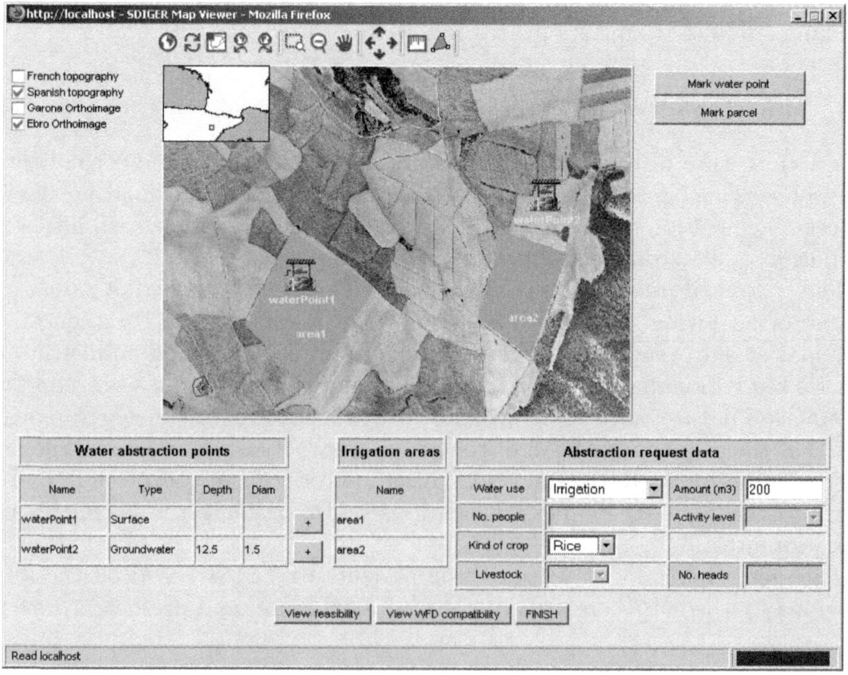

Fig. 2. Graphic user interface for data input

- The visualization tool allows for the selection of the reference data that is more suitable to input the geographical information (administrative boundaries, settlements, river network, transport network, ...) and from the most appropriate source: services from the hydrological SDI or services from a mapping agency SDI.
  Provided the scales at that the work is done, raster imaging and orthophotos are used as background in order to do it properly, together with cadastre parcels.
- The determination of certain geographic elements that have an impact on the request (such as municipality, river subbasin, hydrogeological domain, aquifer, ...) is done by making requests to a web feature service of either the hydrological SDI or the mapping agency SDI.

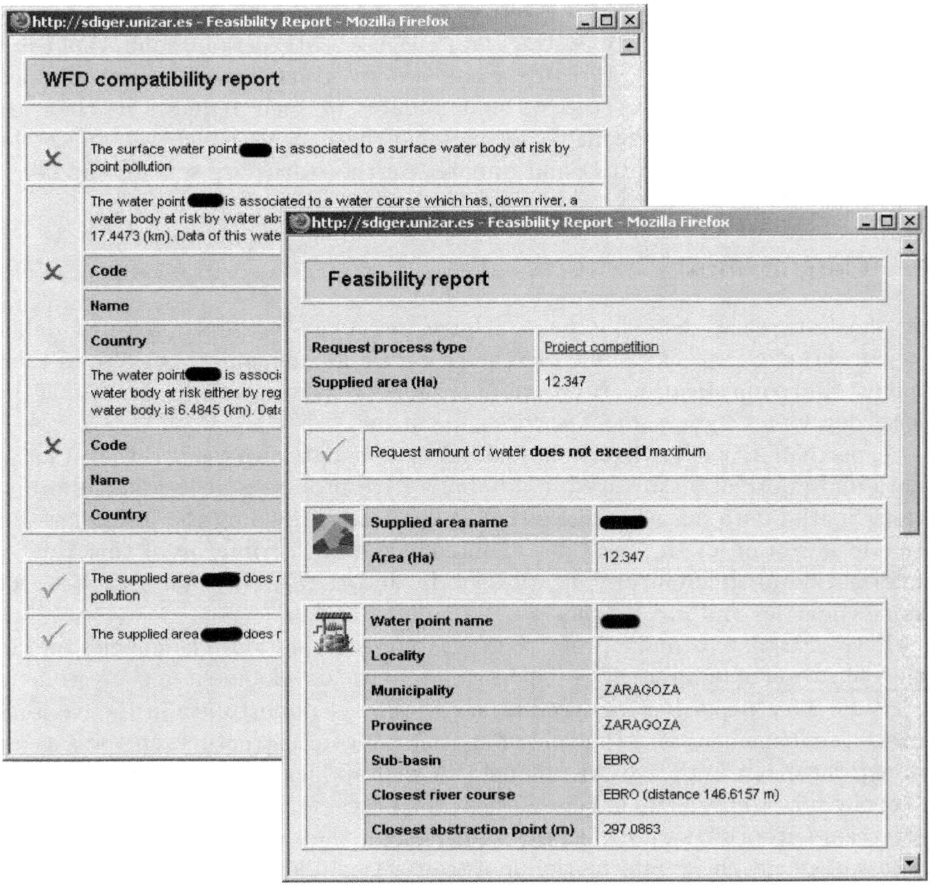

Fig. 3. Feasibility report

Data obtained during the request is included into the information systems of the Ebro River Basin Authority and it is used to provide the user with a feasibility report and information of the administrative process that will be followed (Fig. 3). To achieve a full transactional service, the web application integrates an electronic signature applet, in order to formalize administratively the whole process by using a certification tool valid in Spain (digital certificate or electronic identity card). The electronic signature service validates the signature by checking it against a certificate authority. It is the existence of this electronic signature service what makes the water abstraction request service a *transactional* one. Nevertheless, without them, the application could be used just to help the user to generate the documentation and paper work needed to submit the request in a traditional way, resulting the electronic service in a *one-way communication* or just *interactive* e-government service).

Finally, some services and functionality are included in the infrastructure in order to provide a globally positive user experience by increasing usability (help functionality and process tracking) and user satisfaction monitoring (user feedback and reporting) [15]. Regarding process tracking, users are informed about the administrative statuses and updates of their requests as they are processed. These administrative statuses can be consulted via web (once the user has been authenticated) and updates on the status are sent to the user's e-mail or mobile phone.

5 Conclusions

In the last years, there has been a huge increment not only in the number of e-government services offered to the citizens and companies, but also in their quality and sophistication. However, environment-related permits are among the least developed e-government services in Europe.

A particularity of environmental, administrative management is that a lot of data and information involved in administrative process is geographic information. Spatial data infrastructures (SDIs) are being providing the framework for the optimization of the creation, maintenance and distribution of this kind of information at different organization levels, and they are a legal obligation for some countries and institutions.

It is necessary to make profit of geographic information technologies and of the obligation of building SDIs to contribute to the development of e-government services. This paper has analyzed an e-government opportunity in the environmental management and the role of spatial data infrastructures in the success of e-government initiatives in this field. A real application has been presented, showing how to use SDIs in this context: the process of applying for a water abstraction authorization. SDI services are used for the capture, management, and assess of geographical information in a transactional level e-government service. The tool improves this administrative process and allows for the elimination of the paper work, the reliability of the data and parameters provided with the request are increased and users are provided with immediate feedback about the request about the kind of processing needed and the feasibility of the request.

Future work will deal with extrapolating the application to other River Basin Authorities and with the implications of cross-border (administrative vs. hydrographic limits of basins) and international approaches in the interoperability of the services belonging to the SDIs that support the tool.

Acknowledgments. This work has been partially supported by the Spanish Government (projects "España Virtual" ref. CENIT 2008-1030, TIN2009-10971 and PET2008_0026), the Aragón Government (project PI075/08), GeoSpatiumLab S. L. and Zeta Amaltea S. L.

References

1. Ancarani, A.: Towards quality e-service in the public sector: The evolution of web sites in the local public service sector. Managing Service Quality 15(1), 6–23 (2005), http://www.emeraldinsight.com/10.1108/09604520510575236
2. Baum, C.H., Maio, A.D.: Gartner's four phases of e-government model. Research note TU-12-6113, Gartner Group (November 21, 2000), http://www.gartner.com/DisplayDocument?id=317292
3. Brown, M.M., Brudney, J.L.: A "smarter, better, faster, and cheaper" government: Contracting and geographic information systems. Public Administration Review 58(4), 335–345 (1998), http://www.jstor.org/stable/977563
4. Buehler, K., McKee, L. (eds.): The OpenGIS guide. Introduction to interoperable geoprocessing. Part I of the Open Geodata Interoperability Specification (OGIS). OGIS TC Document 96-001, OGIS Project 6 Technical Commitee of the OpenGIS Consortium Inc. (1996)
5. Deloitte, T.: The citizen as customer. CMA Management 74(10), 58 (2001)
6. Department of Economic and Social Affairs Division for Public Administration and Development Management: United Nations e-government survey. From e-government to connected governance, Survey, United Nations, New York (2008), http://unpan1.un.org/intradoc/groups/public/documents/un/unpan028607.pdf
7. European Commission: Guidance on public participation in relation to the Water Framework Directive. Active involvement, consultation, and public access to information. Guidance document no. 8 for the Common Implementation Strategy for the Water Framework Directive (2000/60/EC), European Commission (2002), http://circa.europa.eu/Public/irc/env/wfd/library?l=/framework_directive/guidance_documents/guidancesnos8spublicspar/_EN_1.0_
8. European Commission: Guidance for reporting under the Water Framework Directive. Guidance Document no. 21 for the Common Implementation Strategy for the Water Framework Directive (2000/60/EC) Technical Report 2009–029, European Commission (2009), http://circa.europa.eu/Public/irc/env/wfd/library?l=/framework_directive/guidance_documents/guidance_guidance_report/_EN_1.0_
9. Directive 2000/60/EC of the European Parliament and of the Council establishing a framework for Community action in the field of water policy. Official Journal of the European Union (October 23, 2000), http://eur-lex.europa.eu/JOHtml.do?uri=OJ:L:2000:327:SOM:EN:HTML

10. Directive 2007/2/EC of the European Parliament and of the Council of 14 March 2007 establishing an Infrastructure for Spatial Information in the European Community (INSPIRE). Official Journal of the European Union (March 2007), http://eurlex.europa.eu/JOHtml.do?uri=OJ:L:2007:108:SOM:EN:HTML
11. Evans, D., Yen, D.C.: E-government: Evolving relationship of citizens and government, domestic, and international development. Government Information Quarterly 23(2), 207–235 (2006), http://www.sciencedirect.com/science/article/B6W4G-4J8D90P-1/2/abde50c4ac5a5d4c6f82bf173ba730e7
12. Goodall, J.L., Horsburgh, J.S., Whiteaker, T.L., Maidment, D.R., Zaslavsky, I.: A first approach to web services for the National Water Information System. Environmental Modelling & Software 23(4), 404–411 (2008), http://www.sciencedirect.com/science/article/B6VHC-4R05JG3-1/2/4e4f5eadc14e7f0a6290ae5f5e0d0f3c
13. Hiller, J.S., Bélanger, F.: Privacy strategies for electronic government. Report, The PricewaterhouseCoopers Endowment for The Business of Government (January 2001)
14. Layne, K., Lee, J.: Developing fully functional e-government: A four stage model. Government Information Quarterly 18(2), 122–136 (2001), http://www.sciencedirect.com/science/article/B6W4G-42YDMD9-5/2/30868b3dd22c204a80fd62628d50ab9c
15. Lorincz, B., Colclough, G., Tinholt, D., van Oranje, C., Cattaneo, G., Jacquet, L.: Smarter, faster, better eGovernment. In: 8th eGovernment benchmark measurement. Tech. rep., European Commission Directorate General for Information Society and Media (November 2009), http://ec.europa.eu/information_society/eeurope/i2010/benchmarking/index_en.htm
16. Marchionini, G., Samet, H., Brandt, L.: Digital government (introduction to the special issue). Communications of the ACM 46(1), 24–67 (2003)
17. Moon, M.J.: The evolution of e-government among municipalities: Rhetoric or reality? Public Administration Review 62(4), 424–433 (2002), http://www3.interscience.wiley.com/journal/118944801/abstract
18. Nebert, D.D. (ed.): Developing Spatial Data Infrastructures: The SDI Cookbook v.2.0. Global Spatial Data Infrastructure (January 2004), http://www.gsdi.org/docs2004/Cookbook/cookbookV2.0.pdf
19. Nogueras-Iso, J., Zarazaga-Soria, F.J., Muro-Medrano, P.R.: Geographic Information Metadata for Spatial Data Infrastructures – Resources, Interoperability and Information Retrieval. Springer, Heidelberg (2005), http://www.springer.com/earth+sciences+26+geography/geography/gis+cartography/book/978-3-540-24464-6
20. Nogueras-Iso, J., Latre, M.Á., Muro-Medrano, P.R., Zarazaga-Soria, F.J.: Building eGovernment services over spatial data infrastructures. In: Traunmüller, R. (ed.) EGOV 2004. LNCS, vol. 3183, pp. 387–391. Springer, Heidelberg (2004), http://www.springer.com/computer+science/general+issues/book/978-3-540-22916-2
21. Pokorný, J.: Database architectures: Current trends and their relationships to environmental data management. Environmental Modelling & Software 21(11), 1579–1586 (2006), http://www.sciencedirect.com/science/article/B6VHC-4K8SC6K-1/2/87ebea752a7483136aafe12492af7be5
22. Rajabifard, A., Williamson, I.P., Holland, P., Johnstone, G.: From local to global SDI initiatives: a pyramid of building blocks. In: Proc. of the 4th GSDI Conference. Cape Town, South Africa (March 2000)

23. Siau, K., Long, Y.: Synthesizing e-government stage models – a meta-synthesis based on meta-ethnography approach. Industrial Management & Data Systems 105(4), 443–458 (2005), http://www.emeraldinsight.com/10.1108/02635570510592352
24. United Nations Division for Public Economics and Public Administration, American Society for Public Administration: Benchmarking e-government: A global perspective. Assessing the progress of the UN member states. Tech. rep., United Nations – DPEPA and ASPA (May 2002)
25. Usländer, T.: Trends of environmental information systems in the context of the European Water Framework directive. Environmental Modelling & Software 20(12), 1532–1542 (2005), http://www.sciencedirect.com/science/article/B6VHC-4GNTG17-3/2/1890a0c844b92517469638002a3b117c
26. Vogt, J.: Guidance document on implementing the GIS elements of the Water Framework Directive. Guidance document no. 9 for the Common Implementation Strategy for the Water Framework Directive (2000/60/EC), Commission of the European Communities (2002), http://circa.europa.eu/Public/irc/env/wfd/library?l=/framework_directive/guidance_documents/guidancesnos9sgisswgs31p/_EN_1.0_

Note. All links in the reference section checked June 10, 2010.

Towards Interoperability: An Architecture for Pan-European eID-Based Authentication Services

Arne Tauber[1], Bernd Zwattendorfer[1], Thomas Zefferer[1],
Yasmin Mazhari[2], and Eleftherios Chamakiotis[2]

[1] E-Government Innovation Center*
{Arne.Tauber,Bernd.Zwattendorfer,Thomas.Zefferer}@egiz.gv.at
[2] Gov2u
{yasmin,lexam}@gov2u.org

Abstract. In the last years several EU Member States have rolled out smart-card based electronic ID (eID) solutions to their citizens. Not all of these solutions are directly compatible to each other. However, with respect to the i2010 e-Government initiative and the upcoming EU Services Directive, cross-border identification and authentication is now on the agenda of all EU Member States. In this paper we present a smart-card based eID identification and authentication solution, which supports smart-cards from different Member States. The proposed solution can be easily integrated into existing authentication and identity management solutions and does not necessarily require any additional client software to be installed by citizens.

Keywords: Authentication, Identification, Interoperability, Smart Card, eID, CAS.

1 Introduction

Enabled by the success story of the Internet, numerous aspects of everyday life have been shifted to or have been adapted for the World Wide Web. This has resulted in a continuously increasing number of services being offered online nowadays. National government agencies of various European countries have reacted to this trend and provide a considerable number of web based services for citizens as well. The electronic provision and improvement of administrative procedures is commonly known under the term "e-Government" and includes services for income taxes, personal documents, change of address, and many more.

One basic challenge of e-Government applications is the secure and reliable identification and authentication of citizens. As administrative procedures usually involve security- or privacy-sensitive data, it is crucial that this data is processed by, and disclosed to, authorized parties only. Therefore, government agencies have to be aware that a citizen involved in an online administrative procedure is really the person they

---

* EGIZ is a joint initiative of the Austrian Federal Chancellery and the Graz University of Technology.

K.N. Andersen et al. (Eds.): EGOVIS 2010, LNCS 6267, pp. 120–133, 2010.

claim to be. When carrying out such procedures conventionally face to face in an office, citizens can easily be authenticated by verification of a presented ID document, e.g. a passport or identity card. In e-Government applications, where citizens usually interact with an online application remotely over the Internet, the reliable and secure authentication of citizens is no trivial task.

The widely used username/password based approaches provide weak authentication only. A number of vulnerabilities are known for these authentication mechanisms [1]. Hence, several EU Member States rely on smart-card technology to identify and authenticate citizens in e-Government processes. Most of these Member States have already rolled out smart-card based electronic IDs (eIDs) to their citizens and several others are in the preparation stage of a country-wide roll-out. An overview of current smart-card based eID solutions of different EU Member States has been provided by Siddhartha Arora [2].

In the last years, many smart-card aware eID applications and solutions have been put in place in several EU Member States on a national level. Unfortunately, most of these solutions are only applicable in a purely domestic scenario, for which the respective solution has been designed. Interoperability between different Member State specific solutions is usually not supported. This is a major drawback since an increasing number of administrative procedures has to be carried out on a pan-European level, especially in the context of the European Services Directive [4]. Hence, the cross-border interoperability and the mutual recognition of national eIDs are of great importance for the next steps towards a European Administrative Space (EAS). The importance of this topic is emphasized by the efforts and focus put by the European Commission into the accomplishment of the European STORK project [21], which aims to establish a pan-European eID interoperability platform.

In this paper we address this issue by presenting a smart-card based authentication and identification solution that supports eIDs of different EU Member States. Any online application that relies on the proposed solution is able to authenticate users from different Member States. Our approach relies on qualified electronic signatures created with the citizen's national eID card ensuring cross-border authentication backed by the mutual recognition of qualified certificates.

In the last years, Austrian e-Government initiatives have created a set of tools for online identification and authentication of citizens using the Austrian citizen card, the national eID. In the remainder of this paper we present a solution based on an adapted version of these tools being able to authenticate citizens of other EU Member States. So far, several different models of identity systems have been established. We discuss these models in Section 2 and show which model fits our solution. In Section 3 we briefly introduce a popular example for each of these models to outline benefits and shortcomings. We discuss the system architecture of our eID identification and authentication approach in detail in Section 4. In order to demonstrate the applicability of our solution in practice, we implemented an authentication plug-in for a popular and widely-used authentication management system. We briefly present this case study in Section 5. Thereafter, we give some remarks on our solution in Section 6. Finally, conclusions are drawn.

2 Models of Identity Systems

Identification and authentication of digital identities are not new problems. Hence, various approaches for identity systems and identity management systems already exist. However, not all identity systems follow the same methodological approach. For instance, some solutions focus more on central storage of identification data; in contrast others rely on federated data repositories. To get a better understanding of how our solution can be classified, we briefly present theoretical models of identity systems in this section. Palfrey and Gasser [5] distinguish between three major types of identity models which are outlined below in a nutshell. The distinctive criterion, in fact, is who has control over the identification data.

2.1 User-Centric Model

Figure 1 illustrates the basic setup of the user-centric model. A user attempts to access a protected resource or application of a service provider. Usually, the service provider initiates an authentication process by forwarding or redirecting the user to an identity provider. An identity provider is responsible for managing and issuing identity information to service providers. Hence, the identity provider handles the identification and authentication process with the user and transfers the identification data back to the service provider. Identification data depicts all user related information like unique identifiers or other user attributes such as name or date of birth.

In this model, the user always carries the responsibility for releasing identification data to the identity provider and service provider respectively. Personal information is only transferred to a requesting service provider if the user explicitly gives his consent to do so. At any time, the user remains the owner of the data and not the identity provider.

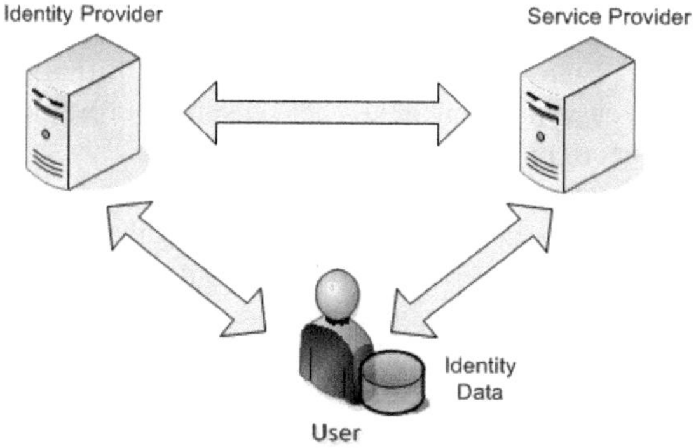

Fig. 1. User-Centric Model

2.2 Centrally-Controlled Model

This type of model is the dominant approach currently used in the Internet. Usually - if users want to access a certain service – they are requested to provide appropriate identity information for registration. This identity information is then stored centrally in data repositories of the identity provider. When requesting a protected application of a service provider, the user has to first authenticate with the identity provider, who then forwards the appropriate authentication information to the service provider.

Regarding privacy, the user is not in control anymore, e.g. of which data is kept in the identity provider's database or which information is transferred to the service. Figure 2 shows such a centrally-controlled model.

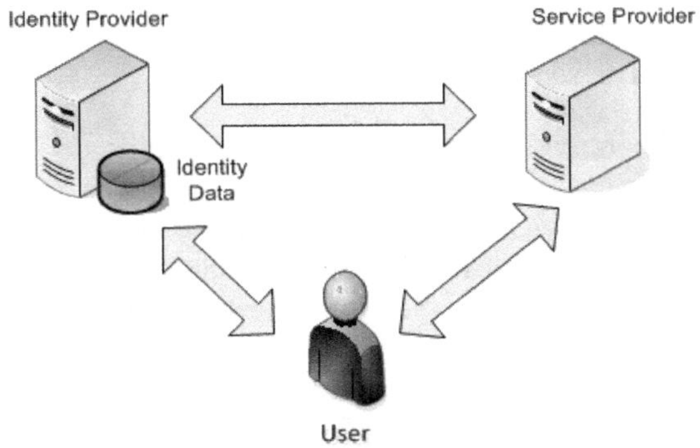

Fig. 2. Centrally-Controlled Model

2.3 Federated Model

In this model, user data is distributed over various identity providers. In contrast to the centrally-controlled model, identity information is not stored in a central location. However, the identification data can be easily shared between identity providers via linkage of the data repositories. Thus, the identity data of a user is stored in a federated way. Usually, identity federation is achieved by special trust relationships between identity providers and the agreement on a common identifier for a specific user. The federated model is illustrated in Figure 3.

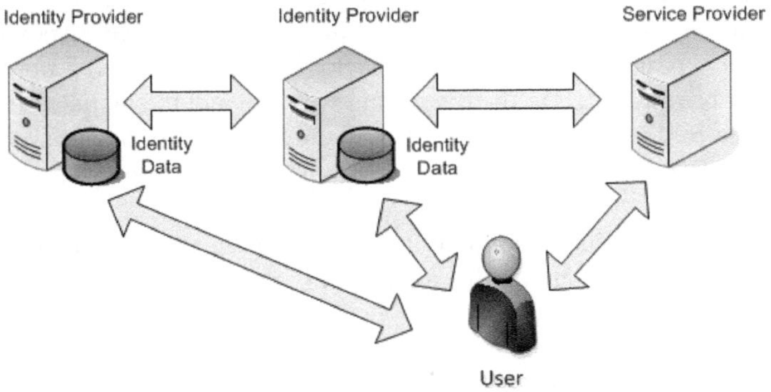

Fig. 3. Federated Model

3 Related Work

Taking the three different identity models into account, many approaches addressing identification and authentication already exist. In order to give an overview of existing solutions and to identify the relative benefits and shortcomings of different approaches, this section gives examples of existing and implemented models that the authors consider relevant.

3.1 Information Cards - Windows CardSpace

Information Cards representing personal digital identities define a technology for decentralized identity management within a so-called identity meta-system [6]. The concept of Information Cards can be realized by so-called Identity Selectors that manage various digital identities. Windows CardSpace [7] defines a well-known implementation of such an Identity Selector. CardSpace has been developed by Microsoft and is included in Microsoft Windows Vista and Microsoft Windows 7. However, other Identity Selector implementations such as the Higgins project [8] also exist.

By adopting Windows CardSpace, users should be provided with a more secure identification and authentication mechanism by using security tokens rather than e.g. simple username/password schemes. CardSpace's main aim is to facilitate user identification and authentication processes on web sites or web services and to enhance the achievable level of security.

Information Card's analogies in non-electronic environments are different IDs and plastic cards in a user's wallet. A so-called Identity Selector running on the user's client represents the user's wallet that contains various virtual identification and authentication cards (Information Cards). Information Cards only contain meta-information about how personal information can be retrieved from an identity provider that actually stores this information. For authentication at Web sites e.g. supporting Windows CardSpace (being denoted as "relying parties"), the user is requested to select an appropriate card satisfying the requested claims by the web site out of his virtual wallet. The InfoCard is transmitted to the corresponding identity provider, which issues a security token including the requested information. This security token is transmitted to the requesting web site and the included information is verified by the relying party. In case of successful verification, the user is authenticated without any additional user interactions such as typing in usernames or passwords.

Since only the user has the possibility to select the desired InfoCard, and thus releases only required identity information, this model can be classified as a user-centric one.

3.2 Google Accounts Authentication

Google released its accounts authentication service [9] in 2006, with the help of which service and application providers no longer need to host or maintain a separate authentication service of their own. The provided services can be protected by a user's Google account. Access to a web application is granted if the user presents valid Google authentication data (username/password). Hence, the authentication process can be seen as outsourced to Google with no need for the application provider to handle any login information. Instead, the service provider receives an authentication token indicating a successful login.

The complete user's identification and authentication data is stored in central repositories managed by Google. Thus Google accounts authentication can be seen as a centrally-controlled identity model.

3.3 Liberty Alliance Project

The main objectives of the Liberty Alliance project [10] are:

- Development of open-standard-based specifications for federated identity management and identity-based web services, independent from the network architecture
- Providing an open and secure single sign-on solution using de-centralized authentication and authorization
- Secure management of user data and personal information for enterprises, considering privacy and policy issues

The Liberty Alliance Project has already released many frameworks covering such diverse topics as identity federation, identity web services, identity governance or identity assurance. The focus of the Liberty Alliance project lies on identity management and identity federation and thus can be seen as an example of a federated model.

4 System Architecture

In this section we discuss our proposed eID based authentication architecture and introduce its basic building blocks and design concepts. The entire system follows a smart-card based user-centric approach as discussed in Section 2.1. Hence, all relevant authentication and identification data are stored on smart-cards that are under the sole control of the respective user. This section shows how smart-cards (eIDs from several EU Member States) act in concert with corresponding central server-side authentication components and afford service providers and users a comfortable way to carry out identification and authentication processes.

Our approach is based on several open-source authentication and identification components being frequently used within Austrian e-Government solutions. Relying on established and approved components guarantees a high level of security of our authentication system. Basically, these components form the identity provider (IdP) that is used by service providers to carry out operations that involve a user's smart-cards for authentication. Thus, the IdP can be regarded as a middleware between service providers (hosting online applications) and the user's local system.

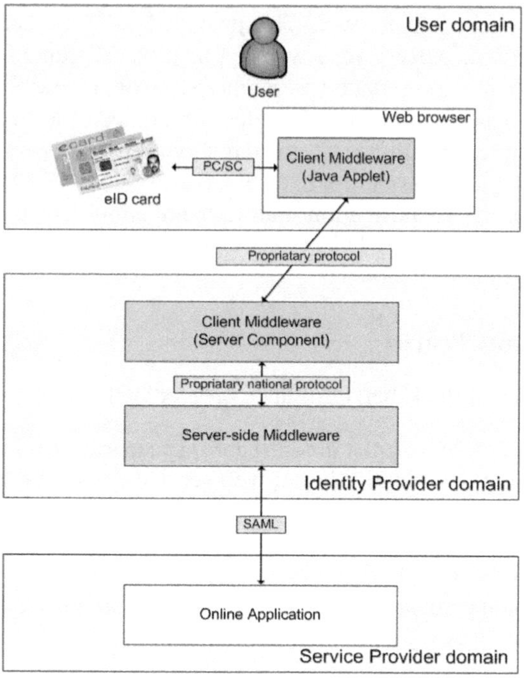

Fig. 4. eID based Authentication Architecture

Figure 4 shows the basic architecture and main components of our authentication system. The entire setup can be split up into three separate domains. The Service Provider domain contains the protected online application that can be accessed via common web browsers and requires user authentication. On the contrary, the User domain comprises the user's local system including the smart-card and a web browser that serves as interface between the user and the protected online application. The user does not directly authenticate with the service provider. The IdP domain acts as trusted intermediary authentication middleware and carries out the whole authentication process with the user.

The IdP consists of three components. Besides the two major server-side components residing in the IdP domain, we can find a small client component in the User domain as well. All components communicate with each other over well-defined protocols. In order to guarantee confidentiality and integrity of the transmitted data, all interfaces provide support for TLS/SSL, which contributes to a higher degree of security of our solution. In the next subsections we discuss all single components of our IdP that build up the authentication path from the user's eID to the service provider.

4.1 Server-Side Middleware

The server-side middleware is the only component of our IdP that directly interacts with the service provider. If an unauthenticated user requests a protected resource of an online application that requires user authentication, the service provider calls the server-side middleware component in order to trigger an appropriate user authentication process. The server-side middleware component is based on the open source module MOA-ID (Modules for Online Applications - Identification) [12], which is a project developed for user authentication and identification based on the Austrian national eID, the Austrian Citizen Card. When MOA-ID is triggered for starting an authentication process with an Austrian citizen, actually two process steps are carried out. In a first step, MOA-ID requests the user's identity information (identification process). This identity information is stored in a special XML data structure on the Austrian citizen card. After having successfully read the identity information from the card, the user is asked to create a qualified electronic signature indicating her willingness to authenticate at the online application (authentication process). The digital signature is verified by MOA-ID and on success, an authentication token (SAML assertion [11]) containing a unique identifier as well as additional relevant identity information (e.g. given name, family name and date of birth) is passed to the service provider. All communication between the server-side middleware MOA-ID and the user's eID is carried out using a client middleware, which we discuss in the next subsection. A well-defined communication interface called Security Layer hereby conveys XML commands from MOA-ID to the user's browser and thus to the client middleware in order to access the eID. The security architecture of the Austrian citizen card and the Security Layer interface is discussed in detail in [13].

In order to also support foreign eID cards, we adapted the identification and authentication components of MOA-ID. Foreign eID cards usually store identity information as part of their qualified signature certificate and not in a special data structure like in the Austrian case. Hence, in the identification process step, MOA-ID must distinguish between Austrian and foreign eID cards. In case of a foreign eID card, the identity information is read out of the digital certificate instead of a special XML structure. The authentication process step remains the same since foreign users are prompted to create a qualified electronic signature as well. Our modifications in MOA-ID mainly affect signature verification and the creation of a unique identifier for foreign citizens. For successful signature verification, all root and intermediate certificates of certification authorities of the various Member States must be installed in the certificate- and trust-store of MOA-ID in order to be able to build a trusted certificate chain. Enhancements such as ETSI Trust Status Lists (TSL) [14] would facilitate this integration. Due to data privacy protection reasons, unique national identifiers (e.g. tax number) of foreign citizens will not be directly used for user identification and passed to the application. A secure one-way-derivation of these identifiers is transmitted to the requesting online application instead.

4.2 Client Middleware

The client middleware is the second core component of our IdP and complements the authentication system. The client middleware is in charge of preparing the creation of XML signatures, accessing the user's smart-card, performing required smart-card based operations, and providing the server-side middleware with relevant smart-card related data and created XML signatures. Our client middleware implementation is based on the Modular Open Citizen Card Architecture (MOCCA) [15]. MOCCA is a

Java based open source project that has originally been developed for the Austrian e-Government. For our IdP, the functionality of MOCCA has been extended in order to achieve compatibility with other European smart-card based eID solutions as well.

The client middleware of our IdP solution basically consists of two components. A server component residing in the domain of the IdP is responsible for the communication with the server-side middleware MOA-ID, while smart-card access is implemented by a Java Applet running on the user's local system. In the following subsections, these two major components and their interactions are described in more detail.

4.2.1 Server Component

During an authentication process, the server component directly communicates with the server-side middleware over the Security Layer protocol interface. Whenever the server-side middleware MOA-ID needs to access the user's smart-card (e.g. to read certificate data or to create an electronic signature), it sends an appropriate XML request to the server component of MOCCA, which decodes the obtained request. The server component subsequently initiates the requested smart-card based operation, which is forwarded to the client component of MOCCA.

In general, the server component of MOCCA, the server-side middleware MOA-ID, and even the service provider's online application can be deployed on the same server. Since all interfaces between the main components of our authentication system can be secured by TLS/SSL, all components can also be deployed on different servers and connected over public networks without a loss of usability or security.

4.2.2 Client Component (Java Applet)

To access smart-cards that reside in the User domain, Java Applet technology is used by our authentication system. The Java Applet, which runs in the user's web browser environment, basically forms the second component of the client middleware. Once started in the user's web browser, the Java Applet receives requests from the server component via a well-defined interface. These requests specify what data to read, or operations to perform, on the user's smart-card. Results of the performed smart-card based operations (e.g. read certificates, computed signature values, etc.) are returned to the server component over the same interface. Basically the whole client middleware may run as an applet in the user's browser. However, in order to minimize the processing load on the user's side, e.g. XML digital signature processing operations like canonicalization etc., these operations are carried out by the server component of MOCCA. The applet itself is only in charge of processing the small amount of data required for card-based operations. All smart-card communication relies on the PC/SC protocol [16] and the exchange of appropriate application protocol data units (APDU). In order to interact with the PC/SC stack, the Java SmartCard I/O API - and thus a Java 6 runtime - is required on the user's browser.

While the basic functionality of the Java Applet has been provided by MOCCA, several adaptations of this open source solution were necessary. To support cards other than the Austrian eID card, the existing card recognition mechanism has been extended. Furthermore, existing methods for the accomplishment of smart-card based operations have also been enhanced so as to achieve compliance with different European eID cards. In the next section we show how these eID IdP components can be applied in practice together with popular and widely-used authentication solutions.

5 Integration in Central Authentication Service

In this section we show how our eID identity provider solution can be integrated into the Central Authentication Service (CAS) identity management system. By combining the centrally-controlled CAS authentication model with our user-centric approach, we established a hybrid solution resulting in a kind of federated authentication model.

CAS is a popular identity management solution, originally designed and developed by Shawn Bayern of Yale University, meanwhile maintained as open-source project by the Java Architectures Special Interest Group (JA-SIG) [17]. Its hallmark is a single-sign-on (SSO) protocol that allows users to access multiple services by requiring them to provide their authentication credentials only once. However, in contrast to Liberty Alliance or Shibboleth [18], CAS does not support trust federation with multiple identity providers.

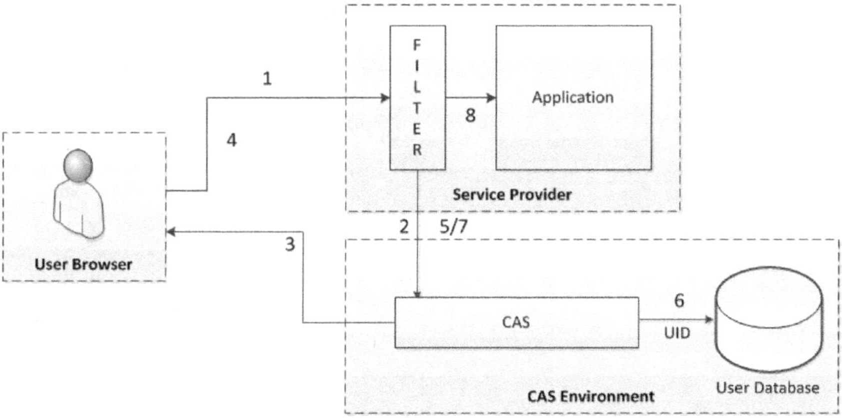

Fig. 5. General CAS authentication process flow

As illustrated in Figure 5, CAS authentication requires a central SSO or ticketing server, which has to be called before gaining access to the protected area of a service provider (SP) (1). Users have to provide their authentication information to the CAS server (e.g. by entering username/password) (2), which issues a SP-specific ticket after successful authentication (3). Users have to provide this ticket to the application of the SP (4), which must then validate the ticket against the CAS server (5/6). After successful authentication, the user gets access to the requested application (7/8) and is automatically authenticated when requesting applications of other service providers protected by this CAS instance. Applications with legacy authentication mechanisms can easily be *"CAS-ified"* by installing a so-called authentication interceptor. For instance, for the Java Servlet API there is a servlet filter available that handles all authentication parts and integrates seamlessly into each web application. Similar implementations are available for web servers (Apache etc.), special web applications (content management systems etc.) or server-side technologies (PHP, JSP, etc.).

The modular CAS architecture allows third parties to integrate custom authentication handlers that have to deal with two basic items: credentials and principals. Credentials are some kind of evidence in order to authenticate users. Some examples are the well-known username/password credentials, an X.509 certificate, a SAML token, etc. A principal represents the authenticated user. An authentication handler must thus evaluate if the user can be authenticated using the given credentials and if an associated principal can be resolved. Our proposed solution provides a custom authentication handler, which is invoked when CAS is accessed using a SAML ticket passed by our eID identity provider as credential. In general, principals may be of any kind. In our case study we used an LDAP user entry as principal data.

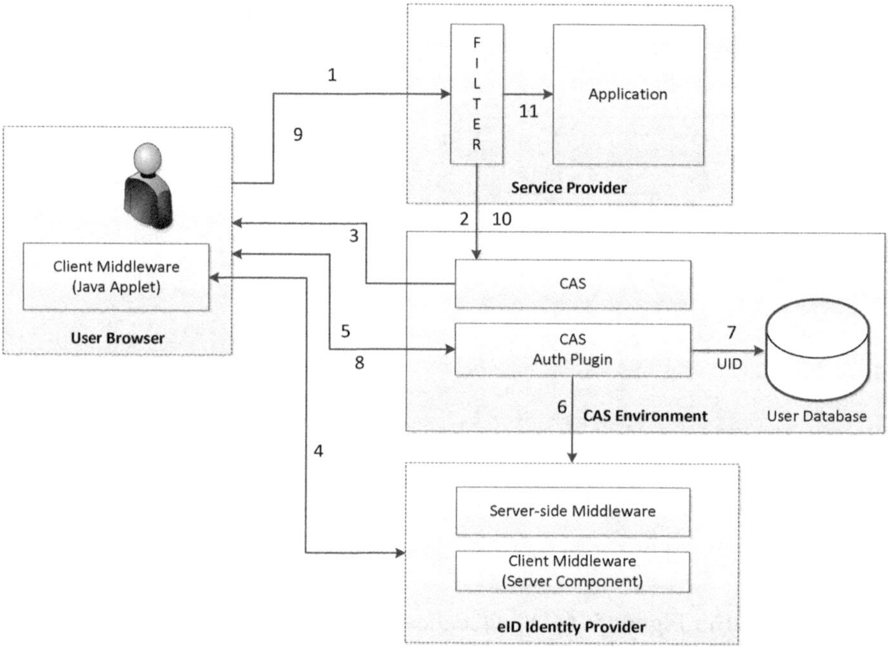

Fig. 6. CAS security architecture for eID based authentication

Figure 6 illustrates our CAS security architecture for eID based authentication with its four entities: user, service provider, CAS authentication server and eID identity provider. The authentication process works as follows: a user trying to access the web resource of a service provider is intercepted by an authentication filter (1). The filter determines that the user is not yet authenticated and thus has to be redirected to the central CAS login page (2). The user has the choice to login either with username and password or with an eID. When selecting the eID option (3), the MOCCA client middleware starts as an applet, automatically determines the eID card type and requests the user to enter the secret signature PIN code (4). Figure 7 illustrates this step in the case of a Belgium eID card. The user can also optionally display the signature data to be signed in a separate window. After successful signature verification and authentication with the eID identity provider, the MOCCA client middleware redirects the user together with the issued SAML ticket back to the CAS login page (5). Our authentication provider is implemented and hooked into CAS in such a way that it is automatically invoked when the login URL contains a SAML ticket (so-called SAML artifact) as HTTP parameter. The plug-in connects to the eID identity provider and fetches the SAML assertion belonging to the SAML ticket (6). In case of an invalid ticket, an appropriate error message is returned to the user. Otherwise, the assertion contains the unique ID (UID) of the authenticated user, which is used to query the LDAP database to determine the associated user's principal data (7). If no principal can be resolved, the user is redirected to a registration page with pre-filled form data extracted from the SAML assertion. Otherwise, the user is redirected to the service provider (8, 9) with a valid CAS authentication ticket as HTTP parameter. The authentication filter of the service provider validates this ticket against the CAS server (10) and in case of success, access to the web resources is granted (11).

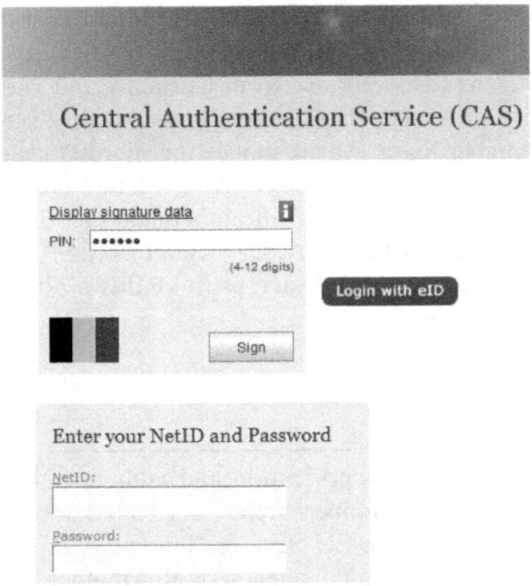

Fig. 7. CAS login sample with Belgium eID

Some remarks on eID based registration: in contrast to the default username/password authentication mechanism, an eID based registration does not necessarily require any user interaction and may be carried out seamlessly. The unique ID enables each user to be recognized and uniquely identified again at each login. A similar registration-less eID approach has been introduced in [20].

The CAS authentication plug-in is able to pass personal data to a particular registration page so that web forms can be pre-filled for the user. The range of personal details depends on their availability from the eID token. In case of an Austrian citizen, UID, given name, family name and date of birth are available. Other examples are Belgian and Estonian eIDs, which hold the same values as the Austrian eID, except for date of birth.

6 Remarks

Due to an open architecture and open interfaces, our solution can be easily integrated in existing environments. This way, access control to already existing online applications can be significantly increased in terms of security and usability.

Due to our modular design, basically any eID card that stores appropriate unique identifiers and which is capable of creating qualified electronic signatures can be easily integrated in our solution with minimal effort. So far, we have implemented card support for the Belgian and the Estonian eIDs, among others. Given the required card specifications, including the respective APDU sequences, any eID card (e.g. Slovenian or Spanish eID) can be integrated into our solution.

Our solution follows a user-centric approach and is only suited to Member States with smart-card based eID solutions. The European large scale pilot STORK [21] (Secure idenTity acrOss bordeRs linKed) aims at enabling cross-border recognition of eIDs by establishing a platform for European eID interoperability. Due to its decentralized interoperability model, it will support any kind of governmental eID. In the STORK case, all citizens (except those from Germany and Austria) are redirected to their national identity provider when authenticating with a service provider that resides in a foreign Member State. Albeit supporting more kinds of governmental eIDs, this approach will depend on decentralized infrastructure components of other Member States. In our solution, by contrast, all authentication components can be located within the domain of the service provider. Under certain circumstances, this may ensure a continuous operation and faster process flows compared to decentralized approaches.

7 Conclusion

In this paper we discussed an identification and authentication solution, which supports eIDs from several EU Member States. As called for by the European i2010 initiative, and with respect to the EU Services Directive, cross-border authentication and eID interoperability is now on the agenda of all Member States.

The authors have based their work on several open source approaches, mainly the Austrian e-Government modules MOA-ID [12] and MOCCA [15], and the Yale University's CAS [17], respectively. These modules, which have a specific focus on a national smartcard environment (MOA-ID, MOCCA) and on username password authentication (CAS), have been combined.

The foreign eID card integration concerned to a great extent the modification and adaption of the Java applet code residing in the user's domain, i.e. card recognition and cryptographic functions, as well as the signature verification adoption in the server-side middleware MOA-ID. In order to show applicability in practice, we implemented an authentication plug-in for the popular and widely-used CAS identity management solution. The result was enhancing a CAS (i.e. username and password) based environment with different smart-card based national eIDs.

Nevertheless, due to the open architecture and open interfaces, our solution can also be easily integrated in other environments.

References

1. Kessler, G.C.: Passwords – Strengths and Weaknesses. In: Cavanagh, J.P. (ed.) Internet and Networking Security, Auerbach (1997)
2. Arora, S.: National e-ID card schemes: A European overview. Information Security Technical Report 13(2), 46–53 (2008) ISSN 1363-4127, Doi: 10.1016/j.istr.2008.08.002
3. The European Parliament and the Council of the European Union: Directive 1999/93/EC of the European Parliament and of the Council on a Community framework for electronic signatures (December 13, 1999)
4. The European Parliament and the Council of the European Union: Directive 2006/123/EC of the European Parliament and of the Council on services in the internal market (December 12, 2006)
5. Palfrey, J., Gasser, U.: Digital Identity Interoperability and eInnovation, Case Study, Berkman Publication Series (November 2007)
6. Microsoft Corporation, Microsoft's Vision for an Identity Metasystem (May 2005), `http://www.identityblog.com/stories/2005/07/05/IdentityMetasystem.htm`
7. Microsoft Corporation, Windows CardSpace, `http://www.microsoft.com/windows/products/winfamily/cardspace/default.mspx`
8. Higgins, Open Source Identity Framework, `http://www.eclipse.org/higgins/`
9. Authentication for Web Applications, `http://code.google.com/apis/accounts/docs/AuthForWebApps.html`
10. The Liberty Alliance Project, `http://www.projectliberty.org/`
11. OASIS TC, Security Assertion Markup Language (SAML), `http://www.oasis-open.org/committees/tc_home.php?wg_abbrev=security`
12. Modules for Online Applications – Identification (MOA-ID), `http://egovlabs.gv.at/projects/moa-idspss/`
13. Leitold, H., Hollosi, A., Posch, R.: Security Architecture of the Austrian Citizen Card Concept. In: Proceedings of 18th Annual Computer Security Applications Conference (2002)
14. ETSI TS 102231 – Electronic Signatures and Infrastructures (ESI); Provision of harmonized Trust-service status information, v3.1.1 (October 2009)
15. Center, M., Orthacker, C., Bauer, W.: Minimal-Footprint Middleware for the Creation of Qualified Signatures. In: Proceedings of WEBIST 2010, International Conference on Web Information Systems and Technologies (2010)
16. Interoperability Specification for ICCs and Personal Computer Systems, `http://www.pcscworkgroup.com/specifications/overview.php`
17. Central Authentication Service (CAS), Java Architectures Special Interest Group (JA-SIG), `http://www.jasig.org/cas`
18. Shibboleth, a project of the Internet2 Middleware Initiative, `http://shibboleth.internet2.edu/`
19. Ivkovic, M., Leitold, H., Rössler, T.: Interoperable elektronische Identität in Europa. Information Security Konferenz 7, 175–190 (2009)
20. Orthacker, C., Zwattendorfer, B.: Seamless eID Integration into Web Portals. In: Electronic Government: Proceedings of ongoing research and projects of EGOV '09, pp. 297–304 (2009)
21. Secure Identity Across Borders Linked (STORK), `https://www.eid-stork.eu/`

SocialSupervisor: A Geographically Enhanced Social Content Site to Supervise Public Works

Luciana Cavalcante de Menezes, Hugo Feitosa de Figueirêdo,
Ricardo Madeira Fernandes, Tiago Eduardo da Silva, and Cláudio de Souza Baptista

University of Campina Grande, Information Systems Laboratory,
Campina Grande - Paraíba, Brazil
{luciana,hugoff,madeira,hugo,
tiagosilva,baptista}@dsc.ufcg.edu.br

Abstract. In the Web 2.0 users may freely contribute with information on several topics. Hence, public agencies can take advantage of this fact by creating communication channels with society. This paper presents the SocialSupervisor, a geographically enhanced social content site, where citizens can be notified about public works nearby. Moreover, they are able to post complaints related to any irregularity in public services. Such information forces the government to promote an immediate investigation of the facts.

Keywords: Social content sites, GIS, Web 2.0.

1 Introduction

The Social Web, best known as Web 2.0, has leaded to huge modifications in the way people relate and share information with each other. Applications developed using Social Web technologies, such as blogs, wikis and social networks ease the production, consumption and share of the information [1]. In this context, social content sites may enrich users experience through the integration of both traditional information and functionalities presented in social networks [2]. In such environments, users may contribute by posting contents. These contents are shared with other users that may either have similar interests or belong to the same friendship network.

Due to people's participation, the social content sites have become an ideal environment to broadcast complaints. Hence, these sites have the potential to encourage the communication between the society and public agencies.

In Brazil, some public agencies make use of the participatory budgeting mechanism. The latter consists of meetings with community leaders, where citizens expose their needs, requests and complaints so that more financial resources might be allocated to solve citizens' requests. However, after the budget decisions are made, it is difficult for the citizens to track the proposal progress. For instance, regarding public works, there are public agencies that supervise their development, such as the Auditor Court of the States. Nonetheless, when a citizen wants an information about a particular work, she finds extremely hard to get it because there is no mechanism to easy this process.

K.N. Andersen et al. (Eds.): EGOVIS 2010, LNCS 6267, pp. 134–141, 2010.

Furthermore, Goodchild [3] points out the importance of applying geographic information in the Web 2.0 services. In this new model, the participants are called 'citizens as sensors', since they are responsible for giving location details of their observations and experiences. This is already a tendency mainly after the rise of map mashups. These maps are web applications that combine data and functionality from different online sources via publicly available interfaces [4]. Therefore, the employ of location together with traditional information might improve the citizens' perception of a social environment, since it enables spatial searches for information and complaints. Besides, the Web 2.0 eases the visualization of spatial query results through the use of map mashups.

This paper presents SocialSupervisor that aims to narrow the communication between public agencies and the society. SocialSupervisor is a social content site geographically enhanced that enables: 1) the public agencies to expose transparently the information about works either finished or in progress, in a given geographic region; 2) the citizens to act like a work supervisor, sending complaints through multimedia files; 3) the society to have access to the information about how money has been invested in a specific geographic region.

The remainder of this paper is organized as follows. Section 2 addresses related work. Section 3 focuses on Web 2.0 and mobility issues. Section 4 presents our system. Section 5 discusses relevant aspects of the proposed system. Finally, section 6 concludes the paper and points out further work to be undertaken.

2 Related Work

There are several works on providing software tools to improve the citizen-government communication. Teerling and Pieterson [5] presented a study on how to lead people to use these Web systems as most of people are not used to explore this efficient communication channel.

The Smartocracy project [6] enables users to pose their problems and solutions to the community. These proposals will receive votes to indicate what is the best solution from the community to a given problem. This work also addresses a trust-based social network to represent the relationship among users. Nonetheless, this trust process might be enhanced through the use of geographic location of the problem posed by the community. Also the location of users who vote in a solution for a specific problem is an interesting issue.

Boldi et al. [7] also deal with trust issue by using votes in electronically mediated social networks. They propose that the voting system in such social networks should be configured in a way that users may express their preferences through only one person to which she is directly connected to.

Wiki Government [8] is a project that uses Wiki technology to design a collaborative democratic government. Although this project enables public decision making through public participation, it focuses only on the particular field of patent examination process.

Maciel et al. [9] present a pilot case study on the Democratic Citizenship Community project. Their approach provides interaction and communication resources such as citizens' profiles, debate, voting, information library, socialization space and users' help. Again, this system does not address the geographic location of the problems and users.

Hiendiger et al. [10] propose a web-based tool for promoting collaborative impact assessment aiming to better evaluate policies, norms or regulations currently under development by legistators. They found out that the success of such tool depends on interface usability. Of course, if they enhance their Web interface with spatial capabilities they will get better results.

In the field of information management and discovery, the work presented by Amer Yahia et al. [11] presents a logical architecture to deal with the challenges to perform information management and discovery in social content sites. The proposed architecture, called SocialScope, consists of three tiers: content management, information discovery and information presentation. Again, they do not address the spatial dimension at all.

Naaman [12] is one of the first works to explore spatiotemporal issues on social networks. Monclar et al [13] have proposed a tool called MEK (Mobile Exchange of Knowledge) which aims to provide a mobile infrastructure to exchange knowledge among people who share the same interests, regarding the geographic aspect of the people involved. However, their approach has not been applied to citizen-government communication.

3 Web 2.0 and Mobile 2.0 Supporting the Supervision of Public Works

The Web 2.0 exploits the collective intelligence to produce enhanced tools. Typical examples are blogs and wikis, where users can share their experiences and knowledge. Besides, people may verify whether the content posted is reliable.

These features can be employed to assist governments in the supervision of public works. Their build or reconstruction might be seen or monitored by those who stand nearby. Despite the government responsibility of monitoring and supervising these works, the society can help in the identification of irregularities, i.e., creating a collective supervision.

In Brazil and several other countries, there are already specialized agencies to receive complaints concerning irregularities on works in progress. The complaint may be sent via communication media, such as phones. This helps to make the supervision more effective. Nonetheless, this kind of media has its limitations because the complaints can only be expressed through speech, which is more difficult to check its accuracy.

However, the Web 2.0 enables the use of different types of media to make complaints (i.e., videos, photos, audios and texts). Hence, they are more likely to prove possible irregularities. Additionally, the employ of maps can surely aid the user in the process of identifying occurrence locations.

The contents posted in social networks are not always truthful. With the purpose of enhancing the information confidence, auditing might be applied by the government, or by people who simply use the Web. In both cases the person responsible for auditing can utilize people's comments to check the accuracy of the complaint.

On the other hand, the Mobile 2.0 paradigm provides the advantages brought by the Web 2.0 to the mobile devices. This is possible as the most recent mobile devices have access to the Internet and also can capture photos, videos and audios. Another essential issue is the mobile devices sensors. For instance, if the GPS (Global Positioning System) sensor is attached to the device, its location can be added to the metadata of the multimedia captured files. As such, mobile devices have become an essential complaint tool. Users can capture multimedia files and broadcast them in order to justify their objections.

The aspects described in this section are suitable for supporting the supervision of public works. Thus, the next section will present the SocialSupervisor, a social content site for monitoring public works. This approach uses the benefits brought by both Web 2.0 and Mobile 2.0.

4 The SocialSupervisor Approach

The SocialSupervisor is a public work manager, where public sector employees can register public work descriptions along with multimedia files that identify their progress. Moreover, it enables people to access the site and make complaints about irregularities that might occur. These complaints can also make use of multimedia files to help the user in justifying his accusation.

Fig. 1 presents the system architecture. Basically, it is composed of three layers: (i) the data layer; (ii) the business logic layer and (iii) the presentation layer. The presentation layer represents the user interface, which can be Web (developed in Flex [14]) or mobile, which enables users to make complaints through Web browsers or cell phones. The Google Maps service is employed to display maps.

The business logic layer contains the logic methods to deal with social content sites. Specifically, a few modules were developed to manager: i) the results presented to the user (Presentation Service); ii) the registered complaints (Complaint Service); iii) the works inserted into the system (Works Service); and iv) the system users (Users Service). In addition, an access control module was built to monitor users' activities. A format conversion service was developed to display the information in a proper way, regarding the media type. Finally, there is the data and file service, which is responsible for providing, respectively, access to the database and the file system management.

The communication between the presentation layer and the business logic layer is implemented through REST (Representational State Transfer) and XML. These technologies were used to facilitate the presentation of the content in the web browser and mobile clients.

The data layer managers the storage of metadata and spatial information used in the SocialSupervisor. The database system employed was the PostgreSQL with its extension for geographical objects, called PostGIS. These objects might be either points or polygons, which may refer to works or complaints.

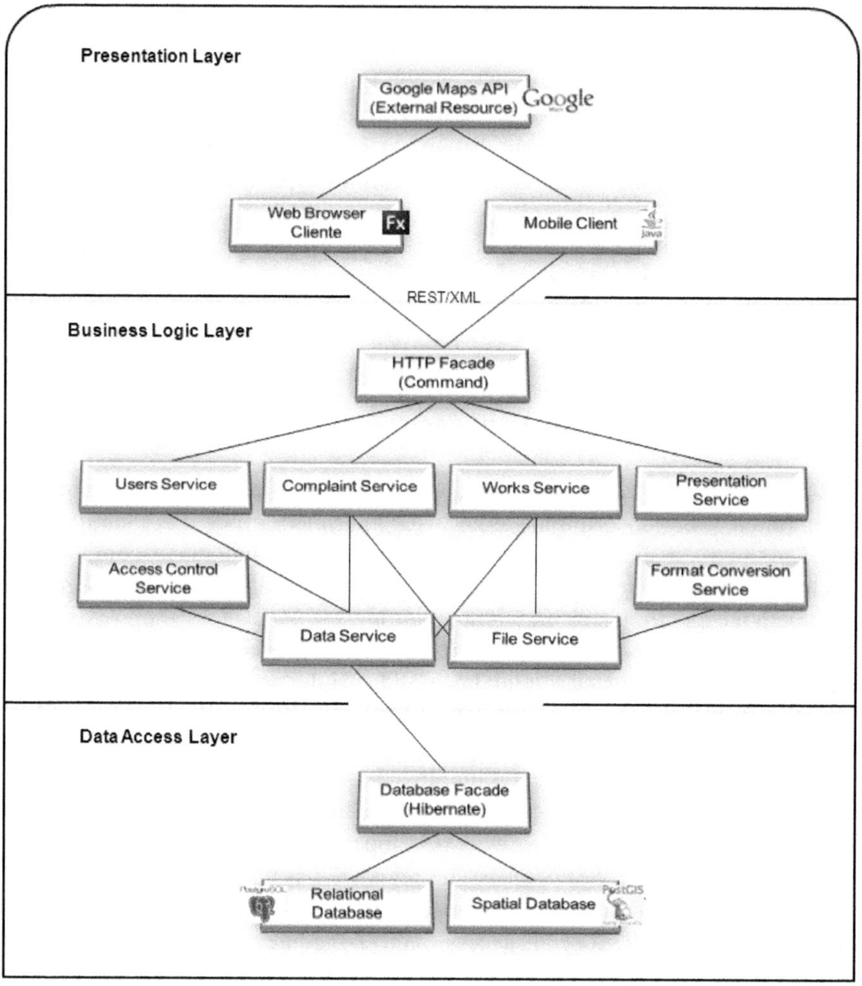

Fig. 1. SocialSupervisor architecture

The interface to register works is presented in Fig. 2. It is restricted to authorized users, for instance, public agency employees. Users can make complaints about registered public works, attach multimedia files together with their geographical position and visualize all the complaints that had already been made. The mobile device interface enables the user to realize the same tasks as in the Web Interface.

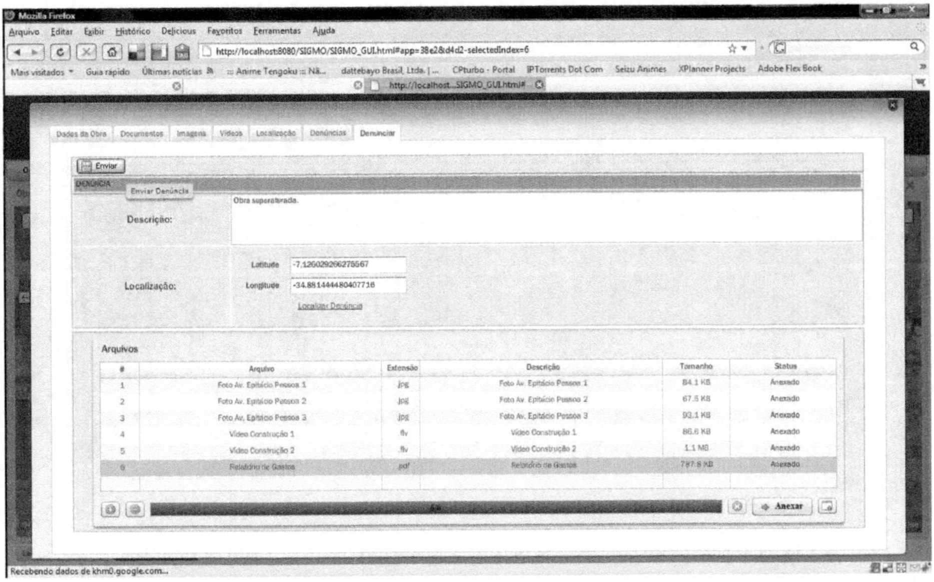

Fig. 2. Interface to insert works into the SocialSupervisor

5 Issues on the Accuracy of the Complaints in the SocialSupervisor

An important issue to consider is the accuracy of a complaint, since it is possible to make it anonymously. On the whole, the SocialSupervisor contains moderators, who shall be authorized users, so that they can evaluate the complaints in order to accept or reject them. The accepted ones can be visualized in a map, along with the works.

In Fig. 3, there is a map containing works and complaints, where number 1 indicates complaints and number 2 registered works. As explained before, the works and complaints are represented through geographical objects, such as points or polygons. When more than one point or polygon is applied to represent the work or complaint location, the map presents the icon and the geometry formed by its points. For instance, in Fig. 3 is possible to notice that A and B form a line, which represents a road work. In A there is an icon that marks the work initial point and C marks a complaint about a specific work location.

In Brazil, the work monitoring is verified through photos, which are appropriate to display work progress. This photo acquisition process is not part of the supervisor agency job, but those who are in charge of the work. Randomly, a supervisor agency employee checks the work personally. As the photos are registered in the SocialSupervisor, any citizen might have access to them. Thus, a person who lives near a certain work is able to contribute by checking if the inserted multimedia files are truly related to this work and if they are not, he can alert the agencies by using the SocialSupervisor.

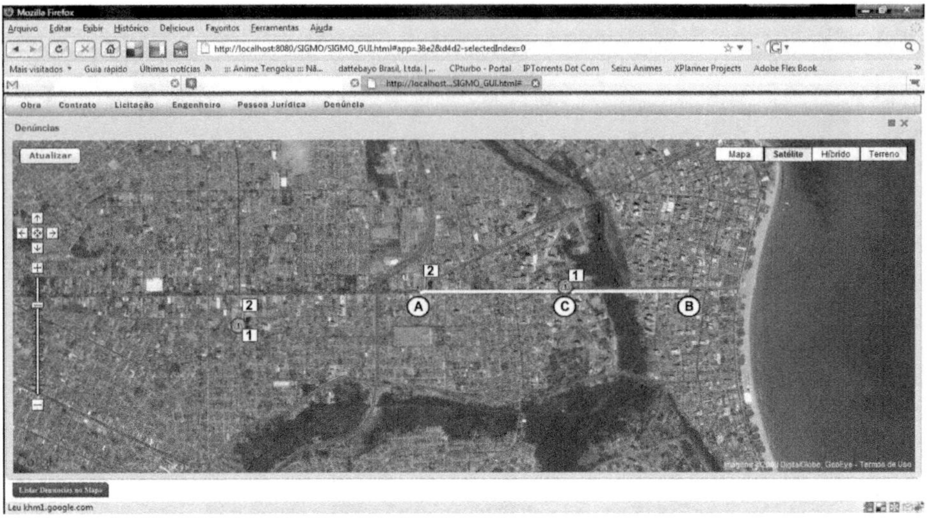

Fig. 3. The SocialSupervisor map visualization of works and complaints

6 Conclusion and Future Work

This paper presented the SocialSupervisor, a social content site that enhances the communication between the citizens and public agencies, which are responsible for performing work supervisions. In the site, any citizen can access the data about works in progress that are registered by authorized users from the public agencies. Besides, this citizen can contribute acting as a supervisor of both finished and in progress works close to his home or office.

In order to exploit the data produced by users, the SocialSupervisor provides map visual interfaces via Web 2.0 facilities and mashups, where exposed complaints of certain works might be visualized. This approach enriches user perception about what is happening around his geographical position.

As further work, recommendation techniques based on users preferences and their experiences using the SocialSupervisor can be applied [15]. Consequently, a person could be advised only about complaints of his interest. Moreover, domain ontologies shall be used to better distinguish the types of complaints that can be described by users. Finally, we plan to deploy the system in a public agency to observe and evaluate its effectiveness.

Acknowledgement

The authors would like to thank the CNPQ - Brazilian Research Council for funding this research, under the grant CNPQ-477948/2009-0.

References

1. Sheth, A., Nagarajan, M.: Semantics-Empowered Social Computing. IEEE Internet Computing 13(1), 76–80 (2009)
2. Amer-Yahia, S., Huang, J., Yu, C.: Jelly: A Language for Building Community-Centric Information Exploration Applications. In: IEEE 25th International Conference on Data Engineering, pp. 1588–1594. IEEE, Shanghai (2009)
3. Goodchild, M.F.: Citizens as sensors: Web 2.0 and The Volunteering of geographic information. In: GeoFocus, pp. 8–10 (2007)
4. Merrill, D.: Mashups: The new breed of Web app. IBM Web Architecture Technical Library (2006), `http://www-128.ibm.com/developerworks/library/x-mashups.html`
5. Teerling, M.L., Pieterson, W.: Multi-channel marketing: an experiment on leading citizens to online public services. In: Proceedings of The 10th Annual International Conference on Digital Government Research, pp. 104–112. Digital Government Society of North America (2009)
6. Rodriguez, M., Steinbock, D., Watkins, J., Gershenson, C., Bollen, J., Grey, V., de-Graf, B.: Smartocracy: Social Networks for Collective Decision Making. In: 40th Annual Hawaii International Conference on Systems Science, pp. 90–90. IEEE, Hawaii (2007)
7. Boldi, P., Bonchi, F., Castillo, C., Vigna, S.: Voting in Social Networks. In: 18th ACM Conference on Information and Knowledge Management, pp. 777–786. ACM, Hong Kong (2009)
8. Noveck, B.: Social Networks: Making Connections between Citizens, Data and Government. In: 10th Annual International Conference on Digital Government Research, p. 1. Digital Government Society of North America (2009)
9. Maciel, C., Roque, L., Garcia, A.C.B.: Democratic citizenship community: a social network to promote e-deliberative process. In: 10th Annual International Conference on Digital Government Research, pp. 25–34. Digital Government Society of North America (2009)
10. Heidinger, C., Buchmann, E., Böhm, K.: Towards collaborative web-based impact assessment. In: 10th Annual International Conference on Digital Government Research, pp. 190–198. Digital Government Society of North America (2009)
11. Amer-Yahia, S., Lakshmanan, L., Yu, C.: SocialScope: Enabling Information Discovery on Social Content Sites. In: Conference on Innovative Data Systems Research (2009)
12. Naaman, M.: Spatio-Tempo-Social: Learning from and about Humans with Social Media. In: 11th International Symposium, Advances in Spatial and Temporal Databases, pp. 1–2. Springer, Aalborg (2009)
13. Monclar, R., Tecla, A., Oliveira, J., de Souza, J.M.: MEK: Using spatial-temporal information to improve social networks and knowledge dissemination. Information Sciences 179(15), 2524–2537 (2009)
14. Flex, `http://www.adobe.com/br/products/flex/`
15. Schenkel, R., Crecelius, T., Kacimi, M., Neumann, T., Xavier Parreira, J., Spaniol, M., Weikum, G.: SocialWisdom for Search and Recommendation. IEEE Data Engineering Bulletin 31(2), 40–49 (2008)

Transforming the Greek e-Government Environment towards the e-Gov 2.0 Era

Prokopios Drogkaris[1], Stefanos Gritzalis[1], and Costas Lambrinoudakis[2]

[1] Laboratory of Information and Communication Systems Security,
Department of Information and Communication Systems Engineering,
University of the Aegean Samos, GR-83200, Greece
{pdrogk,sgritz}@aegean.gr
[2] Deptartment of Digital Systems,
University of Piraeus, GR-185 34, Greece
clam@unipi.gr

Abstract. Modern e-Government environments across the public sector have achieved significant interoperability and coherence but are now in front of the next leap forward, which is the adaptation of Web 2.0 technologies. This transition towards e-Government 2.0 will not only improve participation, transparency and integration but it will also speed up the pace of innovation through collaboration and consultation. This paper presents an enhanced Greek e-Government Framework that fully incorporates Web 2.0 technologies along with an identification mechanism that retains compliance with existing authentication sub-framework taking into account the specific needs and requirements of the Greek Governmental Agencies.

Keywords: e-Government 2.0, Web 2.0, Security, Privacy, Identification.

1 Introduction

During the last decade e-Government environments have undergone considerable transformations in an attempt to satisfy the incessant demand of improved interoperability, acceptance and systems coherence. Currently, they are called to make the next leap forward by embodying technologies and methodologies that will not only improve participation, transparency and integration but also speed up the pace of innovation. The second incarnation of Web named "Web 2.0" or "Social Web" can facilitate towards this direction through public interaction, collaboration and consultation.

The term "Web 2.0" was first introduced in 2003 by Oreily Media and referred to a second generation of the World Wide Web which would provide the platform for Web-based services and communities of social interaction. A formal definition of Web 2.0, given by Hoegg in [3], is "the philosophy of mutually maximizing collective intelligence and added values for each participant by formalized and dynamic information sharing and creation". The tools of Web 2.0 include blogs, wikis, social

K.N. Andersen et al. (Eds.): EGOVIS 2010, LNCS 6267, pp. 142–149, 2010.

networking platforms, syndication, discussion groups, machine automated content and topic analysis based on open standards and technologies. Terms such as "e-Government 2.0", "Government 2.0" and "eGov. 2.0" are used to describe the incorporation of Web 2.0 fundamentals in e-Government environments. These fundamentals include public participation, deliberation, and engagement to government consultation along with transparency.

In this paper we propose an enhanced Greek e-Government Framework which fully incorporates Web 2.0 technologies along with an identification mechanism that retains compliance with existing authentication sub-framework and identity assurance levels. The rest of the paper is structured as follow. Section 2 provides an insight in worldwide endeavors relating to government interaction attempts with Social Web. Section 3 discusses the identification issues emerging in e-Government 2.0 environments. Section 4 presents the current state of Greek e-Government environment, which constitutes the basis for our proposal, while Section 5 presents the proposed model and identification mechanism for Greek e-Government 2.0 environment. Finally, Section 6 concludes the paper providing thoughts on future work.

2 Related Work

One of the first governmental initiatives towards e-Government 2.0 was by the German government in 2005 [9] as part of a universal strategy for the modernization of federal administration. The scope of this initiative was to identify the objectives for further expansion of electronic services, improve cooperation between citizens and public administration, introduce an electronic identification mechanism (e-ID) and finally provide a secure communications infrastructure. In 2006, European Union issued the EU *i*2010 – *Information Society and the media working towards growth and jobs initiative* [10] and the *eGovernment action plan* [11] which provided guidelines and goals for member states towards ameliorating public services and administration transparency, effectiveness and efficiency. President Obama in 2009 signed a memorandum for "*Transparency and Open Government*" [12] which actuated implementations of social media technologies to improve central governance engagement with public. In 2009, as well, Australia has issued a report [13] regarding the engagement of Australian Government with Government 2.0. This report derived from the results of nineteen different projects that were designed to "provide insight into key Government 2.0 issues" [13]. An alternative representation of the transition being conducted and the effort towards e-Government 2.0 is provided by a wiki titled "*Government 2.0 - Best Practices Wiki*"[1], which catalogs official and unofficial worldwide initiatives that involve social media and central government. Currently, this list consists of six countries and it is continuously updated, enriched and improved by user contributions. Table 1, below, summarizes the approximate number of official Web 2.0 tools that are currently available, through ministerial departments and government organizations, in each country.

[1] Government 2.0 - Best Practices Wiki:
`http://government20bestpractices.pbworks.com`

Table 1. Official e-Government 2.0 Initiatives Worldwide

	Blogs	*Disc. Groups*	*RSS*	*Wikis*
AUSTRALIA	●●	●●	●	●
CANADA	●	●●●	●●●	●●●
NETHERLANDS		●		
NEW ZEALAND	●●●	●		●●
U. K.		●		
UNITED STATES	●●●●	●	●●	●
Legend	● *1-5*	●● *6-10*	●●● *11 -15*	●●●● *16 - 20*

3 Identity Assurance in e-Government 2.0

The security risks emerging in e-Government 2.0 environments do not significantly vary from those identified in traditional e-Government environments. Unauthorized access, modification, loss, destruction or disclosure of data that are transmitted, processed and stored, are the risks that have to be confronted through the deployment of appropriate measures and procedures. This is also supported by a report from the secure enterprise 2.0 forum [17], published in 2009, which identifies Web 2.0 security threats and vulnerabilities along with known incidents and possible exploit scenarios. However, issues related to user identification do have a significant diversion.

For the provision of traditional electronic services, a certain level of assurance for user's identity is required. For informational services almost no identity assurance is required while for transactional services there is need for high assurance level for the identity of the user. The required level of assurance is accomplished through the employment of the appropriate registration and authentication procedures which are specified in the corresponding authentication sub-frameworks. For Web 2.0 services, though, almost no assurance for user's identity is required, since no transaction or two way data exchange is taking place. In existing commercial Web 2.0 services and applications, user identification and authentication is performed through the utilization of username/password authentication mechanisms. These credentials are issued through web registration procedures where only user's email address can be verified. For the purposes of these commercial applications, such a level of user's identity assurance may be adequate but this is not the case for governmental applications. For instance, how can central governance take into account public opinion if she cannot distinguish between opinions that do represent public feelings and those aiming to misdirect the conclusions and findings? It is therefore clear that depending on the significance and impact of the service and its results, central governance should be either able to weight different opinions or, alternatively, predefine the levels of identity assurance that are necessary for the establishment of the required level of confidence. No matter what the selection will be, the necessity for guidelines and policies that will be used to determine the required level of assurance, prior to the implementation of the services, is evident.

4 e-Government in Greece: Current Status

4.1 Greek e-Government Environment

Greek public sector has moved to the e-Government era, in an attempt to improve the quality of the provided services. Currently, several ministerial departments offer their services electronically through a comprehensive e-Government framework [4]. The main objective of this framework is the support of common authentication and registration mechanisms for accessing all available electronic services as well as the development of a Central Portal, namely "Ermis"[2], that operates as a *one-stop shop* providing to Greek citizens a common interface for all electronic services offered by the public sector. Framework's main characteristics are briefly described next;

- *Uniform Registration and Authentication Procedures*: The registration and authentication procedures required for accessing the offered electronic services are provided through Ermis Portal.
- *Classification of electronic services to Levels of Trust*: All electronic services offered through the Ermis Portal have been classified to pre-determined trust levels; these trust levels are understood as "The level of confidence of an end-user's electronic identity along with the assurance achieved by the security measures and procedures employed for safeguarding the access, processing and transmission of data" [4].
- *Per Sector Identifiers*: The identification of the users wishing to utilize one of electronic services is accomplished through sectorial identifiers. These identifiers are given to each citizen the first time she requests to use a service (through the registration process) of a particular sector, identifying her uniquely within that specific sector. The bonding of these identifiers, for the provision of user-centric *Single Sign-On* is accomplished through identifier's encryption in a pre-defined sequence, along with an identifier assigned by Ermis itself.

5 Greek e-Government 2.0: Proposed Model

In this paper we propose an enhanced Greek e-Government Framework which fully incorporates Web 2.0 technologies along with an identification mechanism that retains compliance with the existing authentication sub-framework. Our proposal is based on the existing Greek e-Government Framework, as described in Section 4, in an attempt to ensure backwards compatibility with implemented services, procedures and normative regulations through the exploitation of framework's open architecture while taking into account the specific needs and requirements of the Greek Governmental Agencies. In order to keep the Ermis portal as the interface between users and ministerial departments and thus maintaining the One Stop Shop characteristics, Web 2.0 services will be provided through the existing central portal, as demonstrated in Figure 1. Each Web 2.0 Service will be offered through a specific Service Provider that will be responsible for specifying the required level of assurance on users' identity, the data required for the registration process as well as the data utilized during

[2] Greek Public Administration National Portal Ermis: `http://www.ermis.gov.gr`

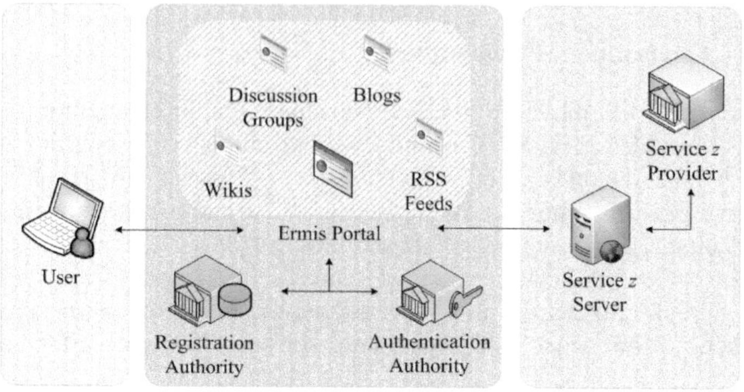

Fig. 1. Greek eGov 2.0 Proposed Architecture

the execution of the electronic service itself, based on the Greek Authentication Framework's guidelines [4]. In this way the desired level of security and trust are maintained.

5.1 Proposed Identification Mechanism

In order to maintain compatibility with identification and authentication procedures, we employ the notion of account linking along with the utilization of the underlying PKI infrastructure of the Greek Public Sector. In a way similar to the existing e-services, user identification in Web 2.0 services is based on identifiers. As described in Section 4, the Greek Public Sector does not utilize an all-embracing identifier (e-ID) due to legal impediments. On the contrary, each sector identifies users through sectorial identifiers. In Web 2.0 services, we propose the preservation of this mechanism in order to overcome Legal barriers imposed by the Greek Legal Framework [18][19] regarding data interconnection that would results from the introduction of a unique identifier. Our proposal is to utilize each department's encryption key pair for storing the corresponding Web 2.0 identifier to the Ermis portal, in a predefined sequence, as an extension of the mechanism described in Section 4 for the sectorial identifiers. Figure 2 below depicts the sequence of User's A encrypted identifiers for traditional e-Services and Web 2.0 services.

The first identifier "*User A Ermis Identifier*" is employed for the users' unique identification by the Ermis Portal, during the authentication procedure, and it serves as the linking mechanism to all per-sector and Web 2.0 identifiers of the specific user. The remaining blocks in the sequence consist solely by encrypted identifiers, each one of them corresponding to a specific service. Since each block is encrypted with the Public Key of a Service Provider, only the specific Service Provider can decrypt it and thus identify the user. Consequently, each encryption is performed by the Service Provider that is responsible for the provision of the corresponding service. The number of these blocks must be at least equal to the number of Service Providers that offer their services electronically and not greater than the available electronic and Web 2.0 services.

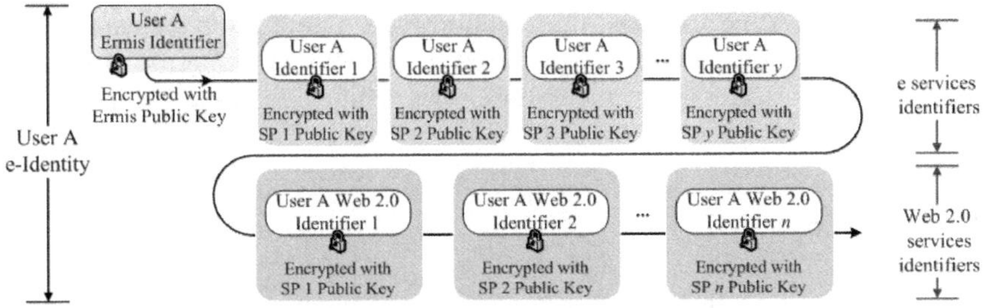

Fig. 2. User's Identifiers Bonding

5.2 Proposed Model of Operation

An overview of the operation of the proposed model and identification mechanism is provided in Figure 3 below. First, the user completes successfully the authentication procedure (*1*) and requests the Discussion Group *a* service (*2*). The authentication procedure depends on the Level of Trust that the specific service has been linked. After the Ermis portal has identified the user, through the aforementioned authentication procedure, it looks up which Service Provider is responsible for the provision of the requested service and knowing the sequence that the identifiers are stored, retrieves the appropriate encrypted identifier (*3*). The encrypted identifier and user's service request are forwarded to the corresponding Service provider (*4*). The Service Provider decrypts the identifier using his private encryption key and is now able to identify the user who requested the service (*5*). After user identification, the Service Provider can grant user access to the requested service (*6*) and thus the user can start interacting with the requested service (*7*).

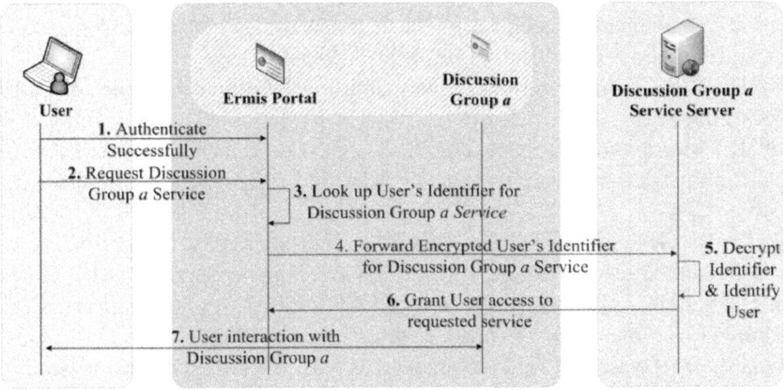

Fig. 3. User Identification in Proposed eGov 2.0 model

In cases where the user requests multiple services, the proposed model proves its efficiency and effectiveness. After a successful authentication the user can be identified by each Service Provider without the need to submit the corresponding identifier each time a new service is requested. Moreover, the authentication procedure is not directly related with the services, thus supporting Single Sign-On functionality. The compilation of user's e-identity, as proposed in Section 5.1, is performed every time the user completes successfully a registration procedure submitting, at the same time, the corresponding identifier.

6 Conclusions

Motivated by the belief that the employment of new governance models which utilize Web 2.0 capabilities will promote user participation and increase the overall effectiveness of the public sector, we have proposed an enhanced Greek e-Government 2.0 model. The expected results of this transition will be the improvement of quality and responsiveness of the Greek government policy making and service delivery.

However, the success of such a model does not solely lie on implementing and redesigning processes. A cultural change is necessary so that users will realize the extent of the participation they are allowed to, along with the responsibilities and obligations that come along with such involvement. As stated in an unofficial Australian Google group[3] "Government 2.0 is not specifically about social networking or technology … It represents a fundamental shift in the implementation of government — towards an open, collaborative, cooperative arrangement where there is (wherever possible) open consultation, open data, shared knowledge, mutual acknowledgment of expertise, mutual respect for shared values and an understanding of how to agree to disagree. Technology and social tools are an important part of this change but are essentially [just] an enabler in this process."

References

1. Osimo, D.: Benchmarking eGovernment in the Web 2.0 era: what to measure, and how. European Journal of ePractice 4 (2008) ISSN: 1988-625X
2. Osimo, D.: Web 2.0 in government: why and how? Technical Report. JRC, EUR 23358, EC JRC (2008)
3. Hoegg, R., Martignoni, R., Meckel, M., Stanoevska-Slabeva, K.: Overview of business models for Web 2.0 communities. In: Dresden (ed.) Proceedings of GeNeMe, pp. 23–37 (2006)
4. Drogkaris, P., Geneiatakis, D., Gritzalis, S., Lambrinoudakis, C., Mitrou, L.: Towards an Enhanced Authentication Framework for eGovernment Services: The Greek case. In: Ferro, E., Scholl, J., Wimmer, M. (eds.) EGOV 2008 7th International Conference on Electronic Government, pp. 189–196. Trauner Verlag (2008)
5. Ostergaard, D., Hvass, M.: eGovernment 2.0 – How can Government benefit from web 2.0? (2009)
6. German Federal Ministry of the Interior, eGovernment 2.0 The Programme of the Federal Government (2006)
7. Lundy, K.: Public Sphere 2: Government 2.0 Briefing Paper (2009)
8. Government 2.0 Best Practices Wiki, `http://government20bestpractices.pbworks.com`

[3] Australia Government 2.0 Google Group: `http://groups.google.com.au/group/gov20canberra`

9. Germany's Federal Ministry of the Interior in, titled eGovernment 2.0 – The programme of the Federal Government (2005)
10. EU i2010 – Information Society and the media working towards growth and jobs initiative (2006)
11. EU i2010 eGovernment Action Plan - Accelerating eGovernment in Europe for the Benefit of All (2006)
12. Obama, B.: Memorandum for the Heads of Executive Departments and Agencies Transparency and Open Government (2009)
13. Australian Government Information Management Office, Engage Getting on with Government 2.0 - Report of the Government 2.0 Taskforce (2009)
14. Seifert, J.: Reauthorization of the E-Government Act: A Brief Overview. CRS Report RL34492 (2008)
15. Baumgarten, J., Chui, M.: E-Government 2.0, Public Sector Practice (2009)
16. Eched, Y., Billiaert, E., Veyret, E.: e-Government 2.0 Identification, Security and Trust. Exploring European Avenues (2007)
17. Ofer, S.: Top Web 2.0 Security Threats, Secure Enterprise 2.0 Forum (2009)
18. Articles 8 & 2b of the Greek Data Protection Law (Law 2472/97), `http://www.dpa.gr`
19. Greek Constitution Articles 2 § 1 (human dignity) and 9 A (right to protection of personal data)
20. Suriadi, S., Foo, E., Jøsang, A.: A User-centric Federated Single Sign-on System. In: IFIP International Conference on Network and Parallel Computing – Workshops (2007)

Geographic e-Services Development through Product-Line Engineering and Standardization

Agustina Buccella* and Alejandra Cechich

GIISCO Research Group
Departamento de Ciencias de la Computación
Universidad Nacional del Comahue
Neuquen, Argentina
{abuccel,acechich}@uncoma.edu.ar

Abstract. Software product families provide an efficient means of reuse between a set of related products. Feature models have been widely adopted in domain requirements capturing and specifying. However, there are still few cases applying software product families to develop geographic services for citizens. This paper presents a framework that uses standard geographic information to model a product line. From this basis, it is possible to reuse different assets building new products easily. We illustrate the use of our framework through a case study that integrates geographic information of two governmental agencies.

Keywords: Geographic Information Systems, Software Product Lines, Services.

1 Introduction

Nowadays, information about geographic aspects is being regarded in both private and public entities. Specifically in public entities as municipalities or other governmental organizations, the set of new services that can be provided to ordinary citizens is really attractive. Services about finding a specific place on a map, or evacuation routes in case of a flooding can really improve the relation between citizens and the public state. Identifying this common set of services and making them flexible to be implemented by the organizations might help reduce costs in development, staffing, maintenance, etc. With this goal in mind, we looked at two main areas of different research lines: *software product line engineering* and *geographic information systems (GIS)*.

The software product line engineering (SPLE) has emerged from the advances in the software architecture area. Here, a system decomposition into high-level components is defined by considering the concepts of reuse and of family of products (introduced firstly by Parnas [1] in 1976). The main characteristics involved in the SPLE discipline are [2]: *variability*, in which individual systems

* This work is partially supported by the UNComa project 04/E072 (Identificación, Evaluación y Uso de Composiciones Software).

K.N. Andersen et al. (Eds.): EGOVIS 2010, LNCS 6267, pp. 150–157, 2010.

are considered as variations of a common part; and *commonality*, in which the software must be developed by considering the similarities among individual systems.

In the second area to be analyzed, GIS have emerged to allow the storage and manipulation of geographic information in spatial domains or with geographic characteristics. There have been many research and industrial efforts to standardize many aspects of GIS technology, particularly by the Open Geospatial Consortium[1] (OGC) and the ISO Technical Committee 211[2] (ISO/TC 211, Geographic Information/Geomatics).

In this work we define a methodology for creating software product lines for GIS applications by combining the advantages of two widely referenced methodologies in the literature [3,4]. The main goal is to create a software product line taking into account a set of common services of GIS software. The implementation of software product line tries to help new and previous GIS applications by joining development efforts in the creation of geographic systems. Development and maintenance costs, and time-to-market are reduced because several services are already implemented. In addition, quality of the products is improved due to components are previously tested. Our work emerged as a solution to different public organizations that implement geographic services to citizens in North Patagonia.

This paper is organized as follows: next Section presents related work in the literature and describes our methodology to create the product-line for GIS applications. Then, we describe the instantiation of the product line applied to an integration project. Future work and conclusions are discussed afterwards.

2 A Software Product Line Specification

Our proposal combines two different research lines in which several works can be found. Within the first research line, the GIS development includes the defiition of several standards. The two main organizations working on defining them are the OGC and ISO. For many years, these two organizations had worked independently to reach overlapping goals, but nowadays both converge towards a common solution. The ISO/TC 211 deals with long-term, abstract, static standards, and the OGC works on industry-oriented, technology-dependent, evolving standards. Thus, the development of GIS applications can be done by following these standards in order to improve the interoperability among systems. However, special efforts must be done to reach effective reuse.

The other research line proposes different methodologies for SPLE. In the literature there exists several techniques proposing methodologies to develop a software product-line. Some of the most referenced proposals in the literature are [3,5,2,4]. All of them propose a division into common and variable aspects of the product line, and a set of tasks or activities that must be done to specify and implement these aspects. Other recent proposals are analyzed in [6].

[1] `http://www.opengeospatial.org`

[2] `http://www.isotc211.org/`

To the best of our knowledge, the two sets of work, GIS standards and software product lines, are not related in the literature. In this way, our work is based on the creation of a software product line to be used by several public organizations that are interested in implementing geographic services. Geographic software shares a set of common services that are essential for every application. These common services must be identified and modeled as part of the product line together with different variations. In addition, each product of the line contains a set of product-specific services that are not part of the line. Each organization will be responsible for instantiating the architecture in order to fulfill its own requirements.

In order to build the software product line we combined characteristics of two methodologies defined in [3,4]. The main process to be performed, named *domain engineering process*, is modified from the software product line engineering framework defined in [4]. Within this framework we define a different set of six subprocesses by applying activities defined in both methodologies. Figure 1 shows these subprocesses together with their main tasks.

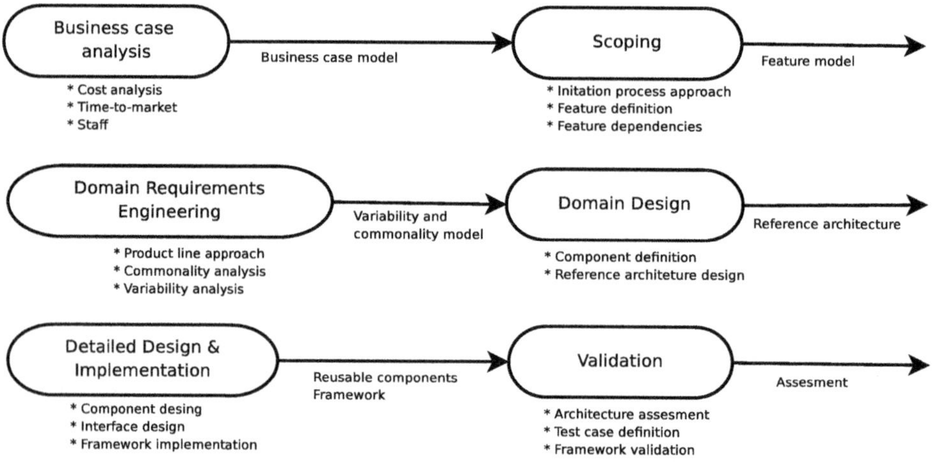

Fig. 1. Domain engineering process

Following, we briefly describe how these tasks were applied to create the software product line for a GIS application.

- *Business case analysis*: To perform this subprocess, the situation of the different organizations was analyzed. In general, only few municipalities had applications involving geographic information. They had used software tools only for administration tasks and some of them had only a web portal with static information. Therefore, the costs and staff needed were analyzed by taking into account two main phases. In the first one, we analyzed the aspects needed to implement the product line and its supporting application framework. In the second phase, we analyzed what we needed to implement future product lines by the instantiation of the framework. The outputs of this subprocess are two business models considering these two aspects.

- *Scoping*: We applied an evolutionary approach as a starting point for the development of the product line architecture. In this way, we started from a set of existing software products. However, considering the aspects analyzed in the previous subprocess, we could not take the organizations' software products, which were incomplete and unreliable. Instead, we used a set of geographic open source software tools for GIS providing features needed by our architecture. To do so, we analyzed several open source tools (extracted from Internet) in order to know the set of services that they provide. Then, we defined the features that were candidate for inclusion in the product line by using firstly the ISO 19119 standard. Table 1 shows part of the resultant features; for brevity reasons we do not include here all of them.

Table 1. Geographic services required by our architecture

Categories	Service	Specific Features
Geographic human interaction	S1. Geographic viewer	S1.1) Show and query data of geographic features. S1.2) Show/hide layers. S1.3) Zoom tool. S1.4) Panning tool. S1.5) Scale. S1.6) Navigation buttons (previous/next)
	S2. Geographic feature editor	S2.1) See, query and edit geographic features graphically. S2.2) Add new geographic features by using the graphic interface
Geographic model/information management services	S3. Feature type service	S3.1) Use a metadata catalogue to reach integrability retrieving information about geographic features
	S4. Feature access service	S4.1) Perform queries to a geographic feature repository. S4.2) Manage data of the geographic features
	S5. Map access service	S5.1) Access to geographic maps
	S6. Gazetteer service	S6.1) Access to instances of a class or classes of real-world phenomena
Spatial processing services	S7. Proximity analysis service	S7.1) Obtain all geographic features within a specific area
Metadata processing services	S8. Statistical calculation service	S8.1) Generate statistics with data of geographic features
	S9. Geographic annotation services	S9.1) Add additional information to a geographic features. S9.2) Add additional information to a map

- *Domain requirements engineering*: We used a minimalist approach in which only the features used in all products are part of the product line. This approach allowed us to fully implement only common features and let the product-specific features be implemented by each different organization. Thus, our software product line is seen as a *platform* [3]. Table 2 shows the subset of features that are part of the product-line and the subset of features that are product-specific features.

Table 2. Features that are part of the product-line and specific-product features

Products/Features	S1	S2	S3	S4	S5	S6	S7	S8	S9
Product-line	X	X		X	X	X	X	X	
Product 1			X						
Product 2									X

As we can observe, features S1, S2, and S4-S8 are part of the product-line. S3 is a product-specific feature that will be implemented only by Product 1, and S9 is part only of Product 2. Remember that each of these products belongs to different municipalities or agencies; thus, each of them has to face the costs for implementing the product-specific features. In addition, within each feature we determined the commonality and variability models. For example, for the feature S8.1, the variability model describes the two variants of implementing statistics by using histograms or tables.

- *Domain design*: We reorganized the features into two sets of requirements to separate functional from non-functional (quality) needs. These sets were the basis to define our architecture's components. We chose a layered architectural style to facilitate dealing with modifiability and scalability requirements. Then, the reference architecture is composed of three main layers: the *geographic model layer*, in which we implemented the geographic model that allows the access to a geographic database; the *geographic processing layer*, in which features involving processing are implemented (features S4-S8); and the *user interface layer*, in which we implemented the S1-S2 features involving graphical aspects.
- *Detailed design and Implementation*: In addition to defininig the architecture of the product line, we created an application framework to be used as a platform for each product of the product line. The framework covers the behaviour that is common for all products and allow developers to add the product-specific features.
- *Validation*: There are several aspects to analyze within this subprocess. Firstly, some test cases were defined in order to test the framework and the specification of the product line. Secondly, we tested the instantiation of the product line by creating a new GIS product (as we will describe in the next section). The instantiation allowed us to test the application of our framework and the effectiveness of the development process. Some conclusions of these aspects are described afterwards.

3 Instantiating the Product Line: A Case Study

In this section we show an instantiation of the product-line previously described. In this case, we build the Product 1 (Table 2) containing features of the product line plus a set of product-specific ones (S3). Product 1 emerges from an integration project between two public organizations, which manage overlapped and non-overlapped geographic information of several areas of the Neuquén Province, Argentina. One of the organizations is the AIC (Autoridad Interjurisdiccional de Cuencas) entity that is in charge of managing, controlling, using and preserving the basins of the rivers Neuquén, Limay and Negro in Patagonia, Argentine. The covered area includes the Río Negro, Neuquén and part of Buenos Aires provinces (about 140.000 Km^2 representing the 5 % of the Argentinean total territory). The other organization is the Provincial Office of Territorial Cadaster (DPCT - Dirección Provincial de Catastro Territorial), which stores all information about buildings, streets, and parcels of the Neuquén Province (about 94.068 Km^2).

The main goal of our project is to create an integrated system in which both organizations work together providing a set of services to citizens. Table 3 shows the features of Table 1 redefined according to the requirements of the product. For example, the feature S1.1 is redefined as a set of new features (a-c) to show different geographic features of the sources; and the feature S1.2 allows the user to show and hide layers. In this product we implement four layers – rivers, shorelines, buildings, and roads. For brevity reasons, we only include here a subset of the instantiated features within each feature category.

Following, the variability models must be also instantiated. For example, the feature S8.1 is implemented by using histograms (not by using a table). Finally, we have to create the architecture based on the reference architecture defined in the last section. In this case, two new layers and new components are added to the reference architecture. As this product is based on integrated sources, an integration process of geographic sources (AIC and DPCT) must be firstly performed. In previous works [7,8] we have proposed an semi-automatic integration approach, which we applied here by using a *feature type information* component implementing the S3 feature to obtain metadata of the geographic features of the sources.

Then, the architecture of Product 1 is used to provide a set of different services to citizens [7]. As an example, we describe here one of them, the *Flood Areas* service. It returns information about flood areas within a specific area. The input of the service is an area of interest defined by the user (represented by a bounding box, circle or polygon), which must include a river section. The service uses the concepts of a shared vocabulary in which the information about rivers and neighborhoods must be overlapped to determine which buildings are within a flood area. The flood area is calculated from the shorelines of a river basin which are determined by the AIC entity and the governments of the provinces the river crosses. The output of the service is a combination of three main layers: *the river and shoreline* layers determining the flood area, and *the building* layer determining the buildings that are within it. Thus, it is possible to know

Table 3. Instantiated features required in Product 1

Categories	Service	Instantiated Features
Geographic human interaction	S1. Geographic viewer	S1.1) a) Show roads. b) Show a specific neighborhood. c) Show data about public entities. d).. S1.2) a) Show/hide the building layer. b) Show/hide the river layer. c)...
	S2. Geographic feature editor	S2.1) a) Show a map with the river basins b).... S2.2) a) Add new evacuation roads. b) Add new shorelines. c)...
Geographic model/information management services	S3. Feature type service	S3.1) a) Retrieve information about geographic feature datatypes of two geographic sources b) Retrieve information of relations of geographic features. c)...
	S4. Feature access service	S4.1) a) Query thematic attributes of public buildings. b) Query the places a river crosses. c) Query the shoreline of a river. d)...
	S5. Map access service	S5.1) a) Allow to create an image of the building map. b) ...
	S6. Gazetteer service	S6.1) a) Obtain the location of public organisms. b)...
Spatial processing services	S7. Proximity analysis service	S7.1) a) Obtain the river and the buildings and roads within a specific area. b)...
Metadata processing services	S8. Statistical calculation service	S8.1) Generate a bar chart with information of the flooding within a period. b)...

which neighborhoods are in danger of flooding when the river flow increases. In addition, this service help citizens to know which areas next to the river are not allowed to live in. Figure 2 shows the output map when a user executes the *flood area* service. As we can observe, red lines denote the shorelines of the Limay River and the set of building (or neighborhoods) that are in danger of flooding. In this case, the buildings are painted with red color.

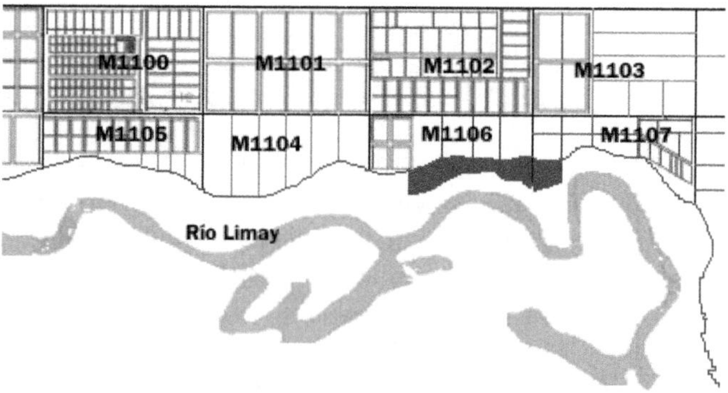

Fig. 2. A map representing the output of the Flood Area service

4 Conclusion and Future Work

In this work we have introduced a framework for building geographic information systems from a software product line, and we have illustrated the process through a case study. Our main goal is to reduce the development effort involved in the creation of this type of systems for government agencies. In this way, two main requirements of every GIS software might be fulfilled. On one hand, *flexibility* might be improved because new products can easily perform changes in the requirements by means of instantiating variable aspects of services. On the other hand, *reusability* might be reached because components of the architecture are created for that purpose.

As future work, the methodology and the framework need more validation, but we are aware that developing management guidelines is also crucial for sucessfully applying the approach.

References

1. Parmas, D.: On the design and development of program families. IEEE Transactions on Software Engineering SE-2(1), 1–9 (1976)
2. Van Der Linden, F., Schmid, K., Rommes, E.: Software Product Lines in Action: The Best Industrial Practice in Product Line Engineering. Springer, New York (2007)
3. Bosch, J.: Design and use of software architectures: adopting and evolving a product-line approach. ACM Press/Addison-Wesley Publishing Co., New York (2000)
4. Pohl, K., Böckle, G., van der Linden, F.: Software Product Line Engineering: Foundations, Principles and Techniques. Springer, Heidelberg (2005)
5. Clements, P., Northrop, L.: Software Product Lines: Practices and Patterns. Addison-Wesley Professional, Reading (2001)
6. Matinlassi, M.: Comparison of software product line architecture design methods: Copa, fast, form, kobra and qada. In: Proceedings of the ICSE '04: 26th International Conference on Software Engineering, pp. 127–136. IEEE Computer Society Press, Los Alamitos (2004)
7. Buccella, A., Cechich, A.: A semantic-based architecture for supporting geographic e-services. In: Proceedings of the ICEGOV'09: 3rd International Conference on Theory and Practice of Electronic Governance. ACM International Conference Proceeding Series, vol. 322, pp. 27–35. ACM, New York (2009)
8. Buccella, A., Cechich, A., Gendarmi, D., Lanubile, F., Semeraro, G., Colagrossi, A.: GeoMergeP: Geographic information integration through enriched ontology matching. New Generation Computing 28(4) (2010)
9. Buccella, A., Cechich, A., Fillotrani, P.: Ontology-driven geographic information integration: A survey of current approaches. Computers & Geosciences Special Issue on Geoscience Knowledge Representation in Cyberinfrastructure 35(4) (2009)

Governmeter: Monitoring Government Performance. A Web Based Application Proposal

Artur Afonso Sousa[1], Pedro Agante[2], and Luís Borges Gouveia[3]

[1] Polytechnic Institute of Viseu, Viseu, Portugal
ajas@di.estv.ipv.pt
[2] Libertrium, Viseu, Portugal
pedroagante@libertrium.com
[3] University Fernando Pessoa, Porto, Portugal
lmbg@ufp.edu.pt

Abstract. Governmeter is an innovative Web application that provides the opportunity for citizens to follow and monitor the national and local government in an easy and convenient way. The Governmeter allows monitoring in relation to three aspects: key statistical indicators, government objectives, and government measures. This paper presents the main functionalities of this application, which we believe will contribute to a higher engagement of the general community and its citizens in the political deliberation.

Keywords: Governmeter, eDemocracy, eParticipation, Deliberation.

1 Introduction

The current economic and social conjuncture appeals to civic engagement and politicians seek to recover public confidence and interest in the democratic process. The Internet's potential for increasing political participation has been debated in the last years [1, 2]. Although skeptics exist [3, 4], we believe that Internet-based technologies have the ability to change and improve the way all stakeholders in the democratic process interact with each other.

In the emerging field of e-democracy, there are several applications using the Internet as an enabling starting point [5]. Within this context, we propose a specific platform, Liberopinion (available at http://www.liberopinion.pt), consisting of a group of online applications covering the main issues of the democratic process with the aim of addressing the major problems faced by all its stakeholders.

At this point, the Liberopinion platform supports two different web applications: Elections and Governmeter. The former, based in the close interaction between voters and candidates of an election, enables voters to submit questions and send proposals, by topics, directly to all candidates. It is then possible, in a single place, to compare and debate the candidates' answers in order to clarify the voting decision. Current work and use of the Elections application, in particular results from the recent Portuguese national and local elections, has been reported in [6].

K.N. Andersen et al. (Eds.): EGOVIS 2010, LNCS 6267, pp. 158–165, 2010.

In this paper, we describe the other Web application of the platform, Governmeter, designed to monitor and debate, in an independent and objective way, the governmental and legislative activity.

The Governmeter application was developed at a national level. However, it is important to note that the same monitoring concepts and principles are equally applicable to local governments with minor modifications. In this case it is possible to monitor the performance in the same way as in national level, for instance the measures undertaken by the local government can be monitored and their objectives can be listed and verified.

Traditional actors covering assessment of Government performance include: political parties, traditional media, unions, groups of interest, among others. Typically, these actors take advantage of general purpose technological tools such as TV, blogs, newspaper, and political websites. However, these usually suffer from ideology and political bias and cannot be considered as an objective and reliable source for assessment of the Government's performance. The media have also taken the task of political fact-checking with the objective of monitoring governing politicians [7]. However, the role of citizens is very limited, being the analysis and conclusions usually drawn exclusively by journalists or political analysts supporting in a very limited manner, if any, the citizen's point of view. For fulfilling these gaps, we propose the Governmeter.

Governmeter is a Web application based on eParticipation [8] that seeks to provide the citizen with a straightforward and clear way of following and monitoring the government performance in relation to three main areas: key statistical indicators, government objectives, and government measures. Within these areas the citizens will find a place for civilized and structured debate about questions such as: how is the country evolving in different areas (economy, health care, education, justice) in light of the corresponding key statistical indicators? Are the objectives defined by the government in its electoral program being fulfilled? Are the measures proposed by the government good or bad for the country?

We consider that it would be convenient to have an online presence that promotes, in a single, neutral and civilized place, ongoing monitoring and debate about the government activity in the three main areas specified above.

The open debate fostered by this website allows the community to present all points of view that could help the analysis of the three components cited above, the indicators, the government objectives and government measures. It is not the objective of Governmeter to directly answer these questions but to provide all relevant information to do so. The final answers themselves are left to each citizen.

This paper is structured as follows: Section 2 describes the major functionalities of Liberopinion-Governmeter, while section 3 describes future work. Finally, the section 4 presents the paper conclusions.

2 Governmeter

The report "Government online" made by The Pew Research Center refers that almost one-quarter of online Americans (23 percent) have participated in online debates concerning government issues by publishing their own commentary or media, attending an online town hall meeting, or joining an online group focused on influence government policies, although much of that is currently occurring outside of the context of "official government channels" [9]. This is the case of Governmeter.

The Governmeter is a Web application that provides the citizen with an easy and clear way of following and monitoring the government activity in relation to three aspects:

1) Evolution and analysis of key statistical indicators;

2) Monitoring and analysis of government objectives;

3) Monitoring and analysis of government measures.

A key feature of this application is the information architecture. All sections, indicators, government objectives and measures are organized according to governmental areas. This way the users will always be faced with a familiar structure and can immediately identify the governmental unit responsible for the visited section. The idea is to provide a simple and straightforward relationship between those governmental areas and the organic structure of the government (both at primary level – ministers, and second level – secretaries of state; which compounds the top structure of Portuguese executive government).

The Governmeter comprises also features that allow social and citizen interconnection: any citizen can follow other citizen's analysis, whereby when a followed citizen submits a new analysis, the follower will receive a notification of such event with direct access to that analysis; a particular analysis submitted can also be followed, in which case, any new comment to it will trigger a notification to all citizens that signaled their interest in following that particular analysis. For convenience, it is possible to filter from the list of analysis the ones that a registered user is following, enabling the user to monitor and visualize in a convenient way the most relevant analysis to that particular user.

Since all data displayed such as Government objectives and measures strongly depend on the economic, political and social context, in each item, there is an extensive analysis section that supports any relevant contextual information. The data used in the Governmeter is retrieved from publicly available data sources. For statistical indicators these include the Portuguese National Statistics Institute and Eurostat, whereas for the government measures and objectives are retrieved from official Government publications and electoral programs. As for the data produced by the Governmeter users in the form of comments, it is publicly available.

Fig. 1 illustrates the main functionalities and actors of the Liberopinion platform and two of its applications (Elections and Governmeter). The platform consists of enabling solutions that are seamless integrated and used across e-democracy applications, as well as custom development to meet specific needs of the stakeholders involved in democratic process. These common solutions include debate, moderation, rating, user management, social networking, and all reusable across applications, whereas the custom development addresses technical solutions about specific aspects of the democratic process such as elections and government performance.

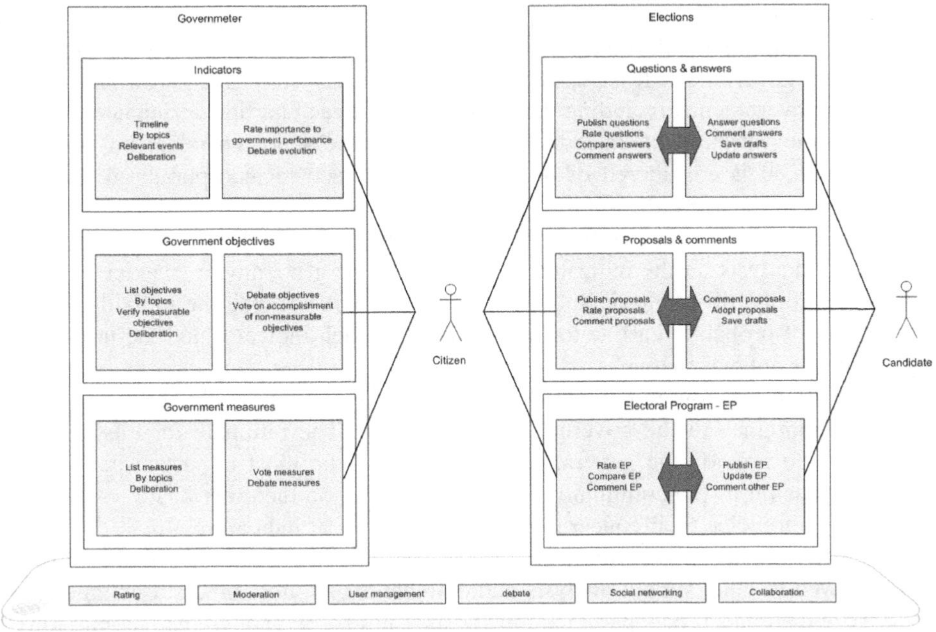

Fig. 1. Liberopinion platform and applications

It is important to note that in the Liberopinion platform we regard citizens as consumers as well as producers of information. In Fig. 1, it can be observed that a citizen, as a producer, can submit questions and present their suggestions to political actors and provide his opinion about the government activity. As a consumer, a citizen can analyze and compare the different proposals and information from all political actors. On the other hand, politicians in this platform act not only as producers when they present, for instance electoral programs and comments, but also as consumers when they receive feedback from questions, suggestions, concerns and comments sent by citizens. In summary, in the Liberopinion platform there is a real bidirectional communication between citizens and politicians, and potentially other actors involved in the democratic process.

Next, we will present in more detail the major features of Governmeter.

2.1 Key Statistical Indicators

In this area of the platform, it is foreseen that the citizens can find their answers to important questions: how is the country or region evolving according to key statistical indicators? What are the indicators the community believes to be most important? Did these key indicators improved or not during the current government? Why did the indicators evolved in such way? To which degree is the government responsible to the indicator's evolution?

Each indicator is associated with a chart where the values over time are depicted. A differentiating factor in relation to conventional reports from public institutions is the overlay of additional information along with the indicator value. In a first stage, the chart illustrates the ruling period for the current and past governments, as well as values in important milestones, government change and the date of inauguration of the current government. It is possible therefore to easily verify the performance of the different governments, including the current one, for each particular indicator.

Since the variation of an indicator is to a great extent dependent on contextual information, it is considered of the utmost importance to incorporate an "analysis" component with each indicator.

Moreover, deliberation is fostered by enabling the general community to provide their own analysis on the indicator in the light of the government or external actions [10]. Hopefully, different viewpoints and analysis will provide the individual citizen with a set of probable reasons for the behavior of each indicator and the influence of government policies therein.

In addition, the community is also encouraged to vote, in a scale of 0 to 5, the indicator's importance to the government performance. The rationale for this is, on the one hand, to provide the government with a list of the most important performance indicators as far as the community is concerned, and, on the other hand, to enable the community to voice their concern about the relevancy of indicators.

In order to actively contribute and participate in this website, only registered users are allowed to vote, submit analysis and comments or follow others users and analysis. To encourage broad participation the possibility of anonymous submissions is also foreseen [11]. All substantive contributions such as analysis and comments are subject to moderation to prevent misuse or abuse, independent whether they are anonymously submitted or not [12].

2.2 Government Objectives

In this area, the list of objectives of the government are monitored and deliberated upon according to different governmental sections, including economy, education, health care, justice, among others. The objective of this section is to find answers to the following questions: Are the objectives set by the government being fulfilled? What is the importance of these objectives?

The objectives include the ones from the electoral program presented by the political party in power, as well as the ones defined during the legislative period in the face of new problems faced by the government. It is considered important to represent this distinction in the website, so that the electoral program can be verified by a check list of the government objectives as defined by the political party for the legislature.

According to their nature, objectives are divided into measurable and immeasurable objectives. The measurable objectives are monitored being the current value for that objective monitored and the government target displayed, along with the deadline when available. Examples of objectives falling into this category could be: public deficit lower than 3% of the GDP by 2013, unemployment lower than 4% of active population, GDP above 2% at the end of the year, and so on.

In relation to the immeasurable objectives, they are listed and made available for deliberation among the community to judge in which measure are these objectives being fulfilled and how. These objectives could be: improve health care system, better access to information technology, among others.

As in the indicators section, each objective has an associated analysis component where the community can expose their point of view about whether the objective has been fulfilled and present reasons why. All analyses are subject to rating by all users and the filtering and ordering possibilities cited for the indicators also apply. The community is also enabled to present comments on these analyses, supporting this way a structured debate around the government objectives.

It is not an objective of this section to reach conclusions about the government achievements. These conclusions are left to the community and to the individual citizen. On the other hand, it is objectively possible to account for the measurable government objectives.

2.3 Government Measures

The third section is dedicated to the government measures. In this section, the actions and decisions made by the government in different governmental areas are monitored and open for discussion. It is an objective of this section to help the citizen answer the following questions: are the government measures good or bad for the country? How important are they and how can I voice my support to them?

Covering all major government departments, the measures are permanently monitored, listed and open for debate among the community. The application is completely independent from any political site and is completely agnostic about the analysis being published by the community members. The main objective is to provide the means for the community to debate in a structured and open way all measures being proposed by the government and deliberate their advantages and disadvantages. In order to assess the community opinion, registered voters can rate their support to the measures and how important they are to them.

The measures include the ones proposed in the electoral program, as well as the ones undertaken during the legislative period. The measures included in the electoral program are highlighted, enabling easy verification whether they have been executed and to which extent. This serves in addition as an indication of the measures still to be implemented according to the proposals during the electoral campaign.

Besides the measures proposed by the government, this tool is also suitable for incorporating the measures proposed by the political parties with chair in the parliament. Similarly to known e-rulemaking approaches [13], it is possible to achieve a comprehensive and time-framed debate about each measure, from the moment of its proposal to the time it is approved by parliament and, when applicable, by the President.

This section comprises a zone for the community to analyze the measures and provide feedback on their approval. For that, the citizen can provide the advantages and disadvantages which, in the citizen's point of view, are associated with each measure. This way it is possible to collaborative compile in a single place the set of advantages and disadvantages to the measures proposed and implemented by the government as identified by the civil society.

3 Future Work

In a project as ambitious as this, there are certainly many improvements possible and many directions for future development and research.

Seamless integration of the platform with existing social networks is also of paramount importance for this project [14]. For this reason, it will be possible for a citizen to publish his analysis and comments to Facebook and Twitter directly from the Governmeter. This will therefore result in an open deliberation interface designed to foster citizen participation.

Data produced is of public domain. Under the consent of the data creator, in the future, all data is planned to be accessed either by a web service or by a public API in order to encourage data mash up with other applications.

Another identified area of future work is the interconnection of the three different areas and the user interface providing semantic meaning to it. For instance, each indicator chart could have associated one or several government measures meaningful to the performance of that indicator, or an objective can comprise a set of measures that contribute to its achievement or, in case measurable objectives are present, they can be graphically depicted in the corresponding indicator. Methods to derive such relationship and criteria for semantically associating the three areas are also a key topic for future research.

Along with monitoring of government measures and proposals, one of the important directions of future work concerns the channels used by citizens to provide their own proposals to problems faced by the government, either by suggestions on how an indicator could be improved or by providing alternatives to the proposals presented by the government. This would direct the website to higher degree of interaction and participation between civil society and government.

4 Conclusion

We believe Internet-based tools to support eDemocracy such as the one presented will become mainstream, and will provide a significant contribution to reverse the current disengagement from political debate [15].

In traditional democratic systems, citizens express their opinion and viewpoint in discrete moments by casting a vote in elections or referenda. We believe that an online presence that promotes and encourages continuous citizen participation will create a new independent, structured and collaborative medium for democratic innovation and will contribute to restore public confidence and interest in the democratic process. In the light of these principles we propose a new monitoring tool for analyzing the government performance according to three parameters: key statistical indicators, the objectives set by the government and the measures taken by the government.

Through rating of the government measures and objectives, in addition to the analysis submitted by the plurality of citizens, it is possible to derive a community-based comprehensive perspective on how the government is performing.

Many open questions and future research topics arise from the challenging goals of this project. These range from what should be the role and scope of user moderation, management of possibly large quantity of historical data from ongoing and past analysis and comments, how to achieve high degree of usability and efficient information architecture, among others.

In conclusion, we hope tools such as the one presented in this paper will contribute for a closer relationship between the political sphere and the civil society, and a higher degree of engagement of the citizen in the ongoing political issues managed by the local and national government. We are deeply convinced that the Governmeter Web application can be an effective tool for engaging the community in structured deliberation about the performance of an elected government.

References

1. Coleman, S., Blumer, J.: The Internet and Democratic Citizenship - Theory, Practice and Policy, pp. 166–197. Cambridge University Press, Cambridge (2009)
2. Chadwick, A., Howard, P.: New Directions in Internet Politics Research. In: Chadwick, A., Howard, P. (eds.) The Routledge Handbook of Internet Politics, pp. 1–9. Routledge, Taylor & Francis Group (2010)
3. Putnam, R.D.: Bowling Alone: The Collapse and Revival of American Community. Simon & Schuster, New York (2000)
4. Sunstein, C.R.: Republic. com. Princeton University Press, Princeton (2001)
5. Participate DB, `http://participatedb.com/projects` (accessed June 8, 2010)
6. Afonso Sousa, A., Agante, P., Borges Gouveia, L.: Liberopinion as an enabling Platform for Elections 2.0. In: Proceedings of the 8th Eastern European eGov Days 2010: Changing Concepts & eGovernment as a Service, Prague, Czech Republic (2010)
7. Polifact, `http://www.politifact.com/` (accessed June 9, 2010)
8. Macintosh, A., Coleman, S., Schneeberger, A.: eParticipation: The Research Gaps. In: Macintosh, A., Tambouris, E. (eds.) ePART 2009. LNCS, vol. 5694, pp. 1–11. Springer, Heidelberg (2009)
9. Smith, A.: Government online. Pew Research Center (2010)
10. Coleman, S., Gøtze, J.: Bowling Together - Online Public Engagement in Policy Deliberation. Information Polity 7(4), 247–252 (2002)
11. Peixoto, T.: Beyond Theory: e-Participatory Budgeting and its Promises for eParticipation. European Journal of ePractice 7, 55–63 (2009)
12. Wright, S.: Government-run Online Discussion Fora: Moderation, Censorship and the Shadow of Control. British Journal of Politics and International Relations 8(4), 550–568 (2006)
13. Schlosberg, D., Zavestoski, S., Shulman, S.: Democracy and E-Rulemaking: Web-Based Technologies, Participation, and the Potential for Deliberation. Journal of Information Technology & Politics 4(1), 37–55 (2007)
14. Taylor-Smith, E., Lindner, R.: Using Social Networking Tools to Promote eParticipation Initiatives. In: Prosser, A., Parycek, P. (eds.) Proceedings of EDEM 2009 - Conference on Electronic Democracy, Vienna, pp. 115–121 (2009)
15. Macintosh, A., Davenport, E., Malina, A., Whyte, A.: Technology to Support Participatory Democracy. In: Gronlund, A. (ed.) Electronic Government: Design, Applications & Management. Idea Group Publishing (2002)

Policy Incentives for Innovation Diffusion: An Agent-Based Simulation

Enrico Ferro[1], Brunella Caroleo[2], Marco Cantamessa[2], and Maurizio Leo[2]

[1] Istituto Superiore Mario Boella, Technology to Business Intelligence Unit,
Via Boggio 61, 10138 Torino, Italy
enrico.ferro@ismb.it
www.enricoferro.com
[2] Politecnico di Torino, Department of Production Systems and Business Economics,
Corso Duca degli Abruzzi 24, 10129 Torino, Italy
{brunella.caroleo,marco.cantamessa,maurizio.leo}@polito.it

Abstract. Policy makers are increasingly required to play a proactive role in the stimulation of innovation creation and diffusion. Such a role poses serious challenges having to do with the design and implementation of effective policies, which requires a deep understanding of diffusion processes.

This paper presents an agent-based decision support tool for policy makers, providing useful insights in the design of incentive policies aimed at maximizing the diffusion of a generic innovation among a population of potential adopters. Such public intervention is tested in an agent-based framework in order to assess its efficiency and effectiveness.

The results show the opportunity to give incentives in order to stimulate a particular diffusive phenomenon, giving useful insights to policy makers as regards the target to address specific policies.

Keywords: Diffusion of innovation, incentives, policy simulation, agent-based simulation, ICT governance.

1 Introduction

The diffusion of Information and Communication Technologies (ICTs) coupled with the increase of the competitive pressure brought by globalization have significantly contributed to make a high level of innovation absorption capacity an essential ingredient for the competitiveness of any socioeconomic system. At the same time, the strain on government budgets - recently exacerbated by the world wide economic crisis - calls for a more efficient and effective allocation of public resources, leaving very little room for mistakes.

Policy makers are thus required to play a proactive role in the stimulation of innovation creation and diffusion. This role requires the development of policy intelligence skills, including the potential impact of alternative policy measures. In this scenario, the possibility to conduct *what-if* analyses could become very important for

K.N. Andersen et al. (Eds.): EGOVIS 2010, LNCS 6267, pp. 166–173, 2010.

avoiding unaffordable and costly mistakes. However, making this kind of analysis familiar to policy makers requires a significant reduction in the complexity linked with the use of simulation tools.

In this perspective, Agent-Based Simulation (ABS) constitutes a good candidate, since 'agents are a natural and powerful ontology for many social problems' [1] and because of its flexibility. Agent-based simulation models enable policy makers to easily build alternative policy scenarios and to evaluate them, thus constituting a decision support tool that allows a low-cost exploration and evaluation of different policy alternatives.

Starting from these considerations, this paper deals with the effectiveness and efficiency of policies aimed at accelerating diffusion of a given technology. To this aim, a policy based on variable monetary incentives is implemented and simulated in an agent-based framework. Such policy is assessed based on the estimation of utility produced as a function of the aggregate economic costs and benefits produced over time.

The article is structured as follows: in the next Section a brief review of the literature on policy analysis and simulation is proposed; Section 3 focuses on the model, describing how and under which assumptions the agent-based model works; the monetary incentive policy is introduced and a policy measurement procedure is proposed. Finally, some preliminary results and conclusions are drawn, and some implications for further research and practice are discussed.

2 Literature Review

The subjects discussed in this paper lie at the intersection of four literature strands: technological diffusion of innovation, policy analysis, policy simulation and the literature on incentives management.

The literature on technological diffusion of innovation is wide and abundant. Surely Rogers' theory [2] and Bass model [3] are among the milestones as far as the literature on the diffusion of innovation is concerned. The Bass framework has been applied in various contexts and fields to model technological diffusion and to analytically forecast adoption patterns [4, 5]. Some authors, starting from Bass framework, have recently derived agent-based models to study and analyze the *S*-shaped curve of diffusion [6, 7], thus simulating and forecasting the adoption process.

Concerning policy analysis in the field of technological diffusion, literature review shows that several rigorous tools have been proposed for quantitative policy analysis, but few of them have been successfully used for a complete analysis: this is mainly due to the complexity of such systems. Furthermore, few inquiries have been made into the status and the impacts of policy practices for technology diffusion [8]. Some attempts are present, for instance, in studying the impact and effectiveness of scenario planning in public policy making [9].

Conventional research methods and tools used in traditional policy analysis [10] e.g. statistical analysis, economic models and linear programming, have been effective in identifying relevant factors and patterns at a certain time and in a given context. Given that policy analysis requires substantial contextual knowledge, policy analysis tools need to be flexible in incorporating such contextual knowledge in many different policy settings [11]. Both the unsuitability of sophisticated modeling formalisms to address such problems of policy science and the need of a what-if approach could be overcome by policy simulation [12].

Policy simulation models are useful because "they accelerate creation of scenarios, allow rapid changes in parameters, and provide a test bed for concepts and strategies" [13]; furthermore, they can assist policy makers in prioritizing and targeting policy interventions [14]. Several authors found in Agent-based Simulation (ABS) a good tool to deal with policy simulation [1, 15].

As regards the specific case of incentives as a policy tool to promote the diffusion of a certain technology, the literature is wide, especially the context of environmental and energy-related technology [16-18]. Contributors to these strands of literature agree that economic incentive-based instruments (e.g., pollution taxes and tradable pollution permits) can provide more efficient incentives for technology adoption than conventional regulations (e.g., technology and performance standards), but these conclusions could be strictly context-dependent. Finally, little or no theoretical work at all has been performed on the influence of incentive parameters (e.g., time and duration of incentives, target categories to whom incentives should be addressed, etc.) on the efficacy and effectiveness of a policy.

3 The Model

This model simulates the adoption rate of a new technology in a population of agents and aims to recreate at a macro level the diffusion mechanisms described by Bass [3] starting from the modeling of the behavior of each agent at a micro level, thus allowing a finer level of detail than the one achievable with differential equations. A brief description of the model framework is given in the next section.

3.1 The Model Framework

Each agent represents an individual decision maker, whose adoption decision depends -as in the Bass model- on the relationship with the technology supplier (i.e. the so-called innovative diffusion effect) and on the interactions with the other agents (i.e. the imitative, or word-of-mouth, effect).

The state variable of the dynamic system is represented by each agent's attitude to adoption $0 < A_j(t) < 1$, that could be interpreted as the utility that agent j perceives to gain at time t by adopting the technology. We suppose that the price of the technology is 1, so that when $A_j(t) = 1$, the agent becomes an adopter. Heterogeneity in the population is represented by the distribution of this state variable across agents at the start of the simulation. Attitude to innovation can be correlated to physical location, thus emulating both populations in which different classes intermix and populations in which they are segregated.

At each time step of the simulation, each agent is supposed, with a given probability, to be exposed to information coming from the technology supplier and to information coming from other agents picked at random from the population, who may already be adopters of the technology. Such events lead to an increase in the attitude to adoption, until this variable eventually exceeds the price of the technology, which transforms a non-adopting agent into an adopter. Further parameters considered in the model are p_{inn} (probability of innovation) and p_{im} (probability of imitation), that represent the odds of being influenced either through the exposure to an innovative or imitative event, respectively.

A plan of 1440 experiments was thus carried out allowing to explore the space of possible outcomes. The simulation was aimed at testing the behavior of a population of 1000 agents in a number of different scenarios obtained by varying the simulation parameters. The model was coded in a standard Java environment using the Eclipse Java editor.

3.2 Modeling Monetary Incentives

In this scenario, the agent-based system is modified by introducing a policy maker that provides monetary incentives to agents willing to become adopters. In order to model incentives, the price of the technology decreases by a fixed amount at specific time buckets, set by the policy maker.

The variables involved in a monetary incentive policy are basically four:

1. to whom: is it more effective and efficient to target incentives to all of the population, or to a target category only?
2. how much: as an example, an incentive policy applied some years ago in Italy provided a government contribution up to 10% of the sale price to purchase a PC;
3. when and how long: the time window of the policy must be defined according to policy makers' objectives;
4. budget: it is usually limited, and known *ex-ante*.

In order to understand when, how long and to whom give incentives (innovators? early adopters? laggards?), it is necessary to assess both the efficacy and the effectiveness of this policy. These issues will be deepened in the following subsections.

3.3 Economic Value of a Policy

In order to evaluate the societal value of a policy it is necessary to perform a cost-benefit analysis, i.e. compare the social benefits with the incentive policy cost itself. We suppose that social benefit is present from the moment an agent adopts the technology on.

In order to measure the benefits provided by the implementation of a certain policy, its utility should be compared to the utility of the adoption without any policy.

The utility U_t borne by the policy in each time bucket t is therefore proportional to the extra adopters derived from its implementation:

$$U_t = \beta \cdot (N_{policy,t} - N_{no\_policy,t})$$

where:

- the coefficient β represents the economic value to society of each adopter over one time unit; for the sake of simplicity, β is supposed to be equal to 1;
- $N_{policy,t}$ represents the number of adopters at time t in the case of policy implementation;
- $N_{no\_policy,t}$ is the number of adopters at time t if the policy is not implemented.

The cost of the policy in each time bucket t can be defined as:

$$A_t = c \cdot \tilde{n}_t$$

where:

- c represents the incentive amount given to an agent in time bucket t;
- $\tilde{n}_t$ is the number of adopters having benefited from incentive c in t.

Under these hypotheses, since social benefits of adoption are cumulative, an incentive leading to adoption in t provides more benefits to society than one leading to adoption during a subsequent time bucket; at the same time, time value of money suggests that expenditure should be postponed. We can therefore balance these two opposing requirements by discounting cash flows and utilities:

$$NPV = \sum_t \frac{U_t}{(1+i_{VAN})^t} = \sum_t \frac{N_{policy,t} - N_{no\_policy,t}}{(1+i_{VAN})^t}$$

$$C = \sum_t \frac{A_t}{(1+i_c)^t} = c \cdot \sum_t \frac{\hat{n}_t}{(1+i_c)^t}$$

where i_{VAN} (inflation rate of utility) and i_C (cost of public money) are the annual discount rates, set for simplicity equal to 5%.

Finally, it is possible to calculate α_{BEP}, which defines the cost-benefit ratio of the policy. The more efficient the policy, the smaller the value of α_{BEP}.

$$\alpha_{BEP} = \frac{C}{NPV}$$

4 Results and Discussion

The aim of the analysis is to test both the effectiveness (in terms of *NPV*) and the efficiency (in terms of α_{BEP}) of a policy for different scenarios, described by the combination of the following four variables, that come into play:

Table 1. Description and levels of the variables taken into account in the model

Variable	Description	Levels
START [*t*]	first time bucket in which incentives are provided, expressed in terms of Rogers' threshold (e.g. START=16% means that the incentive policy begins in the time bucket in which the threshold of 16% of adopters has been reached)	2.5 % 16 % 50 % 84 %
BUDGET [€]	money amount available by the policy maker to roll out the policy (it could be seen as the cost to be met to incline a certain percentage of the potential market towards the adoption)	10 (2%) 25 (5%) 50 (10%)
SIZE [%]	size of individual incentives, expressed in terms of percentage reduction of the technology price	5 % 10 % 15 %
SPAN [*years*]	time span of incentives (SPAN='0' corresponds to the scenario without policy implementation)	0 1 3 5
Number of multiple runs for each combination of parameters		10
TOTAL RUNS (TOT. = $10 \cdot 4^2 \cdot 3^2$)		*1440*

The policy has been tested on a curve with innovative and imitative parameters equal to p_{inn}=0.03, and p_{im}=0.38, respectively. Such parameters have been chosen as they are representative of the coefficients of innovation and imitation of a generic technology [19].

From the simulations it results that in the case of incentives given at the very beginning of technology diffusion (START = 2.5%) -with the budget being constant- the maximization of the policy effectiveness is obtained by giving incentives of little size, in order to cover as many potential adopters as possible. This is probably due to the fact that increasing adopters at the initial stage of the curve activates the imitative stage earlier, hence anticipating subsequent adoptions.

At the end of the diffusion process (START = 84%), it is worthwhile to have a large budget, in order to ensure incentives to almost all remaining potential adopters. This combination maximizes the *NPV*, granting at the same time the minimum α_{BEP}.

As far as the variable START is concerned, maximum efficiency results for investments in the middle phases of the diffusion process (START=16%, 50%). Otherwise, investments increase the costs/benefits ratio. A high BUDGET guarantees better values of policy efficiency (Figure 1).

In conclusion, the simulations suggest that policy efficiency strictly depends upon available resources. If there is enough budget to stimulate up to 10% of the potential adopters it is recommended to operate in the earlier stages of the diffusive phenomenon.

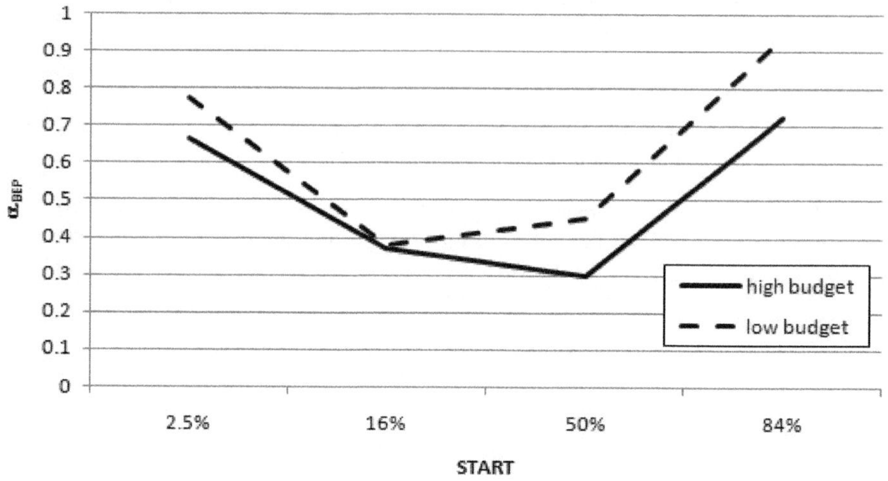

Fig. 1. α_{BEP} as a function of START

On the other side, when a limited budget is available to policy makers, it is preferable to act at a later stage. It is essential that majority has already adopted and the other agents have a propensity to adoption high enough to become adopters receiving a small incentive. Spending a low budget in the earlier stages results in a less efficient policy since it would probably not generate the sufficient thrust to reach a critical mass in terms of adopters to significantly increase the impact of the imitative effect.

In conclusion, the simulations show the opportunity to give incentives in order to stimulate a technology diffusion. It should be remembered that the current work is a research in progress, therefore the above outcomes should be considered as preliminary results, that are still object of validation and verification.

Obviously, the choice of the 'best' policy depends also on the context: policy analysis tools need to be flexible in incorporating the contextual information in different policy settings. This interesting issue could give rise to future works.

References

1. Bankes, S.C.: Agent-based modeling: A revolution? Proceedings of the National Academy of Sciences of the United States of America 99, 7199–7200 (2002)
2. Rogers, E.M.: Diffusion of innovations, 5th edn. Free Press, New York (2003)
3. Bass, F.M.: A New Product Growth for Model Consumer Durables. Management Science 15(5), 215–227 (1969)
4. Abaye, A.R., Babbitt, J., Best, B., Hu, R.Q., Maveddat, P.: Forecasting Methodology and Traffic Estimation for Satellite Multimedia Services. In: Proceedings of IEEE ICC'99, Vancouver, Canada, pp. 1084–1088 (1999)
5. Guidolin, M., Mortarino, C.: Cross-country diffusion of photovoltaic systems: Modelling choices and forecasts for national adoption patterns. Technological Forecasting and Social Change 77(2), 279–296 (2010)

6. Guseo, R., Guidolin, M.: Modelling a dynamic market potential: A class of automata networks for diffusion of innovations. Technological Forecasting and Social Change 76(6), 806–820 (2009)
7. Liu, M., Xiao, Y.: Simulation on the consumer innovation diffusion behavior in the environment of electronic commerce. In: IEEE International Conference on Management of Innovation and Technology (2006)
8. Park, Y.T.: Technology diffusion policy: a review and classification of policy practices. Technology in Society 21(3), 275–286 (1999)
9. Volkery, A., Ribeiro, T.: Scenario planning in public policy: Understanding use, impacts and the role of institutional context factors. Technological Forecasting and Social Change 76(9), 1198–1207 (2009)
10. Georghiou, L., Roessner, D.: Evaluating technology programs: tools and methods. Research Policy 29(4-5), 657–678 (2000)
11. Kim, Y.: Enriching Policy Analysis: The Role of Agent Based Models. In: The 9th Public Management Research Conference, Tucson, Arizona (2007)
12. Zagonel, A.A., Rohrbaugh, J., Richardson, G.P., Andersen, D.F.: Using simulation models to address "what if" questions about welfare reform. Journal of Policy Analysis and Management 23(4), 890–901 (2004)
13. Anderson, J., Chaturvedi, A., Cibulskis, M.: Simulation tools for developing policies for complex systems: Modeling the health and safety of refugee communities. Health Care Management Science 10(4), 331–339 (2007)
14. Berger, T., Schreinemachers, P., Woelcke, J.: Multi-agent simulation for the targeting of development policies in less-favored areas. Agricultural Systems 88(1), 28–43 (2006)
15. Bankes, S.C.: Tools and techniques for developing policies for complex and uncertain systems. Proceedings of the National Academy of Sciences of the United States of America 99(suppl. 3), 7263–7266 (2002)
16. Coad, A., de Haan, P., Woersdorfer, J.S.: Consumer support for environmental policies: An application to purchases of green cars. Ecological Economics 68(7), 2078–2086 (2009)
17. Diamond, D.: The impact of government incentives for hybrid-electric vehicles: Evidence from US states. Energy Policy 37(3), 972–983 (2009)
18. de Haan, P., Mueller, M.G., Scholz, R.W.: How much do incentives affect car purchase? Agent-based microsimulation of consumer choice of new cars - Part II: Forecasting effects of feebates based on energy-efficiency. Energy Policy 37(3), 1083–1094 (2009)
19. Sultan, F., Farley, J.U., Lehmann, D.R.: A meta-analysis of applications of diffusion models. Journal of marketing research 27(1), 70–77 (1990)

E-Government Services Using Customer Index Knowledge

Sung Ho Ha[1,*] and Min Jung Lee[2]

[1] School of Business Administration, Kyungpook National University, 1370 Sangyeok-dong, Buk-gu, Daegu, 702-701, Korea
hsh@mail.knu.ac.kr
[2] Technology Policy Research Center, Korea Industrial Technology Foundation, Seoul, Korea

Abstract. Public sectors have tried to improve service quality for their customers. However, there are still several hurdles in the execution of customer-oriented service production and delivery by the public sectors. On this account, most public sectors thus far have made little progress in making themselves more customer-friendly, when compared with private sectors. The business environment surrounding public sectors has been rapidly changing, such as private sectors rushing into competition, customers demanding their rights, and the self-consciousness of public sectors paying attention to a customer-driven mind. To cope with these challenges, this study suggests a framework of developing knowledge-intensive services based on customer indexes (KISCI) in the e-government scheme, which combines panel information and marketing research information to improve the service quality of public sectors toward citizens. The framework, KISCI, is applied to one of the public sectors and the results are enumerated.

Keywords: E-government; customer service; service quality; public sector; service process.

1 Introduction

For years, customer service in public sectors has been widespread, although the service production and delivery in public sectors remain undeveloped. The importance of customer service in private sectors has been emphasized earlier than in public sectors, since services being purchased by customers directly contribute benefit to the private sector. Recently, customer service has been expected as much from public organizations as it is from private organizations. A recent study of the relationship between citizens and public sectors across 11 countries found that the majority of public sectors had invested in the service technology [1].

At all events, the public sector is the part of economic and administrative life that deals with the delivery of goods and services by and for the government, whether national, regional or local [2]. Regardless of country, agency, or type of customers,

* Corresponding author.

K.N. Andersen et al. (Eds.): EGOVIS 2010, LNCS 6267, pp. 174–188, 2010.

pressure is intensifying for the public sector to change the way it does business by government. A number of forces are driving these changes: Rising expectations of better treatment from and interaction with government agencies; being asked to provide more services on a shrinking budget; mandates for improved access by legislation, such as directives to provide an Internet access; and calling for leverage past investments in e-government.

Regardless of this environment, most public sectors thus far have made little progress in making themselves more customer-friendly, when compared with private sectors. Private sector companies have brought necessary competition into the industry and spearheaded the changes towards a higher utilization of technology, improved customer service, and innovative products. Furthermore, customers have now become increasingly conscious of their rights and are demanding more than ever before [3]. It is natural that citizens expect the public sectors to change the way from agency-driven to customer-driven quality management. Public sectors have also started to pay attention to a customer-driven mind because they expect some possible benefits: Improving the quality of service to the individual customer/constituent; improving inter-agency cooperation at government and local levels; changing the business structure of an agency or department more effectively; improving multi-channel accesses for customers; and benchmarking excellent private enterprises.

However, there are still several hurdles of customer-oriented service delivery of the public sector [4]. First, government agencies find it hard to justify investments in service technology. Second, the primary drivers for customer-oriented services in the private sector, including customer retention and increased profit per customer, are absent in the public sector. Third, government is in lack of competition. The fourth, and possibly the biggest, hurdle is privacy. A customer-oriented purpose is to provide both organization and customer with a single view of the other. Thus, to improve the service quality of a public sector to customers (i.e., citizens), because various surveys on the public sector have been conducted to identify customer needs and wants, in this study a framework of developing knowledge intensive services based on customer indexes (KISCI) in public sectors has been devised, which combines panel information and marketing research information. The accrued benefits derived from the framework are briefly described as follows: Acquiring reliable respondents (i.e. panels) to obtain high-quality customer data for a public sector; improving internal and external customer processes based on a variety of surveys; and upgrading the quality of e-government services to customers through a key process analysis.

This paper is organized as follows. Related studies on quality improvement in customer services are presented in Section 2. Especially this section shows some drawbacks out of which these researches pointed. In Section 3, a framework of KISCI is presented and a detailed analysis procedure based on KISCI is depicted. In Section 4, KISCI is applied to one of the public sectors and the results are enumerated. Section 5 concludes this paper.

2 Literature Review

2.1 Customer Service in the Public Sector

Taveira et al. examined how a typical total quality management program in the public sector interacts with the work environment of employees of four departments in a municipal government organization [5]. Hsieh et al. found a significantly positive relationship between job standardization and service quality [6]. It has become a generally accepted principle that an organization in the public sector should become customer-oriented if it is to deliver better service quality and enhance customer satisfaction [7].

A review of literature revealed that it has been reported that the public sector has lower employee satisfaction level than the private sector [8]. The presence of support at work, the amount of control an employee had over their job, the perceptions of pay, and the perception of a lack of human resources were found to be key predictors of employee-level outcomes [9].

Greasley demonstrated a process-based approach with process mapping and business process simulation with regard to the implementation of an information system for road traffic accident reporting in a UK police force [10]. King presented the UK electronic government CRM programs and proposed an alternative model of CRM which encourages citizens to co-produce the public services they consume [11]. Janssen et al. developed taxonomy for analyzing Web-based business models for e-government based on a survey of 59 e-government Web sites in the Netherlands [12].

Governments start to provide constituents with information and services online over the Internet. Kaliontzoglou et al. developed a secure e-government platform based on Web Services, which addresses the requirements, such as interoperability, security and user friendliness, faced by small to medium sized public organizations [13]. Johnson settled pricing decisions of e-government service, which should be tailored to meet the demands of constituent groups and the revenue needs of government [14]. Dias and Rafael defined a set of requirements for one-stop e-government and a distributed architecture for its implementation [15]. Vassilakisa et al. developed knowledge-based tools that allow the automated production of different versions of the electronic service, each targeted to each channel platform [16].

2.2 Quality Improvement in Customer Services

Even though, during more than 40 years, research activities for quality improvement in customer services have been conducted, those researches have still had several drawbacks [17][18]. The shortcomings can be summarized as follows: Insufficient Customer Satisfaction Index (CSI) surveys conducted by only a few of the possible departments; inefficient relationship analysis among several kinds of customer researches; a lack of efficient strategies for service quality improvement within departments; and insufficient consideration of service process management regarding service stages conducted by departments.

Insufficient CSI surveys. Usually, companies or organizations conduct surveys with customers who buy or use their final services. A department is a part of a larger organization which pursues collective goals with a boundary separating it from its environment. All the departments have their own customers and have their responsibility which their customers expect, and have to meet their customer needs and expectation. On the other hand, a customer may be an internal customer or an external customer. Internal customers refer to departments and employees who are supplied with services in the same organization, which in turn are utilized to create a deliverable for the external customers outside the company [19]. As the internal customers, employees of an organization are also looking to get their needs satisfied [20]. If there are poor internal services, then the final service to the external customer could shrink [7][21][22][23][24]. In order to recognize specific characteristics of all customers who want a diverse array of things, departments should conduct surveys at their own levels. After analyzing these surveys, each department can learn about their customers, which can be helpful in formulating appropriate strategies for service quality improvement.

Inefficient relationship analysis among customer research. A company usually conducts three kinds of independent customer researches. They are a CSI survey to know customer needs and complaints, an Employee Satisfaction Index survey (ESI survey) to identify job satisfaction and the working environment surrounding employees, and a Customer-Oriented Index survey (COI survey) to measure the extent to which an organization listens to its customers and identifies current and future requirements to improve its services. These customer indexes have much to do with each other. Slack et al. argued that every part of an organization contributes to external customer satisfaction by satisfying its own internal customers [25]. If employees are part of a solid service culture and receive management support for delivering improved customer service, this experience will lead to increased job satisfaction. It has been empirically demonstrated that properly constructed customer orientation in an organization produces better service quality and customer satisfaction [21][26]. Under this circumstance, a framework is needed which utilizes all these indexes together.

Inefficient strategies for service quality improvement. Each department has limited capability on self-improvement. Accurate customer satisfaction measurement enables departments to identity important customer requirements [27]. In addition, departments should understand that customers perceive the performance of departments in meeting the requirements. Priorities and areas for improvement in performance should be identified to produce the greatest gain in customer satisfaction. Each department must set goals and strategies for service improvement and monitor the progress of the customer satisfaction index. This leads the department to a profit increase through improved customer loyalty and retention [28][29].

Insufficient service process management. Researches on service quality improvement, so far, have not considered the service process management much. To complement this, two techniques are adopted to consider the service process management. We choose to use the Process Classification Framework (PCF) for an internal CSI survey which has been developed by the American Productivity & Quality Center. PCF is employed in practical ways to understand organization processes better and it serves as a common reference about the business process between different departments. For the external customers, a method called Quality Function Deployment (QFD) is chosen to focus on the characteristics of a new or existing service from the viewpoints of external customers. QFD is applied in a wide variety of service configuration and deployments [7].

3 Knowledge-Intensive Services Based on Customer Indexes

KISCI makes three kinds of analyses as follows: Deriving key service processes from quality variables (QV) to recognize a key retention process (KRP) and a key maturity process (KMP); building customer retention and maturity strategies by using KRP and KMP; and comparing services between service providers to draw synergy strategies of a public sector.

3.1 Deriving Key Service Processes from Quality Variables

Fig. 1 represents the procedure of extracting key processes. A key process should be identified because the manager who is in charge of process improvement can not try to enhance all the processes.

First of all, all quality variables are extracted from the questionnaire. KISCI reduces the set of variables in a survey dataset and derives representative variables from respective components through a factor analysis and partial correlation analysis. A factor analysis explains the variability among observed quality variables in terms of fewer unobserved variables called factors. The observed variables are modeled as linear combinations of the factors. A partial correlation analysis computes linear relationship between a QV and customer satisfaction variables (i.e., overall satisfaction, intention to recommend, and intention to purchase again) while controlling the effects of other QVs included in the same component [30].

After reducing quality variables, KISCI determines priorities of processes by using importance, contribution, and satisfaction measurement. In doing so, KISCI needs two indexes, referred to here as an Importance Index (I.I) and a Contribution Index (C.I) to set the priorities of key processes. The Importance Index (I.I) is a correlation coefficient which is the extent of linear association between reduced QVs and customer satisfaction (CS) variables:

$$\text{Importance Index (I.I)} = \frac{\sum (\mathrm{QV}_i - \overline{QV}) \sum (\mathrm{CS}_i - \overline{CS})}{\sqrt{\sum (\mathrm{QV}_i - \overline{QV})^2 \sum (\mathrm{CS}_i - \overline{CS})^2}}, \quad -1 < \mathrm{I.I} < 1 \tag{1}$$

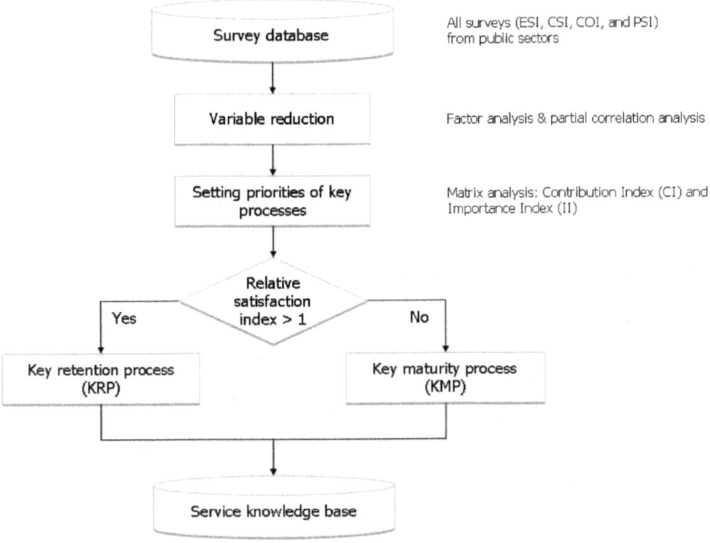

Fig. 1. A procedure of extracting KRP and KMP

The Contribution Index (C.I) measures how much the CS improves when a public sector performs improvement activities to enhance the level of a QV. The contribution to customer satisfaction of a QV is enumerated as following in Equation 2. It indicates how much overall customer satisfaction increases as a result of improving customer satisfaction from a specific QV. When a C.I is equal to one, the overall CS increases linearly as the CS of a customer improves from the QV. If a C.I is less than one, the overall CS does not increase efficiently when compared with the increase of CS from the QV. When a C.I is larger than one, the overall CS improves more than the effort for QV improvement.

$$\text{Contribution Index (C.I)} = \lim_{\delta CSonQV \to 0} \frac{\delta \text{ Overall CS}}{\delta \text{ CS on QV}}, \quad -\infty < \text{C.I} < \infty \qquad (2)$$

A key process with a high value of Importance Index and a high value of Contribution Index should be assigned high priority. After setting priorities of key processes, a Relative Satisfaction Index (R.S.I) is used to classify a key process into a key retention process (KRP) or a key maturity process (KMP). The Relative Satisfaction Index (R.S.I) explains a revealed comparative advantage. The R.S.I is based on the average of each QV value from panels and is enumerated as following in Equation 3. When a R.S.I is less than one, a key process is classified as KMP, since there is a good possibility to improve QV and then improve CS. When a R.S.I is larger than one, a key process is classified as KRP.

$$\text{Relative Satisfaction Index (R.S.I)} = \frac{\frac{\sum_{i=1}^{n} QV_{i,j}}{N}}{\frac{\sum_{i=1}^{n} CS_{i,k}}{N}}, \quad 0 < \text{R.S.I} \tag{3}$$

3.2 Building Retention and Maturity Strategies by Using KRP and KMP

Fig. 2 presents the procedure of building retention/maturity strategies by using KRP and KMP. KISCI chooses *k*-means to derive *k* clusters and determines the characteristics of each group by looking at the socio-demographic features of panels. Among *k* clusters, clustering with KRP can grasp a high-value group with high values on KRP and CS variables. Clustering with KMP can catch a low-value group with low values on KMP and CS variables.

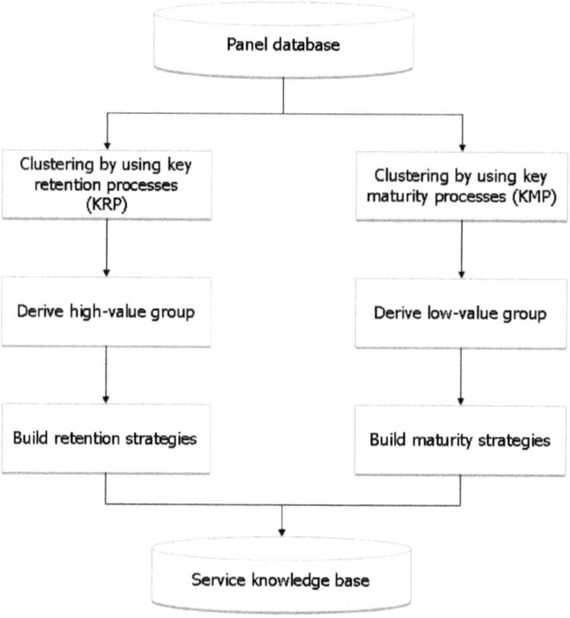

Fig. 2. Building retention and maturity strategies through using KRP and KMP

A high-value group is helpful in building customer retention strategies. The group provides the service provider with its socio-demographic features and behavioral information of the customers. A low-value group is helpful in building customer maturity strategies of the service provider. After retention and maturity strategies are determined, KISCI archives them into the service knowledge base and feeds them back to the service provider. Then the service provider encourages finding and doing an appropriate course of action to maintain/reinforce KRP or improve KMP.

3.3 Comparing Services between Service Providers of a Public Sector

Analyzing the similarity of services between service providers can draw synergistic services, such as cross-selling, cross-delivering, between service providers. Fig. 3 explains a procedure of analyzing similar processes between different service providers or departments of a public sector. It also summarizes possible synergy strategies for two public services.

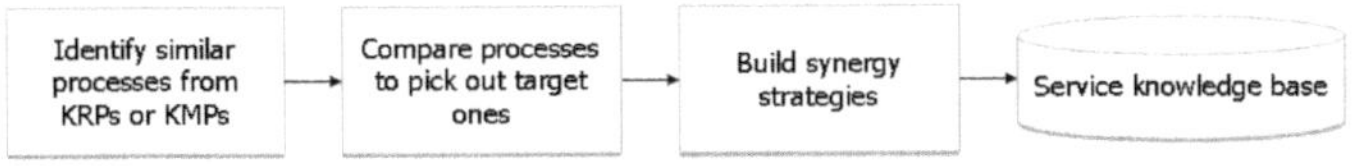

Synergy strategies for two public services

service provider \ service provider	Key Retention Process (KRP)	Key Maturity Process (KMP)
Key Retention Process (KRP)	• Sharing customer information • Retention-strategy-maintaining actions	• Benchmarking • Opportunity of cross-selling, cross-delivering
Key Maturity Process (KMP)	• Benchmarking • Opportunity of cross-selling, cross-delivering	• Sharing customer information • Maturity-strategy- improving actions

Fig. 3. Deriving synergy strategies through a different service analysis

An organization lists up KRPs or KMPs from all the departments, and picks out similar processes from the listed KRPs or KMPs, even though the departments are different. The organization can group more than one department which has similar processes together. Departments in the same group can share customer information, co-work to improve KMP and to maintain KRP so that the organization as a whole can anticipate synergy effects. When a department has KRP, which is KMP to another department, the KMP department can benchmark retention strategies of the KRP department. If that is the case, there are opportunities of cross-selling or cross-delivering between departments.

In order to judge services to be similar, a Similarity Index (S.I) is calculated. The S.I indicates the extent to how correlated a service is with other services. In other words, the S.I identifies the extent to which one service is similar with other services under the same customer behaviors or socio-demographic features. When the values of CS variables, such as overall satisfaction, intention to recommend, and intention to purchase again, are categorized from scale-1 to scale-5, the distribution of each categorical variable is calculated as a Similarity Index.

$$\text{Similarity Index (S.I)} = \sum_{k=1}^{5} \min(d_k(S_i), d_k(S_j)) \tag{4}$$

where S_i and S_j denote services *i*, *j* respectively at an organization or a public sector, *d( )* represents distribution percentages in each of 5 scales, and *k* represents one of the values a CS variable takes.

To measure S.I, KISCI uses an Index of Dissimilarity, which indicates the percentage level of dissimilarity in categorical scales (i.e. 1 to 5) of a specific service is different from others with respect to the same combinations of socio-demographic features or customer behaviors. The Dissimilarity Index (D.I) is equal to the summation over the percentage difference of component units from scale-1 to scale-5:

$$\text{Similarity Index (S.I)} = 100 - \text{Dissimilarity Index (D.I)}$$

$$\text{Dissimilarity Index (D.I)} = \frac{\sum_{k=1}^{5} \left| d_k(T_i) - d_k(T_j) \right|}{2} \tag{5}$$

The minimum value of D.I is zero and the maximum value is 100. If S.I is high (i.e. D.I is low), every distribution of a CS variable between two surveys corresponding to combinations of socio-demographic features is very similar, even though they are totally different surveys about different services.

4 Application of KISCI

The KISCI has been applied to the Korea Tourism Organization (KTO) as one of commercially-oriented public sectors in Korea. KTO performs CSI, COI and ESI surveys every year. Especially those marketing researches conducted from 2004 through 2007 were collected for this study. The Web-based system has been developed by using HTML, Java Script, JSP, and Java Beans as development languages. Table 1 shows a sample list of surveys conducted by KTO.

Table 1. A sample list of surveys

Survey	Panel size	Date
Wireless Internet contents (1)	500	2004. 1
Wireless Internet music contents (1)	450	2004. 2
Wireless Internet MMS contents (2)	450	2004. 12
Baduk pieces	500	2004. 2
Online study	420	2004. 3
Gifted education (market, orientation)	560	2004. 4
Effect on data communication	1200	2004. 5
Strategy for new service	2000	2004. 12
MP3 phone	300	2004. 6
Effect on liver story book	300	2004. 7
Remind service of card company	350	2004. 12
2005 Golf club in Jeju	100	2005. 12

Table 1. *(continued)*

2005 Content management team	880	2005. 12
2005 ESI	105	2005. 12
2005 COI	538	2005. 12
…	…	…
2006 Golf club in Jeju	100	2006. 12
2006 COI	608	2006. 12
2007 ESI	322	2007. 3

4.1 Deriving Key Retention and Key Maturity Processes

Through a factor analysis and partial correlation analysis, KISCI has extracted key processes in 2005 and 2006. KISCI, then, calculated the I.I, C.I, and R.S.I., and drew the matrix of key processes to determine the priorities of KRP and KMP. Fig. 4 illustrates the matrix analysis of KMP and KRP in 2005 and 2006.

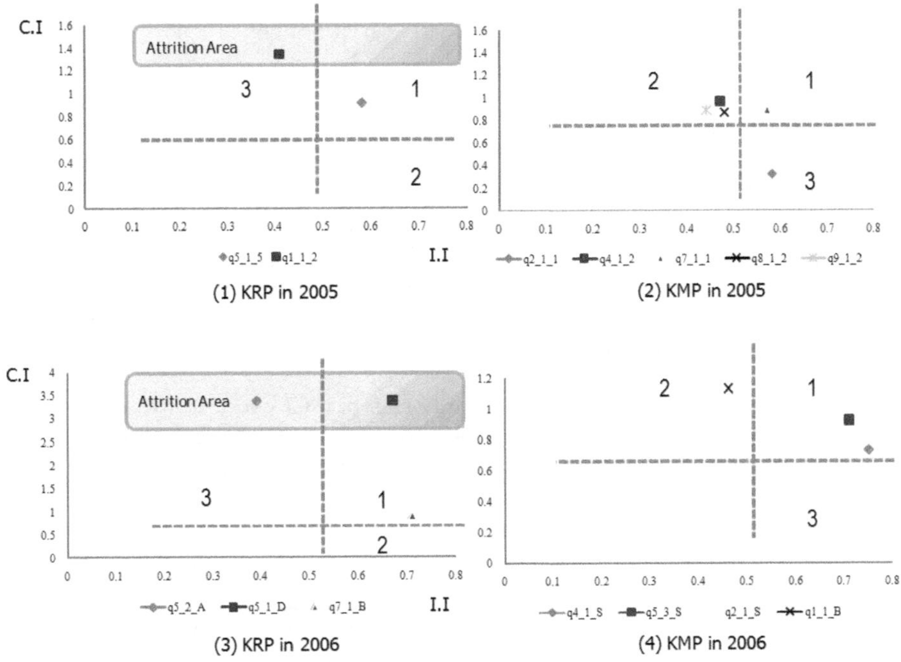

Fig. 4. Matrix analyses of KRP and KMP at 2005 and 2006

Table 2 summarizes strategies for key retention processes and key maturity processes from 2005 to 2006. The "KRP (Attrition)" indicates the KRP with a high R.S.I rate. For example, the "Convenient transportation" process had a medium I.I and a high C.I values. However, it had a high R.S.I value and there was possibility of an attrition risk. For this process, KRPs with attrition strategies need to be developed.

Table 2. Strategies for KRP and KMP from 2005 to 2006

Year	Process description	I.I	C.I	R.S.I	Priority	Strategy
2005	Finding ball with sincerity	0.58	0.92	1.01	1	KRP
	Convenient transportation	0.41	1.34	1.01	2	KRP (Attrition)
	Easy reservation procedure	0.58	0.32	0.88	2	KMP
	Clean locker room	0.47	0.96	0.92	1	KMP
	Suitable tee off time	0.57	0.89	0.96	3	KMP
	Suitable green fee comparing other golf clubs	0.48	0.86	0.96	4	KMP
	Manners and behavior of parking staff (loading the golf supplies to the car)	0.44	0.89	0.98	5	KMP
2006	Scenic view of resort	0.39	3.39	1.07	2	KRP (Attrition)
	Bringing an appropriate iron customer requests	0.67	3.38	1.05	1	KRP (Attrition)
	Manners and behavior of parking staff (loading the golf supplies to the car)	0.71	0.90	1.00	3	KRP
	Overall satisfaction about subsidiary facilities	0.75	0.73	0.95	2	KMP
	Overall satisfaction about golf game progress	0.71	0.92	0.96	1	KMP
	Overall satisfaction about reservation	0.54	0.94	0.97	3	KMP
	Convenient transportation	0.46	1.13	0.99	4	KMP

4.2 Maturity Strategies by Using KMP

In order to show how to build maturity strategies, KISCI chose to use *k*-means clustering with CS variables and key maturity process. KISCI obtained three customer groups as shown in Table 3, which enumerates the characteristics of socio-demographic features of each group.

Table 3. Distribution of socio-demographic features through *k*-means clustering

		Total	Segment 1	Segment 2	Segment 3
Respondents		100	45	1	54
% of respondents		100%	45%	1%	54%
KMP: Average of overall satisfaction about subsidiary facilities		4.33	5	1	3.8
CS: Overall satisfaction		4.55	4.933	2	4.278
Gender	Female	22%	22.20%	0%	22.20%
	Male	78%	77.80%	100%	77.80%
Age	Over 60	3%	4.40%	0%	1.90%
	50~59	22%	20%	0%	24.10%
	40~49	57%	57.80%	100%	55.60%

Table 3. *(continued)*

	30~39	12%	11.10%	0%	13%
	20~29	6%	6.70%	0%	5.60%
Education level	College graduate	10%	13.30%	0%	7.40%
	3-4 years of college	62%	51.10%	100%	70.40%
	College student	7%	8.90%	0%	5.60%
	high school or less	21%	26.70%	0%	16.70%
Average monthly income (M won)	700~	26%	28.90%	100%	22.20%
	600~699	8%	6.70%	0%	9.30%
	500~599	17%	15.60%	0%	18.50%
	400~499	24%	28.90%	0%	20.40%
	300~399	15%	11.10%	0%	18.50%
	200~299	7%	6.70%	0%	7.40%
	100~199	2%	0%	0%	3.70%
	~99	1%	2.20%	0%	0%
Job	No occupation	1%	0%	0%	1.90%
	Housewife	10%	11.10%	0%	9.30%
	Student	5%	6.70%	0%	3.70%
	Technician	0%	0%	0%	0%
	Sales/Service	11%	8.90%	0%	13%
	Professional (Doctor, lawyer etc)	9%	11.10%	0%	7.40%
	Office/management	13%	6.70%	0%	18.50%
	Administration	2%	2.20%	0%	1.90%
	Self-employed	49%	53.30%	100%	44.40%

The "Segment 1" had the highest average values of CS and KMP, and can be defined as a satisfied group. The "Segment 2" was an unsatisfied group with the lowest average values in the CS variable (i.e. Overall satisfaction) and key maturity process (Overall satisfaction about subsidiary facilities). Because, however, the number of respondents was one, the "Segment 3" was chosen as an unsatisfied group, instead. Big differences can be found in the socio-demographic features and customer behaviors between "Segment 1" and "Segment 3." When focusing on a target group which consists of the unsatisfied with KMP, the "Segment 3" had such characteristics as high school or less level of education, more than 0.1M expense on golf play, Jeju residential area, and more than 10 months since the last golf game. New maturity strategies are needed for this target group, such as improvement of the quality of subsidiary facilities.

4.3 Different Services Analysis

Let's assume that KTO tries to start an online education at the Korea Tourism Education Center. It is necessary for KTO to find the related services from the survey database collected by several marketing surveys. Table 4 shows the similarity between different services from a sample of seven surveys. After preprocessing the "Online study" survey data, KISCI identified similar processes under the same socio-demographic features as the "Online study" survey. The "Strategy for new high speed Internet" survey showed the highest Similarity Index with the "Online study" survey. The respondents in the EDU6 (High school graduate level of education) and JOB7 (Technician) were most similar with those of the "Online study" survey.

Table 4. Calculating Similarity Index with the "Online study" survey

Survey name	CS	Category1	Category2	Category3	D.I	S.I	No. of respondents
Strategy for new high speed Internet	CS1	EDU6	JOB7		2	98	111
Strategy for new high speed Internet	CS1	JOB7			5	95	147
Strategy for new high speed Internet	CS1	AGE2	EDU7		6	94	221
Strategy for new high speed Internet	CS1	AGE2	EDU7	JOB8	6	94	124
Effect on data communication	CS1	AGE2	JOB8		6	94	52
Online game of Baduk	CS3	AGE3	JOB6		76	23	59
Online game of Baduk	CS3	EDU6	JOB6		79	21	81

5 Conclusion

In this article, a framework of knowledge-intensive services based on customer indexes (KISCI) was devised. There are two major objectives to be addressed by the KISCI: A public sector can obtain a list of reliable respondents by constructing a panel database and survey database from different departments in the public sector; and efficient, high-valued services can be given to the public by sharing panel information and survey analysis information.

KISCI consisted of three parts: 1) to derive key processes; 2) to build retention and maturity strategies; and 3) to compare different services. Each analysis result was archived in the service knowledge base. The analysis of surveys made it possible for a public sector to identify customer tastes and needs, and then to develop new service strategies to cope with changes in the environment. Many market researches achieve their aims. Service managers, however, occasionally overlook the relationship among survey results. This study has made the public sector better understand the relationship between different marketing research results.

In this study, a Web-based KISCI system has been applied to one of public sectors in Korea. Through the application, KISCI made it possible for service providers to monitor problems in customer services continuously and to resolve them to achieve improvement in service quality. When the KISCI was used in practice, it gave the public sector a new opportunity of cross-selling or up-selling between different services. It could derive new strategies to improve the quality of services, maintain loyal customers, and accordingly, enhance the competitive power of the public sector.

References

1. Accenture, Customer Relationship Management–A blueprint for Government, http://www.accenture.com/Countries/Canada/Research_And_Insights/BlueprintGovernment.htm
2. Greenberg, P.: CRM at the speed of light: Essential strategies for the 21st century, 3rd edn. McGraw-Hill, Osborne (2004)
3. Chesbrough, H.: Toward a science of services. Harvard Business Review 83, 16–17 (2005)
4. Andersen, K.V.: E-government and public sector process rebuilding: Dilettantes, Wheel Barrows, and Diamonds. Kluwer Academic Publishers, Boston (2004)
5. Taveira, A.D., James, C.A., Karsh, B.-T., Sainfort, F.: Quality management and the work environment: an empirical investigation in a public sector organization. Applied Ergonomics 34, 281–291 (2003)
6. Hsieh, A.-T., Chou, C.-H., Chen, C.-M.: Job standardization and service quality: a closer look at the application of total quality management to the public sector. Total Quality Management 13, 899–912 (2002)
7. Chen, C.K., Yu, C.H., Yang, S.J., Chang, H.C.: A customer-oriented service-enhancement system (COSES) for the public sector. Managing Service Quality 14, 414–425 (2004)
8. Desmarais, M.: Contact Center Employee Satisfaction & Customer Satisfaction Link, https://brc.manpower.com/BRC/files?name=Contact_Center_WhitePaper2.pdf
9. Noblet, A., Teo, S.T.T., McWilliams, J., Rodwell, J.J.: Which work characteristics predict employee outcomes for the public-sector employee? An examination of generic and occupation-specific characteristics. International Journal of Human Resource Management 16, 1415–1430 (2005)
10. Greasley, A.: Using process mapping and business process simulation to support a process-based approach to change in a public sector organization. Technovation 26, 95–103 (2006)
11. King, S.F.: Citizens as customers: Exploring the future of CRM in UK local government. Government Information Quarterly 24, 47–63 (2007)
12. Janssen, M., Kuk, G., Wagenaar, R.W.: A survey of Web-based business models for e-government in the Netherlands. Government Information Quarterly 25, 202–220 (2008)
13. Kaliontzoglou, A., Sklavos, P., Karantjias, T., Polemi, D.: A secure e-Government platform architecture for small to medium sized public organizations. Electronic Commerce Research and Applications 4, 174–186 (2005)
14. Johnson, C.L.: A framework for pricing government e-services. Electronic Commerce Research and Applications 6, 484–489 (2007)
15. Dias, G.P., Rafael, J.A.: A simple model and a distributed architecture for realizing one-stop e-government. Electronic Commerce Research and Applications 6, 81–90 (2007)
16. Vassilakisa, C., Lepourasa, G., Halatsis, C.: A knowledge-based approach for developing multi-channel e-government services. Electronic Commerce Research and Applications 6, 113–124 (2007)
17. Anderson, E.W., Sullivan, M.W.: The antecedents and consequences of customer satisfaction for firms. Marketing Science 12, 125–143 (1993)
18. Kotler, P., Keller, K.: Marketing management, 13th edn. Prentice-Hall, NJ (2008)

19. Gremler, D.D.: The internal service encounter. Logistics Information Management 8, 28–34 (1995)
20. Vilares, M.J., Coelho, P.S.: The employee-customer satisfaction chain in the ECSI model. European Journal of Marketing 37, 1703–1722 (2003)
21. Hartline, M.D., Maxham III, J.G., Mckee, D.O.: Corridors of influence in the dissemination of customer-oriented strategy to customer contact service employees. Journal of Marketing 64, 35–50 (2000)
22. Beazley, H., Harden, D.G., Boenisch, J.: Continuity Management: Preserving Corporate Management and Productivity When Employees Leave. John Wiley and Sons, England (2002)
23. O'Riordan, J., Humphreys, P.C.: Developing an effective Internal Customer Service ethos. Institute of Public Administration, Ireland (2003)
24. Korunka, C., Scharitzer, D., Carayon, P., Hoonakker, P., Sonnek, A., Sainfort, F.: Customer orientation among employees in public administration: A transnational, longitudinal study. Applied Ergonomics 38, 307–315 (2007)
25. Slack, N., Chambers, S., Johnston, R.: Operations Management, 3rd edn. Prentice-Hall, London (2001)
26. Jiang, B.C., Chen, C.K.: A study of customer-oriented service culture–concepts and approaches. Research Development and Evaluation 26, 93–101 (2002)
27. McFadyen, K., Harrison, J.L., Kelly, S.J., Scott, D.: Measuring service quality in a corporatised public sector environment. Journal of Nonprofit & Public Sector Marketing 9, 35–51 (2001)
28. Fountain, J.E.: Paradoxes of public sector customer service. Governance 14, 55–73 (2001)
29. Giannoccaro, R., Costantino, N., Ludovico, A., Pietroforte, R.: Measuring citizen satisfaction with aspects of public services from a local authority and determining their importance: A case study. Public Organization Review 8, 1–15 (2008)
30. Woo, J.Y., Bae, S.M., Park, S.C.: Visualization method for customer targeting using customer map. Expert Systems with Applications 28, 763–772 (2005)

The Bangladesh National Biometric Database: A Transferable Success?

M. Sirajul Islam and Åke Grönlund

Örebro University, Swedish Business School
Fakultetsgatan 1, 70182 Örebro, Sweden
{sirajul.islam,ake.gronlund}@oru.se

Abstract. Having a reliable voter list for conducting free and fair elections in Bangladesh was earlier considered unachievable due to political instability, widespread corruption, and weak and demoralized leadership. However, in 2008 the PERP project succeeded in building the world's currently largest biometric database covering the entire Bangladeshi voting age population, 80 million people. This paper describes the PERP project as well as the history of failed projects and analyses success factors based on the IS implementation literature. This is an interpretive case study where both primary and secondary data have been used. The key finding is that the major reason behind the success was to get the project done in a 'politically controlled' environment where the people worked in a highly structured management system following a concrete and realistic roadmap. The implications of this finding are discussed.

Keywords: Biometrics database, Preparation of Electoral Roll with Photographs (PERP), Bangladesh Election Commission, Bangladesh Army, UNDP, Controlled democracy, eGovernment.

1 Introduction

The road to parliamentary democracy in Bangladesh has not been straightforward. Political stability is one of the key factors of national development, and in this respect Bangladesh has been badly affected for a long time under the external suppression and colonial repression and subsequent rulers until the bloody war of independence in 1971. After independence, the new country experienced devastating famine in 1973-74 followed by recurrent natural disasters, dictatorships, martial laws, military coups, political assassinations, non-functional parliaments, entrenched corruption and weak judicial and law enforcement agencies. This history has formed a climate of instability and mistrust among the political organizations. As one of such consequences, a three-month tenured non-party and politically neutral caretaker governmental system headed by a Chief Adviser (equivalent to a Prime Minister) has been introduced since 1991 in order to hold a free and fair parliamentary election. Following the dissolution of the 8th Parliament in October 2006 the two major political alliances confronted dreadfully in the streets of Bangladesh for electoral reforms and for a 'really neutral' head of interim government in order to hold free and fair 9th National Parliament elections. Subsequently, the series of political violence paved the way for an

K.N. Andersen et al. (Eds.): EGOVIS 2010, LNCS 6267, pp. 189–203, 2010.

unelected and military backed caretaker government to take power on 11 January, 2007 (known as the 1/11 Government), for two years. This tenure was termed by many a 'controlled democracy' [1]. The election which was scheduled for 22nd January of 2007 was suspended and rescheduled to December 29, 2008. To hold the widely demanded free and fair elections, a credible voter list was an essential prerequisite; 'The successful completion of the photo (biometrics) voters list will eliminate duplicate records, prevent fraudulent entries and greatly reduce the occurrence of vote theft. It will also build the nation's confidence in the credibility of the parliamentary elections' [2, p.2].

As there was a serious dispute over the list that had been prepared by the then (2005) Election Commission, having an accurate and authentic voter list was one of the main issues under the demand of electoral reforms being raised by the opposition alliance and other civil society groups. The National Democratic Institute (NDI) once commented [3] that the new voter list covered over 93 million names which was inconsistent with the 2001 national census data where the voting age population was approximately 80 million people. Part of the problem of such an unrealistic voters list stemmed from the convoluted process by which it was assembled. NDI therefore suggested that the process should be computerized in order to have more reliable list. Following a nation-wide series of debates during the tenure of the 1/11 government, there was general consensus that the new voters list should use biometric technology and be implemented as a centrally controlled modern computerized system. This would as a byproduct add the capability of issuing a national ID card to each voter and help to implement e-government initiatives efficiently at a later time.

The expectations were fulfilled with the completion of the main phase of voter registration by the project 'Preparation of Electoral Roll with Photographs (PERP)', conducted in coordinated efforts by the Bangladesh Election commission (BEC), the Bangladesh Army and UNDP. The project was widely considered a success which can be evident with the following statement: "The task was mammoth, time frame was tight and technological and logistical challenges were huge. ...... The end result is a highly accurate voter list, a verifiable individual ID card and a citizens database which will have huge positive impact for good governance and national security. The model of this UNDP aided success story could easily be replicated to any developing region of the world". [4]

This project has produced world's largest biometrics database as well [5], [6]. Having this context in mind, the *main objective of this paper is to find the major reasons behind the success of PERP project in Bangladesh.* We do that by first surveying the literature for critical success and failure factors, then examining both the PERP project and previous attempts to establish a voter list in Bangladesh. This will contribute to bridging the often suggested research gap of a lack studies of project success factors in the public sector (projects carried out by governments) [7, p.1400]. In order to operationalize this main research objective, the following objectives are addressed: (1) to explore the earlier initiatives for developing voter list and project governance; and (2) to understand the reasons behind the failures and success of implementing a government initiated project in Bangladesh.

2 Literature Review: Project Management and Success Factors

'Good project management can contribute towards project success but is unlikely to be able to prevent failure' [8, p.164]. The tendency of presenting project success fatcors as general findings can be considered 'an illusion' [8] as there have been a multitude of objectives in the project lifecycle associated with multiple stakeholders. In general, a project engages various stakeholders having various interest and stakes and can be partially used or even rejected by them in any phase of the project life cycle and outcomes if their needs and demands are not adequately addressed. Mitchelle et al. [9] define the scope of this stake with the extent of power, legitimacy and urgency. These three dimensions of each individual stakeholder create a complex environment in the lifecycle of a project which aims to achieve certain objectives within a certain time frame. This environment is in fact is the constellation of several factors related to the project itself, the project manager and team members, the organization and the external environment [10]. Gow and Morss [11] identify 'nine notorious' elements that create discomfort in the project environment and implementation process; macro constraints, institutional realities, personnel constraints, technical assistance shortcomings, decentralization and participation, timing, information systems, differing agendas, and sustainability. Political influence, defined by Hulme [12] as pressure from politicians, bureaucratic politics, and professional self-interest, is one of the impairments of project implementation. Because of politics, even a technically sound or well implemented project may be perceived to be a failure by the intended users [13]. Conversely, productive use of power and politics could be a critical success factor [14]. However, the extent of impact of this influence is more or less dependent on leadership. A good manger can judiciously tackle politics in the project management. According to Pinto [15, p.85], 'while most of us view politics with distaste, there is no denying that effective managers are often those who are willing and able to employ appropriate political tactics to further their project goals '.

Jó and Barry [7] find 'political support' as a top priority factor followed by the availability of technical experts and stakeholder involvements in the successful implementation of public sector projects. The Hossain et al. [16] study on the perceptions of government officials in Bangladesh regarding the success and failure of projects reveals politics as the most dominating factor. Government officials generally think that lack of internal political desire, lack of visions, dominance of politics, poor change management, lack of competencies and inadequate technological infrastructure are the major failure factors for project implementation in Bangladesh. However, the ongoing shift of the public service delivery mode from the bureaucratic model to the e-government self-service model entails changes in the process organization, management principles and leadership style in the management [17]. Gichoya [18] also identifies leadership styles, culture and bureaucracy as some of the major barriers that can hinder the project implementation process. In particular, this leadership should be process facilitating, coordinating and having the ability of innovative entrepreneurship [17] which should at least be sustained during the project period in order to avoid the failures [19], [20].

There have been a number of theoretical frameworks that explain the success and failure of individual project in developing countries [20]. Failure, as Heeks [21] finds, can be total or partial and is based on an evaluation focusing on the certain aspects.

However, very few of the theoretical frameworks are generalizable. Heeks' [22] 'design-reality gaps' is one commonly cited [23] model that explains the extent of gaps among the various dimensions of an Information system (IS) project and corresponding likelihood of the success of this project. Heeks model is basically the gaps between project goals or objectives and attainments. In fact, the factor project 'goals and objectives' has been cited by many authors with due importance [24], [11], [8], [24], [25], [26], [21], [7].

Success factors of a project can be termed as drivers or enablers whereas the failure factors are characterized as barriers or inhibitors [18]. Saurer [27] identified five types of failures, categorized as correspondence (project objectives), process (system production), interaction (user satisfaction), terminal (complete termination) and expectation (stakeholders' demands) failures. Project failure, especially in the context of poor countries, may come at a very high price in terms of several types of costs [22], such as direct financial costs, indirect financial costs (time and efforts), opportunity costs (loss of 'face' and images), political costs, beneficiary costs, and future costs (loss of morale, credibility and trust).

3 Method

This paper is an interpretive case study [28, p.76]. Primary data sources include telephone interviews with relevant actors, such as voters as participants, Army personnel who worked for PERP project, and a data entry operator. Secondary data sources are mainly reports of the development agencies and newspaper articles, printed and online. In addition, as one of the beneficiaries (one of the authors as a voter) of the PERP project, a 'participant observation' approach [29, p.214] was also used. This helped to provide 'rich insights into social settings'. The other author is from another country, hence helping achieve also a 'sense of detachment' which demands 'purposeful and independent way of setting the things' [29, p. 211].

Project assessment was made considering theoretical arguments for success and failure factors as discussed in the literature review.

4 Earlier Initiatives by the Bangladesh Election Commission (BEC)

The Bangladesh Election Commission (BEC) is a constitutional body responsible for administering the elections of national and all level of local governments. The commission consists of a Chief Election Commissioner (CEC) and usually two other commissioners appointed by the President for a five year term. A Secretariat headed by a Secretary to the government provides necessary assistance in order to execute the decisions of the Commission. BEC has a high degree of autonomy given by the Constitution and the Representation of the People Order 1972. According to article 118 (4) of the Constitution [30], BEC is 'independent in the exercise of its functions and subject only to this Constitution and any other law' of the country. This further implies that the Commission is free from influence from the government, parties or individuals in exercising its power. However, despite this constitutional stance, BEC 'still lacks an overarching law, which clearly states the powers of the BEC in relation to the government and an unambiguous redressal mechanism if the Government fails to comply with or distorts the implementation of the BEC's directives [31]'

Since independence in 1971, the role of the BEC has been assumed imperative in setting the future direction of politics and governments. Its role in preparing a reliable Voter ID card list for a credible election and stable democracy has been debated and discussed a lot, especially before the elections. Prior to holding the 6th parliamentary election in 1996, the first Voter ID card was initiated by BEC in August 1992 under the two pilot programs. Based on the lessons learned from these programs, BEC undertook a 15 month project in 1995 with almost no foreign technical or financial assistance [32] in order to prepare and issue nationwide voter ID cards before the 1996 election. It had initial a budget of BDT 3 billion, later reduced to BDT 1.87 billion (1 USD = 40 BDT, approx. in 1996). 'However, this project was not completed and the whole fund used in this project was wasted' [33]. Soban et al. [32] describe the 1995 project as a management and strategic failure rather than a technological failure. However despite continuing voter list anomalies, two general elections were held in 1996 and in 2001 without any ID cards.

Before having a biometrics based ID, a last but very crucial attempt was made to have a reliable and transparent voter list in 2006 based on the list of the 2001 by the then EC who was alleged to have been influenced by a political alliance then in power. However, the election was not held in due time because of gross irregularities in the voter list. According to UNDP [34] - 'This figure [of faults voters] comes roughly to 13% of the total number of voters and exceeds the traditional 5% margin of error; the major source of error in the updated Electoral roll is migration. It was also found that rural centers were more prone to error'.

This history shows that having a reliable voter list in the socio-economic, political and technological contexts of Bangladesh was very challenging. After a through investigation of all the post-independent national elections until 2001, Mannan [35] suggests that only the participative and competitive nature of elections can produce and promote democracy. More particularly, according to him, elections held under the neutral caretaker governments were found more meaningful than those held under party governments so far.

5 Towards a Credible Biometrics Voter List: The PERP

The following description of the implementation part of the PERP project is organized by the six-stage model for project lifecycle proposed by Munns and Bjerimi [36]; conception, planning, production, handover, utilization and closedown.

Conception

A biometric ID card is similar to traditional laminated paper cards but contains some biometric information which is stored digitally in a tiny microchip or barcode (magnetic strip). The card is used as a tool for uniquely identifying a living person by using their enduring physical and behavioral characteristics. The most commonly used biometrics data used are fingerprints, photos of face and eyes, and signature. In many instances hands, feet, ears, teeth, veins, voices, typing styles, gaits, odors [37] and even DNA data are used. Biometric ID cards are comparatively more secure than the traditional one as they are harder to forge. However, there are enormous debates over the security and privacy issues of the biometrics card especially in the western world. While the security issue is concerned with the unauthorized and inappropriate use, access and changes of the card and database, privacy is concerned about what sort of personal information can be provided, how, when and to whom.

There are yet only a few countries who have adopted biometrics ID cards, including South Korea, Brazil, Iraq, Italy, Senegal, Malaysia, and very recently Bangladesh. Notably, India will develop the world's largest repository of personal information by issuing around 1.2 billion biometric ID cards by 2011. The microchip of this card will contain personal data such as criminal records and credit histories, and proof of identity such as fingerprint or iris scans [38].

Preparing a Biometrics Voter list for over 80 million (80,508,311) citizens only within 11 months was not so easy in the context of Bangladesh. BEC acted as implementing agency to implement the activities outlined in the project guideline as formulated by the Executive Agency. Having an extensive experience in conducting elections and managing complex projects in UN peace keeping missions in Asia and Africa, the Bangladesh Army was given responsibilities under an operation called '*Operation Nabajatra*' (New start) with the aim of contributing management, technical and logistic support services under the supervision of the Election Commission. Operation Nabajatra was lead by a Chief Coordinator of the Bangladesh Army with the rank of Major General and a Project Director with the rank of Brigadier General.

The total allocated budget for the whole project was US$ 84,672,262 (of which around 41 % was funded by the Government and the rest from international donor agencies) for a period of 1 July 2007 to 30 June 2010 with a prime target to complete the biometrics voter list before holding the 9th parliamentary election.

Planning

PERP had two phases; to enable holding fair elections in 2008 by means of providing a credible voter list with photographs, and to maintain and update the nationwide list until the end of 2010. The following implementation activities were set out in the project guideline for realizing the desired output [34, 39]:

- Develop required software to support photo voter list data entry and storage (Allocated fund US$ 186,500)
- Establish ICT infrastructure at the Central, District, Upazila and field data collection teams (Allocated fund US$ 4,468,100; 5% of total budget)
- Provide training to field workers who will facilitate the creation of the photo voter list, including enumerators, data entry operators and data collection officers (Allocated fund US$ 6,097,000; 7% of total budget)
- Data collection and integration (Allocated fund US$ 58,137,658; 69% of total budget)
- Printing and distribution of photo voter list (Allocated fund US$ 4,886,56; 6% of total budget)
- Prepare project evaluation (Allocated fund US$ 150,000; 69% of total budget)
- Prepare project audit (Allocated fund US$ 60,000)
- Project management and implementation (Allocated fund US$ 10,686,438; 13% of total budget

The principle post-implementation (i.e. after holding the National Election in December, 2008) activities include [34]:

- To maintain the central and countrywide technology infrastructure established under the project;
- To institutionalize the Printed Voter List (PVL) and ICT skills capacity developed under the project at the central and field levels

Based on the lessons learned from a pilot project in June 2007 at Sreepur Poroshobha (Municipality), the PERP field level operation formally started on October 1, 2007 and completed on October 14, 2008 including the following fourteen stages: Form distribution and data collection, data verification, going to registration centre with the forms, registration centre, completing data entry, data export to server, proof reading/editing, preparation of proof voter list and verification, verification of proof voter list and handing over, ID card preparation and handing over for distribution, ID card distribution, correcting mistakes in ID cards, preparation of draft voter list and distribution, and data safeguarding and distribution.

In order to cover around 80 million voters across the country massive training projects were launched to build the capacity of half a million election workers which included around 309,000 enumerators, 104,000 computer operators of which 25% were women, 62,000 supervisors, 6000 officers and various technical experts and support staff. Over 10,500 laptops with webcams and fingerprint scanners with 5000 desktop computers/servers and 3,000 stand-by power generators were distributed to 90,000 registration centers throughout the country.

Comprehensive but careful planning and innovative methodology made the project overcome geographical challenges by reaching out to the people living in every corner of the country. Every means of transportation were used; walking, human haulers, speed boats, and even helicopters.

Production & handover

A brief about the system

There is an integrated large scale Automated Fingerprint Identification System (AFIS) and multi-biometrics Face-fingerprint Recognition Systems –FRS (please see Figure 1) developed jointly by TigerIT Bangladesh Ltd and DohaTech. This integrated system is designed in the Client Server paradigm and is organized around three areas: advanced solutions for voter registration and authentication for a wide range of government applications, finger print data checking for duplicate entries and Card management system - CMS [40]. The MegaMatcher technology 2.0 is used in this system that allows the use of either a fused face-fingerprint recognition algorithm with a capacity of up to 400,000 records per second or fingerprint and facial recognition engines separately [41]. The CMS server can import data from the client software, verify the data through Biometrics matching and facilitate to get the printout. The vetting server of AFIS is used for matching of fingerprints and facial images which can be taken through any webcam having windows drivers. In order to capture the facial images, a Cognitec Facial Recognition Software had been used. The resulting outputs in the form of ID cards include: (1) a two-dimensional barcode, encoded with

ISO fingerprint templates and PKI digital hash printed on each card including name, gender, birth date, and fingerprint template data for verification. This can include any data up to 4KB in size [40]; and (2) picture, signature and fingerprint images.

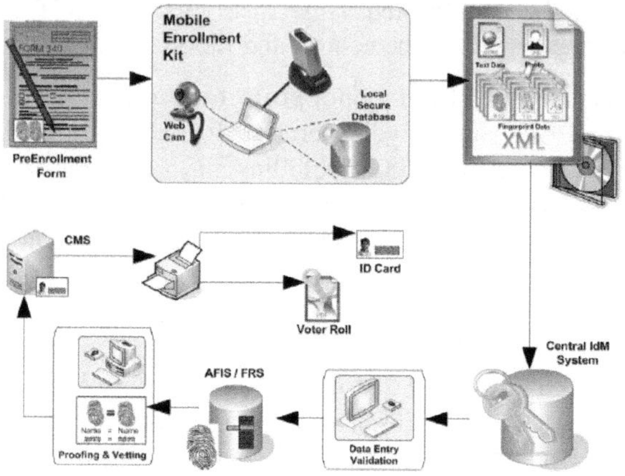

Fig. 1. Basic flow diagram of the Registration process [42]

The field level process and local mobilization

The data collection process was carried out in two phases: (1) before coming to the registration centre in which the enumerators (one for each for 3-400 people in an area) used to visit each home to distribute pre-numbered Registration Forms and to assist with filling in those forms; and (2) during the Registration period at the centers when the voters appeared in person before the data entry operators and had their completed forms recorded in the laptops. During this process, data verification was carried out followed by taking photographs and signatures through webcams and finger prints through scanners.

For the smoothest possible operation, registration equipment was mobilized even at remote places on demand by individual voters who were to travel due to age or disability. Well trained female data entry operators were assigned and separate areas were setup so as to properly adapt to privacy and religious values of the women as necessary. Local Imams (Muslim religious leaders) also worked for the Election Commission for educating the women to allow their photos to be taken for official purposes. In addition, 34 local NGOs were mobilized under a collaboration named Election Working Group lead by the Asia Foundation for raising awareness at the grassroots level and to encourage women and minorities to participate.

Data transfer process

After collecting data at the local centers, the data collection teams returned to the Upazila (sub-district) Election Office and uploaded data from their notebooks to the Upazila servers, after which all data was deleted from the notebooks. In the server, data accuracy was checked and fingerprints were matched for avoiding data redundancy for a particular voter. After this verification, a draft voter list was printed; the individual cards were laminated and subsequently distributed from the assigned locations. The draft voter lists were posted within the voter area for two weeks for getting feedback from the voters for finalization. Later, the final version of the *Upazila* (sub-district) databases were copied to DVDs and sent to the central Election Commission Data Center.

The detail tags of the DVDs being received were recorded in the Central Data Centre manually into the version control application and subsequently the data uploaded into the central database. Finally, electronic copies of the final voter lists were sent back to the respective District Election Officers for uploading to the District database.

Major implementation challenges

The implementation challenges as perceived by the project initiators and coordinators ([43], [44]) were addressed in the following ways:

Selection and customization of software: local development partners were invited to develop standard enrolment server and matching software which integrated multiple biometric features. This reduced the unit cost per ID card and overcame the risk of sharing copyright of the software and database to foreign vendors.

On-time startup, selection and procurement of appropriate and cost effective hardware: to be able to start on time (July 1, 2007) UNDP allocated US$ 5.1 million from its own funds even before signing the formal agreement on August 27, 2007. UNDP's direct procurement of hardware made it possible to proceed with the start-up activities in due time. Use of additional digital signature capture devices was supplanted by webcam snapshots which saved money and logistic hassles. For maintaining the longevity, each laptop was complemented with a low priced keyboard. A computer troubleshooting chain throughout the country was also ready for quick maintenance of the faults of any system involved.

Natural disasters: The project had to overcome two devastating cyclones (e.g. SIDR) with the help of Bangladesh Air force and Navy, which badly affected the communication infrastructure of the southern part of the country.

Utilization and evaluation

Despite some constraints and problems, the overall assessments are unanimously stated as 'success'. This success has initially and generally been defined by holding the most credible and fair election in the history of Bangladesh on December 29, 2008. UNDP [45] describes this outcome as a 'groundbreaking exercise in both scale and scope'. There have been some independent formal evaluations or audits in 2009 on part of the donors and other implementing agencies who had assisted the project. Beside the government and BEC's audits, the International Foundation for Electoral Systems (IFES, USA), the Department for International Development (DFID, UK) and UNDP were also among them. According to IFES [46] "The data was captured with a high degree of accuracy, The list includes only legitimate voters, High accuracy rates were geographically uniform, There were no discernible differences by gender in the accuracy of the list, Almost all photos are of good quality and nearly all eligible voters are on the list".

Furthermore, according to the audit report of UNDP [44], "Not only did it [PERP] develop a credible roll within the tight timeframe and against enormous challenges, it came in on time and under budget. ..... It has a nationwide technological infrastructure in place and functioning that has placed the BEC in the forefront of e-governance within Bangladesh. [....] The PERP project was an extraordinary achievement. It brought international and GoB support together to directly achieve the registration of over 80 million Bangladeshi citizens in eleven months and developed a voter list with photograph database with an accuracy rate of 98%."

6 Privacy and Security

The national identity database of Bangladesh containing the biometric and personal data of more than 80 million people is indeed a sensitive warehouse where privacy and security are important issues to concern. As for proper handling of database of the PERP, the then caretaker government promulgated 'the National Identity Registration Authority Ordinance 2008' in order to facilitate the national identity registration authority which will work with the Ministry of Home Affairs for ensuing secure use of the database. However, this ordinance was lapsed in the subsequent session of the parliament in 2009 and in lieu of this a new act entitled as 'the National Identity Registration Bill 2010' was passed on January 28, 2010. According to this law, BEC has become the custodian of this database and can ask for any data and information from any individual and institution. The third chapter of this law ensures punishments for any illegal activities which include providing false information to the database, possessing of more than one identity card, distorting and mishandling of the data in the database by the officials, forgery and usages of others cards. Notably, there is no clause for protecting privacy of personal information in this law. In fact, presently there is no privacy law at all in Bangladesh.

7 Conclusion

Table 1 compares the earlier initiatives of BEC until 2008 ([32], [47], [48], [34]) and the PERP project on the critical success factors discussed in the Literature Review section. The 3rd column summarizes on our analysis and the evaluation reports of the participating donors ([2], [45], [44], [46]).

Table 1. Comparison between earlier initiatives and PERP on critical success factors

Critical success factors	*Earlier initiatives*	*PERP project (Reasons of Success)*
Realistic goals	Goals were there but not so realistic in terms of political, bureaucratic, managerial, technical and socio-economic contexts.	A concrete project roadmap was there

Table 1. (*continued*)

Time-bound strategic planning	A segmented (phases) rather than holistic national approach to the project Poor planning and execution and unrealistic target settings. Too many anomalies in its preparation and distribution process. Lack of campaigning for creating mass awareness for participation Problems with locating the migrated voters and distributing the cards to Present addresses as was recoded initially	There was a time-bound strategic planning with a clear road map.
Management support	Management support was not adequate and persistent, and found ambiguous.	Very enthusiastic support from all across the management.
Efficient leadership	Lack of motivation of election staff and inadequate arrangements by the EC to visit door to doors to locate the legitimate voters. Failing to reach a majority of the population in due time means a risk of loosing credibility	The heads of all the units of the project were highly motivated and personally involved in achieving the goals. They had adequate sense of ownerships. All of them excelled at crisis and risk management, staff mobilization, staff motivation and effective partnerships and coordination.
Stakeholder involvement	Lack of consideration to culturally sensitive issues, such as taking photographs of conservative women.	An effective partnership and ownership among the various stakeholders with BEC was observed, such as political parties, Support to the Electoral Process in Bangladesh Project (SEPB), UNDP, Armed Forces, Electronic and print Media, Election Working Group (EWG), other civil societies, religious and community leaders, and even with the individual voters through mass awareness.
Resource mobilization	Too many errors and mismatch of voter details because of absence of an integrated central database.	Adequate resources in terms of money, personnel and technologies were mobilized as and when required in a highly coordinated working environment. For quick and uninterrupted start-up, UNDP allocated fund without any formal signing and mobilized computer hardware without any time consuming channel.

Table 1. *(continued)*

Progress review	Lack of periodic progress reviews.	In consistence with the project roadmap, there were regular and on-demand progress review meetings at the various units and at various levels. Formal committees holding such meetings included the Project Steering Committee (PSC), Project Implementation Committee (PIC) and Technical Voter List meetings. There was an annual progress meeting as well.
Positive power and politics	Inadequate political and bureaucratic commitment. Politically motivated self-interests	As the overall project environment was politically controlled and had less opportunity of emerging multiple interests from multiple directions, there were positive exercises of power and politics directing towards the same interests to hold a free and fair election through a credible voter list.
Urgency	Lack of perceived urgency for meeting the goals by the implementing agencies	The urgency was strongly shared by all
Users' expectations	Users expectation were not so vigilant due to lack of awareness by political institutions and civil society	Due to a massive awareness campaign and a certain political reality and restoration of parliamentary democracy, users' expectation for a credible voter list seemed high
Congenial bureaucracy	Strong bureaucracy of the Election commission secretariat and the apparently politically motivated BEC contributed to a complex and time consuming implementation process	Same bureaucratic structure, but now ran though a varied style of leadership with a concrete strategic planning which was congenial for the smooth implementation of the project.
External pressure and donor support	Donors' support was there in some cases but apparently had low and unvigilant pressure due to lack of perceived urgency especially from the demand side stakeholders	As the project was largely donor depended and as the donors apparently had the sincere intention to strengthen the electoral process and transparency both pressure and support were evident
Drive for modernization	Lack of urgency for modernization of process and output, which was one of the causes of having inefficient management	There was a strong drive for modernization in terms of project management and output, resource mobilization, and use of technologies.

Table 1 shows that having only a good vision, goals or objectives will not suffice for a success. Major differences, no doubt contributing enormously to the success are that PERP included: (1) a concrete time bound strategy; (2) competent and effective managerial leaderships; (3) adequate levels of technical and financial recourses; (4) Stakeholders, especially end-users support; and above all (5) firm political and bureaucratic commitment.

These are traditional project success factors, but in national large-scale public sector projects with a sensitive nature, in particular the fifth factor is worthy of some discussion. In particular so, a sone of the key themes of the appraising evaluations specifically pointed to the possibility to copy the project in other countries. There may be reasons for doubt about such transferability. Certainly technical details of the project can be easily transferable. However, the arguably most significant factor was the determination from the interim government – working in a 'politically controlled' environment. It was the inability of earlier governments that paved the way for several failures, and the ability of the military backed government that made the major difference. An issue, hence, is if a project like this is transferable to other countries with weak democratic governments. There are weak democratic governments in many developing countries, and given the Bangladeshi history as presented here it seems a risk that projects like this are more easily transferable to countries with stronger regimes, which are often not democratic.

Why would this be worrying? Isn't it always good with a credible citizen registration system? The debate over registration in the industrialized world holds at least two very different views on this issue which must be balanced. On the one hand, registration is necessary and good for administrative purposes, certainly when governments turn to electronic services. But electronic government services depend enormously on citizen trust; it is the single most important factor determining use in voluntary situations. There is no doubt that the new database will be useful in many ways, not just for voting but also for identification purposes relating to all government services. But registration is also useful for surveillance for many purposes ranging from fraud detection to combating terrorism. Whatever the purpose, not only the citizen's privacy is at risk but also their trust in government. The less citizens trust their government the more likely will they be to interpret the registration as a means for government surveillance purposes rather than for serving the citizens. The PERP has succeeded in supporting a successful election, which is indisputably an achievement. To be successful in the long run the government must also make sure to use the system for improving government services to citizens so it will become a tool for a trusted government.

References

1. Collier, D., Levitsky, S.: Democracy 'with Adjectives': Conceptual Innovation in Comparative Research. Working Paper 230, Kellogg Institute for International Studies, University of Notre Dame, USA (August 1996)
2. UNDP: Fact Sheet for PERP. United Nations Development Program, Bangladesh (2008)
3. NDI- National Democratic Institute: Report on Pre-election delegation to Bangladesh's 2006/2007 parliamentary elections. NDI for International Affairs, Dhaka (2006)
4. ID World International Congress: An overview and impact analysis of biometric voter registration and issuance of National ID card in Bangladesh. Wise Media SpA, Italy (2008)
5. Shaptahik-2000: Present Status of the National ID Cards project (12), Dhaka (2007)

6. New Age (the daily): National Id Cards. In: the interest of surveillance? Dhaka (July 22, 2008)
7. Jó, P.A., Barry, M.L.: The Most Important Success Factors for Implementation of Government Projects in Developing Countries. In: PICMET 2008, South Africa (2008)
8. Wit, A.D.: Measurement of project success. Intl. J. of Project Management 6(3) (1988)
9. Mitchell, R.K., Agle, B.R., Wood, D.J.: Toward a Theory of Stakeholder Identification and Salience: Defining the Principle of Who and What Really Counts. Academy of Management Review 22(4) (1997)
10. Belassi, W., Tukel, O. I.: A new framework for determining critical success/failure factors in projects. International Journal of Project Management 14(3), 141–151 (1996)
11. Morris, P.W., Hough, G.H.: The Anatomy of Major Projects. John Wiley, USA (1987)
12. Hulme, D.: Projects, Politics and Professionals: Alternative Approaches for Project Identification and Project Planning. Agricultural Systems 41, 211–233 (1995)
13. Yeo, K.T.: Critical failure factors in information system projects. Intl. Journal of Project Management 20, 241–246 (2002)
14. Pinto, J.K., Slevin, D.P.: Critical success factors in R&D projects. Res. Techno. Management, pp. 31–35 (January-February 1989)
15. Pinto, J.K.: Understanding the role of politics in successful project management. International Journal of Project Management 18, 85–91 (2000)
16. Hossan, C.G., Habib, M.W., Kushchu, I.: Success and Failure Factors for e-Government projects implementation in developing countries: A study on the perception of government officials of Bangladesh. In: Proceedings of the 2nd European Conference on Mobile Government, Mobile Government Consortium International (2006)
17. Ho, T.K.: Reinventing Local Governments and the E-Government Initiative. Public Administration Review 62(4), 434–444 (2002)
18. Gichoya, D.: Factors Affecting the Successful Implementation of ICT Projects in Government. The Electronic Journal of e-Government 3(4), 175–184 (2005)
19. Heeks, R., Bhatnagar, S.C.: Understanding Success and Failure in information age reform. In: Heeks, R. (ed.) Reinventing Government in the Information Age: International Practice in IT-enabled Public Sector Reform, pp. 49–74. Routledge, London (1999)
20. Kumar, R.: Making E-Government Projects in Developing Countries More Successful and Sustainable: Lessons from Two Case Studies from India. Information Technology in Developing Countries 17(3) (2007)
21. Heeks, R.: eGovernment for Development: Success/Failure. Case Study No.24, IDPM, University of Manchester, UK (2003)
22. Heeks, R.: Most eGovernment- for-Development Projects Fail: How Can Risks be Reduced? iGovernment Working Paper Series, IDPM. University of Manchester, UK (2003b)
23. Pucihar, A., Bogataj, K., Wimmer, M.: Gap analysis methodology for identifying future ICT related eGovernment research topics. In: 20th Bled eConference, Slovenia (2007)
24. Baker, B.N., Murphy, D.C., Fisher, D.: Factors affecting project success. Project Management Handbook. Van Nostrand Reinhold Co., New York (1983)
25. Ewusi-Mensah, K.: Critical issues in abandoned information systems development projects. Communications of the ACM 40(9) (September 1997)
26. Martin, C.C.: Project Management. Amaco, New York (1976)
27. Sauer, C.: Why information systems fail: a case study approach. Alfred Waller Ltd. (1993)
28. Walsham, G.: Interpretive case studies in IS research: nature and method. European Journal of Information Systems (4), 74–81 (1995)
29. Oates, B.J.: Researching Information Systems and Computing, 1st edn. Sage, Thousand Oaks (2006)

30. CPRB- Constitutions of People's Republic of Bangladesh, Part VII (Election). Ministry of Law, Justice and Parliamentary Affairs, Bangladesh (2010)
31. Hasan, M.: How assertive has the Election Commission been? Daily Star, Dhaka, Special issue (February 25, 2010)
32. Sobhan, F., Shafiullah, M., Hossain, Z., Chowdhury, M.: Study of eGovernment in Bangladesh. Bangladesh Enterprise Institute, Dhaka (2004)
33. Akram, S.M., Das, S.K. (eds.): TIB - Transparency International Bangladesh: Bangladesh Election Commission: A Diagnostic Study, TIB, Dhaka (2007)
34. UNDP: Preparation of Electoral Roll with Photographs. Final version, United Nations Development Programme - UNDP, Dhaka (2007)
35. Mannan, M.A.: Elections and Democracy in Bangladesh, vol. XIV, p. 194. Academic Press and Publishers Library, Dhaka (2005)
36. Munns, A.K., Bjeirmi, B.F.: The role of project management in achieving project success. International Journal of Project Management 14(2), 81–87 (1996)
37. EFF - Electronic Frontier Foundation: Biometrics: Who's Watching You? Issue - September, USA (2003)
38. Times: India to issue all 1.2 billion citizens with biometric ID cards. Online edition, UK (July 15, 2009)
39. BEC - Bangladesh Election Commission: Electoral Roll with Photograph Project. Dhaka, Bangladesh (2009), `http://www.ecs.gov.bd/` (accessed September 12, 2009)
40. TigerIT: National ID and Voter Registration Project for Bangladesh. TigerIT, Bangladesh (2009), `http://www.tigeritbd.com/` (accessed September 12, 2009)
41. Dohatech: Product and Services. Dhaka (2009), `http://www.dohatec.com/portfolioVRID.htm` (accessed September 10, 2009)
42. Bio-Key International: Empowering People and Commerce. Bangladesh Voter Registration and National ID Program, USA (September 2008)
43. Islam, S.M.: Getting the Impossible Done. Star Magazine (50) (December 26, 2008)
44. UNDP: PERP Evaluation Report. Evaluation Resource Centre, United Nations Development Program - UNDP, Dhaka, Bangladesh (2009)
45. UNDP: Celebrating the end of Photo voter Registration: Challenges Overcome. United Nations Development Program - UNDP, Dhaka, Bangladesh (2008)
46. IFES - International Foundation for Electoral Systems: Assessment of the Photo Voter List in Bangladesh, Washington DC, USA (November 30, 2008)
47. Raihan, A., Habib, S.M.A.: bd Bangladesh. Digital Review of Asia Pacific. Sage, Thousand Oaks (2007)
48. New Age: Voters' ID cards won't take a long time, claims vendors' forum. Dhaka (March 1, 2007)

E-Government and Geographical Information Based Collaboration Patterns

Lise Schrøder[1], Line Hvingel[1], and Henning Sten Hansen[2]

[1] Aalborg University, Department of Planning and Development, Fibigerstr. 11, 9220 Aalborg Oest, Denmark
[2] Aalborg University, Department of Planning and Development, Lautrupvang. 2b, 2750 Ballerup, Denmark
lisesch@plan.aau.dk, hvingel@land.aau.dk, hsh@plan.aau.dk

Abstract. In order to achieve an efficient e-Government many factors must be considered. In the UN e-Government Survey from 2008 a holistic approach is recommended incorporating human capacity, infrastructure development and access to information and knowledge. In the same survey Denmark is ranked second in regard of e-Government readiness. In Denmark the development of e-Government is characterised by a very informal, bottom-up approach, with a focus on standardisation, the use of geographic information systems (GIS) and IT-architecture. The organisational aspects have not been an issue of much attention. A national survey conducted by the University of Aalborg and Geoforum Denmark shows that the way the different players actually collaborate is a determining factor for a successful development in the field of e-Government.

Keywords: E-Government, Spatial Data Infrastructure, geographical information systems, knowledge management, innovation.

1 Introduction

The role of information and communication technologies (ICT) in e-Government can be regarded as changing into a new e-Government-as-a-whole concept which focuses on the provision of services at the front-end supported by integration, consolidation and innovation in the back-end processes and systems to achieve cost savings and improved service delivery [1]. The UN e-Government Survey from 2008 refers to the whole-of-government concept as a holistic approach to ICT-enabled public sector governance [1]. Achieving successful connected governance demands a re-engineering of technology, processes, skills and the mindsets of officials within a holistic framework, though in general governments in recent years have primarily focused on improving citizen e-Services rather than organising government agency functions and services.

Due to the UN the process of developing e-Government can be framed by three phases, where the first phase is focused on creating information infrastructures gradually moving towards a second phase characterised by integration of information,

K.N. Andersen et al. (Eds.): EGOVIS 2010, LNCS 6267, pp. 204–218, 2010.

services and governance models followed by a phase of transformation. A basic and continually upgraded infrastructure is required to facilitate integrative opportunities for delivering services and engaging citizens, whereas the exploitation of such opportunities demand engagement and participation among all stakeholders in order to foster more systemic transformation individually, organisationally and institutionally. The challenge is how to establish an organisational culture based on more collaborative and participative mindsets to facilitate the necessary transformation. Denmark and the other Nordic countries are topping the list in the UN ranking of e-Government readiness and the Nordic approach to establishing digital infrastructures is emphasised as an important conceptual way to e-Government [1][2].

In a broader European context the need of accessing environmental data has since 1998 resulted in legislation that focuses on public access to information about and the possibility of participation in the decision making in local, national and international environmental cases [3]. The focus on the interrelationship between the public sector and the citizens lead to the implementation of the Public Sector Information directive in 2005 [4] and the necessity of seamless interoperability of European data lead to the INSPIRE directive in 2007 [5]. INSPIRE does not only focus on the standardisation of geographical data, but also focus on a Spatial Data Infrastructure (SDI). During the previous ten years the Danish society has moved steadily towards an SDI by collecting data, making institutional arrangements and adopting standards – but without any overall strategy. However, the INSPIRE process has facilitated the development of a formal national SDI. December 2008 the Danish Parliament adopted a new law concerning the setup of an Infrastructure for Geographic Information, and geographic information is now considered as a key component in e-Governance [6].

In Denmark the development of e-Government is characterised by a very informal, bottom-up approach, with a focus on standardisation, the use of geographical information systems (GIS) and IT-architecture. The organisational aspects have not been an issue of much attention at the management level, though the actual situation shows that the way the different players actually collaborate is a determining factor for a successful development in the field of e-Government. During summer 2009 The University of Aalborg and Geoforum Denmark – the Danish national GI organisation – carried out a web based survey amongst Danish local, regional and national institutions to study the level of readiness for INSPIRE implementation in Denmark. This survey shows that the Danish model of organising the actors result in a close connection between the technicians and the decision makers, and also results in a general overall knowledge of new initiatives, for instance the INSPIRE Directive.

The aim of this research is to analyse the collaboration potentials regarding employee-driven innovation, knowledge sharing, cooperation and consensus creation between the various partners as opposed to a top-down model with implementation of detailed national strategies or working plans. The paper uses the Danish e-Government as a point of departure and is divided into four parts. After the introduction follows a description of the theoretical framework used in this paper. Next we describe and analyse the Danish context and some of the findings from the survey. Finally we end up with a conclusion and an outline for the next steps in our research.

2 The Theoretical Framework

Referring to the UN-report ICT-based connected governance efforts are aimed at an improved cooperation between governmental agencies, allowing for an enhanced, active and effective consultation and engagement with citizens, and a greater involvement with multi-stakeholders regionally and internationally [1]. Researchers in the field of geographical based ICT is emphasising how a SDI developed within the framework of e-Government contributes to ensure interoperability as means of developing the service part of the SDI and to create value due to the geographic and spatial dimension of e-Government [7]. Referring directly to the implementation of the INSPIRE directive it has also been pointed out how the political-organisational factors rooted in historical practises, legacy systems and dominating standards influence the practice of cooperation with geo-information which among other counter effects include a resistance towards top-down-steered standards [8]. This increasing tendency to focus on decentralisation and local matters is seen within e-Government as well [9]. In the following the UN perspective on the concept of Government-as-a-whole will be introduced followed by an illustration of how the development of e-Government can be seen as part of the threes step progression: Infrastructure, integration and transformation.

2.1 Government-as-a-Whole

E-Government can be defined as "the use of information and communication technologies (ICT) to improve the activities of public sector organizations and their agents" [1]. The UN e-Government Survey 2008 points out how the role of ICT in government is changing from the provision of services into a new e-government-as-a-whole concept which focuses on the provision of services at the front-end supported by integration, consolidation and innovation in the back-end processes and systems to achieve cost savings and improved service delivery [1]. It is pointed out how a more holistic approach is required in this process where the focus on creating information infrastructures gradually is moving towards integration of information, services and governance models followed by a phase of transformation. It is furthermore emphasized how a more collaborative and participative mindset is a must when dealing with this kind of transformation and how the organisational culture and the people element is crucial in the translation of back-end processes.

The distinguishing characteristic of the whole-of-government approach is that government agencies and organisations share objectives across organisational boundaries, as opposed to working solely within an organisation [1]. Due to this approach the focus on the e-Government has shifted from the provision of services to the use of ICT to increase value of services the citizens as illustrated in figure 1.

Traditional government	→	**e-Government**	→	**Connected government**
↓		↓		↓
Traditional Modes of Service Delivery	→	**e-services**	→	**Value of Services**

Fig. 1. Evolving approach to public service delivery [1]

To achieve greater value in service delivery and reduce costs, integration and re-design of government organisation and processes is a necessity. The concept of connected government is derived from the whole-of-government approach which is increasingly looking towards technology as a strategic tool and as an enabler for public service innovation and productivity growth.

1. Intra-Government Process Re-engineering → efficient, responsive and tailored government to reflect citizen needs

2. Inter-Government Process Re-engineering → efficient, joined-up borderless government:

- **Vertical cooperation/integration between levels**
- **Horizontal cooperation/integration between agencies at the same level**
- **Multi-stakeholder cooperation (with private and third sectors)**

3. Re-engineer legacy technology, processes, skills and mindsets

Fig. 2. Achieving Connected Governance: What the Government Does [1]

A basic and continually upgraded infrastructure is required to facilitate integrative opportunities for delivering services and engaging citizens, whereas the exploitation of such opportunities demands engagement and participation among all stakeholders in order to foster more systemic transformation individually, organisationally and institutionally [1][10].

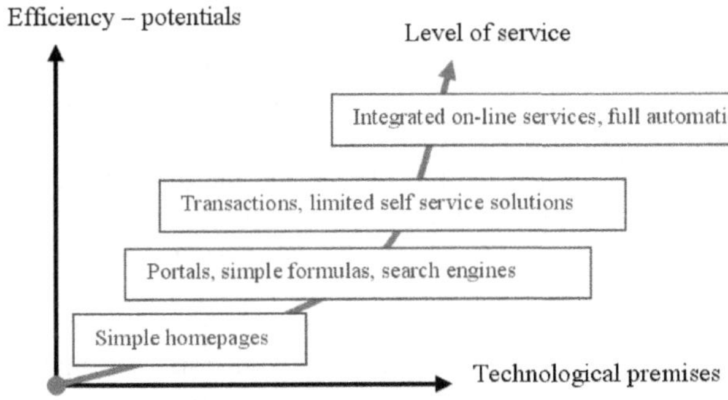

Fig. 3. Development of e-Government as visualised by the Danish Ministry of Science, Technology and Development [11]

As the geographic component is essential in most governmental issues, a well organised SDI is an important component of e-Governance, but it requires legal, institutional and technological frameworks facilitating the information flow between agents. Designing, building, implementing and maintaining an SDI draws on many different disciplines and requires examination of a large number of factors and issues. Organisational aspects are often overlooked in SDI assessments. SDI strategies are most often shaped by technical and economical aspects. However, the organisational issues are in many ways a much bigger challenge.

2.2 The Role of Spatial Digital Infrastructures in Developing E-Government

Though moving towards new concepts of e-Government focusing on integration of information, services and governance models followed by a phase of transformation well functioning information infrastructures is the basic foundation [1].

Infrastructure:
Creating an information infrastructure

Fig. 4. The first phase: The information infrastructure is fundamental [1]

A Spatial Data Infrastructure (SDI) can be defined as a framework of policies, standards and technology that enables data providers to publish, and users to access and integrate, distributed heterogeneous geospatial information [12]

An SDI hosts geographic data and attributes, sufficient documentation (metadata), a means to discover, visualize, and evaluate the data (catalogues and Web mapping), and some method to provide access to the geographic data. Beyond this are additional services or software to support applications of the data.

Fig. 5. The definition of an SDI set by the Global Spatial Data Infrastructure Association [12]

As formulated by Keith Murray, former Vice-Chair of FIG Commission 3, the SDI model can reflect all kinds of things: a "one stop shop" for GI information, a data clearing house, access to free data, visualisation of information/mapping, electronic services supporting GI and so on [13]. The Global Spatial Data Infrastructure Association points out how the spatial infrastructures provides the ideal environment to connect applications to data – influencing both data collection and applications construction through minimal appropriate standards and policies – even if the core SDI concept includes within its scope neither base data collection activities or a myriad of applications built upon it [12].

The Global Spatial Data Infrastructure Association emphasises how the organisational agreements on a local, regional, national, and on trans-national scale must be included to make an SDI functional [12], which is in contrast to a number of examples regarding the INSPIRE implementation. As de Vries points out there is a growing resistance of top-down steered standards due to the needs for autonomous decisions on the local level, which arise out of increasing influence of constituencies [9]. As he sees it there seems to be a tendency to an ongoing cyclic process regarding the acceptance or adherence of standards:

1. Centralisation of standards, formalisation of data regulations, grouping of authorities or centralising authorities
2. Decentralisation – opposition to standards, alternative standards, autonomous solutions, flexible solutions
3. Re-centralisation (new associations, new manoeuvring) – inter-agency cooperation changes from reciprocity relations to more top-down/principle-agent relations

2.3 Integrating Geographical Data in Citizen-Centric Governance Models

It has been pointed out how a more holistic approach is required in this process where the focus on creating information infrastructures gradually is moving towards integration of information, services and governance models followed by a phase of transformation [1].

Integration:
Leveraging this new infrastructure within the public sector and across society in order to better share information (internally and externally) and bundle, integrate, and deliver services through more efficient and citizen-centric governance models encompassing multiple delivery channels

Fig. 6. The second phase: Integration of information, service and governance models [1]

Although the core SDI concept includes within its scope neither base data collection activities or myriad applications built upon it, the infrastructure provides the ideal environment to connect applications to data – influencing both data collection and applications construction through minimal appropriate standards and policies [13]. Many of the ideas and concepts promoted over the last 10-15 years have been developed from a technical stance or academic perspective with very little influence by potential users [12].

De Vries emphasises how geoICT is changing public sector interactions and can be considered an agent in its own right [9][14]. Based on a series of case studies he concludes that the more inter-organizational ICT practices are institutionalised, the more complex the political nature of ICT becomes, which makes any evaluation of government-to-government achievements more complex [15].

2.4 E-Government, Knowledge Management and Collaboration Patterns

The whole-of-government concept has been described as a holistic approach to ICT-enabled public sector governance. Due to this approach the focus on the e-Government has shifted from the provision of services to the use of ICT to increase value of services, which furthermore is leading to a drive towards more collaborative models of service delivery. It is furthermore emphasized how a more collaborative and participative mindset is a must when dealing with this kind of transformation and how the organizational culture and the people element is crucial in the translation of back-end processes [1].

Transformation:
Pursuing service innovation and e-government across a broader prism of community and democratic development through more networked governance patterns within government, across various government levels and amongst all sectors in a particular jurisdiction

Fig. 7. The third phase: Transformation [1]

In recent years governments have primarily focused on improving citizen e-services rather than organising government agency functions and services. Achieving successful connected governance demands a re-engineering of technology, processes, skills and the mindsets of officials within a holistic framework. Changing skills and mindsets within a holistic framework demands on one hand a change from a technical view to optics known from theories concerning organisational learning, knowledge management, and human factor based innovation [16]. Dealing with the translation of back-end processes the understanding of the term *communities of practice* as conceptualised by Wenger [17] seems useful as means of grasping diffuse premises as organisational culture and the people element. Wenger characterises communities of practice as formed by people who engage in a process of collective learning in a shared domain of human endeavour, which could be a tribe learning to survive as well as a group of engineers working on the same problem known from various contexts as learning networks, thematic groups et cetera.

Communities of practice are groups of people who share a concern or a passion for something they do and learn how to do better as the interact regularly

Fig. 8. Communities of practise as defined by Wenger [17]

Wenger points out three crucial characteristics:

1. The domain – membership implies a commitment to the domain, and therefore a shared competence that distinguishes members from other people
2. The community – in pursuing their interest in their domain, members engage in joint activities discussions, help each other, share information, and build relationships that enable them to form each other
3. The practice – members of a community of practice are practitioners and develop a shared practice based on a shared repertoire of resources

Though there is an increasing focus on the need for focusing on user needs in innovation processes the potential in the community of practice approach could be seen as dealing with the crucial people element in the translation of back-end processes, which also leads to the actual discussion concerning user driven verses employee driven innovation.

3 Danish GI-Based Collaboration and E-Government

Denmark comes in second in the 2008 e-Government Readiness Index [1]. This indicates that Denmark is on the right track in regard of a successful e-Government approach. But what are the determining factors in this success?

One of the initiatives pointed out in the survey is the portal http://borger.dk/ ("borger" means citizen). This portal has together with http://virk.dk/ ("virk" is short for "virksomheder" which means companies) been key issues in the Danish development of front-end services. The two portals have been tools to achieve fully digital communication between the citizens, the private sector and the public sector. The other Scandinavian countries have similar portals working as a primary site that is informational and a tightly integrated, gateway site for e-services. Using this approach, each of the Scandinavian countries scored very high on the availability of services and transactions, the clear area where they excelled compared to most other countries [1]. In regard of Web Measurement Assessment (consisting of infrastructure development, citizen-friendly portals, online applications and back office integration) Denmark comes in first.

In 2009 a national survey was conducted by the University of Aalborg and the Danish national GI organisation Geoforum Denmark. Questionnaires containing 63 questions were sent to all public organisations in Denmark – i.e. ministries, national agencies, universities, regional authorities, and local authorities (municipalities). The survey gives a more detailed explanation of the Danish way of developing e-Government.

3.1 Development of Spatial Data Infrastructures in Denmark

The backbone of e-Government, represented by data and providers, has been in place for many years in Denmark. Already from the 1970ties and 1980ties the use of electronic data processing (EDP) to automate processes and make better use of information was been seen as a way of making the public service more efficient. Hence there is a lot of data available (digital maps and digital registers) with a geometry covering the whole country (fig. 9).

The first strategy for the Danish e-Government was given in 1994 under the heading "Information Society by the year 2000" [18]. But the real change came in 2001 with the creation of a Digital Taskforce, dedicated to enhance e-Government across the public sector. In a strategy from the same year e-Government was a focus area with the use of ICT as a way of improving and making the public sector more efficient to the benefit of citizens, private companies and the public sector itself [20]. There is no specific focus on SDI in the strategies. But together the elements represented in figure 9 form a national SDI [20].

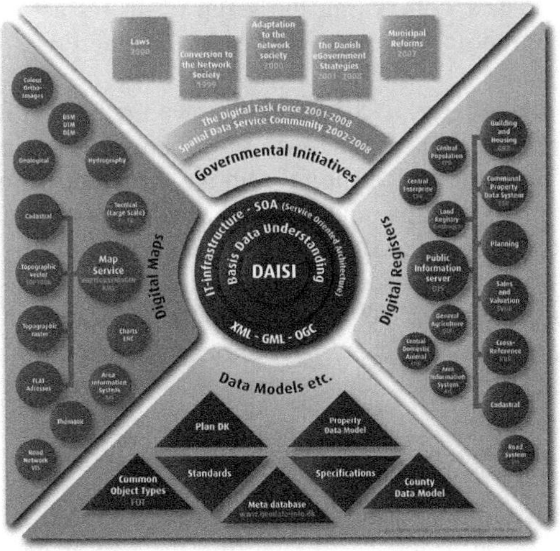

Fig. 9. An outline of the existing Danish registers, maps data models and governmental strategies [20]

The use of Geographical Data is an integrated part of the Danish SDI. By using a common geographic basis for administration, it is possible for example to link relevant data about the environment, traffic, health, property, companies and people.

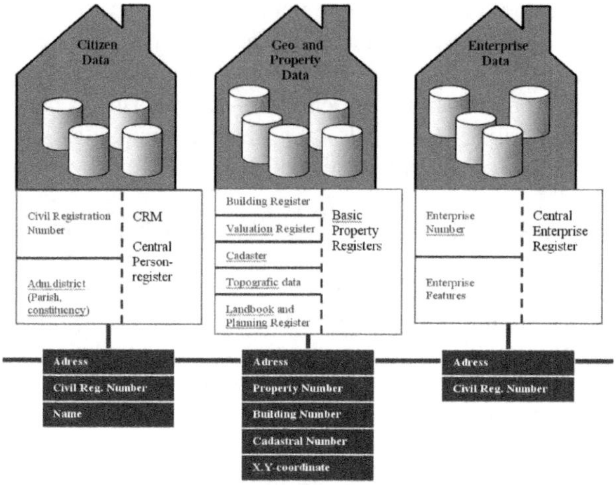

Fig. 10. The cohesion between geographical data and the existing registers in Denmark [21]

The INSPIRE-directive does not only focus on the standardisation of geographical data, but also focus on the SDI. The INSPIRE directive means implementation of net services, standards, metadata, portals and free access to the most essential data – all elements that is seen as a part of a SDI. Hence the INSPIRE process is facilitating the development of a formal national SDI in Denmark. December 2008 the Danish Parliament adopted a new law concerning the setup of an Infrastructure for Geographic Information, and geographic information is now considered as a key component in e-Governance [6].

One of the more challenging INSPIRE principles mentioned in the Directive deals with access to information. In order to make information from various levels of public authority available, Member States should remove the practical obstacles facing public authorities at national, regional and local level when performing their public tasks that may have a direct or indirect impact on the environment [6]. To remove this obstacle the Danish Government decided to let spatial information flow freely between all public bodies from 1 April 2010. Thus having paved the road for local SDI implementation in various parts of the public sector, the various organisations can start building their local SDIs.

3.2 GI-Based E-Government Initiatives in Denmark

A national Spatial Data Infrastructure (SDI) is often regarded as one of the prerequisites for an efficient e-Government and handling the new dependencies. But there is no official national SDI in Denmark. Though, as shown in the centre of figure 9 there is an actual functioning SDI in Denmark. The data integration is established though the use of XML, GML, WMS and WFS cookbooks etc. Information value of the data is obtained thought the use of metadata (ISO standards, INSPIRE compliant), map-services and portals (for instance a public environmental and area information system and a Digital Map Supply). Finally the overall IT-architecture is conceptualised through the Service Oriented Architecture-model (SOA). It may seem odd that there is a functioning SDI, when it is not a result of an overarching strategy.

The explanation lies in the Danish way of organising the development in the e-Government field and in general the way of organising the public sector. As mentioned in the UN-survey: Importantly, Denmark is not a federation but rather a unitary state [1]. Multiple levels of government thus coexist in an environment viewed by both the public and governments themselves as interrelated components of a single system. This sort of starting point is therefore more conducive to charting a collaborative, integrative course based upon more seamless governance architectures. Indeed, the Danish e-Government and related service strategies have been based since day one on formal intergovernmental planning and coordinating mechanisms to proceed in this manner [1].

As mentioned earlier The Digital Taskforce is working on endorsing e-Government. The implementation strategy is a combination of facilitating the development by establishing supporting services and pushing the development in a chosen direction by setting goals and making recommendations. This work is supported by another interrelated public project – The OIO-project – a more technical approach to the ongoing e-Government development. OIO is an acronym for Public Information Online. The OIO-project is to be seen as the toolbox for e-Government. It is through the OIO-project the choice of XML and SOA as the recommended concept has been made.

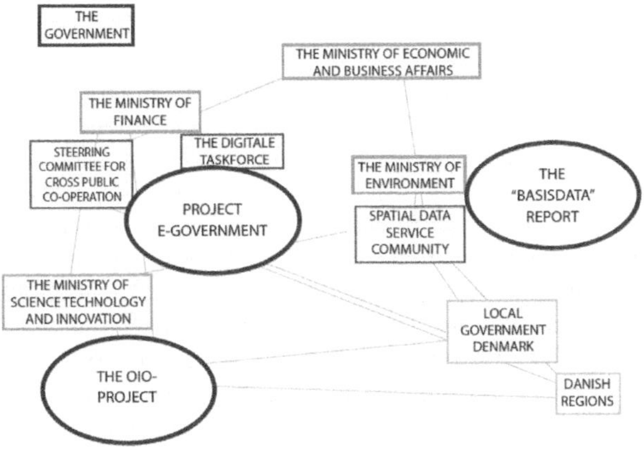

Fig. 11. A model showing the tangled interaction between actors in the national e-Government development

As a consequence of the INSPIRE implementation process national GI stakeholders made a report on Base Data [22]. This report is a very essential report, because it describes the interrelationship between data. As shown in figure 11 some data can be appointed as "Geographical Reference Data" which means data that is used as a base for the creation of other data, – for instance the cadastral parcel, the address, roads or buildings.

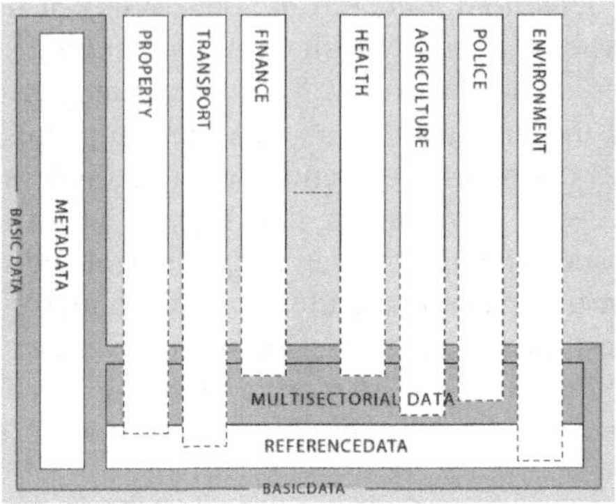

Fig. 12. The basic concepts of data interrelationship [22]

Other data is created solemnly for the use in one sector and is hence defined as Sector Specific Data. The appointment as "Geographical Reference Data" results in a higher demand of quality, coverage, metadata and so on than the single use data. This concept is broadly accepted on the Danish scene. The report is a result of the work in a committee under the Spatial Data Service Community (a good example of the Danish model understood in terms of communities of practice). Delegates from public and private users and producers of spatial data are assigned to the committee work. Researchers and professional associations (for instance Geoforum Denmark) are regularly invited to join the work.

The development of e-Government and SDI in Denmark reflects the technological possibilities and is to a great extend a result of engagement and shared responsibility among the players. This way of working implies a short way from the technicians to the decision makers, and often ideas born on one level is quickly adapted on the other levels – for instance the FOT-project (FOT is a Danish acronym for Common Object Types referring to common public geographical administration data) [23]. Together with the Spatial Data Service Community and Local Government Denmark, the National Survey and Cadastre has launched FOT-Denmark to develop a set of Common Object Types in order to establish a national base map for use at all administrative levels by combining the nationwide topographical TOP10DK database, which has a specified accuracy of 1 meter in all three dimensions, and large-scale technical maps with an accuracy requirement of 10-20 cm used by local government administrations.

3.3 Employee Driven Innovation in E-Government Facilitating Transformation

The distinguishing characteristic of the whole-of-government approach is that government agencies and organizations share objectives across organizational boundaries, as opposed to working solely within an organization. Regarding the web based survey carried out by Aalborg University and Geoforum Denmark to study the readiness for INSPIRE implementation in Denmark the response rate was 81 % and among 98

Danish municipalities 75 have answered the questionnaire as well as 47 other public organisations at the regional and national level. The overall conclusion of the survey is that geographical information is an important component of e-Government, and is seen as an integrated and inherent part of the public administration in Denmark.

Although there is no national strategy for SDI more than fifty percent of the municipalities have a strategy for the use of geographical information and the development of better administration systems and in the end better public service. The survey conveys a picture of a model with a strong emphasis on the sub-national levels where implementation is done by technicians in cooperation with leaders. The survey shows in general that the price (both regarding data and software), accessibility (fast and simple), data quality and accuracy are all important factors.

INSPIRE supports the ongoing development by implementing national standards for SDI, which of course will affect the local SDIs. The survey shows that approximately 75 % of the participants are aware of the INSPIRE Directive, and more than half (nearly 60 %) is familiar with the Danish Law concerning Infrastructure for Geographic Information. Considering the sources of information about INSPIRE the responses illustrates that 68 % of the municipalities obtain knowledge by the national GI organisation Geoforum Denmark, 24 % are participating in special seminars on INSPIRE, 38 % of the municipalities are consulting the Danish INSPIRE homepage, whereas only a few answers from the municipalities points out the official EU INSPIRE homepage as the main source to information. Only 11% of all answers mentions the official INSPIRE homepage as the main source to information – and not surprisingly this groups represents universities and governmental agencies. The share of organisations using Geoforum Denmark decreased to 55 % when regarding all respondents. Additionally, 25 % of the organisations are member of the national INSPIRE network stimulating discussions regarding INSPIRE among Danish organisations.

According to the survey INSPIRE is discussed to a great extend at the technical level, as 37 % answers that only the technical staff is involved, 10 % are having discussions at the technical level as well as at the management level, while only 15 % experience it as a matter solely handled by the top level. Almost half (44 %) the answering organisations points out that they have a local GI Strategy, and 70 % are having a GI-coordinator, while only one organisation (a national agency) has made a specific strategy concerning the implementation of SDI.

An educated and trained workforce is an important component in building SDIs. According to the answers in the Danish survey further education of the existing staff in order to meet the need for further competence is of great importance. 72 % will upgrade staff to be able to perform at a simple GI use level, 62 % will upgrade perform at an advanced GI use level, and 48 % will upgrade teaching, management, and support functions.

3.4 The Danish Experiences

Based on the discussion above it is evident that one important factor in order to obtain a successful implementation is dissemination of information, which in this Danish case is being carried out most successfully through NGO interest groups, and by continuing education of the workforce. The main interest for SDI and INSPIRE comes from groups of GI- and IT-technicians, whereas SDI still lacks focus from the top management level. Nevertheless, we expect that particularly the Danish Law on Infrastructure for Geographic Information and the national e-Government strategy will improve this situation, and move geographic information into a key position in e-Governance. The Danish case shows how Geographical Information Systems have proved to be an interlinked and essential part of the e-Government. It is shown as well how the informal network is very efficient in spite of the low degree of hierarchy. The Spatial Data Service Community itself is a good example of the Danish approach.

4 Conclusion

The aim of this research has been partly to explore the way to an efficient e-Government partly to analyse the potentials in the Danish approach based on employee-driven situated innovation, knowledge sharing, cooperation and consensus creation between the various partners as opposed to a top-down model. Framed by the emerging whole-of-government concept and the need for a holistic approach to ICT-enabled public sector governance the Danish GI-oriented e-Government has been analysed as an example of modern collaboration patterns based on knowledge sharing and a creative and highly skilled workforce.

It is important to understand that a focus on organisation and transformation in organisations is not the same as formalising and institutionalising the development. The Danish case shows that the very informal environment with cross ministerial projects and a close co-operation between public and private actors and interest group is a profitable constellation. The key in this regard is the knowledge dissemination and innovation through these communities of practises. Based on our analysis we can conclude that the Danish approach has proven its strength as a collaborative bottom-up approach to e-Governance implementation. The other way around the Danish approach has proven its worth as the INSPIRE and PSI directives has been relatively easy to implement. Many data, metadata and services are already in place. Especially the use of GIS to develop e-Government is an illustrative case of successful bottom-up collaboration patterns. The challenge in the Danish model is the lack of awareness – awareness of the justification regarding this way of working, and awareness of a more common objective of the work with focus on the different demands to front-end and back-end services.

Subsequent research has to be conducted in interdisciplinary fields of employee driven innovation, organisational learning and knowledge management to be able to facilitate the collaborative working environments shaping the future e-governance concepts. Especially there seems to be a potential in the theory of communities of practise as means of framing diffuse collaboration patterns in the ongoing phase of transformation.

References

1. United Nations Department of Economic and Social Affairs: UN E-Government Survey 2008 – From E-Government to Connected Governance. United Nations Publication, New York (2008)
2. World Economic Forum, INSEAD: The Global Information Technology Report 2008-2009. Geneva (2009)

3. UNECE: Aarhus Convention – UNECE convention on Access to Information, Public Participation in Decision-making and Access to justice in Environmental Matters (1998)
4. European Union: Directive 2003/98/EC of the European Parliament and of the Council of 17 November 2003 on the reuse of public sector information the Public Sector Information. Official Journal of the European Union (2003)
5. European Union: Directive 2007/2/EC of the European Parliament and of the Council of 14 March 2007 establishing an Infrastructure for Spatial Information in the European Community (INSPIRE). Official Journal of the European Union (2007)
6. Danish Government: Lov om infrastruktur for geografisk information (implementation of Directive 2007/2/EC of the European Parliament and of the Council of March 14, 2007). Ministry of the environment, Copenhagen (2008)
7. Georgiadou, Y., Harvey, f.: A Bigger Picture. In: Information Systems and Spatial Data Infrastructure Research Perspectives. In: The Proceedings of the 10th AGILE International Conference on Geographic Information Science, Aalborg University (2007)
8. De Vries, W.T.: INSPIRE obscured by clouds of inter-organizational cooperation with geoITC? International Journal of Spatial Data Infrastructures Research 4, 117–133 (2009)
9. De Vries, W.T.: e-GOV and SDI: The common grounds and missing links. In: The proceedings of the 8th Annual International Digital Government Research Conference, Philadelphia (2007)
10. Danish Government, Local Government Denmark and Danish Regions: Towards Better Digital Service, Increased Efficiency and Stronger Collaboration – The Danish e- Government Strategy 2007-2010. Copenhagen (2007)
11. Danish Government: Hvidbog om IT-arkitektur (Whitepaper on IT architecture). Danish Ministry of Science, Technology and Development, Copenhagen (2003)
12. Nebert, B. (ed.): The SDI Cookbook, Vers. 2. The GSDI-Technical Working Group (2004)
13. Murray, K.: What is an "SDI"? National SDIs are needed if GIS is to reach its full potential. Geomatiocs World 14(1), 33–34 (2005)
14. Georgiadou, Y., Geordiadou, Y., Miscione, G., Lance, K., de Vries, W.T.: Framing the use of geoinformation in government: A tale of two perspectives. Earth SCi Inform. 2, 271–282 (2009)
15. De Vries, W.T.: A review of the political nature of ICT in G2G integration – based on 3 cases from the geoICT domain. In: The Proceedings of the 9th Annual International Digital Government Research Conference, Montreal (2008)
16. Snyder, W.M., Wenger, E.: Our World as a Learning System: a Communities-of-Practice Approach. In: Conner, M. L., Clawson (eds.): Create a Learning Culture: Strategy, Practice, and Technology. Cambridge University Press, Cambridge (2004)
17. Wenger, E.: Learning for a small planet – a research agenda, Etienne Wenger Research and Consulting, `http://www.ewenger.com/research/`
18. Danish Government: Information Society by the year 2000, Ministry of Research, Copenhagen (1994), `http://vtu.dk/filer/publikationer/1994/rapport-fra-udvalget-om-informationssamfundet-aar-2000/english-version/html/preface.html`
19. Danish Government: Projekt Digital Forvaltning (Project Digital Government), Copenhagen (2001)
20. Brande-Lavridsen, H., Jensen, B.H.: Development of a Danish Infrastructure for Spatial Information (DAISI) – under the wings of digital Management. In: Proceedings from the Nordic GIS Conference in Helsinki. National Survey of Finland, Helsinki (October 2-4, 2006)

21. The Danish Department of Taxes, The Danish Survey and Cadastre: Undersøgelse af adressefællesskabet mellem CVR og BBR (Common addresses in the Central Enterprise Register and the Register of Buildings and Dwellings), Danish Ministry of Internal Affairs and the Danish Ministry of the Environment, Copenhagen (2000)
22. Servicefællesskabet for geodata: Basisdata (basic datasets), Copenhagen (2004)
23. FOTDanmark: Specification FOT 4.0. Copenhagen (2010), `http://www.fotdanmark.dk/Materiale/Files/Specifikation+4.0+p%c3%a5+engelsk`

Participatory Design of Public Sector Services

Alan Hartman[1,*], Anshu N. Jain[1,*], Jay Ramanathan[2], Antonis Ramfos[3], Willem-Jan Van der Heuvel[4], Christian Zirpins[5], Stefan Tai[5], Yannis Charalabidis[6], A. Pasic[7], T. Johannessen[8], and T. Grønsund[8]

[1] IBM Research India Bangalore, India
{ahartman,anshu.jain}@in.ibm.com
[2] Ohio State University Ohio, USA
[3] Intrasoft International Luxemburg
[4] University of Tilburg, Netherlands
[5] Karlsruhe Institute of Technology, Germany
[6] National Technical University of Athens, Greece
[7] Atos Origin, Spain
[8] Ignitas, UK

Abstract. This paper describes a methodology for the participatory design of services in the public sector. The stakeholders participating in the design include three major players, the public which uses the service, the government body which sponsors and finances the service, and the organization (government or third party) that delivers the service. We propose a method for a) gathering the – possibly conflicting – requirements for a service from the three stakeholders, b) representing the design alternatives and their levels of requirement satisfaction, and c) generating a simulation model of the service delivery process for the different design alternatives. The method is illustrated by a practical example based on a real government service.

Keywords: Service design; value; modeling; simulation.

1 Introduction

A service system is a system for creating an experience which provides value for both the consumer and provider of a service. Service systems in the public sector are often created by ad hoc methods and frequently suffer from defects that impair their capabilities to provide value in a systematic and predictable way [14]. A service design process that introduces engineering rigor can help alleviate these problems by exploiting engineering techniques including modeling, simulation, testing, and prototyping.

Historically, most public enterprises have been organized around hierarchical principles with decision-making concentrated at the apex of the organization. Centralization ensures fairness of treatment for both service recipients and employees, clear chains of accountability, and minimizes the exposure of service delivery to political

* Corresponding authors.

K.N. Andersen et al. (Eds.): EGOVIS 2010, LNCS 6267, pp. 219–233, 2010.

forces. However, institutions organized as hierarchies also find it challenging to address non-routine problems that demand networked solutions and responsiveness to external public forces. In response to criticisms that centralized hierarchies are stultified and inefficient, some public organizations have moved towards decentralization. More recently, organizational boundaries in the public sector have become porous as service delivery becomes the responsibility of a network of public and private organizations – government agencies, private firms, non-profit organizations – bound together by contracts and grants, with a common commitment to addressing relevant services [16].

Looking to the future, as Broadband and social media encourages citizen participation and more targeted identification of needs, we will see government organizations and networks with wide-ranging service responsibilities strive to become more adaptive. That is, by fine-tuning service delivery to the very specific needs of communities, greater efficiencies can be achieved by hierarchies, federations and networks.

A public service has multiple stakeholders, each deriving some value. Three key stakeholders are: the public; the government leadership; and the operations or delivery organization. A design based approach exposes the value trade-offs, and enhances the ability to adapt to changes in the value expectations of the stakeholders. Our work focuses on this design methodology with emphasis on the gathering of requirements and tradeoffs between the design alternatives using a valuation function which balances the stakeholders' interests.

Section 2 discusses the background and related work. We then introduce the details of the design methodology in Section 3. The next three sections go into more details of our approach to gathering requirements, representing design alternatives, and creating simulation models from them. We conclude in Section 7 with an illustrative scenario.

2 Background and Related Work

There have been several attempts at building conceptual tools and languages to model service businesses. Shostack [2,3] made one of the earliest attempts at emphasizing the uniqueness of services as opposed to product manufacture. She proposed the blueprinting concept which was later developed by several researchers including Zeithmal and Bitner [4] and Zeithmal et al. [5] who added a service quality model based on gaps in service quality to the blueprinting framework.

In the public sector, Cole and Parstons [7] have described a model for determining the value of public service outcomes and described methods of measurement for the value and efficiency of public services. Substantial results have been certainly achieved in specific fields [8]: for example, the most important services are available on the Internet to all citizens [9], the majority of income tax declarations are made electronically, and huge savings have been achieved through eProcurement. However, according to EUROSTAT, in 2007, just above 10% of European citizens used public services through the Internet at the transaction level [8], despite the fact that the number of services available online has grown considerably over the previous few years and included the majority of basic public services [10].

Ramanathan et al. [17] have used an Adaptive Complex Enterprise (ACE) architecture framework for decision-making in a multi-year interdisciplinary industry-university collaboration with the City of Columbus (Ohio, USA) which implemented a successful 311[1] system.

The case for the 311 was based on viewing the City as a complex of service transactions - the Adaptive Complex Enterprise (ACE). This architecture framework treats the city organizations and IT in a holistic manner to create a sense-and-respond view of networked service capability. ACE consists of a number of nested dimensions, each of which represents stakeholders with similar performance interests regarding each type of service transaction:

- The **strategic** dimension: consisting of the citizens, the mayor's council and other stakeholders that are recipients of deliverables. With emerging social media tools, a new opportunity to sense external requirements and assess satisfaction exists.
- The **business** dimension: consisting of the financial stakeholders that make decisions related to investments, value creation of ACE transactions, and prioritizations that align this to respond to the external requirements.
- The **operations** dimension: consisting of managers that use the infrastructure and align it to maintain and improve transaction quality, costs, and satisfaction,
- The **infrastructure use** dimension: consisting of stakeholders that perform services in response to incoming requests. Rules are applied so that the needed transactions are operationalized into detailed tasks using resources, and deliverables are produced.

The methodology described in the next section extends the ACE view and adds a number of qualitative and quantitative aspects to improve the engineering rigor and formalize the participatory nature of public service design. We are also indebted to the anonymous reviewer who drew our attention to the extensive literature in participatory design, cooperative design, and socio-technical design especially the work of the late Enid Mumford [28].

3 Public Service Engineering Methodology

The focus of the methodology proposed in this paper is to involve all stakeholders including policy makers, governmental administrators, public/private service delivery managers/staff, software architects and engineers, and most importantly the citizens into the conception and/or reinvention, analysis, design and optimization of public services. This requires a new way of public service engineering that is substantially more interactive and agile than traditional software and service engineering approaches. Large groups of individuals need to be consulted frequently up to a point

---

[1] A 311 system is a central, one-stop-shop for requesting non-emergency City services (such as bulk trash pickup), reporting non-emergency information (such as potholes, water leaks, and dead animals) and receiving information – such as open routes to Fourth of July fireworks displays.

where they act as co-designers in the engineering process. The challenge is to provide adequate channels, modes, models and methods to effectively and efficiently engage large groups of people into a rigorous engineering process that has to consider legislative and budgetary constraints.

Building on various Web-based communication channels for direct and indirect modes of interaction with large groups of stakeholders, the focus of our service engineering approach is on appropriate models, methods, processes and tools that leverage mass collaboration for public service design. This not only accommodates the development of new services, but also, and probably more importantly, the modernization or overhaul of the existing public service portfolio.

We build on sophisticated service modeling techniques that combine multiple social and technical dimensions to be considered in the engineering approach. To this end blueprints play a pivotal role. Public service blueprints are logical extensions to existing service modeling standards that define a) common patterns of public service delivery to be reused for new designs and b) associations between different models that describe these patterns with respect to various social and technical dimensions. Among others, such blueprints integrate

- service models, defining interfaces and service collaborations,
- process maps, defining abstract models of standard public service processes,
- performance models, defining a logically cohesive set of process-, service- and resource performance indicators in terms of collaborative KPI and QoS levels,
- value models, defining costs and benefits associated to public services, and
- lifecycle models, defining deployment descriptors and monitoring requirements.

Underpinned by service models and blueprint abstractions, our public service design approach comprises a number of engineering methods that consider preferences and constraints of large societal groups and communities as well as governmental policies, rules and regulations alike. On the one hand, our project will devise mass-collaboration methods for participatory decision making based on costing and valuation of public service designs. Public service costing leverages a framework for static analysis of cloud service total cost of ownership [18] that we refine and extend for the case of public service delivery. This is complemented by our approach to public service simulation, which enables dynamic analysis of key performance indicators. Subsequently, we adopt and extend multi criteria valuation methods like the analytic hierarchy/network process [19] in order to translate citizens' opinions and wishes into categories of decision-making and conduct pairwise comparisons of design choices for public services. Categories reflect technology, societal, and economic factors. On the other hand, we also consider regulatory compliance of public service designs. By offering means to formalize the public services and rules alike, compliance-checking services will be offered to ascertain that public services do in fact adhere to critical and relevant constraints.

Finally, our service engineering includes a specific lifecycle methodology. True co-creation requires much more intense and frequent stakeholder interaction than would be the case in traditional service development processes. Public service design involves fast cycles of continuous (re)designing, costing, checking and valuating many service aspects in order to keep all parts of a blueprint in sync and evolve them in terms of public opinion. This is complemented by less frequent cycles of simulating, representing and deliberating more complex service characteristics. However, the concrete level and methods of interaction vary from case to case. Hence we consider life histories that interrelate the lifecycles of public service networks, models and instances. In particular, we advocate a recursive method that leverages our participatory engineering approach for bootstrapping the engineering process of public services itself including customization of the engineering methodology under consideration as well as existing policies and regulations.

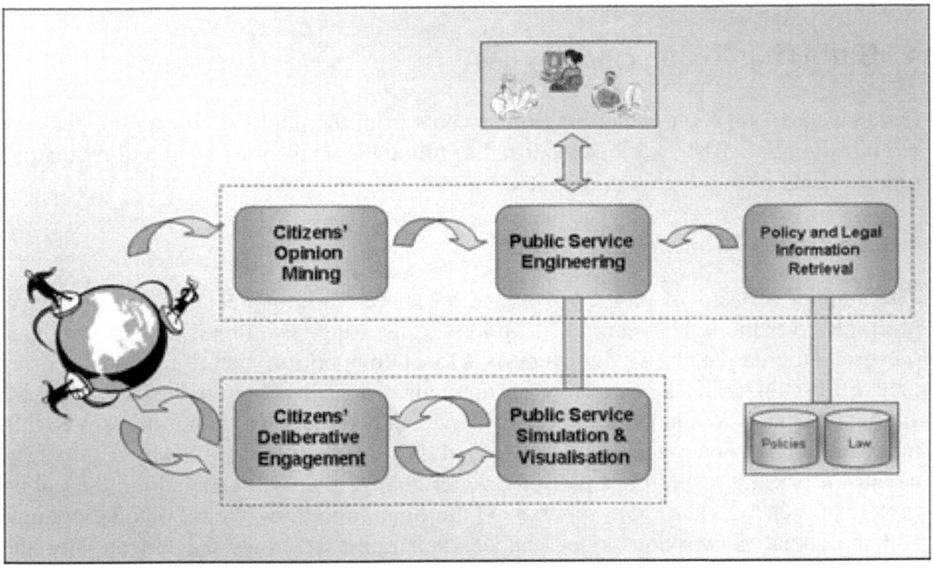

Fig. 1. Data flow in the design methodology

The best way to illustrate the methodology is to describe its flow of information, as shown in Figure 1, which includes the following steps:

1. Citizens' interactions with Web 2.0 social media are monitored for their opinions and needs on public services in a specified domain. These requirements are fed into the initial service design process.
2. Government decision makers start modeling the service using our public service engineering tool. They input the high level requirements for the service outcomes. Citizens' opinions and wishes on the selected public services are available to the decision makers to be taken into consideration.

3. During specification of the service, the existing policy and legal framework related to the corresponding service is consulted using existing text retrieval technology on policy and legal digital libraries.
4. Experts in service delivery input their constraints related to resources and infrastructure requirements.
5. The output of the public service engineering tool is fed into the public service simulation and visualization tools in order for the decision makers to make adjustments that will reflect budgetary and operational constraints.
6. Once decision makers have arrived at a specification for the delivery of the public service, citizens will be presented with a visual simulation of the service in a deliberative platform.
7. Citizens' informed judgment on the simulated operation and related costs of the selected public services are expressed and returned to the decision makers for further consideration and final decisions.

4 Gathering Requirements

Our current focus is on gathering requirements from the public and from the delivery organizations. Further work is proposed to refine the analysis of legal and regulatory requirements from the government itself.

4.1 Gathering Public Requirements

The number of users of blogs, wikis, and social networking websites has grown explosively over the last 3 years [11]. Moreover, the long-term trends of customer empowerment, creative knowledge workers, global competition, flatter and looser forms of work organization, and user-driven innovation are all being enabled by Web 2.0 applications [12]. While there are certainly elements of hype in the notion of Web 2.0, many underlying socio-economic trends lead us to conjecture that the key features are not just a passing fashion but part of a wider change that will carry along the public sector. In fact, we share with others [13] the opinion that, as Web 2.0 collaboration- and the social networking-savvy younger generation becomes the citizenry of the future; it will increasingly turn to Web 2.0 social media in order to express its opinions and wishes about public services delivery.

There are many definitions of Web 2.0 and other terms describing it (social software, social computing, participative web, and user-generated content), each one capturing some dimensions and missing others [24]. This paper adopts an operational definition of what is included in the definition of Web 2.0, and defines Web 2.0 as composed of a set of:

- **Values:** openness to broader audience and transparency, sharing of information and knowledge, and value co-creation, ease of use
- **Applications:** e.g. blogs, wikis, Podcast, social networks, collaborative filtering, recommender systems, and bookmark sharing (tags, RSS)
- **Technologies:** e.g. Ajax, XML, OpenAPI, Microformats, Flash/Flex

Citizens' opinion mining will involve two major steps:

- **Content collection** - constructing the analysis (mining) space, i.e., collecting and managing the appropriate content in which citizens' opinions (sentiments) about aspects of a public service can be tracked.
- **Content analysis** - performing the analysis and identifying citizens' sentiments on particular aspects of a public service.

Content collection: Opinion mining is based on publicly available data sources like blogs, fora, newsgroups, msn, and YouTube, but excludes social networking sites that require membership, a password and authorization to access data. The mining bases itself on existing collections of content or develops its own content collection. Key factors are the scope of the subject matter of the services, the geographical scope of the services, and the citizens affected by the services. In both cases specifically targeted content collection activities are undertaken:

1. Identification of potentially relevant Web 2.0 sources: for this a robot (crawler) is used that crawls on RSS feeds and recognizes structure (blog, forum, etc) and initial content. The robot stores URLs and metadata.
2. The second pass is the relevance analysis of the stored URL and metadata in two steps. Step one filters spam and noise, followed by a semantic and keyword analysis to determine relevance. The relevant URLs are kept, while the irrelevant URLs are stored as a reference to be excluded in new searches.
3. The relevant Web 2.0 sources are downloaded in their entirety and stored in a database for further analysis.
4. Through the RSS, feeds updates of the Web 2.0 sources are continuously captured

Content analysis: The analysis of the stored Web 2.0 content is specified for each policy and public service domain. Analysis of the stored content includes the following steps:

1. A definition of the policy and public service domain specific key concepts scheme. This scheme is not a formal ontology but is based on terms used by citizens for referring to public service delivery in the public debate in Web 2.0 blogs and fora.
2. Matching of the scheme with the service design formal representation
3. Building the queries that perform the analysis, and refine the queries.
4. Running the analysis queries on the stored content.
5. Interpretation of the analysis results as citizens' opinions on public service delivery.
6. Mapping of the analysis results into a suitable input form to the public service modeling tool.

In the analysis of the stored content to identify citizens' opinions, the method applies a combination of supervised and semi-supervised learning techniques, as well as symbolic methods based on rules and patterns. The supervised learning is used to classify textual fragments from blogs, newsgroups texts and forums based on a training corpus built from the same kind of data. The semi-supervised approach is less reliant on annotated training data and is used to automatically learn subjective words and patterns that are good indicators for sentiment and to classify new fragments of text based on the patterns learned.

Our prior work in gathering public service requirements from the public was based on analysis of the call logs from 311. These logs are a rich source of information collected from the citizen calls since 311 is the single point of contact for non emergency citizen complaints. The information from the 311 call logs provide insights not provided by the standard reporting procedures, and these were used to provide insights into the structure and strategy for service delivery.

4.2 Gather Delivery Organization Requirements

The current practice is to use public administration management information systems to gather statistical data around service request and delivery such as transactions volume, frequency, processing time, delivery time, accumulated costs. This is evaluated and manually incorporated into the service design process. With our methodology and tools much of this is automated.

It is currently the strategy of the Greek government to model and simulate processes related to the provision of services towards the citizens, (e.g., request and delivery of birth, marriage, death certificates, request and delivery of family status certificate, residence license for foreigners, declaration to the police), and businesses, (e.g., payments to the municipality, license to operate an entertainment place), also through the regional and local administrative levels. The latest Greek National Interoperability Framework [21] prescribes the above activities and information points, in accordance also with the European Interoperability Framework [22] and its latest reviews. New services can take advantage of the ERMIS portal, which is the central governmental service gateway, running at www.ermis.gov.gr.

The set of all requirements are consolidated into the public service design model, and where necessary, transformed into constraints on the delivery model, and factored into the service valuation function which is applied to the simulation model.

5 Representing Design Alternatives

To implement the methodology described in Section 3 we introduce the specification of various input parameters which can be configured. This can be achieved by providing the corresponding placeholders in the service design specification. We extend the service design model defined in Dhanesha et al. [25] which provides these placeholders in form of SolutionParameters and SolutionParameterValues. Variants are represented by specifying different values for the SolutionParameter. This section also introduces possible approaches for assigning value to the alternative designs

Representing design choices as attributes: Certain design choices may lead to the creation or elimination of new and unrelated solution parameters. The new designs resulting from these choices are referred to as design alternatives or blueprints, which are distinctly different from each other. This means that the variation of a few parameters will not lead directly from one design to another. It would involve eliminating or including one or more service entities like processes, tasks, resources etc. From a conceptual point of view, a design alternative is a significantly different approach of delivering the same service. While a design alternative includes using distinctly different parameters, to compare designs with each other we represent the design choice as a boolean solution parameter (gi), and a value of 1 or 0 representing whether that design choice was used or not used in the alternative. This is illustrated in Figure 2.

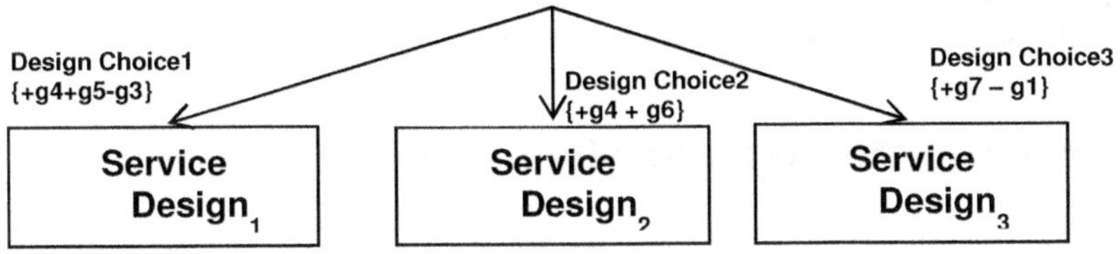

Fig. 2. Solution Space: {g0…g7}

Value function: To create a value function we denote a SolutionParameter by g.

We use a variation of Taguchi's loss function and Cook's value function [26] to determine the value to a stakeholder resulting from the changing values of solution parameters. Our model is based on the multi-attribute value assessment model specified by Downen et al. [27]. For an attribute g we pick a value g_0 which describes the current value of the solution parameter in question or a nominal value in the case of a new solution parameter. Each solution parameter should have a value g_c which represents a critical value beyond which the overall value for the stakeholder goes to zero. And g_i beyond which no more value is added. The value function can then we represented by equation (1). For solution parameters which do not have a continuous value the value function is expected to be a discrete function specified through the design tool by the designer, or predefined in the service design templates.

$$v(g) = \frac{(g_c - g_i)^2 - (g - g_i)^2}{(g_c - g_i)^2 - (g_0 - g_i)^2} \quad or\ f_{discrete}(g) \qquad (1)$$

This is then used to calculate the overall value for a stakeholder s_i based on the formula for relative value RV_{s1} given below.

$$RV_{s1} = v(g_1)^{\gamma_1}.v(g_2)^{\gamma_2}.\cdots.v(g_n)^{\gamma_n}$$

Where γ_j is the exponential weighting factor of the attribute g_j. The above equation is based on the Cobb-Douglas utility function. The system has value 0 if any single attribute reaches the critical point, g_c. The multiplicative relationship among the attributes ensures that the effect of a specific product attribute depends not only upon its own level but also on the levels of the other attributes.

Assuming multiple stakeholders, the overall value delivered by the system, V, is then defined as a weighted sum of value generated for each stakeholder weighed by the relative importance of each stakeholder.

$$V = \sum_i w_i RV_{si} \quad where \quad \sum_i w_i = 1, \quad w_i \geq 0$$

As an alternative to the above value function, we are studying other multi-attribute valuation method based on the analytical network process (ANP) [19]. ANP offers a systematic way to structure and quantify the value contributions of attributes without the need for hard-to-define metrics or quantification by relative comparison, which is especially promising in our participatory context.

6 Simulation Models for Service Delivery

Simulation models of the service delivery process provide an ideal way for all stakeholders to get an appreciation of the solution proposed. We are automating the process for generating simulation models from design artifacts to provide opportunities for all stakeholders to refine their requirements and understand the viewpoints of other stakeholders.

The simulation model for a public service delivery simulation will be based on the following minimal set of quantitative inputs [15]:

- A list of all service requests together with the distribution function for their arrival times. The distribution function may be estimated from the usage pattern of existing services.
- A set of capability types and a set of resources each of which is associated with a capabilities vector.
- A set of service processes for handling each service request – each process comprises a set of tasks, transitions and the transition probabilities.
- Each task is qualified by a capabilities vector which describes the set of capabilities required to perform the task, and a function for estimating the task time, cost of execution, and any other statistics required as outputs from the simulation model.
- A time dependent resource availability function.
- A dispatcher algorithm for deciding how to handle the requests for service and how to allocate resources.

7 Illustrative Scenario

We illustrate our methodology by taking the example of a government service to issuing residence visas to foreigners. In this scenario the government Foreign Residents' Registry Office (FRRO) is expected to overhaul its service to foreign residents under continuous complaints from the citizens on the inefficiencies, bureaucracy and paper work involved. The FRRO Officer (henceforth referred to as FRO) has the public service design tooling (PSD) at his disposal which he can use to aid him in this restructuring and re-engineering the process. Note that we have simplified the scenario and not presented the full iterative process – rather focusing on the first iteration.

Defining the Concept: The FRO starts his restructuring exercise by identifying the problem, defining the keywords of the problem, and also identifying the key stakeholders of the service under investigation.

Opinion Mining: Based on his initial concept definition he and additional inputs like "FFRO Residence Permit Visa Extension" as topic keyword, and "Foreign residents, Foreign employees, Multi-national companies" as stakeholder keywords, the opinion mining toolkit (OMT) is invoked. By providing some more information interactively to the OMT it returns the citizens buzz on the topic based on the content extraction form from the web, blogs, and other sources. The OMT returns with a summary of the buzz on the topic:

7532 Documents found:
7 complimentary
Stakeholder issue breakdown

Requirements Definition: Drilling down into the issues the FRO finds issues of cost to customers, time wastage, imprecise instructions issued by FRRO officials, irrelevance of some documentation required, and several others concerned with poor customer relations. The PSD then prompts the FRO to create a list of high level measurable requirements based on typical requirements for public services as provided by the tool. It offers to create requirements based on the issues identified. At the end of this the requirements look like:

- Issue of permits within 2 weeks of first receipt of validated forms and documents from customer
- Automation of inter-departmental workflows
- 30% reduction in operational costs
- 30% increase in customer satisfaction as measured by web buzz

Process Design: The PSD then assists the FRO in creating the detailed process description of the existing service using the abstract service model. The PSD automatically creates swimlanes in the business process modeling diagram based on the stakeholders and key roles defined in the concept stage by the FRO. A subset of the process diagram is given in Figure 3. The PSD ensures that the designer provides, and thus thinks through, the details like resources, time consumed etc. by various steps in the process.

Touchpoint Modeling: During the creation of the process blueprint, the PSD continues to prompt the FRO for specifying the interaction details whenever there is a communication across the line of interaction. Touchpoints Figure 3 are shown as white dots on the line of interaction. This ensures that the designer thinks through the customer experience aspects of the service.

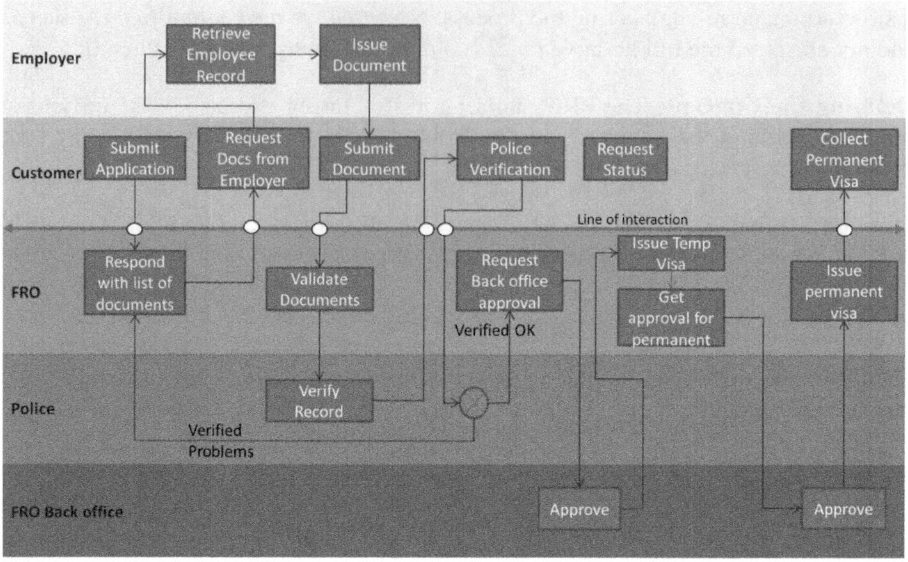

Fig. 3. Partial description of the as-is visa renewal process

Stakeholder Value Modeling: Having identified the primary stakeholders of the service, the PSD tool now asks the FRO to assign the value derived by each stakeholder from each task in the process, as well as each process and service request. The user is expected to fill in the value on a scale from none, very low, low, medium, high, very high. User inputs are also solicited via direct questions regarding the value contribution of various design alternatives with respect to specific requirements. These inputs are then used to provide inputs to the mathematical model described in Section 3.

Policy Law Retrieval: Before proceeding to redesign the service, the tool fetches the current set of policies and laws applicable to the service under investigation. It allows connection to a Policy and Law repository, which can be accessed using metadata that are specified by the FRO. This ensures that the FRO factors in the relevant government requirements before proceeding

Design Alternatives: Based on the inputs so far, and the formal specification of the high level goals, (e.g. increased value to the service consumer, reduced number of touchpoints, or reduced total service time) the tool proposes a small number of design alternatives.

- The tool suggests elimination of certain tasks which are not marked as critical, and do not add value to other stakeholders.
- It suggests replacement of some tasks with similar or related tasks which are available in the library as best practices.

From the alternatives offered, the FRO chooses the following alternatives:

1. Elimination of the task "Request docs from employer" and a direct connection between FRO office and employer.
2. Changing the mode of the touchpoint between the tasks "Submit application" and "Respond with documents list" from manual to online leveraging suggestions from the library on similar touchpoints
3. Eliminating the step of Issue Temp Visa and merge the two "Approve" steps by back office, which take the maximum execution time.

Simulation: Once the FRO has confirmed the design choices, the PSD generates a simulation model. The FRO has to input certain values like the rate of arrival of requests and resource availability. He can then execute the simulations and check the outputs of the simulation. The tool also allows changing certain inputs which were specified as solution parameters in the design, so that the FRO can chose the optimal value by looking at the output. This helps him confirm the impact of his design changes to some extent, after which he can proceed with detailed planning of this service. A public simulation model is also made available on the web and citizens' responses to this model can be gathered by the OMT to assist in further refinement of the service design.

8 Conclusions and Future Work

We have presented a methodology for collaborative service design taking into account the interests of all major stakeholders. We propose to evaluate this methodology in three case studies involving the Greek Ministry of the Interior, the City of Venice, and the City of Tilburg.

The fact that public data is being used by governmental authorities might make citizens reluctant to express themselves freely, so results of opinion mining might not reflect the citizen's opinion or might contain cognitive bias. There is also a danger of discrimination that can emerge when decisions are based upon automatically generated data, leading to different treatment of certain citizen's opinion. In this respect, our methodology addresses not only the architecture and toolkit, but also the privacy of the services as well as necessary legal safeguards. This concern is motivated by cases such as [20] where the Electronic Frontier Foundation and its partners filed suit against several USA government agencies for refusing to disclose their policies for using social networking sites for investigations, data-collection, and surveillance. We are undertaking a Privacy Impact Assessment to elicit privacy and data protection issues that need to be taken into account in the technical design of the architecture and toolkit and will offer guidelines in respect of a privacy friendly design.

Acknowledgements. This work is sponsored by the EU FP7 program as part of the COCKPIT project. The work with the city of Columbus was supported by the National Science Foundation's IUCRC program and the City of Columbus.

References

[1] OECD - Modernising government: the way forward, Paris, France (2005)
[2] Shostack, G.L., Kingman-Brundage, J.: How to design service. In: Congram, C., Freidman, M. (eds.) The AMA Handbook for the Service Industries, AMACOM, New York, pp. 243–261 (1991)
[3] Shostack, G.L.: Designing Services that Deliver. Harvard Business Review 62, 133–139 (1984)
[4] Zeithaml, V.A., Bitner, M.J.: Services marketing, 1st edn. McGraw-Hill, New York (1996)
[5] Zeithaml, V.A., Berry, L., Parasuraman, A.: The behavioral consequences of service quality. J. Mark. 60, 31–46 (1996)
[6] Kingman-Brundage, J.: The ABCs of Service System Blueprinting. In: Designing a Winning Service Strategy: American Marketing (1989)
[7] Cole, M., Parstons, G.: Unlocking Public Value: A New Model For Achieving High Performance In Public Service Organizations. John Wiley and Sons, Chichester (2006)
[8] The User Challenge Benchmarking: The Supply Of Online Public Services, Capgemini, 7th edn. (2007), http://www.epractice.eu/files/media/media1673.pdf
[9] EU: Study on the Measurement of User Satisfaction and Impact in the EU 27 – Draft Final Report (2009), http://www.epractice.eu/en/library/281909
[10] Dunleavy, P., Margetts, H., et al.: New Public Management Is Dead - Long Live Digital-Era Governance. Journal of Public Administration Research and Theory 16(3), 467–494 (2006)
[11] Pascu, C., Osimo, D., et al.: Social computing: implications for the EU social innovation landscape. Foresight 10(1) (2008)
[12] Tapscott, D., Williams, A.D.: WIKINOMICS – How Mass Collaboration Changes Everything, Portfolio, Published by Penguin Group (2008)
[13] Osimo, D.: Web 2.0 in Government: Why and How? European Commission Joint Research Centre Scientific and Technical Reports (2008)
[14] Dietrich, B.: Resource Planning for Business Services. Communications of the ACM 49(7), 62–64 (2006)
[15] Banavar, G., Hartman, A., Ramaswamy, L., Zherebtsov, A.: A formal model for service delivery. Handbook for Service Science (in press)
[16] Agranoff, R., McGuire, M.: Agranoff and McGuire 2003–Big questions in public network management research. Journal of Public Administration Theory and Research 11(3), 295–326 (2001)
[17] Ramanathan, et al.: Adaptive IT Architecture as a Catalyst for Network Capability in Government. In: Saha, P. (ed.) Advances in Government Enterprise Architecture. Idea Group Publisher (2008) (with Ramnath, R., Desai, A.)
[18] Klems, M., Nimis, J., Tai, S.: Do Clouds Compute? A Framework for Estimating the Value of Cloud Computing. In: 7th Workshop on E-Business, WEB 2008, Revised Selected Papers, Paris, France, December 13, pp. 110–123. Springer, Heidelberg (2009)
[19] Saaty, T.: Decision Making with the Analytic Hierarchy Process. Services Sciences 1(1), 83–98 (2008)
[20] Electronic Frontier Foundation, Complaint for Injunctive Relief (2009), http://www.eff.org/files/filenode/social_network/social_networking_FOIA_complaint_final.pdf

[21] Charalabidis, Y., Lampathaki, F., Sarantis, D., Sourouni, A.M., Mouzakitis, S., Gionis, G., Koussouris, S., Ntanos, C., Tsiakaliaris, C., Tountopoulos, V., Askounis, D.: The Greek Electronic Government Interoperability Framework: Standards and Infrastructures for One-Stop Service Provision. In: The Panhellenic Conference of Informatics (PCI 2008), August 25-28. IEEE Publications, Los Alamitos (2008)

[22] IDABC, European Interoperability Framework for pan-European e-Government Services, Version 1.0 (2004), http://europa.eu.int/idabc/en/document/3761 (retrieved)

[23] Charalabidis, Y., Lampathaki, F., Psarras, J.: Combination of Interoperability Registries with Process and Data Management Tools for Governmental Services Transformation. In: 42nd Hawaiian International Conference on System Sciences (HICSS), January 3-5 (2009)

[24] What is web 2.0, http://www.oreillynet.com/pub/a/oreilly/tim/news/2005/09/30/what-is-web-20.html

[25] Dhanesha, K.A., Hartman, A., Jain, A.N.: A model for designing generic services. In: Proceedings of IEEE International Conference on Services Computing, pp. 435–442 (2009)

[26] Cook, H.E.: Product Management: Value, Quality, Cost, Price, Profit and Organization, 1st edn. Chapman & Hall, Boca Raton (1997)

[27] Downen, T.: A Multi-Attribute Value Assessment Method for the Early Product Development Phase with Application to the Business Airplane Industry, PhD thesis, Engineering Systems Division, Massachusetts Institute of Technology (February 2005)

[28] Mumford, E.: Effective Systems Design and Requirements Analysis: The ETHICS Approach, http://www.enid.u-net.com/C1book1.htm

Public Safety Mashups to Support Policy Makers

Sunil Choenni[1,2] and Erik Leertouwer[1]

[1] Dutch Ministry of Justice, Research & Documentation Centre (WODC), Schedelsdoekhaven 131, 2511 EM The Hague, The Netherlands
{r.choenni,e.c.leertouwer}@minjus.nl

[2] Rotterdam University, School of Media and Information Technology, G.de Jonghweg 4-6, 3015 CG Rotterdam, The Netherlands
r.choenni@hro.nl

Abstract. To shape an effective and sound public safety policy, policy makers have a need for statistical insights in factors that may influence public safety. Today, there is a wide variety of sources available that contain data that is related to public safety. The data in these sources varies from register to survey data. There is a growing need to mash data from these sources and to create a coherent and uniform view of public safety. In this paper, we present a tool to create public safety mashups. The tool collects and processes safety related data from relevant sources. Mashups are presented in a uniform and accessible way to support policy makers in developing sound public safety policies. Besides data that is directly related to public safety, also contextual information, such as demographic data, is included in the tool that may help the user to understand the development of public safety aspects in the course of time.

Keywords: Information system architecture, public safety mashups, measuring safety, application.

1 Introduction

Public safety is considered to be one of the corner stones of an affluent and healthy society. Therefore, policy makers have a practical need for statistical insights into public safety at different geographical levels of a society, ranging from national to regional level. These insights help to shape effective and sound safety policies in a country. For example, if it appears that some parts of a country are becoming less safe, while other parts remain as safe as they were, policy makers may decide to spend more resources in the deteriorating parts and less in the stable parts of the country.

After the 9/11 events, we have seen a tremendous increase in the budget for the enforcement of public safety in many countries. Many organizations directly or indirectly involved in the enforcement of public safety intensified their collection and publication of safety related data. On the one hand, we observe a boom in the on line publications of these data, see e.g., www.statline.nl, www.homeoffice.gov.uk/rds, bjs.ojp.usdoj.gov, www.nationmaster.com, etc. On the other hand, Web 2.0 technology, especially mashups, provides web users with the possibility to combine data that

K.N. Andersen et al. (Eds.): EGOVIS 2010, LNCS 6267, pp. 234–248, 2010.

is published on different websites. A mashup is an attempt to move control over data closer to the user and closer to the point of use, by providing a user with a collection of tools to combine data from different sources in order to create relevant content, see e.g. www.programmableweb.com and [5,8]. Content generation in mashups is typically dynamic, i.e. it occurs on runtime on the basis of the information need of a specific user. In [10,16], the authors report the potentials and challenges involved in creating mashups by combining comprehensive statistics that can be accessed on line from different websites. Kalidien et al. [10] argue that the creation of mashups is not without risks; undesired effects, such as violation of privacy, misinterpretation of combined statistics and the disclosure of the identity of a group of individuals, may arise unintentionally. To prevent these effects, [16] proposes a framework to protect the privacy of citizens, while [10] proposes a comprehensive architecture to minimize the undesired effects. However, an implementation and evaluation of both approaches are missing yet and are on the agenda for the future. Furthermore, the authors in [10] argue that in some cases it is better that the government decides which mashups should be developed by itself and which ones can be left to web users. The (potential) sensitivity of a topic and the principle of compliance are mentioned as important parameters in the decision making process. For example, the Dutch Personal Data Protection Act (PDPA) distinguishes a category of sensitive data that requires special attention, namely data on someone's religion or life conviction, ethnic origin, political conviction, health, sexual orientation and memberships of employer's organizations [17]. The PDPA demands the correct and thorough processing and collecting of personal data for clearly defined, explicit and justified goals. Anticipating on sensible topics and taking the PDPA into account may prevent undesired effects in mashing up data.

It is widely accepted that public safety is a broad notion that is determined by a wide variety of social phenomena [11]. Furthermore, subjectivity plays an important role in many of these phenomena. A vast amount of different types of data is collected by different organizations, and made available to gain insights in public safety, see e.g., [9]. However, it is far from trivial to create a uniform and coherent view of public safety from these data. Consequently, misunderstandings may easily arise in the interpretation of the data. Therefore, we have taken the initiative to develop a tool that creates public safety mashups in order to support policy makers in the development of sound public safety policies. Although many mashups are being developed, no substantial research on the issues that may be involved in the development of mashups has been reported yet. So far, most of the efforts only enumerate many of the issues that deserve attention from researchers [5, 8] or are focussed on the potentials of mashups for businesses and web users, see e.g. [12]. The problem of data integration in the context of mash ups is slowly gaining attention [2,3,15].

In this paper, we discuss the development and implementation of a tool that creates public safety mashups. The tool collects and processes safety related data from relevant sources and presents it in an integrated and uniform way to users. During a number of workshops with policy makers, we have identified their information needs. On the basis of the outcomes of the workshops, we have decided which data sources should be "mashed up". Besides data that is directly linked with public safety, it appears that policy makers are also interested in contextual data, i.e. data that might be useful in understanding certain phenomena. Examples of contextual data are time stamps associated with data and population statistics in geographical regions throughout the Netherlands.

Our mashup tool is based on an extensible architecture, which facilitates the updating of included sources and the addition of new sources. The tool extracts data from a number of sources, performs consistency checks on these data and passes the data to a component called Data Access Layer. This layer stores the data that it receives in a data warehouse, handles the execution of queries resulting from a mashup and sends the results to an interface module for presentation purposes. The data warehouse also includes contextual data as mentioned above. Our mashup tool takes care of privacy issues at different modules. The data warehouse records attributes that are in line with the PDPA act [17] and stores *aggregated* data at region level, which hampers the disclosure of the privacy of individuals. Furthermore, whenever it appears that there is a risk for violation of the privacy of an individual at the interface module, the mashup will not or will only partly be shown to a user. To facilitate an adequate interpretation of a mashup (and thus minimizing misinterpretations) we provide users with the ability to determine how a mashup is obtained and which data are used. For example, it should be indicated clearly whether a number in a mashup is based on register or survey data.

The remainder of this paper is organised as follows. In Section 2, we describe our approach to elaborate the notion of safety in measurable variables. Furthermore, we discuss the requirements posed on the mashup. In Section 3, we describe our design for developing a tool to create public safety mashups. Section 4 is devoted to the implementation of the tool. In Section 5, we illustrate the functionality of the tool by means of creating some mashups that are typically used by policy makers. Finally, Section 6 concludes the paper and outlines our plans for future research.

2 Measuring Safety

As noted in the foregoing, public safety is a broad notion that is related to social, psychological, and criminological phenomena. For example, public safety is perceived to increase whenever crime is decreasing and the efforts to enforce the law is increased. In Section 2.1, we make the notion of safety operational by means of a set of phenomena and their corresponding measurable variables. In Section 2.2, we discuss how we use this set in two successive workshops to identify the information need of policy makers. The workshops resulted into three types of questions that are relevant for policy makers.

2.1 From Safety to Phenomena and Variables

Due to the broadness of the notion of public safety and the subjectiveness that might be associated with it, it is hard to give a comprehensive definition of public safety. Therefore, we have chosen the strategy of listing major social phenomena that point to public safety from the view of police and justice. Typical examples of such phenomena are crime, (law) enforcement, resources available for police and justice, etc., see also [1,11]. However, many of these phenomena can not be translated directly into quantitative measures. Therefore, for each phenomenon we have searched for a number of measurable variables that approximate or point to that phenomenon. For instance, crime can be measured by the number of crimes registered by the police in a specific region and period, by the number of victims of crime in that region and period, by the amount of money spent on crime preventive measures undertaken by companies and households, or by the number of people who value the way the police handled their reporting of a crime as satisfactory.

In order to come up with an effective set of variables, we inspected a number of available databases, including the databases at our institute that are used and maintained by organizations involved in safety enforcement. This way, we developed a sense of the information that is stored in the databases with regard to relevant safety measures. We needed this sense to minimize the risk of coming up with sensible variables in theory, while no information is registered with regard to these variables in the available databases.

In Fig. 1, we have depicted the relation between a number of phenomena and a set of measurable variables that may describe (an aspect of) a phenomenon. While in most cases the relationships between safety and the different phenomena pertaining to it, and the relationships between a phenomenon and the measurable variables that describe the phenomenon are obvious, this is not always the case. For example, to understand the relationship between youth and public safety, further differentiations are required. Here, one way of reasoning is that youth leaving school without a diploma run the risk of ending up loitering around shopping centres and other public spaces. Consequently, the public may start feeling intimidated, which means that a neighbourhood will be perceived as less safe by its inhabitants. To measure different possible implications of the phenomenon youth on public safety, the number of school dropouts, the number of youths in prison, the number of youths becoming victim of a crime, and the number of youths entering into the so-called HALT program can be used as variables. HALT is a Dutch extrajudicial program for less serious offences by juveniles, such as vandalism and setting off fireworks, and is aimed at preventing juveniles from deteriorating into heavier types of crime.

Since annoyance may influence the perception of public safety, it is also included as a relevant phenomenon in Fig. 1. Annoyance can be quantified, among others, by the number of people that claims to have good contact with their neighbours, by the number of people who experience aggressive driving behaviour on the road or in their neighbourhood, by the number of people who say they are much disturbed by littering or by the number of people who say they feel insecure in the street. The relationships between the remainder of the phenomena and the attached measurable variables in Fig. 1 are considered straightforward.

In the next section, we discuss how we exploit the collected phenomena and variables in identifying the information need of policy makers.

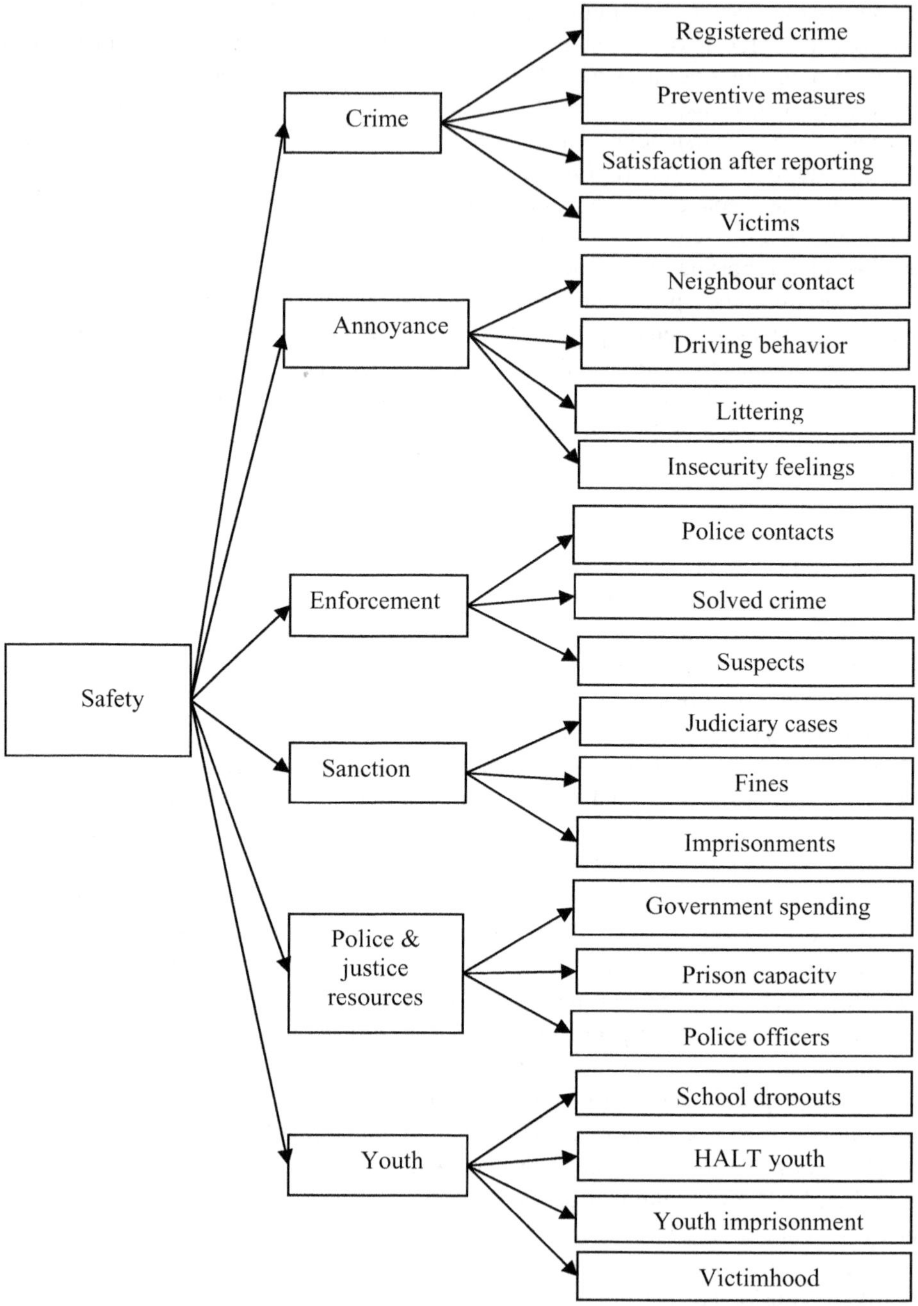

Fig. 1. Relationships between safety, phenomena, and measurable variables

2.2 Information Need

Since a review of public safety literature [1,11], internal documents, and a set of databases that are available at Statistics Netherlands (CBS) and the Research and Documentation Centre (WODC) of the Ministry of Justice revealed a large set of phenomena that is related to public safety, we decided to focus on those phenomena that would meet up with the information needs of policy makers best. During a workshop with policy makers, we presented the set of phenomena and potential corresponding measurable variables to policy makers, to allow them to comment on each phenomenon and its corresponding variables. About thirty people participated in this workshop with positions ranging from (junior) policy makers to directors. Most of them were envisioned as potential users of our tool.

On the basis of the output of this workshop, we elaborated a number of phenomena and their corresponding variables. For each variable, we investigated by which available database attributes it might be described. For example, the value assigned to a variable "registered crime" is derived from different attributes stored in different databases, such as the number of suspects heard by the police, distinguished types of crime by the law, etc.

The results were presented in a second workshop, including an overview of questions that could be answered using the given attributes. The participants of the second workshop consisted of more or less the same people as the previous one. Shortly after the workshop we organized individual meetings with some of the potential users for an in-depth discussion regarding our findings. The workshop and individual meetings with potential users revealed that in order to provide insight into public safety, it is also necessary to provide contextual data along with public safety data. Different users may ask for different kinds of contextual data. The workshops resulted in a set of phenomena with corresponding measurable variables that was recognized as relevant and related to public safety, as well as the following types of questions and mashups that need to be addressed in the development of a tool:

1. Simple quantification. For example, the user could ask how many people in a region within a time period responded in a specific way to a specific survey question. The result can be presented as a single figure, or a table presenting the figures and totals for the underlying regional and temporal levels, possibly showing trends.
2. Contextualisation of a quantifier. For example, how does the growth or decline of a specific figure in a geographical region relate to another figure? For example, a growth in bicycle thefts in a neighbourhood can turn into a relative decline when local population growth exceeds. This contextualisation must be considered in order to understand the public safety data.
3. Similarity queries, i.e. looking for regions that share in some respect the same context. After querying for a specific data set in which some numbers stand out in some way, the user can query the tool for other regions that show similar numbers or trends.

Besides the above-mentioned types of questions and the set of phenomena related to public safety upon which agreement was achieved (which can be found in [13]), an additional number of requirements was needed to be taken into account while developing a tool for creating mashups. An important requirement of the tool concerns user friendliness, which pertains to the interaction with the tool. The tool should not only provide accessible interfaces but, to a certain extent, it should also help to interpret the results. The tool should facilitate the addition of new phenomena, variables and new types of questions in the future. Finally, it was pointed out that the rules and regulations with regard to privacy should not be violated. As a consequence, it is not allowed to collect and/or to store data with regard to or data that may disclose the identity of individuals.

In Section 3, we present a design of a tool that captures these requirements and is able to handle the different type of queries. We note that answering the queries of type 2 requires the creation of mashups, while this may not always be the case for the queries of type 3.

3 Design

As stated in the foregoing, in the design of our tool for mashups we should take care of the rules and regulations with regard to privacy. To fulfil this requirement, we only use aggregated data for creating mashups. The aggregation level is dependent on the information need of its potential users. Since the distinguished types of queries that should be supported by a tool pertain to public safety mashups within a certain region, we collect and store public safety data that is oriented towards regions. The regional level on which the mashup result is available depends on the regional levels of which source data combined in the mashup is available. For instance, if a mashup is created from data on registered crime, which is available on the level of police regions, combined with population data, which is available on the more detailed level of municipalities, the resulting mashup will be on the level of police regions. We note the regions used in the tool are mutually exclusive, and regions on a more detailed level can be converted into regions on a higher aggregation level.

Data collected from different databases at various regional levels will be stored in a data warehouse [6] after cleaning (see Section 4). Conceptually, the data warehouse may be regarded as a universal relation **U** with a region identifier (*regid*) as primary key [4]. The addition of a new set of attributes **N,** representing a phenomenon in a region, to the data warehouse can be performed by joining relation **U** and **N** on the attribute *regid*. In this way, our design is extensible and flexible. Furthermore, the introduction of a data warehouse has the advantage that it creates a uniform view of the data and that all data is region oriented with regard to public safety. Since many people with different backgrounds live in the same region, the possibility that the identity of individuals will be disclosed on the basis of the output of our design is minimized. Nevertheless, in the unlikely event that there is a risk for violation of the privacy of a person, a mashup will not or will only partly be shown to a user. Therefore, the privacy of persons is preserved.

To meet the requirement of user friendliness, we equip the tool with a rich set of interfaces that facilitate the interaction with the user. For example, the tool may contain a menu-oriented structure with click and drag facilities and/or Google like interfaces to define the mashups a user wants to create. The output should be presented in different ways for the convenience of the user. For interpretation purposes, users should be able to determine how a mashup is obtained and which data is used. For example, it should be indicated clearly in what unit a number is expressed and whether the number is based on register or survey data. Information that might be useful for the interpretation will be stored in the tool as well.

In Fig. 2, we present a component-based architecture for our tool to create public safety mashups. In the architecture, we have on the one hand components that are involved in the extraction, transforming and loading of data in a data warehouse (left part of Fig. 2), and at the other hand we have components that are involved in the creation and presentation of a mashup (right part of Fig. 2).

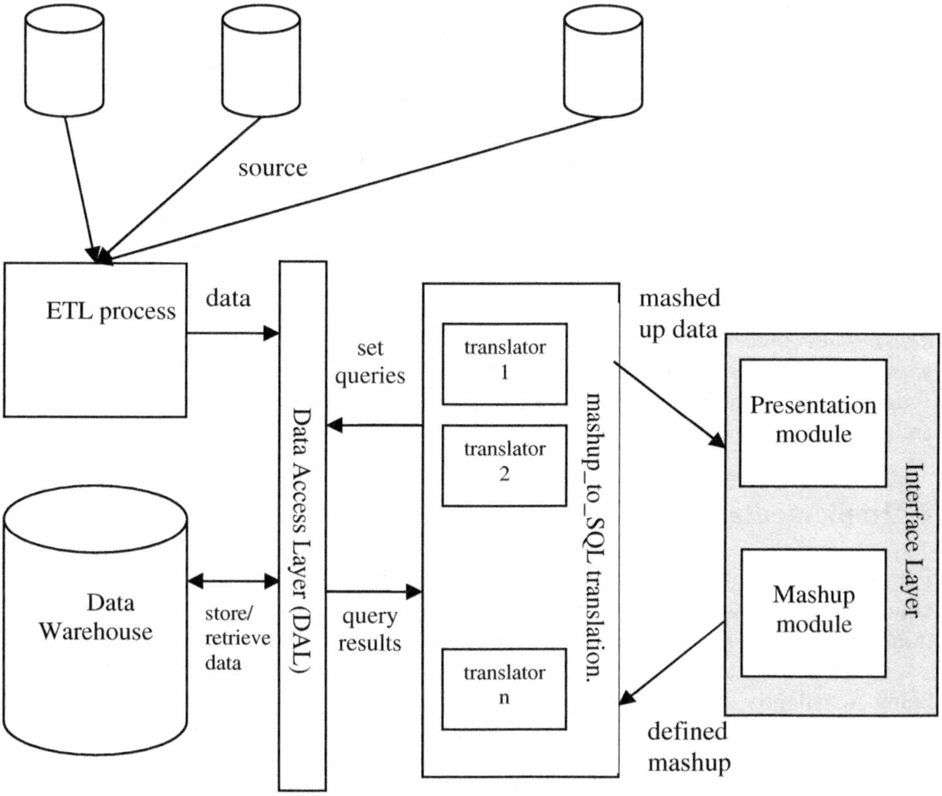

Fig. 2. Architecture of a tool to create mashups

The components for building the data warehouse and the components for creating a mashup are connected by a Data Access Layer (DAL). This layer has two main tasks. First, it is responsible for loading data that is extracted from different databases in the data warehouse. This data is cleaned and transformed in an ETL process [6] into a format that can be accepted by the DAL for loading. The second task of the DAL is to co-ordinate the creation of a mashup. Once a mashup is defined, it is translated into a set of queries by a "mashup_to_SQL translation" component and the set is passed to the DAL. In generating the set of queries, information stored as meta data, such as restrictions posed on the use of data for reasons of privacy, is exploited. This meta data is part of the data warehouse. For example, a highly detailed categorization of data on the country of birth of a person may disclose the identity of certain people if only a small number of people from a specific country is living in the region under investigation.

The queries generated by a translator of the mashup_to_translation component are passed by the DAL to the data warehouse for processing, and the query results are passed to DAL, which composes the query results to the required mashup and passes it to the Interface Layer for presentation purposes. We distinguish two modules within the Interface Layer, a *mashup* and a *presentation module*. The *mashup module* helps a user to define a mashup in a user friendly manner, for example by click and drag facilities or Google-like interfaces. For the user of the tool, no knowledge is needed of either SQL or the underlying data warehouse structure. The user may also specify how the mashup should be presented. We note that, in general, for each interface that may be used to express a mashup, a separate module is required to translate the mashup into a suitable set of queries for the DAL. The interface to express mashups determines how advanced a module will be. For example, providing the user with the possibility to define mashups by means of Google-like interfaces requires an advanced component to translate a mashup in a set of queries, while a less advanced module is required if a mashup is defined by click and drag facilities. The *presentation module* presents a mashup in a suitable manner to a user after consulting the *mashup module* for possible user preferences.

In the next section, we describe the implementation of the core components of our architecture.

4 Implementation

For the implementation of our architecture, we have used open source as well as commercial software. Our ETL process is implemented in the Java 1.5 Standard Edition environment with the Java Persistence API feature [7]. By means of scripts, data is extracted from these sources. A source may be a database or a file. For the time being, we mainly use sources that are coming from Statistics Netherlands (CBS) and our own institute (WODC). For a description and characteristics of the sources, we refer to [9, 13]. The Object Mapper of Java Persistence API transforms the data in a suitable format for loading the data into the data warehouse via the DAL, see Fig. 3. Prior to loading the data, the data is cleaned. Currently, the cleaning activities consist of solving inconsistencies for data from different sources, e.g., arisen due to typing errors, and a uniform handling of NULL values. Attribute values that assume values as "unknown", "to be determined" or " " are treated as NULL values.

For the time being, only data from sources can be loaded that has a unique region identifier or if there is a one-to-one relationship between the region identifier and a set of attributes of the source.

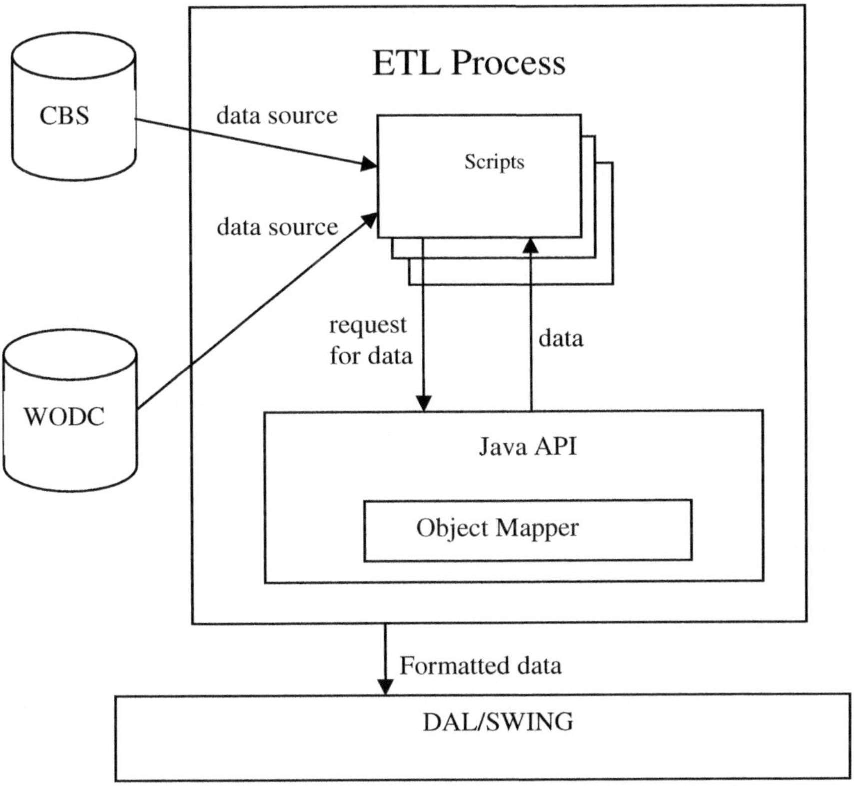

Fig. 3. Elaborated ETL process

The data warehouse is organised as a set of "tables". Three types of tables are distinguished, a so-called FACT table, CUBE tables, and SUBJECT tables. The FACT table is the central table of the data warehouse. It contains the values of the measurable variables, which are referred to as themes or indicators in the user interfaces. CUBE tables contain the attributes that contribute to a measurable variable, on different dimensional levels. For example, *Sanctions* is a measurable variable that is built out of different types of sanctions, e.g. the number of persons that obtained fines, persons that are in detention, and so on. For each group, additional dimensional data is stored, e.g. with regard to sex and age-groups. Data on each type of sanctions is stored in the CUBE table. The SUBJECT table records for each value of a measurable variable to which location and period it pertains. Furthermore, relevant background data of a measurable variable, such as the owner of data, restrictions posed on the use of the data, etc., may be recorded as well in a SUBJECT table. We note that the collection of SUBJECT tables may be regarded as a combination of a data dictionary and a meta database of the data warehouse, which contains data about the data stored in a FACT table. For the time being, the data warehouse is implemented in a SWING environment [14]. The features of our Data Access Layer (DAL) are implemented in

SWING as well. SWING is a software package that combines attractive statistical visualization techniques with data management. The visualization techniques contain, among others, detailed geographical representations of the Netherlands. For data management, SWING supports MSACCESS databases, which may be considered as drawback of SWING. Currently, we are preparing to migrate the data warehouse into an ORACLE environment, which is more flexible and easily extensible. As long as an MS ACCESS database is used and the visualization capabilities are used to define a mashup, there is no need for a "mashup_to_SQL translation" component, since the SWING provides this component.

For the Interface Layer of our tool, we exploit the visualization capabilities of SWING. Users may define their mashups by using the intuitive dragging and clicking facilities of SWING. In a tree structure, measurable variables and the attributes are listed. Users may also drill down to the values that an attribute may assume. We note that SWING is not supporting free search text interfaces, like Google. A mashup can be presented in different ways in SWING, e.g. bar charts on a map, tables, graphs, text and so on.

We note that SWING uses a more intuitive terminology for users, such as Themes/Indicators, Cubes, Dimension, Dimension levels. Themes/Indicators may be regarded as measurable variables. As noted before, a Cube may be regarded as a set of attributes that contributes to a measurable variable. A Dimension can be regarded as an attribute, while a value that an attribute may assume is referred as a Dimension level. In Section 5, we demonstrate how mashups are created by means of the terminology of SWING and how they are used by policy makers.

5 Creating Mashups

In order to create public policy mashups using quantitative information in the application, a user needs to select a subset of the available indicators. On startup of the application, a tree structure presents the main themes in the field of safety, such as registered crime, prosecution, sanctions, etc. From these main themes, more specific subjects can be selected from a list of indicators. If a user cannot find the subject he is interested in, a search function is available.

Once the relevant indicator is selected, a user needs to select the regional level and the time period he is interested in, subject to availability. Depending on the source, data in the application is mainly available nationally, on the level of municipalities and/or on the level of police regions. In some cases, alternative regional levels such as economic regions or provinces are used. All data in the application are annual data, and in most cases a number of recent years is available.

If the selected indicator is part of a cube and thus can be broken down in more dimensions than region and time period, values need to be selected for these additional dimensions as well.

In Fig. 4, a screenshot of the application shows the tree structure and illustrates the selection process of indicators and their different dimensions. We note that the screenshot is displayed in Dutch.

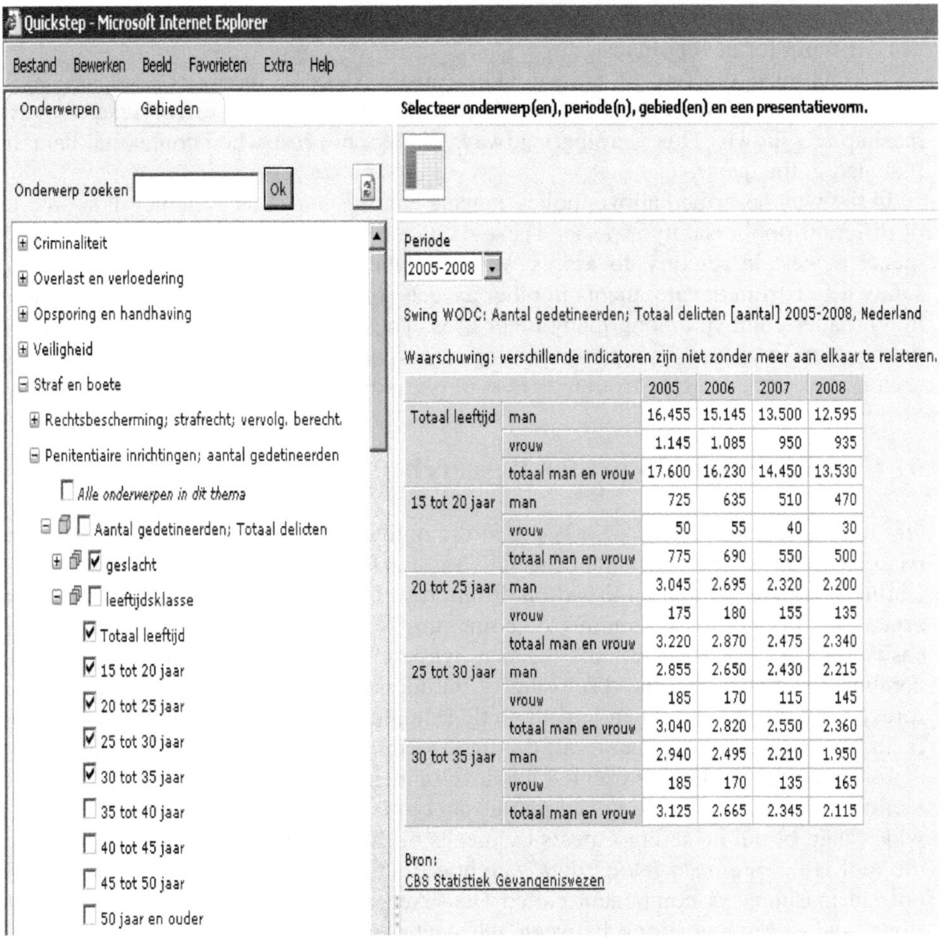

Fig. 4. Screenshot of the application (in Dutch)

In Fig. 4, the user of the application is interested in the number of young men and women (until the age of 35) in detention in recent years (2005 until 2008). Therefore, in the main theme *Sanctions* the subject *Correctional facilities: number of people in detention* is selected. Data on this subject is only available nationally. As the selected indicator is part of a cube, values for the dimensions *Sex* and *Age group* are also chosen. The right hand side of Fig. 4 shows the result of the query in the form of a table. If preferred, alternative presentation forms such as graphs and maps are available.

From the information in the table in this example, recent trends in the number of young men and women in detention can be derived. However, these trends can only be interpreted meaningfully if also trends in the number of young men and women in the overall population are taken into account – for instance, a decrease in the number of young men in detention can be caused by a decrease in the share of young men in the population as a whole. Therefore, also contextual information such as population data is available in the application. If population data for young men and women under 35 in the period 2005-2008 is added to the query, the resulting mashup can be used as input for new policies.

To minimize the risk of users making meaningless or incorrect comparisons, a warning is provided in the right hand side of the screen, where the results of the mashup are shown. This warning is always visible, not just when contextual data are included in the query.

In the way described above, policy makers can use mashups to gather data on a lot of different public safety aspects. These data can be used to gain insight in developments in certain regions, to assess whether developments in one aspect of public safety differ from developments in other aspects, to put developments in public safety in a broader context, among many other uses. These insights are essential to substantiate policy proposals, prepare working visits of government officials to certain regions, answer questions from members of parliament, etc.

6 Conclusions and Further Research

On the one hand, we observe a boom in the online publication of data. On the other hand, Web 2.0 technology, and especially mashups, provides web users with the possibility to combine data published on different websites. However, in [10] the authors argue that besides the potentials of combining data from different sources, it may easily lead to undesired effects, such as violation of privacy, misinterpretation of combined statistics and the disclosure of the identity of group of individuals. Therefore, a government should anticipate on this situation by providing tools to web users, including policy makers, that minimize undesired effects while creating mashups.

In this paper, we have presented the development and implementation of a tool that facilitates policy makers to create public safety mashups. Insights may be gained in a wide range of public safety aspects by means of the mashups. Central components of the tool are *a region oriented* data warehouse and an Interface Layer to define and present mashups. A component called Data Access Layer (DAL) manages the data flows and communications between the central components. The data warehouse contains data that pertains directly to public safety, such as law and enforcement data. Furthermore, it also contains contextual data, such as demographic data, that is used to support the understanding of the developments in public safety issues. To meet up with "user friendliness" demands posed by policy makers, the Interface Layer is equipped with advanced visualization capabilities. Other important features of the tool are its extensible architecture, i.e. new data can be easily added and updated and privacy rules and regulations are preserved. To prevent the disclosure of the privacy of individuals, we record only aggregated data and attributes that meet up with the PDPA act [17]. Furthermore, whenever it appears that there is a risk for violation of the privacy of a person at the interface layer, the mashup will not or will only be partly shown to a user.

For the time being, the tool handles a set of pre-defined mashups that are related to regions. In order to provide the user with more advanced user interfaces and a richer set of contextual data, the following topics are on our agenda for the future. First, the addition of more data sources to the tool to provide users a richer set of contextual data. Second, the extension of the tool with a free text search engine, like Google, such that a wide range of ad hoc queries/mashups can be handled. Both of these extensions may contribute to the scalability of the tool. However, we note that the addition of more sources to the tool may give rise to problem of information overload. Advanced user interfaces may prevent this problem to a certain extent. Therefore, the evaluation of the tool is a topic for further research.

Acknowledgements. The authors are grateful to Diederick de Vries (WODC) and the colleagues of Statistics Netherlands (CBS) involved in the development and implementation of the tool. The authors would also like to thank *Veiligheid begint bij Voorkomen*, the policy division of the Ministries of Justice and Internal Affairs that commissioned the project, and the members of the supervisory board of the project for their valuable contributions.

References

1. Becker, G.S.: Crime and Punishment: an economic approach. Journal of Political Economy 76(2) (1968)
2. Choenni, S., Van Dijk, J.: Towards Privacy Preserving Data Reconciliation for Criminal Justice Chains. In: Proceedings of the 10th International Conference on Digital Government Research, pp. 223–229. ACM Press, New York
3. Choenni, S., Van Dijk, J., Leeuw, F.: Preserving Privacy whilst integration data: appiled to criminal justice, Information Polity. Int. J. Government & Democracy in the information Age (to appear)
4. Elmasri, R., Navathe, S.: Fundamentals of Database Systems. Addison-Wesley, Reading (2004)
5. Ennals, R., Brewer, E., Garofalakis, M., Shadle, M., Gandhi, P.: Intel Mash Maker: Join the Web. SIGMOD Rec. 36, 4 (December 2007)
6. Inmon, W.: Building the Data Warehouse. Wiley, Chichester (2005)
7. http://java.sun.com/developer/technicalArticles/J2EE/jpa/
8. Jhingran, A.: Enterprise Information Mashups: Integrating Information Simply. In: Dayal, U., Whang, K., Lomet, D., Alonso, G., Lohman, G., Kersten, M., Cha, S.K., Kim, Y. (eds.) Proceedings of the 32nd international Conference on Very Large Data Bases, VLDB Endowment, Seoul, Korea, September 12-15, pp. 3–4 (2006)
9. Kalidien, S., Choenni, S., Meijer, R.: Towards a Monitor for Crime and Law Enforcement. In: 3rd European Conference on Information Management and Evaluation Gothenburg, Sweden, September 17-18, pp. 239–247. Academic Publishing Limited
10. Kalidien, S., Choenni, S., Meijer, R.: Crime Statistics On Line: Potentials and Challenges. In: Proceedings of the 11th International Conference on Digital Government Research, DG.O 2010, Puebla, Mexico, May 18-21. ACM Press, New York (2010)
11. Lilly, R.J., Culle, F.T., Ball, R.A., Inciardi, J.A. (eds.): Criminilogical theory, context and consequences. Sage, Thousand Oaks (1995)
12. O'Reilly, T.: What is Web 2.0: Design Patterns and Business Models for the Next Generation of Software, http://oreilly.com
13. Rienstra, M., De Rijk, A., Van den Berg, P., De Vries, D.: In: Dutch: Bevragingsapplicatie Veiligheid Statistisch inhoudelijke documentatie, Statistics Netherlands, The Hague/ Heerlen (2009)
14. Swing manuals upon request available from SWING, http://www.swing.eu

15. Thor, A., Aumueller, D., Rahm, E.: Data Integration Support for Mashup. In: 6th International Workshop on Information Integration on the Web, June 23. AAAI Press, Menlo Park (2007)
16. Warner, J., Chun, S.A.: Citizen Privacy Protection Model for E-government Mashup Services. In: Proceedings of the 2008 International Conference on Digital Government Research, Montreal, Canada, May 18-21 (2008)
17. Winter, H.B., de Jong, P.O., Sibma, A., Visser, F.M., Herweijer, M., Klingenberg, A.M., Prakken, A: Dutch: Wat niet weet, wat niet deert; Een evaluatieonderzoek naar de werking van de Wet bescherming persoonsgegevens in de praktijk, WODC, The Hague (2008)

Intellectual Capital Management Using Knowledge Scorecards: The Austrian National Defence Academy Showcase

Johannes Göllner[1], Klaus Mak[1], and Robert Woitsch[2]

[1] Landesverteidigungsakademie, Zentraldokumentation (ZDok), Stiftgasse 2a, 1070 Vienna, Austria
{klaus.mak,mba.ukm}@bmlv.gv.at
[2] BOC Asset Management GmbH, Bäckerstraße 5, 1010 Vienna, Austria
robert.woitsch@boc-eu.com

Abstract. This paper discusses the applicability of knowledge scorecards and intellectual capital management for monitoring and steering of knowledge-driven organizations based upon a practice project at the Austrian Defence Academy (in particular the School for Atomic, Biological and Chemical Defence). Within this project the model-driven approach PROMOTE® has been applied to develop the knowledge scorecard at the Austrian National Defence Academy. The paper presents the knowledge scorecard architecture, the method and the findings.

Keywords: Intellectual Capital Management, Knowledge Scorecard, Knowledge Management, PROMOTE®.

1 Introduction

New regulations for academic institutions [23] changed the reporting responsibilities for knowledge assets within the Austrian National Defence Academy (LVAk), committing them to issueing intellectual capital reports. The concept of knowledge scorecards assures compliance with the legal reporting obligations and enables furthermore the initial step to monitor and manage the intellectual capital.

The School of Atomic, Biological and Chemical Defence (ABCAbwS) has been selected for the project, since there was pre-existing work in the domain of knowledge management that could be reused. This work consists of a committed knowledge management concept, the specification of a quality management system, initial knowledge management projects such as the acquisition of skill profiles and the definition of knowledge management processes.

Beside the work on knowledge management that is seen as the fundament for intellectual capital management, there is an important aspect that makes the school an interesting testbed. The school not only consists of teaching parts, but also of a research part and a force provision part. This means this school combines research on

K.N. Andersen et al. (Eds.): EGOVIS 2010, LNCS 6267, pp. 249–256, 2010.

ABC topics, the teaching within and outside the Austrian military but also the actual force provision in case of earthquake, water flood or other operations.

This rare constellation of research, teaching and application of knowledge within one organisation in a very complex, high-risk and dynamic environment made the application of an intellectual capital management system an interesting challenge. The project was accompanied by the LVAk as the highest military training- and research institution of the Austrian Armed Forces. It acts as the "brain trust" of the Austrian Armed Forces, and serves the forces and the Ministry of Defence with approx. 240 employees.

In the following some conceptual background will be provided to discuss existing approaches, introduce the idea of the “knowledge product” and outline how the intellectual capital management can be implemented with PROMOTE® [18] by defining the “knowledge product” as the centre point. The paper concludes with an outlook.

2 Conceptual Background

This section discusses related work and introduces three adaptations that were necessary in the aforementioned complex environment. The adaptations are (1) the introduction of the “knowledge product”, (2) the re-arrangement of the balanced scorecard as well as (3) the holistic architecture of the intellectual capital monitor.

2.1 Related Work

Monitoring of knowledge management initiatives and application scenarios within a company is not something unusual, representing just a current hype.

There are various concepts for managing intellectual capital, such as the Skandia Navigator [6], the Intangible Assets Monitor [21], the Intellectual Capital Navigator [19], or more general concepts like the market-to-book ratio [16], [2] or the comprehensive company value [14]. Moreover different approaches have been implemented over the years in order to provide an instrument for evaluating the intellectual capital and can be considered as a holistic management philosophy [11] or can be seen as novel approach bringing competitive advantage [4]. The aims for developing and implementing such an instrument may vary from realising more knowledge management friendly point of view where such tools are used to steer the initiatives as depicted in Aidermark and Sterner [1], to events where such an approach is only used to perform precise calculations of the overall asset value of the company – this view is discussed in [8]. The first obstacle on the road to creating a presentable intellectual capital balance is to perform valuing of the specific knowledge assets. There are many different approaches that tackle the concern of defining the value of the knowledge assets by applying different methods. These methods include valuing of the knowledge assets based on “Tobin's *q*” - which uses the ratio between a company's market value and the replacement value of its physical assets to calculate the value (as depicted in the [25]) - evaluation based on the combination of Fuzzy Linguistics and MCDM[1] method [22], etc.

The next step after the initial measurement method that has been chose and applied is to include the results in a reporting and monitoring mechanism – lately the trend has gone towards the presentation in the adapted balance scorecards (to be inline with the "business" part of the balance sheet). An overview on how these metrics can be connected to business strategy (in form of IC BSC) is depicted in [7].

Studies on how intellectual capital is being monitored/reported in 19 Danish enterprises can be seen in [3], a similar study concerning Finish companies can be found in [24], and UK companies in [20]. Additional reports from Slovenia [15] discussing IC from a two-tier view – customer and non-customer relationships – , the report from Taiwan evaluating what importance levels are assigned to different IC forms by company employees [13] and the historical report on intellectual capital management/reporting from Scandia can be found in [6] – providing insights on development and valuing of the company's own IC.

2.2 Required Adaptations of Existing Approaches

The first challenge of measuring intellectual capital is to identify knowledge in such a form that it can be assessed. As the authors follow the slogan of Karagiannis "knowledge is humanised information" the knowledge needs to be specified in an explicit form. The concept of the "knowledge product" [12] has been introduced that defines the knowledge in a consumable way. The PROMOTE® approach identifies three types of knowledge products: (a) service: implicit knowledge is provided for implicit usage like an expert, trainer or the like, (b) information product: explicit knowledge is provided for implicit usage like books, magazines, and other forms of publications as well as (c) application: explicit knowledge is provided for explicit usage like expert systems, glossaries and the like.

The definition of the "knowledge product" and the identification of services, information products and applications enables to specify the knowledge of the organisation, and hence the intellectual capital in a consumable way. The assumption is that only the consumable and hence applicable knowledge is of interest, therefore the knowledge products have been identified to be the central point of intellectual capital management approach.

The concept of the Balanced Scorecard [17] provides a balanced and flexible steering approach. The second challenge was to measure the intellectual capital using this scorecard approach with the focus on knowledge products.

Therefore the structure of the knowledge scorecard is defined as follows

- Product Perspective: Goals, indicators and measures for the actual knowledge products provided by the organization
- Processes and Structure Perspective: Goals, indicators and measures in relation to processes executed (core processes, supporting processes and management processes) to create the knowledge products.

---

[1] MCDM - multiple criteria decision-making.

- Human Capital, Relations and Competences Perspective: Goals, indicators and measures of human capital and competences required to create the knowledge products.
- Resources and Support Perspective: Goals, indicators and measures of budget, infrastructure, material and tools (incl. structural capital) as well as information access that is seen as the basic resources.

These perspectives have been derived by analysing available measurement criteria and validating them against literature in the domain [10]. These perspectives have been evaluated according to their applicability in a series of workshops and internal reviews. The third challenge was to extend the aforementioned horizontal views with vertical pillars to provide architecture for realising a knowledge scorecard.

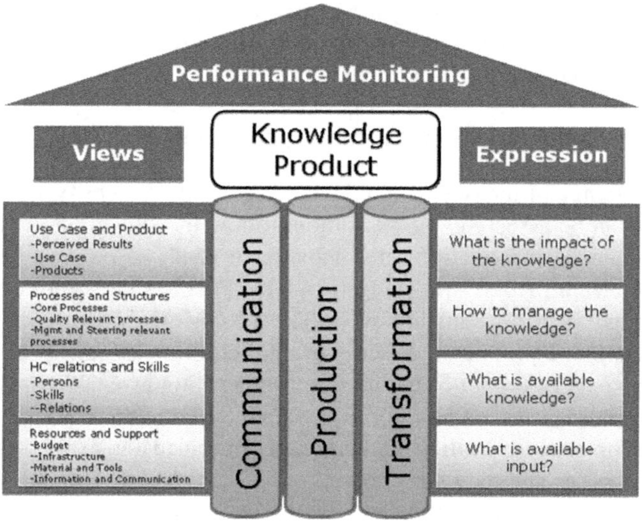

Fig. 1. PROMOTE® Knowledge Scorecard Architecture

Figure 1 depicts the developed architecture for the Knowledge Scorecard [9]. Starting point is the knowledge product that needs to be produced, disseminated and continuously improved through transformation. These three pillars are analysed according their impact, their management processes, the available vs. required skills and the available vs. required input. This matrix has been used as a guideline to identify the critical success factors, the knowledge goals and measurement criteria.

3 The Show Case: Knowledge Scorecards at the Austrian National Defence Academy

In the following the best practice project for knowledge scorecards based upon the PROMOTE® approach is described giving insights in the project results and implementation steps.

3.1 Definition of the Initial Situation

The knowledge product model has been structured according three main categories: *Research-, Training- and Force Provision Products. Research Products* establish the grounding of knowledge related work (e.g. scientific publications in different domains, maintenance of e-Learning, etc.). *Training Products* are the main area within the organization comprising all courses and training products necessary to maintain a long-term availability of forces. *Force Provision Products* are products that are provided when military actions take place. Competences have been mapped by relating the provided knowledge products to the organizational models. By adding identified competences necessary for the provision of products by the organizational unit the analysis concluded with a competence matrix. There are about 950 competences identified, whereas between ten and twenty of these competences are annotated in average to one working place. That approach enabled the identification of competences per workplace, the availability of competences within the organisation and enabled a direct relation of provided knowledge products and the according required and available competence.

3.2 Specification of Critical Success Factors

This step was the most time consuming and most difficult task it aimed to identify the critical success factors and externalise relevant knowledge on steering the school from the management team using the aforementioned architecture of the Knowledge Scorecard. Existing management instruments (Process Management, Balance Scorecard, Quality Management in accordance with ISO9001:2005, CAF [5], Continuous Improvement, Cost accounting) have been investigated.

3.3 Definition of Goals and Their Cause and Effect Relations

Based upon the critical success factors identified in the previous phase, the goals have been grouped according to a set of similar success factors. Cause and effect relations between goals have been identified and enhanced by measurable criteria. The cause-and-effect diagram as depicted in Figure 2 has been defined in multiple discussion rounds condensing the initial goal definition to a final set of concrete goals.

The image shows the four perspectives marked with A, B, C and D as well as indicates the three pillars marked with 1, 2 and 3.

3.4 Quantification of Goals

The identified goals had been detailed described by measurable criteria. A set of indicators were identified that are already subject to operational data available in different systems such as HR management tools, financial controlling systems, etc. In addition to those indicators, criteria have been identified where operational data sources are not yet available and need further investigation. These elements have been highlighted within the model and are out-of-scope for the implementation of the knowledge scorecard at this stage. For the operational indicators a detailed specification has been derived giving all necessary information for the reporting and monitoring system.

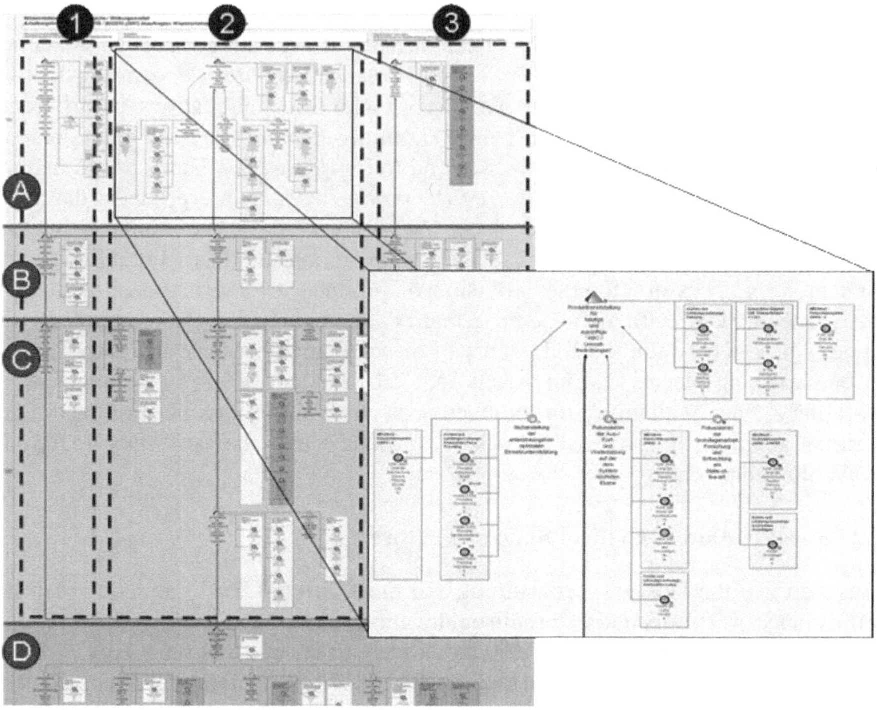

Fig. 2. Cause-And-Effect Diagram

The detailed view of Figure 2 indicates the knowledge goal "Provision of knowledge products for current and future ABC issues" as the blue pyramid. Below there are three sub-goals represented as orange circles for the research, training and force provision. Each of the goals is measured by criteria represented as blue targets that range from concrete financial criteria like "Costs for Research" to fuzzy criteria like "Estimated degree of knowledge goal achievement".

3.5 Operational Data Coupling

The next phase considers the operationalisation of the knowledge scorecard through the coupling of the designed models with operational data-sources. For concrete criteria the operational data sources are typically data warehouse applications, databases in general or spreadsheets that are updated on a regular basis. For fuzzy criteria there is a range of instruments like self-assessments, management assessment, client assessment, questionnaires or the like that provide representative values. The calculation capabilities within the modelling tool allow the definition of complex indicator structures and combine indicators to be used.

3.6 Steering and Management Based on Knowledge Scorecard

As a reporting and performance monitoring tool, the controlling cockpit has been used to visualize the results of the knowledge scorecard to the targeted audience and provide interactive analysis and reporting functions. The reports generated by the knowledge scorecard provide the decision makers with the necessary information.

4 Conclusion

The implementation of the knowledge scorecard at the ABCAbwS resulted in a comprehensive instrument for steering the service provision processes within the organization and built up a transparent framework for evaluation of knowledge assets. The implementation is regarded as a best practice application within the LVAk that proves that evaluation of knowledge assets and continuous monitoring could improve the reaction capabilities and learning structures of Austrian Armed Forces, leading to an increased readiness for duty in the case of military actions.

Acknowledgement

We would like to thank Bgdr. Loidolt, and o. Univ Prof. Karagiannis for supporting the project as well as Bgdr Fürstenhofer, Kdt ABCAbwS, for the possibility to execute the project and the quality feedback.

References

1. Aidemark, J., Sterner, H.: A Framework for Strategic Balancing of Knowledge Management Initiatives. In: IEEE, Proceedings of the 36th Hawaii International Conference on System Sciences (2003)
2. Andriessen, D.: Making Sense of Intellectual Capital. Elsevier Butterworth Heinemann, Oxford (2004)
3. Bukh, P.N., Larsen, H.T., Mouritsen, J.: Constructing intellectual capital statements. Scandinavian Journal of Management 17, 87–108 (2001)
4. Chen, Y.-S.: The Positive Effect of Green Intellectual Capital on Competitive Advantages of Firms. Journal of Business Ethics 77, 271–286 (2008)
5. Common Assessment Framework, `http://www.eipa.eu/en/pages/show/&tid=67` (access 25.10.2008)
6. Edvinsson, L.: Developing Intellectual Capital at Skandia. Long Range Planning 30(3), 366–373 (1997)
7. Fairchild, A.M.: Knowledge Management Metrics via a Balanced Scorecard Methodology. In: Proceedings of the 35th Annual Hawaii International Conference on System Sciences (HICSS'02), vol. 8, p. 243. IEEE, Los Alamitos (2002)
8. García-Meca, E., Martinez, I.: The use of intellectual capital information in investment decisions - An empirical study using analyst reports. The International Journal of Accounting 42, 57–81 (2007)
9. Göllner, J., Mak, K., Trattnig, G., Woitsch, R.: Wissensmanagement und Wissensbilanz im ÖBH am Beispiel der ABCAbwS & ABCAbw, Wien (2008)

10. Peter, H.: Wissensbilanz – Made in Europe. In: Wissensmanagement – Das Magazin für Führungskräfte, Heft (April 2008)
11. Johannesse, J.-A., Olsen, B., Olaisen, J.: Intellectual capital as a holistic management philosophy: a theoretical perspective. International Journal of Information Management 25, 151–171 (2005)
12. Mak, K., Woitsch, R.: Der Einsatz des prozessorientierten Wissensmanagementwerkzeuges PROMOTE® in der Zentraldokumentation der Landesverteidigungsakademie: Entwicklungslinien der ZentDok und die Implementierung von PROMOTE®, Wien
13. Lai, M.-C., Lin, H.T., Wu-Der, T.: The Evaluation of Intellectual Capital in a Taiwan Hospital. In: Proceedings of the Second International Conference on Innovative Computing, Informatio and Control, p. 385. IEEE, Los Alamitos (2007)
14. Lev, B.: Sharpening the Intangibles Edge. Harvard Business Review, 109–116 (June 2004)
15. Nemec Rudez, H., Mihalic, T.: Intellectual capital in the hotel industry: A case study from Slovenia. Internationa Journal of Hospitality Management 26, 188–199 (2007)
16. North, K.: Wissensorientierte Unternehmensführung. Gabler Verlag, Wiesbaden (1998)
17. Kaplan, R., Norton, D.: The Balanced Scorecard: Translating Strategy Into Action. Harvard Business Press, Boston (1996)
18. Woitsch, R., Karagiannis, D.: Process Oriented Knowledge Management: A Service Based Approach. J. UCS 11(4), 565–588 (2005)
19. Stewart, T.A.: Intellectual Capital. Nicholas Brealey Publishing, London (1997)
20. Striukova, L., Unerman, J., Guthrie, J.: Corporate reporting of intellectual capital: Evidence from UK companies. The British Accounting Review, 1–17 (2008)
21. Sveiby, K.E.: The New Organizational Wealth. Berrett-Koehler Publishers, San Francisco (1997)
22. Tai, W.-S., Chen, C.-T.: An Intellectual Capital Performance Evaluation Based on Fuzzy Linguistic. In: Proceedings of the Third International Conference on International Information Hiding and Multimedia Signal Processing (IIH-MSP 2007), vol. 02. IEEE, Los Alamitos (2007)
23. Universitätsgesetz (2002), `http://archiv.bmbwk.gv.at/universitaeten/recht/gesetze/ug02/Universitaetsgesetz_20027727.xml`
24. Vuontisjarvi, T.: Corporate Social Reporting in the European Context and Human Resource Disclosures: An Analysis of Finnish Companies. Journal of Business Ethics 69, 331–354 (2006)
25. Wilkins, J., van Wegen, B., de Hoog, R.: Understanding and Valuing Knowledge Assets: Overview and Method. Expert Systems With Applications 13(1), 55–72 (1997)

Deploying a Semantically-Enabled Content Management System in a State University

Maria Befa[1], Efstratios Kontopoulos[1], Nick Bassiliades[1], Christos Berberidis[1,2], and Ioannis Vlahavas[1,2]

[1] Department of Informatics, Aristotle University of Thessaloniki
GR-54124, Thessaloniki, Greece
{mmpefa,skontopo,nbassili,berber,vlahavas}@csd.auth.gr
[2] School of Science & Technology, International Hellenic University
GR-57001, Thessaloniki, Greece

Abstract. Public institutes often face the challenge of managing vast volumes of administrative documents, a need that is often met via Content Management Systems (CMSs). CMSs offer various advantages, like separation of data structure from presentation and variety in user roles, but also present certain disadvantages, like inefficient keyword-based search facilities. The new generation of content management solutions imports the notion of semantics and is based on Semantic Web technologies, such as metadata and ontologies. The benefits include semantic interoperability, competitive advantages and dramatic cost reduction. In this paper a leading Enterprise CMS is extended with semantic capabilities for automatically importing and exporting ontologies. This functionality enables reuse of repository content, semantically-enabled search and interoperability with third-party applications. The extended system is deployed in semantically managing the large volumes of documents for a state university.

Keywords: Semantic web, metadata, content management, ontology.

1 Introduction

Public institutes, like state universities, often face the challenge of managing vast volumes of (mainly administrative) documents, which are rapidly increasing every day. The need to manage massive volumes of content imposes the deployment of *content management systems* (*CMS*), software applications that allow creating, editing, managing and publishing content, as well as controlling access and versioning [1]. CMSs mainly offer the advantage of separating data structure from presentation, defining user roles, in order to control what (subset of) information each user has access to.

Nevertheless, besides simply managing content, a key functionality is also the ability to efficiently and effectively retrieve information. Paradoxically, most current CMSs offer only basic keyword-based search, similarly to Web search engines [2]. Although several techniques (word occurrence frequency measurement, lexical analysis etc.) have been developed for improving the retrieved results, they have not been adequately evolved yet, in order to offer more advanced features than basic search.

K.N. Andersen et al. (Eds.): EGOVIS 2010, LNCS 6267, pp. 257–264, 2010.

A lot of effort is now concentrated on developing a new generation of content management solutions for efficiently managing the rapidly growing volumes of information, based on the notion of *semantics* (study of meaning) [3]. The use of semantic technologies in content management (referred to as "*Semantic Content Management*") will bring various benefits to organizations working with large volumes of data, like syntactic/semantic interoperability, dramatic cost reductions, revenue improvements and opportunities for competitive advantages. Semantic Content Management methods are based on the *Semantic Web* (SW), an evolving effort towards extending Web content with semantic information (metadata) [4]. A key factor in the development of the Semantic Web are *ontologies* – data models that represent a given domain and are used to reason about the objects in that domain and the relations between them [5]. *RDF Schema* (*RDF/S*) is an ontology language for encoding ontologies [6], providing a vocabulary for describing properties and classes of RDF resources as well as hierarchies among them. Overall, the Semantic Web provides a set of standards for encoding and querying knowledge, so that data integration is facilitated. Therefore, Semantic Web technologies seem promising for improving CMS data handling capabilities and for leading to advantages in all situations, where data integration is beneficial.

Especially in *e-Government* (*e-Gov*) that involves a wide array of IT-related aspects, like human-computer interaction (HCI), software/systems engineering and Web service design, the SW can resolve many HCI- and access-related issues and allow users to facilitate e-Gov processes [7]. Additionally, e-Gov networks are among the largest networks in existence, according to size, number of users and information providers; thus, creating a Semantic Web infrastructure to meaningfully organize e-Gov networks is highly desirable. At the same time, the complexity of the existing e-Gov implementations also challenges the feasibility of Semantic Web development [8].

In this paper we are extending a leading Enterprise CMS, called *Alfresco* [9], with semantic capabilities and, more specifically, the capacity of automatically importing and exporting RDF/S ontologies. The implemented Alfresco plug-in parses the input ontologies and automatically updates the corresponding Alfresco core files that are related with the creation of categories, properties, metadata and their appearance in the Alfresco front-end. The reverse process, namely, exporting content from the Alfresco repository into an RDF/S ontology, is also integrated in the plug-in, allowing third-party applications to use and process Alfresco content. In order to test the implemented extensions, the system was deployed for managing the large volumes of documents for a state university (as in e.g. [10]), also offering semantic interoperability between the university and other education-related organizations.

The rest of this paper is structured as follows: Section 2 gives a brief overview of related work paradigms, followed by a more thorough presentation of the Alfresco CMS. Section 4 comprises the backbone of this work, presenting the test application domain and the proposed semantic extensions implemented in Alfresco, while the paper is concluded with the final remarks and directions for future work.

2 Related Work

SCORE (*Semantic Content Organization and Retrieval Engine*) [11] is a system that offers semantic content organization and recuperation of information. The software has the capability of processing information, by interrelating different pieces of information existing in its repository with the knowledge that a person can possess over a specific subject. These semantics-based information processing capabilities offer a significantly superior performance over syntactic information searching methods. Other vital advantages of SCORE include its high output and extensibility.

Caravela [12] is another CMS that provides dynamic unification and automatic categorization and is mainly used for categorizing published scientific researches and for the on-line creation of bibliographies on issues related to schema evolution and data cleaning. Content and documents of various types from diverse (semi-structured) sources can be unified and categorized in different dimensions. The system offers: (a) dynamic information unification with simultaneous attachment of related sources, (b) automatic interconnection that offers dynamic categorization without any time- or effort-related cost to the user, (c) semi-automatic categorization at length of multiple dimensions, and, (d) flexible and functional points that make search tasks easier.

The *Rhizomer* platform [13] is a CMS based on REST and Semantic Web technologies, offering advanced content management services. All content is described using semantic metadata that is semi-automatically extracted from multimedia content, facilitating publishing, querying, browsing, editing and interacting with semantic data. Rhizomer supports search via semantic queries and the user can navigate through the graph of data, retrieving fragments and rendering them as interactive HTML. Additionally, two or more pieces of metadata about common or similar resources can also be mixed and simple mappings between concepts from different ontologies can be defined. Finally, the user can annotate new semantic metadata describing a resource, or edit existing annotations via user-friendly HTML forms.

A more e-Gov-oriented approach is featured in [14], where a system for multimedia management is proposed. The system supports: automatic information extraction, retrieval, semantic interpretation of the relevant information presented in the document, storing and long term preservation. Since an e-Gov document is typically composed by various multimedia data types (images, text, graphic objects, audio, video etc.), the textual processing phase involves the use of legal ontologies.

The systems described above are semantic-enabled CMSs with possibly more related capabilities than the "semantically enhanced" Alfresco presented here. However, the aim of this work is to convert a "traditional" CMS into a semantically-enabled system, offering the capability of interoperation with other applications via importing/exporting ontologies, which is a feature none of the other systems possesses.

3 Alfresco

Alfresco [9] is an open-source enterprise CMS and is considered a pioneer in its domain. It comprises a client/server application that provides a powerful *Application Programming Interface* (*API*) for web services integration. The server-side of the software resides inside an application server, where the Alfresco application and repository are kept. On the other hand, the client-side does not require installation of additional packages, as it is launched by the user's web browser and runs like a typical web application. This modular architecture provides the advantage that existing components can be replaced, providing better implementation and optimum integration with existing environments/applications. Additionally, unneeded features can be removed, offering a lighter and potentially more flexible version of the system.

Alfresco integrates a variety of cutting-edge open-source technologies and can cooperate with any popular data base repository. Furthermore, Alfresco is fully compatible with *XML*, supporting importation and exportation of content in any XML format (e.g. *Dublin Core*). Moreover, the system is strongly supported by a wide developer community. In order to encourage further development of the system, the Alfresco Company consistently offers the latest Alfresco versions openly to the community and has translated the software in more than 20 languages.

The two most important factors for choosing Alfresco as the development platform were its distributed architecture and open source code. The former is based on a scalable *Service-Oriented Architecture* (*SOA*), while the latter allows for incorporation of further technologies into the system as well as the extension and interoperability with external applications. Additional advantages involve Alfresco being easy to install and use, without requiring any additional third-party applications and its support by well-written documentation as well as an enthusiastic developer community.

4 Implementation: Alfresco Semantic Extensions

A running example will be used throughout section 4, for illustrating the usability of the presented implementation. The *International Hellenic University* (*IHU*) was chosen as the application domain, since it is a newly founded state organization that inevitably faces the challenge of managing large volumes of administrative documents and is currently developing its ICT infrastructure. In addition to improving content management and information search and retrieval, the deployment of a semantically-enabled CMS in organizing IHU will also contribute in the *semantic interoperability* between the institute and other organizations (e.g. Ministry of Education, other universities, international education-related organizations etc.).

4.1 Source Ontology Specifications

The Alfresco extension is designed to accept as input all RDF/S ontologies that comply with the following specifications:

- The input ontology can contain any number of classes, subclasses and properties.
- Only data type properties are allowed in the ontology, since Alfresco cannot handle object properties.
- Each class should have a label that will enclose a human-readable identifier for the class. The tag content is used for representing the class in the Alfresco front-end.
- Hierarchy correlations among classes and subclasses are allowed, but their property counterparts (properties/subproperties) are not, as Alfresco does not support them.

As a sample model, an RDF/S ontology was deployed that was used for testing the Alfresco semantic extensions and represents the organizational chart of IHU, containing 25 classes and 20. The root class in the hierarchy is "*University Branch*" that declares a categorization of the various operational branches of IHU and has four subclasses, "*Administrative Board*", "*Administration*", "*Secretary*", "*Department*", which are further subdivided.

4.2 Importing Ontologies into Alfresco

Initially, the *Ontology Loader* module reads the input RDF/S ontology that conforms to the above specifications and detects all included classes, subclasses and properties, as well as their interrelations. For accomplishing these tasks, the software deploys *the Jena Semantic Web Framework* [15] and the *Pellet* reasoner [16]. Since Alfresco treats classes (represented as "*categories*" in Alfresco) and properties (represented as "*aspects*") separately, the module also follows this principle, generating two separate vectors that include classes (vector V_C) and properties (vector V_P), respectively. Each vector member "is aware" of all relevant information, e.g. a member class $c_i \in V_C$ is aware of all its predecessor and descendant classes, while a member property $p_j \in V_P$ is aware of its domain and range. Eventually, the Ontology Loader passes vector V_C to the *Categories Manager* module and vector V_P to the *Aspects Manager* module, which are the components responsible for updating repository content.

The *Categories Manager* module modifies file *categories.xml* (a core Alfresco XML file responsible for classifying repository content), adding the categories/classes that were extracted from the ontology (vector V_C). The new categories are appended, starting with the root superclass (i.e. the class that has no further superclasses) and gradually proceeding to its subclasses etc. In case of categories with more than one parent category, the corresponding child category is appended more than once into the document. The process terminates, when all members of vector V_C have been added.

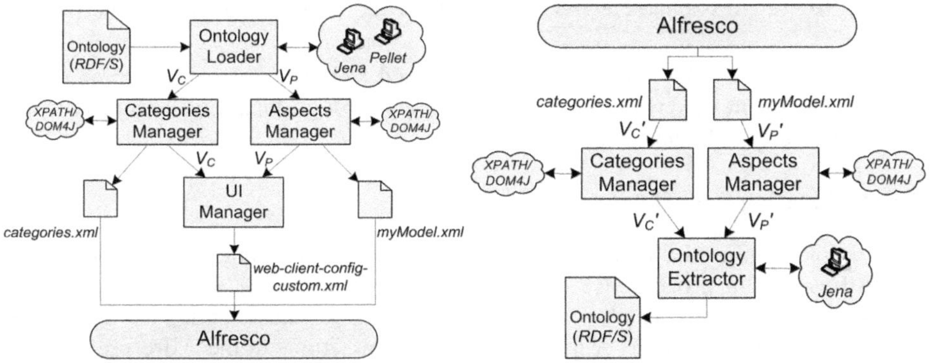

Fig. 1. Ontology import plug-in architecture (left); Ontology export plug-in architecture (right)

The *Aspects Manager* module, on the other hand, is responsible for adding the extracted properties (vector V_P) into *myModel.xml* (another core file responsible for properties, rules and metadata). For every class that appears as domain in (at least) one of the detected properties, a new aspect with the same name is created. The range of the property determines the type of the aspect and the process terminates, when all members of vector V_P have been added.

Finally, the *UI Manager* module is responsible for modifying file *web-client-config-custom.xml* that is responsible for displaying the aspects and categories in the Alfresco web client front-end. The module receives the two vectors V_C and V_P from the previous two modules and proceeds to three basic modifications to the file. Firstly, the classes and their properties are declared. Secondly, the module has to define which classes should appear in the Alfresco wizard for creating rules on the content. The third modification involves the aspects that will be included in the Alfresco search window. Fig. 1 (left) displays the architecture of the implemented plug-in responsible for importing an ontology into Alfresco.

4.3 Exporting Ontologies from Alfresco

The process of exporting ontologies from the repository was integrated as a second plug-in to the system, which implements a similar but functionally inverse approach. Again, the two Alfresco core files that play a major role are *categories.xml* and *myModel.xml*, the former provides the set of RDF/S classes, while the latter is responsible for generating the corresponding set of properties. This process is realized via two of the modules presented previously: *Categories Manager* and *Aspects Manager*.

The *Categories Manager* module initially parses the Alfresco file *categories.xml*, creating a vector of categories/classes V_C'. Each member category $c_i' \in V_C'$ is aware of its direct predecessor, which will be included as the corresponding superclass in the resulting RDF/S ontology. This procedure excludes any root classes, which are considered subclasses of `rdfs:Resource`, the top RDF/S class. The *Aspects Manager* module, on the other hand, parses file *myModel.xml*, searching for properties. A corresponding property vector V_P' is created that contains properties; each member property $p_j' \in V_P'$ is characterized by its name, the property range and the property domain.

The two vectors (V_C' and V_P') are then passed to the *Ontology Extractor* module that actually creates the resulting RDF/S ontology through Jena. Fig. 1 (right) displays the architecture of the ontology export plug-in.

4.4 Integrating into Alfresco

After implementing the two plug-ins, the final task was to integrate the application into Alfresco. This process involves modifying the following Alfresco files: (a) *faces-config-custom.xml*, where the JSF-managed listener beans reside, (b) *web-client-config-custom.xml*, which is responsible for customizations to the Alfresco front-end, and (c) *titlebar.jsp* that contains the statement declarations for the newly developed front-end buttons that will appear on the Alfresco GUI toolbar.

Two frames were developed for assisting the user in importing and exporting an ontology, respectively. The *Ontology Import Frame* (*OIF*) (Fig. 2 - left) requires from the user to enter the path of the input ontology as well as the locations of the three Alfresco core files (*categories.xml*, *myModel.xml*, *web-client-config-custom.xml*), as described previously. The plug-in automatically detects the locations of the respective Alfresco files, but the user also has the option of browsing for a different location. Next to each text field in *OIF* there is an "*Import*" button, for modifying each of the three files separately, but there also exists a choice for mass modification ("*Import All*"), through which the user can merge all three ontology importing steps into one.

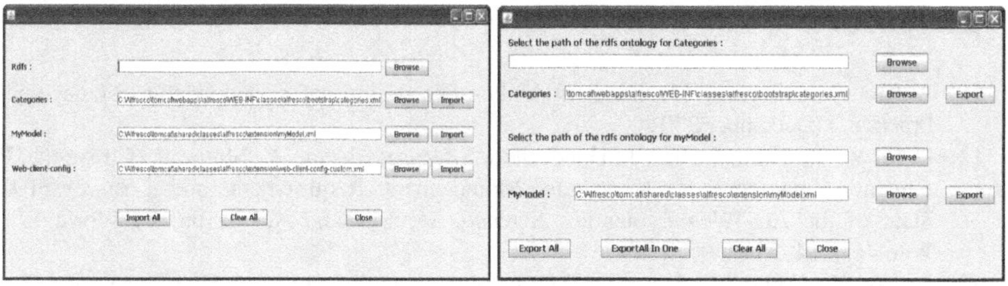

Fig. 2. Developed frames for importing (left) and exporting (right) an ontology

Similarly to *OIF*, the *Ontology Export Frame* (*OEF*) (Fig. 2 - right) consists of text fields, where the user again has to provide file paths. *OEF* operates in two modes: the user can either export the repository content into two separate ontology files (one for classes and one for properties), or, alternatively, a merged export can be performed, exporting the content into one single file. This dual functionality was considered useful, since Alfresco stores representations for classes/categories and properties/aspects in different locations, without ensuring that consistency is maintained. Buttons "*Export All*" and "*Export All In One*" perform these the two distinct operations.

5 Conclusions and Future Work

This paper argued that CMSs offer various advantages to enterprises and organizations for managing the large volumes of information, but also display certain disadvantages. The application of Semantic Web technologies in content management offers various benefits, like semantic interoperability, dramatic cost reductions, revenue improvements and competitive advantages. This paper presented a semantic extension to a leading Enterprise CMS, called *Alfresco* for automatically importing and exporting RDF/S ontologies. The added functionalities enable re-use of Alfresco repository content, semantically-enabled search and interoperability by a variety of other third-party applications. IHU was chosen as the test domain for the implemented system, which was used for managing the subset of managerial and administrative documents.

As for future work directions, an interesting improvement would be to have the system import and export ontologies encoded in a more expressive language, like OWL. Another appealing extension would be the integration of a reasoning engine, which would allow Alfresco to automatically classify content classification. Further operations that Alfresco can cover can be discovered by its application in different environments, such as educational institutes, enterprises and, generally, any organization that deals with voluminous collections of documents. Finally, it would be interesting to study whether the "semantic-oriented" methodologies developed for Alfresco can also be applied in other "traditional" CMSs, like e.g. *Plone* [17].

References

[1] Auffret, M.: Content Management Makes Sense. Journal of Knowledge Management Practice 2 (December 2001)

[2] Uren, V., Cimiano, P., Iria, J., Handschuh, S., Vargas-Vera, M., Motta, E., Ciravegna, F.: Semantic Annotation for Knowledge Management: Requirements and a Survey of the State of the Art. Web Semantics: Science, Services and Agents on the World Wide Web 4(1), 14–28 (2006)

[3] Lytras, M., Garcia, R.: Semantic Web Applications: A Framework for Industry and Business Exploitation-What is needed for the Adoption of the Semantic Web from the Market and Industry. Int. Journal of Knowledge and Learning 4(1), 93–108 (2008)

[4] Berners-Lee, T., Hendler, J., Lassila, O.: The Semantic Web. Scientific American 284(5), 34–43 (2001)

[5] Guarino, N.: Formal Ontology, Conceptual Analysis and Knowledge Representation. Int. J. Hum.-Comput. Stud. 43(5-6), 625–640 (1995)

[6] Brickley, D., Guha, R.V.: RDF Vocabulary Description Language 1.0: RDF Schema (2004), http://www.w3.org/TR/rdf-schema/

[7] Fass, L.F.: The Semantic Web, E-Government and the Digital Divide. In: Abecker, A., Sheth, A., Mentzas, G., Stojanovic, L. (eds.) Semantic Web Meets eGovernment, Stanford University, pp. 14–17. AAAI Press, Menlo Park (2006); SS-06-06

[8] Wagner, C., Cheung, K., Ip, R., Bottcher, S.: Building Semantic Webs for e-government with Wiki technology. Electronic Government 3(1), 36–55 (2006)

[9] Alfresco Enterprise Content Management System, http://www.alfresco.com/

[10] Wales, T.: Library Subject Guides: a Content Management Case Study at the Open University, UK. Program-Electronic Library and Information Systems 39(2), 112–121 (2005)

[11] Sheth, A., Bertram, C., Avant, D., Hammond, B., Kochut, K., Warke, Y.: Semantic Content Management for Enterprises and the Web. IEEE Internet Computing 6(4), 80–87 (2002)

[12] Aumueller, D., Rahm, E.: Caravela: Semantic Content Management with Automatic Information Integration and Categorization. In: Franconi, E., Kifer, M., May, W. (eds.) ESWC 2007. LNCS, vol. 4519, pp. 729–738. Springer, Heidelberg (2007)

[13] García, R., Gimeno, J.M., Perdrix, F., Gil, R., Oliva, M.: The Rhizomer Semantic Content Management System. In: Lytras, M.D., Carroll, J.M., Damiani, E., Tennyson, R.D. (eds.) WSKS 2008. LNCS (LNAI), vol. 5288, pp. 385–394. Springer, Heidelberg (2008)

[14] Amato, F., Mazzeo, A., Moscato, V., Picariello, A.: Semantic Management of Multimedia Documents for E-Government Activity. In: Int. Conference on Complex, Intelligent and Software Intensive Systems, pp. 1193–1198 (2009)

[15] McBride, B.: Jena: Implementing the RDF Model and Syntax Specification. Technical report (2001)

[16] Sirin, E., Parsia, B., Grau, B., Kalyanpur, A., Katz, Y.: Pellet: A Practical OWL-DL Reasoner. Web Semantics: Science, Services and Agents on the WWW 5(2), 51–53 (2007)

[17] Clark, A., Parker, C., Hanning, D., Convent, C., DeStefano, J., Stahl, J., Aspeli, M., Bowen, M., Newbery, R., Knox, S., McMahon, S., Conklin, T., Williams, V.: Practical Plone 3: A Beginner's Guide to Building Powerful Websites. Packt Publishing (2009)

Author Index

GPSR Compliance

The European Union's (EU) General Product Safety Regulation (GPSR) is a set of rules that requires consumer products to be safe and our obligations to ensure this.

If you have any concerns about our products, you can contact us on ProductSafety@springernature.com

In case Publisher is established outside the EU, the EU authorized representative is:

Springer Nature Customer Service Center GmbH
Europaplatz 3
69115 Heidelberg, Germany

Batch number: 10844619

Printed by Printforce, the Netherlands